T0198857

# GUNCRAZY
# AMERICA
A History and Critique of Our Gun Culture

FRANK  N.  EGERTON

authorHOUSE®

*AuthorHouse*™
*1663 Liberty Drive*
*Bloomington, IN 47403*
*www.authorhouse.com*
*Phone: 1 (800) 839-8640*

*Published by AuthorHouse 10/05/2018*

*ISBN: 978-1-5462-4160-7 (sc)*
*ISBN: 978-1-5462-4159-1 (e)*

*Library of Congress Control Number: 2018906027*

*Print information available on the last page.*

# CONTENTS

Introduction .................................................................................. vii
Acknowledgements ...................................................................... xvii

Chapter 1    From Conquest to Independence ............................................ 1
Chapter 2    From Second Amendment to Civil War and Indian Wars ... 14
Chapter 3    Shooting Animals and Targets ............................................. 32
Chapter 4    Making and Selling Guns and Ammunition ...................... 57
Chapter 5    Fear Mongering National Rifle Association ...................... 87
Chapter 6    Guns in Crime ................................................................... 112
Chapter 7    Gun Violence as Entertainment ....................................... 155
Chapter 8    Guns, Politics and Paranoia ............................................. 185
Chapter 9    Laws: Making America Safe for Guns and Dangerous for
             People, including Law Enforcers ................................... 209
Chapter 10   Costs of Gun Violence ..................................................... 234

Conclusions ................................................................................ 239
Escaping Our Guncrazy Culture ............................................... 243
Further Reading ........................................................................ 247
Abbreviations ........................................................................... 271
Endnotes ................................................................................... 273
Bibliography ............................................................................. 301

# INTRODUCTION

Preposterous! The strongest country in the world, of 325,000,000 people, is jerked around by a gun lobby with 5 million members! NRA claims that any more gun laws lead to gun confiscation! I do not advocate government seizure of private guns! That is phony NRA propaganda to scare timid gun owners to pay their NRA dues.

Assassinations of Martin Luther King, Jr. and Robert F. Kennedy in 1968, following the assassination of President John F. Kennedy in 1963, led me to conclude that protesting in Pittsburgh against the Viet Nam War was not enough! What more? Somehow, grappling with that question eventually led to me writing this book.

This book is not primarily about guns—except for manufacturing—and focuses on use of guns amd America's gun culture and its deadly consequences.

The United States is notorious for (1) both an abundance of guns and a high rate of gun casualties. Gun rights have become more important than public safety. Here are other examples of gun-craziness in America:

2. Tens of thousands of shootings yearly, with over 10,000 killed, and tens of thousands more wounded. This must be acceptable to most Americans, since there is little serious effort to stop it;

3. Frequent mass shootings, with government taking tiny steps to moderate, but not stop them;

4. Politicians are more afraid of the NRA than of gun violence;

5. America has the most gun violence of any industrial country, yet America also produces the most numerous books, movies, TV shows, and videogames featuring gun violence for entertainment;

6. Notorious gun criminals become objects of fascination (antiheroes?) and so become characters in dramas for public entertainment;

7. Congress restricts proper authorities' collection and sharing of data on gun violence;
8. Florida in 2011 passed into law a restriction on what physicians can say to patients about guns in the home (struck down by Federal Court);
9. organizations focused on reducing gun violence receive very modest public support;
10. gun and ammunition manufacturing and selling flourishes;
11. NRA is the self-appointed gate keeper of our gun laws and is heavily supported by its membership;
12. NRA propaganda encourages its members to fear government and own guns to protect themselves against government, and this phony propaganda is little challenged by political scientists or other authorities;
13. When NRA was of modest size and influence, our Supreme Court interpreted the Second Amendment as giving states authority to pass their own gun laws; after NRA became our most powerful lobby, our Supreme Court accepted the NRA's interpretation that it gives Americans a right to own guns (neither interpretation is historically correct);
14. with little challenge from society's leaders of NRA's interpretation of the Second Amendment, NRA produces its own scholarship interpreting it;
15. Mexican drug gangs fight their government with American guns, and America has an inadequate (even counterproductive) response;
16. we appropriately mourn the 2403 killed and 1176 wounded at Pearl Harbor on 7 Dec. 1941. We mourn Japan's planes mounting an unprovoked attack on our armed forces, and just as appropriately mourn almost 3000 killed by terrorists on 11 Sept. 01, yet 10,000 to 15,000 are killed annually by other Americans, and unless victims are public figures, they are soon forgotten by all except their families and friends (few monuments);
17. our gun carnage is not only a human tragedy, it is also enormously expensive financially, medically, and in our penal system;
18. concealed carry laws have swept through all 50 states despite disputed evidence it makes us safer.

The first responsibility of government is to protect the people. That requires the passage and enforcement of laws to ensure their protection. When thousands of Americans are murdered every year with guns, government is not performing its primary responsibility. The laws or their enforcement, or both, are inadequate. Fortunately, we live in a democracy, in which we can change legislators, executives, and laws, as needed. Why, then, has our democracy failed in its primary responsibility?

A complex question; a history lesson may help. No Roman ever decided to invent gladiatorial games as an encouragement for building an empire. History rarely works like that, because people are seldom that insightful. However, once gladiatorial games were invented, it became increasingly popular, for it celebrated combat, aggression, blood and gore—values that encouraged Romans to conquer neighbors and skim off their wealth and enslave part of their population to work on Roman plantations. Success led to competing visions of empire, and after assassination of charismatic Julius Caesar, the Roman Republic disintegrated into civil war. A dictatorial Roman Empire emerged, which could at least maintain peace and continue expanding. Yet, despite Rome's aggression, it could not expand indefinitely, and when it could no longer do so, it began a slow decline which no one understood, and so decline continued until the empire disappeared.

Nearly continuous warfare in North America among representatives of European nations, and between those nations and Indians led to a triumphant United States, with an ideology of liberty. As eastern states expanded westward into an American empire, a new ideology was invented to encourage the process: manifest destiny. However, there had never been a master plan for conquest. Americans responded to the challenge in many ways, and those ways that promoted empire became popular. Those ways added up to an imperial ideology and practice, though no one wrote out an explicit guide book for imperialism. Along with success, as among the Romans, competing visions of empire led to civil war, and after assassination of unifying President Lincoln, a mediocre Reconstruction occurred while America conquered Indians in the West, with an industrializing North and a plantation South being forced to get along.

Ever since 7 Dec. 41, USA has annually mourned the 2403 killed and 1178 wounded at Pearl Harbor when Japanese airplanes mounted an unprovoked attack on our armed services. Ever since 11 Sept. 01, USA has annually mourned about 3000 killed by 19 terrorists who commandeered 4 commercial airliners and crashed them into the World Trade Center's twin towers, the Pentagon, and a Pennsylvania field. However, every year

Americans with guns kill 4 to 5 times more than died in either of these two tragedies, and although we mourn them at funerals, the only people who annually mourn them are those who knew and loved them. Exceptions are assassinated prominent public figures—Lincoln, JFK, RFK, MLK, Jr., John Lennon. Ordinary gun victims do not provoke annual national sorrow because they were killed every day in all 50 states, not to mention tens of thousands wounded annually with guns, and some 15,000 who commit suicide with guns.

It's crazy to accept this annual domestic carnage as normal. One might protest that we do not accept this as normal. However, our inaction belies any such protest. If we did not accept the slaughter of 10,000 to 15,000 gun victims as normal, we would take action to stop it—yet we do not. Why not? The answer is obvious to all. The gun lobby, led by the NRA, has paralyzed our democracy concerning gun laws. The NRA's five million members, less than 2% of our population, are gate-keepers of American gun laws. The NRA mantra is that we already have some 20,000 gun laws, so just enforce those already passed.

Once upon a time, the owners of private guns were organized into government militia to protect society. But time passes and situations change. Now the owners of private guns menace society, and every hour of every day Americans are shot with private guns. It is crazy that our legislators are unable to change with the times and provide the protection that society now needs. Although the NRA is the single most important impediment to passage of adequate gun control laws, inadequate legislation is not the only problem.

What passes in America for normal, rational judgment concerning private guns is considered crazy by the rest of the world. It is crazy that private gun ownership is better protected by law than is public safety, and that public safety is, in fact, threatened by private guns. This is such an astonishing situation that one British photographer, Zed Nelson, spent two years documenting it and produced a prize-winning coffee-table book, *Gun Nation* (2000), and another British photographer produced a TV documentary, shown on MSNBC on 19 April 09, on introduction of American children to shooting. In the "Foreword" to Nelson's book he explained to a bewildered world that "Most American gun owners consider themselves normal, law-abiding citizens." Anthropologists tell us that in societies which practice cannibalism, cannibals see themselves as "normal, law-abiding citizens."

There is a difference, however, between these two societies: in a cannibalistic society, all its members see (or saw) cannibalism as normal. In Gun Nation, there is strong disagreement between those who defend gun rights and those who think public safety is paramount. In recent decades the gun rights movement has been winning the debate—if not logically, at least politically, where it matters. Statistics on gun crimes show, however, that gun-rights advocates' dominance has led to a more dangerous, not a safer, society.

How does America get beyond such a dysfunctional culture? There has not been as much ink spilled as blood, but nevertheless considerable ink has been spilled without any significant progress toward a safer America. This is a problem of broad dimensions, and the discussions of it known to me have not been broad enough to address all aspects of it. Guns enjoy special status in American civilization that is not accorded to swords or firecrackers. This special status spills over into our culture, our crime, and our legal system. Since this special status endangers public safety, why does it persist?

Although the problem predates the National Rifle Association and would still exist if the NRA disappeared tomorrow, the gun lobby is a log jam that prevents a normal resolution of the problem. The NRA also enjoys a special status in America. Our political tradition includes the rise of private organizations that articulate particular values that are not shared by all Americans. These organizations can develop an ideology that provides the basis for a political campaign and lobby. The NRA has been more effective than other successful organizations, such as Sierra Club or American Medical Association.

The recreational use of guns predates the NRA. Hunting was an important activity in European colonies, initially to help feed and clothe one's family, but later it persisted as a sport. It involved hiking and camping and displayed manly capabilities. Shooting matches emerged as another sport. It helped pass the time when one was not hunting, and it polished one's shooting skills for hunting or armed conflicts.

Armed conflicts began as early as hunting, or earlier. European settlers came from a warring civilization. World historians have wondered why it was Europeans who rose to dominate the world, beginning in the 1700s and continuing into the later-1900s. The main answer is that the European continent was never unified into an empire, as China was, and therefore the European continent was subject to frequent warfare, usually between neighboring governments, but occasionally due to revolution or civil war.

When Europeans immigrated to America they did not leave behind their warring traditions. The Americas were sparsely settled compared to Europe, but there were people here who possessed the land. There were some conflicts from the start, but even when Europeans bought land from Indians conflicts eventually arose, because Europeans kept coming, and they wanted more land than Indians wanted to sell. Guns helped Europeans settle and survive.

As time passed, guns were traded to Indians, and some Indians used them not just against deer and turkey, but also to shoot back when attacked. However, Indians could never win many conflicts unless they were allied with one European nationality against another, because Indians would soon run out of ammunition and need gun repairs, and only Europeans provided these.

Initially, all guns came from Europe, and American gunsmiths-blacksmiths merely repaired guns. Even when Americans began making guns, they could make only one at a time. Without French muskets, Americans could never have won their War of Independence. However, as the United States continued fighting wars, the two U.S. Army arsenals began helping gun manufacturers improve their productivity. This coincided with the importation of British technology from its industrial revolution. A government-backed munitions industry was strategic for advancing the manufacture of standardized parts for mass production. And mass production led to advertisement, not just to announce what was for sell, but also to persuade customers to purchase guns and ammunition.

As gun production and use became characteristics of Americans, both history and fiction were written to celebrate Americans using their guns to win and protect their freedom. The spread of agriculture, commerce, transportation, and religion were important developments but were not tantalizing fare for historians and novelists. Accounts of armed conflicts attracted readers, and many who read about them were inspired to think of themselves as participating in similar conflicts. They were often inspired, as well, to buy guns to reinforce their aspirations.

The rise of industry not only led to production of abundant goods (including guns and ammunition), it also led to sectional and class conflicts. The slave-holding South felt threatened not only by northern industry and wealth, but also by northern abolitionists. Labor organized, or wanted to organize, to defend its interests against industrialists and their capitalist partners. The American political system evolved to deal with the clash of interest groups and often did so effectively. But not always, and not always impartially. Political compromise between slave and free states worked for a while, but abolitionists were not satisfied with territorial compromise. Industrialists and capitalists used their wealth to achieve political influence disproportionate to their numbers compared to the labor force. Americans discovered limits to the flexibility of their political system. When frustrated by the political process, Americans can and sometimes do resort to armed conflict. The Civil War was the climax of irreconcilable sectional conflict, and the industrial North defeated a slave-dependent South.

The defeated South was poor but still needed cheap labor. Some freed blacks escaped north, but most could not go far. The Klu Klux Klan was a secret terrorist organization that arose among the defeated Confederate veterans to reclaim white political power and to intimidate Black labor force. When Reconstruction ended in 1876, the Klu Klux Klan became an important interest group that articulated an ideology and lobbied in the political process. It also continued terrorists tactics, which often involved use of guns.

The NRA was another private organization that arose after the Civil War, also formed by veterans, but by victorious veterans in the North. It had more limited goals and was slower than the Klu Klux Klan to develop an ideology. Its original goal was merely to train northern city men to shoot as well or better than southern country men who were hunters. The NRA ideology that later developed emphasized that some armed Americans were criminals, and therefore law-abiding Americans needed to be armed to defend themselves.

Because of the NRA's political success, its ideology seems compelling to many citizens and legislators. That is to be expected. Capitalism was articulated as an ideology by Adam Smith in 1776 and seemed invincible until 1929 and again in fall of 2008, when the U.S. economy, and then the world economy, began to collapse. The capitalistic ideology that argues government should get out of the way and let the free market operate no longer seems persuasive to everyone. Karl Marx was an intellectual who developed a subtle ideology that attracted other disgruntled intellectuals until one of them, Vladimir Lenin, seized power in Russia in 1917. Then, his version of Marxist Communism became a compelling ideology that won the support of intellectuals in Russia and in many other countries. But that intellectual support collapsed with the Soviet Empire in 1989 (though many intellectuals had defected earlier). Mussolini and Hitler were regarded as ignorant fanatics by European intellectuals before they gained power in 1922 and 1933 respectively, but then Fascism and Nazism became potent ideologies that attracted educated as well as ignorant supporters—until Italy and Germany lost World War II in 1945. Many people thus find it difficult to distinguish between power and wisdom, and it is especially difficult for politicians who like to please politically powerful interest groups like the NRA.

I am writing this book as a citizen's report to fellow citizens. I am neither criminologist, sociologist, political scientist, nor an authority on guns. Rather, I am a historian of ecology who for thirty years also taught courses in world history and American environmental history. I would not have taken time away from writing my history of ecological sciences (being published quarterly in the *Bulletin of the Ecological Society of America*) if I saw others doing what seems to me necessary to deal adequately with this serious situation. One reason fine books on gun control, and gun control organizations, have not initiated adequate reforms is that they are up against the NRA, and they do not attract an equally-powerful lobby. "Reasonable" reformers could not end slavery or segregation and cannot end America's guncraziness. Who do I know who was shot? No one, directly. What drew my attention to America's gun problem was the inadequate response of government to the assassinations of John F. Kennedy, Martin Luther King, Jr., and Robert F. Kennedy. There are worthy books written about these tragedies, but they focus on what happened, not on how to prevent similar tragedies.

We must stop sacrificing 10,000-15,000 lives a year on the altar of NRA fanaticism and disabuse its paranoid membership of their guncrazy mindset. Can this one book effect changes needed? Only if readers agree with my analysis and conclusions and are then willing to make this cause a national cause.

Newspapers of record are generally understood to be the *New York Times, Washington Post, Chicago Tribune,* and the *Los Angeles Times.* Rarely are any of these cited in this book. Instead, I cite the *Milwaukee Journal Sentinel* and Racine *Journal Times.* My rationale is that these two represent middle America, and they are the ones which I have read regularly.

My extensive bibliography serves to document my arguments and also to provide an entry to readers who wish to pursue an argument in greater detail.

# ACKNOWLEDGEMENTS

I very much appreciate: computer assistance by Jerry Hershberger; broad assistance by Sarah Dowhower with illustration permissions; assistance with chapter 10 by David W. Smith; illustration reproductions by Laura Mason; and general assistance by librarians at the University of Wisconsin-Parkside, Kenosha; assistance by Eric Gunn with two illustrations; and assistance from Buddy Dow, Emily Amos, and April Roma from ArthurHouse with publication. Milton Christensen has had a continuous interest in this project, sending encouragement and relevant material from the news media.

# 1

# From Conquest to Independence

## Contenders: Spanish, French, and English

There was some potential for a gun culture from the start, but it did not develop while guns were complicated, sometimes unreliable, and sometimes dangerous to the user. The Portuguese and the Spanish began building their empires in the early 1500s, and by the late 1500s, the English and French attempted to do likewise. The North American colonial strategy of three Old World neighbors varied: Spanish strategy was to conquer and manage Indians,[1] French strategy was to trade with Indians (except in Louisiana, to some extent),[2] and English strategy was to acquire land from the Indians.[3] The French strategy was best for relations with Indians, but since the English strategy yielded the most settlers, they won the struggle in the long run.

During the 1500s, guns and cannon were major assets for Spanish conquests in America, though swords and horses were also important, and Spanish settlers accidentally introduced European diseases that killed more Indians than Spanish weapons.[4] Spanish settlers also introduced horses north of the Rio Grande, which became an important asset for Indians on the plains. In 1680, pueblo Indians drove their abusive masters from the New Mexico region, but Indian inability to stay united and also fend off nomadic enemies enabled the Spanish to regain control in a divide-and-conquer war, 1692-96.[5] Elsewhere, when Spanish soldiers were insufficient to counter a threat, mission Indians would also use guns. However, Hispanic settlers seldom had guns to spare. In 1719, two Franciscan missionaries reported:

"We do not have a single gun, while we see the French giving hundreds of arms to the Indians."[6] French Protestants established Fort Caroline on the St. Johns River on the Florida coast in 1564, and the colony became a haven for French pirates preying on Spanish galleons. Therefore, in 1565, Pedro Menéndez de Alilés settled San Agustin (St. Augustine) forty miles south. While Frenchmen were away chasing Spanish ships, Alilés marched 500 arquebusiers to Fort Caroline and attacked at dawn. It was raining and the arquebus wicks could not light, but swords were adequate because they caught the settlers by surprise and slaughtered them. Later, he surprised the returning sea-venturing French and slaughtered them also.[7]

When the French began colonizing in Canada, they also withheld guns from Indians. In 1609, Champlain organized a war party of Montagnais, Algonquin, and Hurons and bringing two soldiers to attack Mohawks on southern Lake Champlain, which he named for himself.[8] The deadly fire of three arquebuses panicked the usually fierce Mohawks, who threw down their wooden shields and fled. Champlain wanted to convince Mohawks to stop warfare so peaceful commerce could flourish, but the Indian practice of torturing captives to death made peace difficult. In June 1610, his Indian allies asked Champlain to participate in another battle with the Mohawk. He agreed, and on the 19th they attacked a Mohawk fort on what is now Richelieu River. This time Champlain had four soldiers with arquebuses, which again made the difference, enabling the allies to take the fort and kill the Mohawks whom they did not capture and torture.[9] Those two defeats did curb Mohawk aggression for two decades, allowing trade to develop.

Having trading partners who possessed guns satisfied Indian partners of the French for a while, but then Dutch sailed up the Hudson to trade with Iroquois (including Mohawks), and Dutch had no qualms about trading guns—their most lucrative trade good—for furs.[10] In response, French traded guns only with mission Indians. However, in the winter of 1648-49, Iroquois finally had enough guns to attack and destroy Huron villages, killing or capturing hundreds.[11] French then had to trade guns to all friendly Indians or loose their trade to the Dutch.[12] In 1763, France deeded Louisiana to Spain for its assistance in the French and Indian War (Europe's Seven Years War). In 1779, the Spanish governor of Louisiana decided that French policy of trading guns to Indians had succeeded, and he made it Spanish policy also.[13]

# English Precedents

Colonists brought their customs and traditions to America, where they were adapted to new conditions. For the English colonists, adaptation was especially important, since these colonists would break free and invent a new government, but one influenced by English precedents. Queen Elizabeth I (r. 1558-1603) was popular among her subjects as a leader. She had no heir, and the throne went to the king of Scotland, who became James I of England (r. 1603-25), who was unpopular, not a good leader. He was succeeded by his son, Charles I (r. 1625-49), who was even less popular. Parliament was unwilling to fund a standing army of any consequence, and against King Charles' opposition it passed a Militia Ordinance, enabling it to control militias.[14] Charles' relationship with Parliament deteriorated to the point that they fought a civil war, which he lost to Oliver Cromwell (r. 1649-58). Charles was executed for treason. An unpopular Cromwell ruled with an unpopular standing army. Puritanical Oliver was succeeded by his playboy son, Richard, who abdicated nine months later. The two sons of Charles I had been raised by their French Catholic mother in France, and Charles II (r. 1660-85) learned the lesson of his father's failure: cooperate with a Protestant Parliament. His reign was successful, and he was succeeded by his younger brother, James II (r. 1685-88), who had not learned the crucial lesson. He was more open about his Catholicism, and he aroused alarm in a Protestant Parliament by dismissing Protestant officers in a standing army and replacing them with Catholics. Members of Parliament invited William of Orange in the Netherlands, who had married James II's daughter, to depose James, and he did. Parliament was pleased and offered the throne to William and Mary, provided they accepted a bill of rights which Parliament wrote to be sure it did not trade one difficult monarch for another. With some reluctance, they accepted. Parliament's "Declaration of Rights," 13 February 1689, which listed the transgressions of James II, including: "6. By causing several good subjects, being Protestants, to be disarmed at the same time when papists were both armed and employed contrary to the law."[15] The list of transgressions was followed by a bill of rights, including: "7. That the subjects which are Protestants, may have arms for their defense suitable to their conditions and as allowed by law."[16] A related grievance of Parliament was that James II, "5. By raising and keeping a standing army within this kingdom in time of peace without the consent of Parliament and quartering soldiers contrary to the law."[17]

The practical significance of England's "Glorious Revolution" for its American colonies was slight (perhaps inspiring rebellions in Maryland and New York[18]), but the theoretical importance of Parliament's "Declaration of Rights" was immense, though that importance was not evident for a century.

# English Colonies

English colonists acquired land in three ways: if it seemed vacant, they took it; if not fully vacant, they bought it from presumed owners (though some Indians were unaware of the difference between selling and renting land); and when they fought Indians, they took land as spoils of war. Some wars were started by Indians, others by the English, but in almost all cases Indians lost land.[19] English settlers were dependent upon England for guns and ammunition, and to run out of ammunition was catastrophic.

In 1585 Sir Walter Raleigh sponsored a well-armed colony on Roanoke Island (now in NC), with about half the men being soldiers—too many if the colony was to become self-sufficient. They proved better at shooting Indians than at raising food, and when Sir Francis Drake stopped by in 1586 (after hearing of a Spanish plot to destroy the colony), they gladly went home with him. Raleigh tried again the next year, with different colonists who were as unprepared as their predecessors. When they decided to attack their tormentors, they mistakenly attacked friendly Indians. Their inept leader, John White (an excellent artist), went back for supplies. The supply ship he sent back to America was high-jacked by the Spanish, and before another ship could be launched, the Spanish Armada invaded English waters, and no ship reached Roanoke Island until two-and-a-half years after White had departed. By then, colonists would have depleted their powder and shot and become vulnerable to the will of their Indian neighbors. None of that "lost colony" was ever seen again.[20]

English colonists at Jamestown in 1607 brought along Captain John Smith, a professional soldier, to supervise their protection. Even so, it only survived by receiving regular supplies of guns, ammunition, and colonists (who died at a rate of 50% a year). Samuel Argall was captain of a supply ship that made several trips between England and Jamestown. In 1613, when he was ready to sail back to England, colonists asked him to stop off at French colonies on the Bay of Fundy and destroy them. He was glad to oblige them.[21] Smith occasionally threatened Indians with guns to coerce food from Powhatan Indians. He was once captured and only released when he promised to send chief Powhatan two great guns and a grindstone. Smith forced colonists to work six hours a day, which motivated some to desert to the Indians. If they brought weapons, they were welcomed, but if not, they were killed. Smith's successor, Captain Christopher Newport, traded weapons to Indians for supplies, but later Governor Thomas De la Warr, attacked the Indians to regain the weapons.[22]

CAPTAIN JOHN SMITH'S ENCOUNTERS WITH THE INDIANS.
From Smith's "General History."

Fig. 1 Smith taking King.

Ambivalence over trading guns to Indians was not resolved.[23] When Indians realized there was no end to English colonists and their land hunger, they mounted a surprise attack in 1622 (Powhatan War), killing 3347, nearly a third of those in the Chesapeake Bay area. In 1623, the English invited 250 Indians to a peace talks and killed them with poison and swords. When peace came in 1632, it cost Indians more land. Indians tried again in 1644, killing over 400. However, by then European diseases were decimating Indians, whom colonists outnumbered.[24]

When the Plymouth Colony arrived in 1620, it also had a professional soldier, Myles Standish, in charge of defense. Relations with Indians began peacefully, but when news of the 1622 Indian massacre of Virginians arrived, Plymouth decided to teach local Indians a lesson. In 1623 it lured a band of Massachusetts Indians into a trap and killed seven and posted the head of a sachem atop the Plymouth fort as a lesson to other Indians. Using terror to maintain peace, Plymouth objected to a later arrival, Thomas Morton (c.1580-1647), who traded guns to Indians.[25] By 1627, Indians around Massachusetts Bay were thought to have at least 60 guns, largely supplied by Morton.[26] He ignored a warning to end his gun trade, and in 1628 Plymouth sent Standish to arrest and deport him to England. Those who profited from gun trafficking paid no damages when those guns were used against colonists. That tradition has persisted throughout American history. Morton returned in 1629, was expelled again in 1630, and took revenge by writing *New English Canaan* (1637). In 1643 he returned to Massachusetts yet again and was imprisoned for writing a book unfavorable to colonists.[27] In 1634, Cape Cod pilgrims and Boston puritans had a shooting conflict over the boundary between their respective fur trades, and one man was killed on each side before they made peace.[28]

In 1636, colonial leaders expanded their authority to the Mystic River Valley and demanded that Pequot Indians pay taxes, give up children as hostages, and turn in suspects accused of killing a trader. When they refused, Plymouth, Boston, and Connecticut declared war. In May, 1637, colonists and Indian allies surrounded a village of about 400 Pequots— mostly women, children, and old men, as most men were hunting. At dawn, they set it afire and shot those who tried to escape the flames; only five survived. Before year's end, most other Pequots were either killed or sent to the West Indies as slaves.[29] This behavior was acceptable in America but shocked Puritans in England. In the late 1640s, Rev. John Eliot began converting Indians to Christianity. Many colonists opposed this, and in the next war, many "praying Indians" were massacred.[30] King Philips's War, named for Indian leader Metacom, called King Philip. It started in 1675, after Wampanoag Indians murdered a praying Indian informant and Plymouth executed three who presumably had killed him.[31] This time, Indians were as well armed as colonists, and they inflicted heavy losses until they began running out of powder and shot and needed gun repairs. Indians captured were either executed or sold as slaves. Indians who escaped to Canada were glad to guide French-Canadians to New England when wars between France and England started in 1689.[32] Indians often lost land and lives in conflicts with European colonists, and their lost warriors were more difficult to replace than killed colonists.

Not all conflicts fit into the same mold. Bacon's Rebellion in Virginia in 1676 pitted backcountry frontiersmen against the eastern established government.[33] Settlers on the western frontier were usually poor, often former indentured servants, who had little, if any, money to buy land. Bacon was not poor, and he became leader of the frontiersmen, who coveted Susquehannock lands. When Bacon defended his squatter neighbors, Governor William Berkeley, back east in Jamestown, defended the peaceable Indians whom he wanted to keep peaceable. Bacon's frontiersmen were furious and marched on Jamestown and even burned it, with Berkeley and other officials fleeing. It is unclear how this might have ended had not Bacon died of dysentery, after which the leaderless rebellion collapsed.

There was no permanent solution to the question of arming Indians. Indians sometimes used guns to hunt for game which they traded to colonists. Friendly Indians often had guns and fought with colonists against unfriendly Indians. In 1751, Benjamin Franklin recommended that gunsmiths live among Indians so that Indians would not have to come to town for gun repairs.[34] When Indians ceased tolerating English bullying, they sometimes used their guns against English neighbors, but in the long run, they would need ammunition and gun repairs; they could sometimes manage repairs, but not gunpowder production. On one or two occasions they gained access to cannon and were able to use them, but otherwise, they lacked them.[35] Canada's history was less violent than in the region that became the United States.[36] The French were early settlers of Quebec and they were mainly interested in the fur trade and in converting Indians to Christianity. That less violent tradition continued when the English began settling there, simply because Canadian Indians were less numerous than those south of them, and the land was vast.

Colonial relationships with African-Americans was about as difficult as with Indians. Slavery spread from Caribbean Islands to Virginia in 1619, and guns were used to subdue slaves who ran away or rebelled. All English colonies quickly formed militias, except for Pennsylvania, which did later when non-Quakers gained dominance. Despite the threats of hostile Indians and the French, militia drill and practice were seldom taken seriously, except in the South, where there was always a potential of slave revolts. Militias hardly ever had enough functioning guns for all militiamen, which in itself never stopped the trade of guns to Indians.[37] The earliest slave revolt occurred Virginia in 1691, and a larger revolt occurred in New York City on April 12, 1712.[38] After 1 a.m. in New York, slaves set a house afire and when neighbors came, they attacked them with a gun and knives. Eight or ten colonists were murdered and a much larger number of slaves were killed before the revolt was crushed. On September 9, 1739, 20 miles from Charleston SC on the Stono River, 20 slaves killed two store keepers, stole guns and ammunition, and began marching toward Florida. Along the way, they recruited other slaves, killed 20 colonists, and burned seven plantation complexes. About 100 mounted militiamen attacked the runaways, killing most, and militiamen offered Indians bounties to track down escapees.

English colonies before the War of Independence were constantly either at war or in risk of war, largely because of land hunger. Sometimes European wars spread to America. At least once—our French and Indian War (Europe's Seven Years War)—war started in America and spread to Europe.[39] By 1754, there were 1,042,000 English colonists and only 55,000 French colonists. Both British and French colonists claimed territory along the Ohio River. In July 1749, the governor of New France sent troops to show the French flag.[40] They traveled down the Alleghany and found six English traders trading with Indians. Captain Pierre-Joseph Céleron sent them home, with a letter to Governor James Hamilton of Pennsylvania, explaining they could avoid conflict by keeping English colonists out of lands France claimed. However, English traders were much closer to the Indians than French traders and could offer goods at only a quarter of the French prices. The English were not frightened away, and in 1753 the French governor decided to build a series of forts to keep the English out. On 11 Dec. 53 a Virginian officer, George Washington (1732-99), appeared at one of the forts south of Lake Erie and presented a letter from Governor Robert Dinwiddie explaining that the forts were in English territory, and the French must leave.[41] The French were no more willing to accept their competitor's demands than the English had been in 1749. In spring 1754, Governor Dinwiddie sent Washington to build a fort where the Alleghany and Monongahela meet (now Pittsburgh) to form the Ohio River. He arrived after the French had already build Fort Duquesne there.

Therefore, Washington built Fort Necessity about fifty miles south of Fort Duquesne, only to be expelled by a superior French force. Benjamin Franklin, among others, saw that the colonies could only stand up to the French if they united, and on 9 May 54 his *Pennsylvania Gazette* published his cartoon of a snake divided into 13 parts, with each part having the name of a colony. His caption read: "Join or Die."[42] Delegates from seven colonies met in Albany on June 19 to plan their unification and to confer with a delegation from the Six Nations of Iroquois. The colonies formed a plan for unification which they referred to the British Parliament. Parliament judged the plan too democratic and did not act on it.[43] However, Parliament was willing to build roads into the wilderness to bolster the British cause. Major general Edward Braddock was dispatched to build a southern road to Fort Duquesne. Washington led Braddock and his men but Braddock declined to take precautions which Washington recommended, and he paid for that folly with his life when French and Indians ambushed the expedition.[44] Britain could hardly loose a general and his men (Washington obviously escaped) without responding. This was the first world war, since it spread to Europe and to colonies elsewhere. British dominance of the seas enabled it to win, in 1763.

Britain won the war, then lost the peace. Americans thought they had helped defeat the French so they could gain access to the Ohio River Valley. However, Britain had neutralized Ohio Indians with the promise of a definite boundary to keep Americans out of their lands.[45] Indians were shocked to learn that France had deeded to Britain the disputed lands which Indians felt was theirs, and that the French had no right to give it away. Furthermore, when General Jeffrey Amherst took over French forts, he banned giving presents to Indians, as the French had, which was really paying rent for use of the land. The loss of gifts of powder and shot meant that some Indians would starve. Into this crisis strode a visionary, Neolin, know to English as Delaware Prophet. He preached driving out the English and returning to the old ways before guns. Indian chiefs took up the message, under leadership of Ottawa chief, Pontiac. Pontiac's Rebellion, in spring 1763, involved Indians using surprise to capture several forts which had stored muskets and ammunition.[46] Indians killed over 2000 settlers and soldiers. Amherst countered with the first known instance of biological warfare: he had blankets from smallpox victims given to Indians as presents, which led to an epidemic, killing hundreds of Indians. In response to the rebellion, Britain's Parliament proclaimed a boundary running the length of the Appalachian Mountains, with colonists east and Indians west of it. To ensure peace and give employment to its soldiers, Britain also left troops in America and imposed quartering them on Americans.[47]

The war had been expensive, and since the British felt they had fought it to save the colonies, the colonies should help pay the war debt. A decade of cold war followed, 1764-74, in which Britain tried different tax strategies and tactics, to all of which the Americans responded with what became their mantra: no taxation without representation.[48] (Parliament might have avoided a conflict by giving each colony a representative in Parliament; they could have been outvoted on critical issues.) Continued friction between the two peoples gradually turned the cold war into a hot one. That war is commonly called the American Revolution, but was not a revolution as we now know them, beginning with the French Revolution, as involving class warfare.[49]

The Proclamation Line of 1763 and taxes were major American incentives to war, but there were other grievances as well, such as the "Boston Massacre" (1770), in which a hostile crowd threw stones and snowballs at soldiers occupying Boston to ensure tax collection.[50] The soldiers, without any orders, fired at the Bostonians in self defense, killing three, and two of the six wounded died later. Radical lawyer John Adams defended the soldiers with a self defense plea and had them acquitted. Paul Revere published his drawing after the fact, showing the captain giving an order to fire, turning the "Boston Massacre" into an American propaganda victory.[51] Another famous episode was the response of some Bostonians to the Tea Act of 1773, giving the British East India Company a monopoly on importing tea to American colonies. Fifty or sixty Boston men of all sorts on 16 Dec. 73 dressed as Indians, boarded an East India ship, and dumped 45 valuable tons of tea into the harbor.[52] New York Sons of Liberty soon did the same in their harbor. Britain responded with a series of what Americans called "Intolerable Acts" in 1774, including closure of Boston Harbor. The first Continental Congress from 12 colonies met in Philadelphia, 5 Sept.-26 Oct. 74 and adopted measures to resist British oppression. Patrick Henry in Virginia responded to such oppression on 20 March 75: "Is life so dear, or peace so sweet, as to be purchased at the price of chains and slavery? Forbid it Almighty God! I know not what course others may take, but as for me, give me liberty or give me death!"[53]

# War of Independence

The hot war began on April 18, 1775 when General Thomas Gage in Boston ordered 700 infantrymen to march on Concord and seize a store of ammunition. Both sides had spies, which is how Gage knew of the storehouse and how the Americans knew about the troops sent out at night, allowing Paul Revere to ride through the night to alert militia, the British are coming![54] When the Redcoats reached Lexington about seventy armed minutemen met them but had no plan. When ordered to throw down their guns, they backed away, holding their guns. No order to shoot was given but Redcoats fired, killing eight and wounding ten minutemen. News of that loss spread quickly, and when Redcoats reached the Concord bridge, Americans fired on them, killing three and wounding five.[55] The British decided they could not take the bridge and retreated to Boston, but were followed by almost 4000 militiamen who took shots at them when they could. British casualties were 73 dead and 202 wounded or missing, and militiamen suffered 95 casualties.[56]

Each colony had militia in every town large enough to organize one.[57] England had had militia in its towns also, but they were inadequate fighting forces, and during the 1600s they had been replaced by "select militia," which easily became detested standing armies. American colonies revived an obsolete English custom, requiring militiamen to have their own guns and ammunition, because colonies could not afford to supply them. Some colonies did supply guns to men too poor to buy one.[58] Guns were precarious weapons, frequently broken. Blacksmiths could make some repairs, but a militia or army needed a gunsmith. Before the war, gunsmiths mostly repaired European guns, but during the war some began making guns. At the start of war, Massachusetts had more gunsmiths than government could hire—not a problem for other colonies.[59] Continental Congress asked the emerging states to seize guns from Loyalists, which they did, either paying for them or giving owners an I.O.U. to be paid after the war. Militia could be supplied locally, but a Continental Army could not operate with a variety of local guns. The Continental Army imported 80% of its guns from France and Holland and 90% of its ammunition.[60]

As the Americans became alienated from what they began viewing as a tyrannical government, they awoke to the adage that the enemy of my enemy is my friend. The French also appreciated this possibility, but responded cautiously, waiting to see if Americans might be able to win before openly supporting them.[61] Militia in 1775 repelled Redcoats at Lexington and fought bravely at the Battle of Bunker Hill, but Washington learned militia were unreliable—he called militia "a broken stick"—and he was pleased if militiamen fired one shot before fleeing.[62] In 1777 militia again fought well with a Continental Army under General Horatio Gates against General John Burgoyne as he marched south from Canada through New York countryside.[63] Burgoyne's defeat provided the French with enough confidence to openly support Americans.[64] France provided guns and ammunition for the Continental Army, and on 11 July 80, a French fleet reached Rhode Island, and Count Rochambeau with his army of 5000 disembarked.[65] At times, Washington had commanded 15,000 troops, but by 1780, he may have had fewer men than Rochambeau. Not until spring 1781 did Rochambeau think it safe to join Washington north of New York. Washington's Continental Army had staying power but was unable to defeat Britain. Washington and Rochambeau were able to coordinate their march south to attack General Charles Cornwallis with the movement of a French fleet under Admiral de Grasse from the West Indies to Chesapeake Bay. Cornwallis had led his army through the South, liberating slaves, and winning some battles, loosing others.[66] He could live off the land for food, but not for military supplies, and so he marched to Yorktown, Virginia to await a British fleet with supplies. However, de Grasse's fleet reached the mouth of Chesapeake Bay before Admiral Graves' fleet did and was able to prevent British supplies reaching Cornwallis.[67] The Americans and French besieged Cornwallis' fort, October 1-19, before Cornwallis surrendered. That was the effective defeat of British forces, though some fighting continued into 1782. A peace treaty was negotiated in Paris, 27 Sept.-30 Nov. 82, which was quite favorable for America, since Britain feared a weak America would become a French client.[68]

A complication of this struggle was the existence of different Indian tribes along the periphery of American settlements.[69] A few allied with the

Americans—Oneidas, Tuscaroras, and some Mohawks—some wanted to be neutral, and most allied with the British.[70] As a whole, Indians suffered from this war, especially after their British allies withdrew from the periphery following acceptance of the peace treaty.

## Conclusion

Having enough guns had been essential for Americans to defend themselves from Indians and from colonists of France and Spain, and later, to liberate themselves from British rule, and all those conflicts were successful steps toward the special status of guns in America. Professional Alexander DeConde surveyed this history, but thought that other historians had exaggerated how many guns were in colonial America.[71]

# 2

# FROM SECOND AMENDMENT TO
# CIVIL WAR AND INDIAN WARS

With signing of the "Declaration of Independence" on July 4, 1776, rebellious British colonies officially became United States. To fight for independence, they adopted "Articles of Confederation" (1777), which worked well enough during wartime, with Congress and General Washington sharing executive duties.[1] However, afterwards, it proved unsatisfactory. All thirteen states adopted constitutions in 1776-80, and some constitutions contained bills of rights, inspired by the one presented by Parliament to William and Mary in 1689, which had guaranteed Protestant rights to guns (see ch. 1).[2] After the War of Independence, Congress realized that it had negligible revenues and owed pay to its disbanded army.[3] Congress did allow soldiers to take home their guns from the Continental Army.[4] When army pay did not seem to be Congress' most pressing problem, on 17 June 83, about 80 veterans from Lancaster marched to Philadelphia, where they were joined by about 200 other veterans and demonstrated before Independence Hall. When Pennsylvania did not scatter them, Congress moved its session to Princeton.[5] Shay's Rebellion (Aug.-Dec. 1786) in western Massachusetts was similar to Bacon's Rebellion in western Virginia (1675-76) in being prompted by financial distress to which eastern legislatures responded, in the opinion of rebels, too slowly and too weakly.[6] Massachusetts squashed Shay's, just as Virginia had Bacon's, but this time the rebellion helped states realize the inadequacy of the Articles of Confederation for peacetime, and it helped Alexander Hamilton realize the need for a regular army.[7] A convention to revise the Articles met in Philadelphia on 14 May 87 and soon realized revision was impractical, and it wrote a new constitution.[8] Heated arguments followed, and the resulting document represented a series of compromises, including slaves, women, and Indians being excluded from "all men are created equal."[9] Upon completion, on September 28,[10] Congress sent it to the states for ratification, where debates ensued between those who believed that a strong federal government was needed to ensure domestic tranquility and strength abroad versus those who feared a federal government might tyrannize states, as Britain had tyrannize its American colonies.[11] Firebrand Patrick Henry complained that the Constitution "does not leave us the means of defending our rights, or waging war against tyrants."[12] Another compromise was to add a Bill of Rights with ten amendments and a provision to add others as needed.[13]

Least clear of the amendments was the second: "A well regulated Militia, being necessary to the security of a free State, the right of the people to keep and bear Arms, shall not be infringed." A debate raged throughout much of the 1900s and later over whether the emphasis should be on the first clause, giving states power to regulate militia, or on the second, giving the people the right to bear arms.[14] Of course, guns are only one kind of arms; slingshots and/or swords might satisfy the amendment. During the 1900s, the U.S. Supreme Court nodded toward states, but after the NRA's sustained campaign, a conservative Court in 2008 nodded toward "the people's right to bear Arms."[15] Actually, framers of the Second Amendment had in mind neither state regulation nor individual's rights to guns—they assumed that any reputable white man who wanted a gun would get one. Authors of the Bill of Rights worried about historical examples of abuse by the British government with a standing army: Charles I's attempt to intimidate Parliament, Cromwell's use of one to rule, James II's attempt to establish an Irish army and dismiss Protestant soldiers (1685), and Britain's use of its army and navy to bully American colonies. The Bill of Rights, therefore, provided for state militias to be counterweights to a federal army. However, the poor performance of militias during the past war had convinced Washington and his closest officers that without central instruction and coordination, militias were unreliable and so, of very little use.[16]

One thing is clear: framers of our Constitution expected government to meet the needs of citizens. If those having private guns became a menace to public safety, the Constitution's Article I, Section 8 gave Congress the responsibility to raise armies and "suppress Insurrections," and "To provide for organizing, arming, and disciplining, the Militia."

Europe was able to make peace only after centuries of violent warfare, and America's gun problems seem tied to our constant warfare. One military historian, Geoffrey Perret, entitled his history *A Country Made by War: from the Revolution to Vietnam—America's Rise to Power* (1989), and military historians Fred Anderson and Andrew Cayton entitled theirs *The Dominion of War: Empire and Liberty in North America, 1500-2000* (2005). Perret explained:[17]

America's wars have been like the rungs on a ladder by which it rose to greatness. No other nation has triumphed so long, so consistently or on such a vast scale through force of arms.

To which Anderson and Cayton add: "war has been the engine of change in North America for 500 years."[18] Those wars stimulated our gun industry (ch.4), but success at war also increased the tendency of veterans and others to use guns to resolve peacetime conflicts.

Following the War of Independence, U.S. Federal Government needed to be established. In the Ohio Valley, "Roughly twenty white people were scalped every month in 1790, or carried off to a fate unknown but easily imagined."[19] Secretary of War Henry Knox advised President Washington that the land being fought over belonged to the Indians, despite what the peace treaty with Britain said. However, America could not afford to have its citizens slaughtered without response, so Continental Army veteran General Josiah Harmar led 400 of the Army's 900 regulars and 1100 militiamen from Fort Washington (now, Cincinnati), to the forks of the Maumee River (now, Fort Wayne IN), to show the Indians who was boss.[20] In October, they marched into a trap, the militiamen fled and the regulars were slaughtered. At his court-martial Harmer explained that leading his remnant to safety was all he could do.[21] Those Indians attacking them had traded furs to British traders for guns, ammunition, and gun repairs. Next, Washington sent General Arthur St. Clair, who left Fort Washington in August with 600 Army regulars, 600 militiamen, and 800 volunteers, to march to the headwaters of the Wabash River and attack

Miami Indians. When they arrived only 1400 men were fit to fight. Before dawn on November 4, Miami, Shawnee, and Delaware Indians attacked the Americans, who sustained 890 casualties before escaping, with Indians suffering about 60 casualties.[22]

These two defeats convinced Congress that it needed to both allow Washington to raise the standing army to 5000 and revise the law on militia, as Washington requested, so he could call up militia, as needed.[23] However, the Uniform Militia Act (1792) was so weak that neither Washington nor his Federalist Party liked it.[24] Militia members were supposed to provide their own guns and equipment. Now that the Federal Government was functioning, Congress decided it feared taxes more than it feared Washington. A situation did eventually emerge in which the Federal Government tyrannized southern states—the Civil War—but the Constitution's Article III, Section 3 provided for war against treason. Attempting to leave the Union could be interpreted as treason by the Federal Government, though the southern states would not have agreed, nor would southern states ask the Supreme Court to decide this issue.

Washington increased the Army to 5000 men, with 3-year enlistments. In 1793, after attempts for peace failed, a third foray was commanded by impetuous "Mad" General Anthony Wayne, who had 2000 Army regulars and 1500 Kentucky militiamen.[25] On August 20, they marched down the Maumee River toward British Fort Maumee. They encountered Indians who had gained confidence from the defeat of two previous armies, but this time the Americans did not flee, but charged with bayonets, and it was the Indians' turn to flee, to Fort Maumee, only to find that the British commander would not open the gates from fear of starting a war with the Americans. The Indians could only disperse, and America claimed victory at the Battle of the Fallen Timbers, and in the Treaty of Greenville (1795), the Indians relinquished claim to two-thirds of what is now Ohio.[26]

Meanwhile, Congress imposed a tax on liquor, domestic or foreign made, to pay for war debts, and in July-Nov. 1794 a Whiskey Rebellion occurred in western Pennsylvania,[27] after Wayne's victory but before he had marched back from the Ohio Valley. Backwoodsmen in western Pennsylvania responded to the tax by attacking the tax collectors (repeating a pattern of behavior which had preceded the War of Independence).[28] President Washington sent Attorney General William Bradford to

Pittsburgh to try to make peace. Bradford reported that radicals had sent to Kentucky for ammunition and allies. Washington himself traveled to Carlisle, Pennsylvania to organize an army of militia from four states and remaining Army personnel into an army of 12,950 men under Governor Henry "Light-Horse Harry" Lee of Virginia. With Wayne marching from the west and Lee from the east, the Whiskey Rebellion collapsed without bloodshed, and Washington proclaimed a day of thanksgiving.[29] Twenty men were tried for treason and 18 were acquitted; the two found guilty received a presidential pardon.

Shay's Rebellion (1786) and Whiskey Rebellion (1794) showed the power of the state and federal governments to suppress local disturbances, so that ended that, did it not? Oh, no. In 1798, Congress anticipated war with France, and imposed a property tax, to begin raising revenue to fight it. John Fries (ca. 1750-1818) led a rebellion against that tax in western Pennsylvania, and raised several hundred men from three counties.[30] On 15 January 1799, a Judge William Henry issued subpoenas for activists in the resistance. They were uncooperative and the subpoenas were given to a federal marshal. The men subpoenaed were arrested, and others sought to rescue them from confinement in Bethlehem. The rescue squad was quite large, and so the marshal gave them to Fries, who released them. With no progress by March, President John Adams issued a proclamation on 12 March 99 commanding dispersal and cooperation with authorities. That happened, but Fries was arrested and sentenced to death. President Adams pardoned him. These three rebellions were minor events in American history, but they take on significance in recent decades in relation to militia debates. It seems unlikely that militias 170 years later were aware of this history, and maybe would not even have cared.

Algerian pirates seized two American ships in the Mediterranean in 1785, and eleven more ships in 1793; America agreed to pay a ransom—a new warship— for their release.[31] That made Algeria's neighboring ruler of Tripoli jealous. America needed warships to end the vulnerability of its commerce at sea. The Continental Congress had put ships to sea during the War of Independence, with John Paul Jones being its notable hero, but there had been no holdover fleet between the end of that war and the new government under Washington.[32] In 1794 Congress authorized three 44-gun frigates at $100,000 each with projected building time of one per year.

It took four years to build them, at a cost of over $300,000 each, but "Even a generation later, they could out-sail and out-fight any frigate on any sea."[33]

In the 1790s, during a war between Britain and France, Britain removed its forts and soldiers from the Ohio Valley in exchange for an American promise not to allow French privateers into its ports—which was trading one problem for another, as French ships then preyed on American sea trade in retaliation.[34] British traders in the Ohio Valley continued trading ammunition to Indians in exchange for furs.

It is worth interrupting this historical summary to discuss an important concurrent subject—history of dueling in America.[35] Dueling was a custom in many European countries, a custom that settlers brought with them to America. It seems likely it was less common in America than in Europe, since American society was still developing and so was more flexible than Europe's. Nevertheless, there were two duels of historical significance. First and most famous was between a remarkable Alexander Hamilton (1757-1804) and a less fondly remembered Aaron Burr (1756-1836).[36] Both were prominent statesmen who had known each other for years and eventually became rivals. In 1804, Burr ran for governor of New York State, and Hamilton believed he was unfit for office and campaigned vigorously against his candidacy. Burr became convinced his honor had been impugned and challenged Hamilton to a duel. Hamilton, whose oldest son, Philip, had died in a duel in 1802, defending his father's honor, could have talked his way out of it but, foolishly, did not. He accepted and fired his pistol into the air, and Burr shot him dead. It was a hollow victory, for Burr never recovered his reputation. Both men could have accomplished much more than they did if they had been collaborators instead of rivals. What Hamilton did accomplish was impressive but not much appreciated in public memory until theater genius Lin-Manuel Miranda was inspired by Ron Chernow's biography, *Alexander Hamilton* (2004), to turn this political genius' life into a musical (2016)!

Fig. 2. Aaron Burr (shooter). Alexander Hamilton (victim).

In his recent history of the War of 1812, Alan Taylor called it a "civil war," since substantial numbers of American Tories had moved to Canada during and after the War of Independence, some Irish had joined the British Army while others had immigrated to America, and both Canada/Britain and the United States had Indian allies. "Americans fought Americans, Irish battled Irish, and Indians attacked one another."[37] Taylor made this claim because he focused on men who fought in opposing armies and navies. He also limited his book to war along the Canadian-American boundary, omitting war on the Atlantic and in the South. At the time, Britain was already fighting France and did not want an American war. However, its navy was short of men and were stopping American ships at sea and searching crews for British deserters. That was the explicit cause of the war which Gordon Wood called "the strangest war in American history."[38] The first of several ironies was that New England merchants did not want war, despite it being their ships being searched, because war interfered with trade. Backers of war were Congressmen from the West, where people wanted to seize as much of Canada as possible, and in the South, where people wanted to seize Florida.[39] President Madison hoped that war would unite his squabbling Republican Party before he campaigned for a second term.[40]

America declared war in June 1812; ironically, before then Britain had repealed its law allowing its ships to search American ships, but knowledge of that repeal only reached America later. A British delegation reached Washington to talk peace, but it arrived too late. Despite the British navy being the best in the world, American won naval victories in the Atlantic, where British cannon balls failed to penetrate the *Constitution's* thick wooden hull, and it became known as "Old Ironsides." Americans also won a naval victory under Commodore Oliver Hazard Perry (1785-1819) in the Battle of Lake Erie, near Put-in-Bay, Ohio (where there is now a monument to peace). Britain had built a small fleet on the north shore of Lake Erie and America had built a slightly larger fleet on the south shore. During the battle, Perry's flagship, *Lawrence*, was very badly damaged and many of his men were casualties. He had five seamen row him to another ship, *Niagara*, and continued the fight against already-damaged British ships. After his victory, he repaired his ships and used them to move the army under General William Henry Harrison to the north side of the lake, from which they marched northeast to meet the British, Canadians, and Indians at the Battle of the Thames, which Americans also won.[41] But those victories were followed by a series of defeats as other American armies invaded Canada under incompetent generals leading poorly trained troops. (The U.S. Naval victories enticed Theodore Roosevelt to write *The Naval War of 1812*, in 1882.)

In the South, in August, 1813, Creek Indians and their British allies attacked Fort Mims, to which civilians had fled, and massacred over 300 Americans. In response, Andrew Jackson (1767-1845) led Tennessee and Kentucky militias and Cherokee, Choctaw, and Chickasaw Indians into five battles against the Creeks, whose final defeat on 27 March, 1814, at the Battle of Horseshoe Bend, killed about 3000 Creeks, in the worst defeat of Indians in American warfare.[42] The Creeks also lost half of their land—23 million acres. Jackson became a U.S. Army general in southern Louisiana, and in December 1814 the British attempted to invade New Orleans with 7500 troops under Sir Edward Packenham. Jackson built defenses for his 4500 troops, who lacked the skill and fortitude to fight in the open, and waited for Packenham's charge, on 8 Jan. 1815, which led to 2036 British casualties (including Packenham), with 8 Americans killed and 13 wounded.[43] Tragically, the Battle of New Orleans occurred after the peace of Ghent was signed on December 24, but news of Jackson's victory reached Americans before news of peace did. (If trans-Atlantic telegraphy had existed, the war could have been avoided.) Historians credit this otherwise minor war as having transformed 18 United States into a nation, The United States.[44] It also gave Canadians their first sense of being one people. Regardless of the merits of Taylor's civil-war thesis, this was certainly an imperialistic war. Although the war accomplished little, it "inflicted the biggest defeats on land and sea suffered up to that time by British forces."[45] And the war removed British forces and traders who had supported Indians on the western frontier.

Andrew Jackson had been a lawyer in Tennessee who rose to be a prosecutor in Nashville in 1788. The sarcasm of an opposing lawyer, Avery, led Jackson to challenge him to a duel on 12 August 88. Avery was reluctant, but accepted, and, fortunately, their seconds persuaded both to shoot into the air.[46] Jackson helped write the Tennessee constitution, and when Tennessee was admitted to the Union in 1796, he was elected its first Congressman.[47] In 1797, he became instead a Tennessee Senator. In 1806, Jackson became offended in another argument and challenged Charles Dickinson to a duel. Dickinson accepted, had the first shot and fractured two ribs of Jackson (which never healed properly); Jackson then shot him dead.[48] Enough? No! In 1813, Jackson was a second in a duel, in which both duelists received slight wounds. Jackson then became embroiled in a conflict with Thomas Benton, brother of one dualist, and a spontaneous duel occurred in which Jackson was wounded in his left arm and shoulder.[49] All of Nashville's physicians worked to prevent him from dying from loss of blood. If Jackson had died in either duel, he would never have defeated the British in Louisiana in 1815 or become a president of the United States. Dueling faded away in the northern states before the Civil War and after that war in the South and West. A point to appreciate here is that one aspect of gun carnage in America ended!

Following his decisive victory in New Orleans,[50] Jackson became U.S. Army General of the Southern District. He thought that as long as Indians remained in the South, foreign powers would ally with them against America.[51] He played an influential role in the purchase of lands from the southern tribes. A fort in West Florida 60 miles from the U.S. border had been occupied by runaway slaves who were armed by the British. At the directive of Secretary of War William Crawford, Jackson wrote to the Spanish governor of Florida saying the fort threatened America and should be removed.[52] Governor Mauricio de Zúñiga replied that Jackson could remove it and that he would serve under Jackson in doing so. Jackson directed General Edmund Gaines to build a fort within the American boundary and then attack the fort, which Gaines did. On 27 July 1816, a supporting Naval vessel from New Orleans fired a shot at the fort, and hit its magazine, which exploded, killing 270 and wounding 61. Meanwhile, Indians from lands America had either conquered from Creeks or bought from other southern tribes fled to Florida and became part of a group called by then Seminoles. One or more British agents were arming and advising them. Seminoles at Fowltown were accused of killing Georgians. Gaines sent a brigade to arrest the murderers, but when the soldiers arrived, they were fired upon and returned fire. Indians then fled and Americans burned the town. Nine days later, Seminoles ambushed a boat with 40 soldiers, 7 women, and 4 children, killing 37 soldiers, all children, and either killed or kidnapped the women. In 1817, a new Secretary of War, John C. Calhoun, authorized Jackson to march into Florida and end the Seminole threat.[53] Jackson did, but he felt the only way to permanently end the threat was by America acquiring Florida, as he wrote to President Monroe.[54] Monroe responded by asking Calhoun not to attack any Spanish post, but Calhoun never got around to writing such a letter to Jackson,[55] who was unlikely to have been influenced by it if received.

Jackson's concern over slaves running into Florida and his behavior convinced Spain in 1819 that its realistic choice was to sell Florida to the United States. Jackson became a national hero, which alarmed John Calhoun and Henry Clay, who saw him as a rival for the presidency.[56] A Congressional committee criticized Jackson for executing two British traders in Florida. There was concern that Jackson might become another Napoleon. However, America's population was doubling about every two decades, and territorial imperialism was too popular for the public to pay attention to such political fears. By 1825, Jackson had forced Indians to relinquish lands the size of Western Europe, which lands became the Cotton Kingdom.[57] In the 1824 election, Jackson won 40,000 more votes for president than John Quincy Adams, but the decision had to go to the House of Representatives which made Adams president. (Trump got his presidency from the Electoral College, despite Clinton's winning three million more votes.)

Jackson was an activist who was glad to take charge. He won the presidency in 1828 and again in 1832. A blight on his presidency was Indian removal. It involved the "Five Civilized Tribes" in the South. Although they had already ceded most of their lands, Southerners wanted the rest of it.[58]

By 1828, when Jackson won the presidency, Indians had relinquished most lands east of the Mississippi, yet whites wanted the rest of it. In 1830, Jackson urged Congress to pass an Indian Removal Act.[59] One excuse for removal was the fact that the federal government could not preventing adjacent farmers from invading Indian lands. This is a bit like closing banks because government could not prevent bank robberies. Cherokees resisted in the Supreme Court, and Chief Justice John Marshall ruled in their favor on 18 March 1831 and again on 3 March 1832.[60]

Jackson ignored that ruling, for which Congress should have impeached him. By 1832, Jackson's administration planned to remove Indians not only from the Southeast, but also the Sauks and Fox from what became Illinois and Wisconsin. One leader, Black Hawk, led a resistance in what became known as the Black Hawk War.[61] "The army managed it with a fair degree of humanity and skill, but with distaste."[62] The number of Cherokees who began the journey in 1838 were 16,000; after six months and a thousand miles, only 12,000 survived to reach their new home in Oklahoma. The Battan Death March, April 1942, covered 60-70 miles; 60,000-80,000 Filipinos and U.S. prisoners of war began the march, and there were 5000-18,000 Filipino and 500-650 U.S. deaths along the way. Japanese troops were harsh guards, and their general, Masaharu Homma, was executed after World War II, for having supervised a war crime. U.S. troops supervising the Indian forced trips from the east to Oklahoma were not as inhumane as those Japanese troops much later were.

Seminoles remained in Florida, reinforced by Creeks and runaway slaves, and resisted removal. The Second Seminole War began in 1835; by 1843 nearly 5000 of them were removed, several hundred killed, and about 300 remained in Florida. In the 1820s, Americans began settling in Indian territory in Illinois. Most tribes gave up and crossed the Mississippi, but Sauks in Illinois and Wisconsin under Black Hawk resisted until 1831, when they crossed the Mississippi and had conflicts with tribes already there. In 1832, about two thousand Sauks crossed back into Illinois. When Black Hawk confronted a militia and finally decided to surrender, the militia thought it was a trick and fired. The Sauks fled, and when Black Hawk tried again to surrender, he failed again. At the Bad Axe River at least 150 men, women, and children were killed and the remainder were taken across the Mississippi.[63] The attempt to assassinate President Jackson by Richard Lawrence (c. 1800-61) in 1835 had no connection to Jacksons treatment of Indians; Lawrence was mentally ill.[64]

The Age of Jackson in America was also the Age of Antonio de Santa Anna (1794-1876) in Mexico.[65] Mexico fought a war of independence against Spain in 1821, which gave Mexico a northern boundary problem. Its northern territories were thinly populated and not growing significantly. One solution was to welcome Americans to Texas to become Mexicans. Mexico outlawed slavery but made an exception for the Americans. Mexico did not have a comparable experience of American colonies that had been essentially democratically governed for more than a century before a war of independence. Mexico's government was unstable. In 1835 President Santa Anna declared himself dictator and nullified the Mexican Constitution of 1824.

Americans in Texas, with some Mexicans' help, revolted in 1835. Santa Anna already had experience suppressing revolts elsewhere, and he had an army of 5000 that besieged a force of 187—led by David Crockett, James Bowie, and William Travis—[66] in the Alamo in San Antonio, 23 Feb.-6 March, 1836.[67] The Americans there decided to defend their fort in the face of overwhelming odds, and all defenders were killed, and Santa Anna lost about 600 men. Part of Santa Anna's army marched on and encountered about 400 Americans at Goliad who surrendered. He ordered their execution, and 342 of them were killed. Others escaped and spread the word about what had happened. For Indian revolts which Santa Anna had suppressed, that would have been enough to end this revolt. However, Sam Houston (1793-1863)—who had been an officer under Jackson at the Battle for New Orleans[68]and then a political leader in Tennessee—raised an army of 800 men and laid a trap for Santa Anna on a bank of the San Jacinto River in 1836. Santa Anna had 900 men there and lost 650 of them (in 18 minutes) to Houston's loss of two. Victorious Houston became the first governor of a free Texas.[69]

In the U.S. election of 1844, Jackson's protégé, James K. Polk (1795-1849) defeated Clay with a campaign to annex Texas and Oregon.[70] However, before Polk took office in March 1845, President John Tyler had Congress vote to annex Texas. The independent nation of Texas claimed its southern boundary as the Rio Grande River, even though its settlements were north of the Nueces River. Polk accepted that claim and sent an army to the Rio Grande, opposite to the Mexican city of Matamoros. Mexican troops in the area greatly outnumbered the American troops, and 1600 of them crossed the Rio Grande and ambushed an American patrol of 63 dragoons, killing 16. Mexico, with an army four times larger than Americas, declared war on America, but word of it only reached Washington after Polk persuaded the Senate to declare war on Mexico. Despite Mexico's larger army, the United States won the Mexican-American War with better trained officers, better weapons, and greater national wealth, to take care of its army's needs.[71] After General Scott took Mexico City, Sam Grant wrote to his fiancé on 25 July 46: "About all the Texans think it perfectly right to impose upon the people of a conquered city to any extent, and even to murder them where the act can be covered by the dark, and how much they seem to enjoy acts of violence, too!"[72] The Mexican-American War saw the introduction into warfare of anesthetics, telegraph, and war correspondents.[73] America then forced Mexico to sell it territory in the Southwest comparable in size to the Louisiana Purchase from France (1803).

Polk did not want two wars, and the United States and Great Britain split the Oregon Territory between them at the 49th Parallel, not the Columbia River, but Britain got all of Vancouver Island.

The U.S. Army built roads and forts in the West, and in the 1850s the Army doubled to 16,000 officers and men.[74] The roads and forts were to enable the Army to cope with hostile Indians over a vast territory; the forts became centers for settlers, and few forts were later dismantled. Although Plains Indians got horses and guns, their guns were seldom as effective as those of the Army. In 1858, in the Yakima Indian War, 1000 Indians with muskets faced 500 troops at the Battle of Four Lakes. The Indians had smooth-bore muskets, but soldiers had new rifled muskets, and they began a deadly fire before the Indians were in range to use their muskets.[75] Yakimas tried again at the Battle of Spokane Plain and lost even more men than they had at Four Lakes. That ended the war.

During the 1800s, a number of religious groups arose, many of which did not survive. Mormon religion both survived and flourished.[76] Its charismatic founder, Joseph Smith (1805-44), who grew up in upstate New York, advocated polygamy, which angered "gentiles," who had him arrested at a Mormon settlement, Nauvoo, Illinois.[77] However, an angry mob kidnaped and lynched him. Leadership passed to Brigham Young (1801-77), who consulted a published report from U.S. Army explorer of western territory. Young decided that the fertile, but isolated, Salt Lake region would enable Mormons to settle without harassment.

With the northern and southern boundaries settled, slavery became the burning political issue. There were a few bloody slave revolts,[78] Southern states feared the political power of the abolitionists, who were led by William Lloyd Garrison (1805-79).[79] However, John Brown (1800-59) was the most controversial abolitionist of his time, and he remains controversial for having added violence to the polemic.[80] (One might reply that slavers had added violence, from the start of slavery.[81]) He and a few followers attacked Harpers Ferry Arsenal in 1859, to get guns for a slave revolt, which was a nightmare come true in the South, even though his band of guerillas was quickly defeated and he hanged.[82] When Abraham Lincoln, who had strong abolitionist sympathies, was elected president in 1860, southern states seceded from the Union and formed the Confederate States of America. When South Carolina decided to take Fort Sumter by force, it committed an act somewhat similar to Mexico's killing of American soldiers along the Rio Grande, though no soldiers were killed in the attack on Fort Sumter. Nevertheless, that attack was sufficient provocation for President Lincoln to raise a very large army to reassert control over Federal property.

The Civil War was revolutionary in several respects, most dramatically, ending slavery.[83] The Union Army won the war against a determined Confederacy with more men, more and better weapons, more extensive railroads, and a much stronger manufacturing industry, stimulated by war orders. Officers on both sides included West Point graduates, most notably Ulysses S. Grant and Robert E. Lee. Early in the war Confederate troops raided Harpers Ferry Armory and carried to Richmond its machinery, costing the Union half of its rifled arms production. Confederate war ships also harassed Union commercial ships in the Atlantic. Such tactics kept the war going for four years but could not affect the outcome.

In their textbook, *Out of Many: a History of the American People* (2000), John Faragher and three coauthors give a bar graph[84] showing the assets of North and South in 1861: population, N 71%, S 29%; factory production, N 91%, S 9 %; railroad mileages, N 71%, S 29%; iron production, N 94%, S 6%; farm acreage, N 75%, S 25%; wheat, N 81%, S 19%; cotton, N 4%, S 96%; wealth, N 75%, S 25%; % of eligible men in military service, N 44%, S 90%. The South's only hope was for the North to lose commitment, pick up its marbles, and go home, which never happen.

Fig. 3 Civil Water Battle

This was America's most costly war, in terms of casualties of opposing forces—497,000 (more than all other wars combined)-and lasting negative effects. Indians at Sand Creek, Colorado, 150-200 of whom were massacred by a volunteer force in 1864,[85] were unlikely to have been attacked in peacetime by a regular Army force. The northern economy was little affected by war; the southern economy was in shambles. Its infrastructure was severely damaged, and the wealth tied to slavery vanished.[86] The four million former slaves were only slightly better off, as they were given none of the assets of their former masters (whose main wealth was their slaves) and were often stuck working for them for subsistence wages. Those who escaped to the North did somewhat better.

John Wilkes Booth's assassination of President Lincoln on April

14, 1865, five days after Lee surrendered to Grant, was part of a foolish, desperate plot which he dreamed up and pulled in other Confederate sympathizers.[87] Booth, a professional actor, had acted in Shakespeare's "Julius Caesar," but obviously hoped for a better outcome this time. He gained entry into Lincoln's box at Ford's Theater because he was recognized as a house actor. By shooting Lincoln, he achieved his own death by gunfire, at age 26, and lasting infamy. He also set an example for the assassins of Presidents Garfield (1881)[88] and McKinley (1901).[89]

The end of war was not the end of conflict. Confederate veterans after the war in Pulaski, Tennessee founded the Ku Klux Klan, which did not last beyond the 1800s, but was revived in 1915.[90]

Out West during the Civil War, "Some outposts were abandoned entirely; others were garrisoned by soldiers too old, too sick, or too raw to fight in the regular armies."[91] Since fit soldiers had been sent east from Colorado Territory to places of conflict in the war, Indians became less deferential toward whites than before. In Minnesota, the Dakota Sioux became exasperated at the slowness, and sometimes defaulting, of the Federal Government to live up to its treaty obligations, and began an uprising on 17 Aug. 62 that cost 77 soldiers and 450-800 civilian casualties, with 150 Indian warriors dead and 38 hanged on 26 Dec. 62—the largest mass execution in American history.[92]

Governor John Evans raised a regiment of militiamen for 100 days in summer 1864. These men went out on an extermination mission, yet all they found to kill were about 20 Cheyenne women and children. Not having any more than that to show for their efforts, they went to the Indian sanctuary outside Fort Lyons and massacred those who had been guaranteed their safety. The Indian Wars in the West might be dated to that Sand Creek Massacre, 29 November 1864, before the Civil War ended, in which more than 125 women, children, and elderly Cheyennes and Arapahos were massacred—while Black Kettle waved an American flag to indicate loyalty.[93] Larry McMurtry said about 140 Indians died.[94] A participant in that militia had a different perspective on what the situation was. A former captain of that militia force, Eugene Ware, reported in 1911 that "The Indian idea was to have the Government feed the old people, women and children, while the bucks would ravage the country."[95]

In 1867, Indians massacred 80 soldiers from Fort Phil Kearny, Dakota

Territory.[96] Americans had committed atrocities against Indians in Dakota Territory, so this was not specifically payback for Sand Creek, though it amounted to that.

In 1811, a steamboat traveled down the Mississippi, beginning at Pittsburgh (on the Ohio River) to New Orleans. Steamboat travel on the Great Lakes began in 1817. Steamboats also began traveling up the Missouri. The Oregon Trail was expanded from a horse to a wagon trail in 1836, and the California Trail was in use by 1843. After the war, not all the troops went home, and those still in the army could be deployed out West. The first continental railroad began in 1863 at both Council Bluffs, Iowa and San Francisco, and was completed in 1869 at Promontory Point, Utah.[97] All these innovations were used to move troops. American technology became powerful enough to force nomadic or settled Indians onto reservations, out of the way, allowing Americans to settle everywhere else. The U.S. Calvary facilitated that process when and where needed. Sometimes Indians defied being herded to where U.S. government wanted them to go. That was the case in June 1876, when Sioux and Cheyenne warriors united under the leadership of Crazy Horse (c. 1840-77) in Montana, where about 700-750 of them attacked 1000 Army men plus about 300 Crow and Shoshoni auxiliary as they marched along Rosebud Creek. Indians inflicted casualties, 10 killed and 23 wounded, on the U.S. force, yet, Indians had their own casualties of over 100, and they retreated when they had exhausted their ammunition.[98]

They joined with other Indian tribes and had about 1800 warriors at the Little Big Horn River, MT. George Armstrong Custer (1839-76) was sent to block their leaving to the south while other troops approached from the north. Custer divided his force and proceeded to approach from three directions on 25 June 76. Since the Indians had superior numbers, they met the troops and killed all 210 in Custer's detachment.[99]

Last of the large Indian conflicts occurred at Wounded Knee, SD, on 30 December 1890.[100] The U.S. Army had become concerned over a Ghost Dance semi-religious movement that had spread from the plains. It was not inherently bellicose, but some followers had used it to encourage their hostile feelings toward the U.S. Army, which was monitoring them. The Army decided to ship about 100 Lakota Sioux men and 200 women and children to Omaha. They agreed, but then the soldiers wanted to collect their guns before the trip, which angered the men, who refused. A soldier attempted to take a rifle from one of them, and a rifle fired. That precipitated a massacre, in which 146 Indians and 25-31 soldiers died.

The closest Canada came to having war between Euro-Canadians and Indians were small-scale conflicts between Canadians and Metis, biracial communities of descendants of French fathers and Indian mothers. Carl Waldman listed 14 such incidents, 1816-85.[101]

Conflicts with Indians were not the only troubles in the West. Because of the way Americans settled the West, law enforcers were far apart and few in numbers. Consequently, banditry was a common problem, leading sometimes to shootouts between the lawful and the lawless. Harry Sinclair Drago collected surviving accounts of such troubles in *Road Agents and Train Robbers: Half a Century of Western Banditry* (1973). Even in towns with a law officer, there were saloons where cowhands and others could drink and fight, commonly with guns. Paul Trachtman placed western conflicts in context in *The Gunfighters* (1974), and Carl Breihan focused upon eight notable men and their guns in *Great Gunfighters of the West* (1977).

## Conclusions

This chapter follows U.S. history from independence through a new nation's growing struggles during the 1800s. It fought another war with Britain (1812-15) and a war with Mexico (1846-48) before the ultimate catastrophe, the Civil War (1861-65). After the Civil War, American resumed their push westward, which meant more conflicts with Indians. Histories of this period do not necessarily emphasize the role of guns, since that necessity could be taken for granted. However, the American gun industry was growing along with the country, and the people involved in that history new very well how important guns were to success, and when Custer did not discover until it was too late that the Indians he attacked had better guns than his troops did, he and his men paid the penalty of his ignorance with their lives. There could be no lasting victory for the Indians, who were subsequently defeated in battle and herded on to reservations.

# 3

## SHOOTING ANIMALS AND TARGETS

Hunting, shooting animals that threatened crops or livestock, and target shooting are major reasons why Americans have owned guns. Understand recreational users of guns, their guns, organizations, and commercial suppliers can help end gun violence. However, hunting is not a static aspect of American life. It has changed considerably throughout history in comparison to other uses of free time such as spectator sports, playing games, going to church, going on picnics, or going camping. Presently hunting is controversial and is likely to remain so.[1] Understanding its role in our society requires some historical background. In contrast, sport shooting in galleries or in contests is not controversial. We need to consider whether the hunting controversy is like the Protestant Reformation in which people fought over their beliefs until they realized that everyone should be free to worship as they please, or is it like the slavery debate in which the opponents of slavery never accepted the status quo? In recent decades hunting seems to have stirred up about as much debate as slavery did before the Civil War, but it is safe to say that this debate will not splinter the Union. As we survey the history of hunting in America we can ask why Americans hunted, how they justified it, and how non-hunters viewed hunters and hunting. One critic has classified hunters' motives into six categories: hungry, hired, hostile, happy, holist, and holy, though these categories are not mutually exclusive (a hungry, hired, or hostile hunter might also be a happy hunter).[2] Kheel's list illustrates diverse motives hunters have had and may continue to have, though the last two categories may be more rationalizations than motives (discussed below). There seem to be three reasons for target shooting: to improve one's shooting accuracy, recreation, or to compete in shooting matches.

Early Indians were certainly hungry hunters, and maybe also happy hunters. Since they were subsistence hunters, ethical issues usually did not arise. However, they exterminated many species of large mammals about 13,000 years ago, which today is lamentable.[3] From then until 1500 A.D. there were few additional extinctions, which seems more related to the small Indian population and primitive weapons rather than to conservation concerns. After European fur traders arrived, Indians east of the Mississippi River killed commercially important mammal species faster than they reproduced, leading to their disappearance over much of their range.[4] The introduction of guns and steel traps facilitated this endeavor.

English settlers came from a complex civilization which held diverse views on hunting. Ancient Greeks had viewed hunting as manly and character building. Surprisingly, Roman authors Sallust and Varro disapproved of hunting; it would be interesting to know if they also disapproved of all the blood and gore that occurred in the Coliseum. During the Middle Ages hunting became an aristocratic sport in Europe, and hunting manuals explained protocols and terminology as well as techniques. That ethos was challenged during the Protestant Reformation, beginning with Erasmus' *Praise of Folly* (1511) and Thomas More's *Utopia* (1516). These two authors were reformers, not Protestants, and if the ruling class had heeded their messages, the chances for a Reformation would have been slightly less. Montaigne also attacked hunting in his essay, "Of Cruelty" (1580). In *Don Quixote* (1605), Cervantes has a duke praise hunting, while Sancho Panza dismissed it as killing animals that do no harm to anyone. Puritans generally disapproved of hunting. However, all of those criticisms did not end hunting any more than similar criticisms reformed the Church. Although many New Englanders disapproved of hunting, Virginians were not Puritans and had a different opinion.

Settlers who had crops and livestock usually hunted raccoons, wolves, cougars, and other "pests" or predators. Bounties were paid for killing predators and the skins were also sold.[5] Some settlers became frontiersmen who abandoned farming in order to hunt for food and furs. Farmers viewed them as undependable citizens. The guns they used on deer were easily turned on Indians when conflicts arose, and when whites attacked Indians, there were apt to be reprisals, not against the elusive hunters but against sedentary farmers. Still, towns were glad to have wild animals sold in their meat markets. There were some wealthy planters, like George Washington, who imitated British aristocracy and gentry by introducing fox hunting. There were even a few hunting clubs during the 1700s. However, there was no way to restrict hunting to the upper classes as had been done in Europe. The Declaration of Independence did not complain about restricted hunting since there was none, other than restricted seasons on disappearing species, but frontier hunters certainly believed hunting was an inalienable right. [6] Frontier hunters' image improved during the War of Independence, when they brought rifles into the Continental Army. Although the war was won with muskets, riflemen gained status, and after the war they became folk heroes because of stories about Daniel Boone and James Fenimore Cooper's Leatherstocking novels. Leatherstocking was based on the mythic Boone, if not on the real man. Frontier hunters introduced shooting matches to America. Sometimes targets were inanimate objects, but often animals were targets, and the killer got the carcass. Frontiersmen proved they could live off the land as well as or better than Indians, but that was not enough to recommend hunting to many well-off Americans.

English naturalist Mark Catesby explored southeastern colonies in 1712-19 and 1722-26, collecting specimens which he described and illustrated in *Natural History of Carolina, Florida, and the Bahama Islands* (1729-47). His well-appreciated work set a precedent for others.[7] Adding to a store of knowledge from Catesby's book was an endeavor that appealed to Thomas Jefferson, who published his own natural history observations in *Notes on the State of Virginia* (1787).[8] However, Jefferson was too busy with affairs of state to indulge his curiosity as much as he might wish,[9] but after he became president and then made the Louisiana Purchase in 1803, he authorized his secretary, Meriwether Lewis, to organize an expedition to explore and describe this territory. The Lewis and Clark expedition set a fine example by observing, collecting, and describing many species of plants and animals previously unknown to science and bringing back specimens for museums.[10] Two of the birds discovered were named Lewis' Nutcracker and Clark's Woodpecker by the Scottish-American ornithologist, Alexander Wilson (1766-1813), who also described and illustrated them. Wilson had become enchanted with American birds as he disembarked from Britain in 1794. A red-headed woodpecker flew across his path, and since his few possessions included a gun, he shot it to inspect it more closely. He was impressed by its beauty and regretted having killed it. Yet, he continued killing American birds in order to describe them in *American Ornithology* (9 vols., 1808-14). His was the first prominent voice defending birds from market hunters and from farmers who shot them for eating a few seeds and did not appreciate their importance for eating insects.[11] Once he forgot his crusade and killed more Carolina parakeets than he needed for drawing, not, apparently for the sport of it, but to observe their curious habit of not abandoning their fallen comrades when they were shot.[12] (This habit helps explain why this species became extinct in the early 1900s.[13])

For species seen in vast flocks or herds, the myth of super-abundance undermined restraint. That was certainly true for the passenger pigeon and bison. The disgusting slaughter of passenger pigeons—the most abundant bird in North America—provoked a famous discussion of conservation in James Fenimore Cooper's *The Pioneers* (1823),[14] and a slaughter of bison— the most abundant hoofed mammal in North America—provoked a similar sentiment published in the same year by explorer Edwin James in his narrative of the Long Expedition to the Rocky Mountains.[15]

Wilson's ornithological achievements inspired John James Audubon (1785-1851) to exceed them in his own *Birds of America* (4 vols., 1827-38, no text) and *Ornithological Biography* (5 vols., 1831-39). Audubon aspired to paint all American birds at life size. He conveyed his exuberance for nature in dynamic poses of his bird drawings and in his lively text, which, however, was occasionally less reliable than Wilson's text. Audubon was also a happy hunter for many years before he appreciated Wilson's concern for preservation of wildlife.[16] During a Canada goose hunt, in which he confessed that "the number of geese obtained would seem to you so very large that I shall not specify it," his only lament was, "Oh that we had more guns!"[17] After he finished drawing birds, he turned to American mammals. He and several companions traveled up the Missouri to Fort Union in 1843 to observe and collect prairie mammals, including bison. Audubon himself did not participate in an orgy of bison slaughter, possibly because he felt he was too old to chase them on a horse. But members of his party got carried away with killing bison.[18] Although Audubon penned a pious lament, "that thousands multiplied by thousands of Buffaloes are murdered in senseless play," he did nothing to stop the slaughter by members of the party he led.[19]

In fact, his companions tried to stage their kills where he could watch. With Wilson and Audubon's publications for inspiration, other hunter-naturalists collected and described our wildlife and deposited their specimens and findings in public museums and libraries during the 1800s and 1900s.

Even scientific collecting was not enough to certify hunting as an important ruling class activity. That required importing the aristocratic hunting ethos from England. Henry William Herbert (1807-58) was an aristocrat banished to America in 1831 because of gambling debts.[20] In New York City he became the guru of upper class hunters who absorbed his teachings on sportsmanship. He also claimed that hunting is good training for military leadership. He fashioned a career out of writing hunting narratives in sports magazines and in novels under his pseudonym, Frank Forester. The climax of his writings was *Frank Forester's Field Sports of the United States and British Provinces of North America* (2 vols., 1849). His promising career ended in 1858, when his wife departed and he shot himself. By then, however, his legacy was established and was being embellished by other authors and artists who portrayed hunters and their quarry in landscapes. Thomas Doughty made drawings that were turned into lithographs that he and his brother published in their journal, *Cabinet of Natural History and American Rural Sports* in the 1830s.[21] The Englishman Arthur Fitzwilliam Tait specialized in hunting and fishing scenes, 1850s-70s. Original paintings were often bought by wealthy patrons, but Currier and Ives made engraved copies that were popular in the middle class. They engraved about 140 scenes of hunting, camping, trapping, and wild animals, almost a third of which were from Tait's work.

Fig. 4. Hunting Woodcock. Currier and Ives.

Another factor contributing to the popularity of hunting in the 1800s was a fairly steady improvement in the technology of guns and ammunition. Many of the improvements were made for military use but were easily adapted for hunting.[22] General Jean-Baptiste Vaquette de Gribauval's idea of making guns with interchangeable parts was implemented by a French engineer in 1788 and published by H. Blanc in 1790. Thomas Jefferson brought the idea to America,[23] where it was taken up at the turn of the century by Captain John N. Hall at the U.S. Arsenal at Harper's Ferry and by two neighboring private manufacturers in Connecticut with government contracts, Eli Whitney and Simeon North.[24] According to a historian of hunting weapons, in 1807 Scottish clergyman Alexander Forsyth "took out perhaps the most important patent in the history of firearms."[25] He experimented at the Ordnance workshops in the Tower of London. He learned about a recently developed safe process to make fulminate of mercury, and he used it to convert a flintlock to a percussion lock, utilizing the explosive power of a fulminate powder to ignite the charge in the barrel. He then began making guns to capitalize on his discovery. Breach-loading guns had already been available for some time, but Swiss inventor Samuel J. Pauly invented the modern version in 1812. In 1827 Prussian gun-maker Johann von Dreyse developed the needle-fire cartridge, leading to development of the bolt action breech-loading rifle. That was only the beginning:[26] The middle third of the nineteenth century brought the most rapid period of technological innovation in the history of armaments and warfare. Much like the computer revolution of today, the pace of change was quick, and each season brought forth new, lighter, faster, less expensive, and more powerful weapons.

Revolving barrels and double-barreled hunting rifles were developed, then in 1866 Oliver F. Winchester began manufacturing the repeating rifle which Tyler Henry had developed for the Union Army during the Civil War. Samuel Colt made revolver hunting rifles.[27]

Meanwhile, the frontier custom of holding informal shooting matches spread westward more readily than eastward, but organized groups of marksmen arose. New York firemen hit upon marksmanship contests as a way to spend some of their time between fires. In addition, Germans who fled their failed Revolution of 1848 brought along their guns into the northeast. They held shooting matches, Schutzenfest, with their marksmen in uniforms, and these matches became popular in New York and New England. By 1850, after the Mexican-American War, there were about 10,000 members of target companies in New York City.[28] Shooting matches also became popular among workmen in the three northeastern cities where firearms were made—Hartford, CT, Ilion, NY, and Springfield, MA. Members of the target groups in New York City were suspected of being active in the anti-draft riots of July 1863.[29] Gunfire was part of the July 4th celebration annually in Hartford, and Harriet Beecher Stowe's daughter was accidentally shot on July 4, 1866. Newport, RI was also famous for its pistol shooting galleries.[30] No doubt all these activities declined, but did not disappear, during the Civil War when many participants went off to fight.

Hiram Berdan, an engineer from New York City, was considered the best shot in the state. He responded to President Lincoln's call for volunteers on May 3, 1861 by offering to organize companies of marksmen. The Secretary of War accepted his proposal, but then the Army expected his snipers to use muzzle-loaded muskets. Berdan insisted on Sharp's breech-loaded rifles, which they eventually got (after Lincoln intervened). Berdan's sharpshooters were a valuable asset, but two companies could not tip the scales of battle very often, though they played a significant role at Gettysburg.[31]

Although some hunters continued hunting during that war, periodicals and artwork were discontinued for the duration. Afterwards, hunters not killed in battle sought diversion from that trauma in their previous pastime of hunting, and there were new devotees recruited from former soldiers, who had learned to shoot during the war and brought their guns home. Some 300 sportsmen's clubs formed by the 1870s.[32] In the South, hunting became an economic necessity for some whites and blacks who were left destitute by the war. In addition, vigilantes, such as the Ku Klux Klan, used hunting clubs and outings as covers for their reign of terror against former slaves.[33] As the U.S. Army moved West to contain the Indians, hunters followed. Army officers themselves were enthusiastic hunters who supplemented both their own and their men's rations with fresh meat. They also occasionally sent specimens back to the Smithsonian Institution and welcomed politicians and wealthy businessmen to their military compounds. One such hunt was organized for General Philip H. Sheridan and began at Fort Mc Pherson, NB, on September 22, 1871 and ended at Fort Hays, KS, on October 2. The party included three other generals, a few lesser officers and enlisted men, two newspaper editors, and a financier. They took along 6 wagons of baggage and five greyhounds. Their guide was the esteemed "Buffalo Bill" Cody, who dressed to meet their expectations, and whose skills, tact, and charm enhanced his reputation. The party killed more than 600 buffalo, 200 elk, and many, many rabbits, turkey, and prairie dogs. The Salt Lake *Tribune*, in reporting the kill, worried whether there would be anything left for the Russian Grand Duke Alexis when he arrived.[34]

By then, most Indians were contained on reservations, leaving good hunting for Whites. In 1876, when Indians broke free in order to resume hunting buffalo on the prairie, the Army set out to herd them back onto their territory. General George Armstrong Custer was among the most enthusiastic hunter-naturalists in the Army, but that summer he became too enthusiastic about herding Indians. When he located the naughty Indians, rather than wait for two other armies to arrive, he attacked. There were more Indians than his intelligence indicated, and they were better armed than he thought, and he and his entire army were slaughtered (see chap. 2). That victory could not, however, save the buffalo for the Indians. The transcontinental railroad had been completed in 1869, and it brought an endless stream of gentlemen

Fig. 5. Train ride to buffalo hunt. Dodge, Hunting Grounds of the Great West (1877).

hunters who shot buffalo from train windows and left the carcasses to wolves and to rot. There were also commercial hunters who killed them for their hides which they carried in wagons to the railroad. At first, commercial hunters could only shoot one buffalo from a herd because the sound of the gun discharge frightened the others into running away. The problem was solved by developing buffalo guns that could be fired from a great enough distance that the buffalo could not hear the shot, and then the hunter could kill the entire herd without any of them fleeing.[35] Sharps' Buffalo Rifle could be fired accurately at 500 yards and the bullet could cover 1200 yards.[36] When commercial hunters went out in 1883, there were no buffalo to kill; instead, they collected the bones from previous kills and sold them to fertilizer companies. Fortunately, a few isolated buffalo still lived beyond their reach, and the modest herds that still exist today come from them, largely thanks to William T. Hornaday, director of the New York Zoological Park.[37]

The passenger pigeon was not so lucky. The railroad also helped ensure its doom by carrying market hunters wherever pigeons roamed—they were tracked down by telegraph—and railroads also took the kill to city markets. The last individual died in the Cincinnati Zoo in 1914.[38] Extinction of the once most abundant bird in America and the near extinction of the most abundant mammal were dramatic examples of a broader problem: hunting was taking an alarming toll on native birds and mammals because hunters killed more than they consumed. Of the seven species of birds which Euro-Americans exterminated, five were by hunting and two by habitat destruction.[39] There was a backlash against these excesses.

The German Schutzenbund resumed after the Civil War and continued until America went to war with Germany in 1917, but that tradition was ethnically limited and therefore could not satisfy the concerns for marksmanship which two Army officers had after the Civil War. William Conant Church joined the Union Army in 1862, but resigned in 1863 to become the founding editor of the *Army and Navy Journal*.[40] Before the war, he had been a reporter for a few months in Britain, France, and Germany and had observed their military training. He had been positively impressed with European training of soldiers using guns, and after the Civil War began, he was negatively impressed with the comparable Union Army training. He complained about it in *Army and Navy Journal*, which struck a responsive cord from Captain (later, General) George W. Wingate, who had looked in vain for a shooting manual for training his troops. After Church and Wingate discussed the problem, Church suggested that Wingate do some research and write a manual himself. He did, and it appeared in six successive issues of the *Army and Navy Journal* in 1870-71 and then reprinted as an enlarged separate publication in 1872. However, neither man thought that a manual was an adequate solution to the problem of having a small army in peacetime and a rapidly expanded army in wartime. The British had faced a similar problem in 1859, when France's emperor, Napoleon III, engaged in saber rattling. The National Rifle Association of Great Britain trained civilians in case the country's army had to expand rapidly. The British association became a model for the National Rifle Association which Church and Wingate founded in 1871. The New York State Legislature gave them a charter and funds to buy a farm on Long Island for a rifle range. The NRA held its first shooting competition on June 2, 1873 and then hosted a U.S.-Irish competition in 1874. These matches were well publicized and attracted many spectators. The NRA has been sponsoring or encouraging rifle ranges and matches ever since.[41] In 1903, the NRA received U.S. Military support for rifle clubs and matches, as explained in chapter 5.

The most famous hunter in the 1800s was William Frederick Cody (1846-1917), a frontiersman born in an Iowa log cabin.[42] His father, Isaac Cody, had a typical frontiersman's wander lust, and in 1854 moved his family to the newly-organized (at least on paper) Kansas Territory. A few months later he gave a talk opposing the extension of slavery into Kansas and was stabbed by a pro-slavery fanatic. He lived another three years, but the stab wounds were listed as contributing to his death. At age eleven, Will, who was adored by his mother and sisters, became the main support for a family of six. He inherited his father's Mississippi Yager rifle. He worked as a messenger and a cowboy and then as a Pony Express rider for two months in 1860. He joined the U.S. Army during the Civil War and fought in the Battle of Tupelo (1864), but mostly served as a scout-spy. In 1867, he contracted with the Kansas-Pacific Railroad to kill twelve buffalo a day for its crew laying track, and apparently he did so for eight months, earning his nick name, Buffalo Bill." Otherwise, he served as a guide for the U.S. Army and participated in several skirmishes with Indians and killed a few of them himself. He was a superb marksman, either on the ground or on horseback. By 1867 his exploits became a subject of stories in newspapers, magazines, and books. In 1869, Edward Zane Caroll Judson, who wrote dime novels (under pseudonym Ned Buntline) about hunters, met Cody and wrote an article on his exploits. In 1872, Buntline urged Cody to exploit his fame on the stage, and he first did so in Chicago that December. He played himself in plays Buntline wrote. This succeeded, and for a decade he acted across the country in winter and worked as an Army scout or a hunting guide in summer. In 1883 he launched his outdoor Wild West show that played around the country and in Europe until 1915. Both on stage and in the outdoor shows, gun play was a major source of excitement. It involved marksmanship, simulated hunts, and simulated conflicts between Whites and real Indians, including Sitting Bull for one season. One of the sharpshooters in the show was "Annie Oakley" (Phoebe Anne Moses 1860-1926), who grew up in rural Ohio. Her father died when she was six, and by the time she was eight she began shooting quail and squirrels to help feed the family. She always shot them in the head to avoid damage to the meat. Later she also sold game to a Cincinnati hotel, and when she was fifteen, the hotel keeper arranged a match between her and an exhibition sharpshooter, Frank Butler. When Butler saw his competition, he thought it was a joke, but she beat him in shooting trap-released pigeons, and a year later he married her.[43] Cody hired her in 1885, and she was with his show for 16 seasons. She became a celebrity and an advocate for female shooters and hunters. Capt. Adam H. Bogardus (b. 1833), who was billed as the Champion Pigeon Shot of America, was another sharpshooter in the show. However, Cody worried about offending women and children with live pigeons, and the program for the 1884 Wild West show stated:[44]

In deference to the humanitarian sentiment, [our exhibition] matches are all show at Ligowsky "clay pigeons," an ingenious mechanical contrivance that furnishes an exact imitation of the bird's flight. Ladies and children can, therefore, witness and enjoy this unique exhibition with no violence to the feelings, while the expert and experienced sportsman can still appreciate the excellence of the shooting, the clay pigeons heightening rather than diminishing the sport.

Clay pigeons may have slightly reduced the hunting pressure on live passenger pigeons, but not enough to save them from extinction. Without guns, the show would not have seemed authentic; with guns, it was exciting.[45]

There were also target shooting acts in vaudeville shows. One of these acts made the front page of the *Chicago Tribune* on February 25, 1895, because the marksman, Alfred Rieckhoff, 24, fatally wounded his assistant, William Haberle, 17. Rieckhoff rapidly shot twenty times a steel target strapped to Haberle's chest, but either the rifle or the nineteenth bullet misfired, causing the rifle to move before the twentieth shot. The distraught Rieckhoff was arrested. Both performers were from Milwaukee.

Wearing moccasins and buckskins while hunting enabled American Natives—of whom Theodore Roosevelt was an exemplar—to become symbolic heirs of Native Americans.[46] A New Yorker who, as a teenager aspired to emulate Wilson and Audubon, Roosevelt instead came closer to emulating Jefferson by becoming a naturalist-president. Roosevelt did publish his own nature observations, and instead of sending other naturalists to explore (as Jefferson had), he explored and collected himself.[47] Reading his hunting books, one sees that trophy hunting was more important to him than collecting for science, though he did both.[48] Roosevelt championed another reason to hunt—to maintain the virile manhood of our pioneering ancestors after growing up in an overly domesticated society. Although hunting was often an act of individualism and self-reliance, as the wildlife diminished, élites wanted government to intervene and save it. There were two groups who pushed for conservation, nature lovers or preservationists and sports hunters.[49] The latter group was probably more numerous and more influential. Sportsmen had two goals: (1) to deprive market hunters of their resource in order to save it for themselves, and (2) to legislate and enforce hunting seasons and bag limits in order to ensure that the species hunted did not disappear. This switch from the hungry hunter to the happy hunter meant that the dynamic of the situation shifted from hunting in order to eat to eating the fruits of the hunt in order to justify killing animals. Audubon became a symbol of the preservationists because his occasional expressed concerns about over-hunting were emphasized, not his earlier writings as a profligate happy hunter. George Bird Grinnell, editor of *Field and Stream*, was a founder of both the National Audubon Society in 1886 and, with Theodore Roosevelt, of the Boone and Crockett Club in 1887.[50]

Both organizations were dedicated to restraining hunting to sustainable levels, but the Audubon Society emphasized nature appreciation and the Boone and Crockett Club was an élite hunting club that emphasized trophies.

Regardless of how successful Boone and Crockett members were at lobbying Congress and a few state legislatures for laws to protect wildlife, Roosevelt was able to do far more when he became President of the United States. He established the first National Wildlife Refuge in 1903, he doubled the size of the National Forests, and he added new National Parks and National Monuments. In 1908 he hosted a Conference of Governors at the White House, which one historian called "the single greatest stimulus to resource preservation and management" in American history.[51] Forty states responded to the conference by establishing departments of natural resources in their governments. These departments advised state legislatures on writing hunting and fishing bills and then enforced the ones passed into law. Although these departments worked for all the people of a state, they easily became captive to the minority of citizens who bought hunting and fishing licenses, because much of their operating budgets came from license sales. Similarly, the U.S. Biological Survey in the Department of the Interior became a captive of western ranchers who demanded government rodent and predator control. The relevant agency was run by self-trained naturalists when established by C. Hart Merriam in 1885 as the Office of Economic Ornithology and Mammalogy.[52] Its staff focused on life histories of wild species as long as they could get away with it, but when ranchers complained to Congress, it forced the Biological Survey to undertake pest eradication. Much of it was done with poison and traps, but wolves, coyotes, and cougars were also shot by hunters, ranchers, and government agents.[53] The American Society of Mammalogists, which was organized by Survey staff in 1919, attracted professional mammalogists in universities who raised objections to indiscriminate eradication programs. The balance of nature concept had been a part of natural history teachings since antiquity, but Vernon Bailey, chief field naturalist of the Survey, 1887-1937, scoffed at the idea.[54] The Ecological Society of America was only established in 1915, and ecologists were not yet ready to explain authoritatively the role of top predators in a food chain.[55] Modern ecologists argue that predators actually have a favorable effect upon their prey species by killing the feeble, deformed, and diseased individuals. The U.S. Fish and Wildlife Service eventually ended its pest control program, but then the U.S. Department of Agriculture created an Animal Damage Control program which spends about $36 million annually and seems to do much more harm than good.[56]

Theodore Roosevelt became the American personification of the European "great white hunter," who marched or rode through colonial possessions in Africa and elsewhere killing big game to demonstrate who was in charge. Boys read accounts of these hunts as high adventure stories. Yet, even at the peak of western imperialism, such hunting had its critics. Essayist-novelist Charles Dudley Warner wrote a story in the *Atlantic Monthly* in 1878, "A-Hunting of the Deer," which stated: "The hunters in winter, find [the deer] concentrated in 'yards' where they can be surrounded and shot as easily as our troops shoot Commanche women and children in their winter villages."[57] Mark Twain expressed similar sentiments in several of his works.[58] John Muir, who founded the Sierra Club in 1892, had harsh words on hunting and in May 1903 even asked Theodore Roosevelt, "when are you going to get beyond the boyishness of killing things?" This may have been the only time in his life that Roosevelt ever conceded the high moral ground to anyone else. He replied, "Muir, I guess you are right," but he was only being polite.[59] He expressed his true feelings two years later in *Outdoor Pastimes of an American Hunter*:[60]

> The excellent people who protest against all hunting, and consider sportsmen as enemies of wild life, are ignorant of the fact that in reality the genuine sportsman is by all odds the most important factor in keeping the larger and more valuable wild creatures from total extermination. Of course, if wild animals were allowed to breed unchecked, they would, in an incredibly short space of time, render any country uninhabitable by man—a fact which ought to be a matter of elementary knowledge in any community where the average intelligence is above that of certain portions of Hindoostan.

In 1907, through an interview with a reporter, Roosevelt entered an on-going controversy about whether several nature writers, including novelist Jack London and Rev. William J. Long's accounts of animal behavior went beyond what they actually saw. In response, Rev. Long wondered why

Roosevelt considered himself an authority on animal behavior, since "I find after carefully reading two of his big books that every time Mr. Roosevelt gets near the heart of a wild thing he invariably puts a bullet through it."[61]

About the same time Annie Montague Alexander became one of the first female hunter-naturalists.

Her father was a wealthy co-founder of the California and Hawaii Sugar Co. She accompanied him on a big-game hunt to Kenya in 1904, and afterwards she decided to found the Museum of Vertebrate Zoology at the University of California-Berkeley. She and her companion, Louise Kellogg, spent part of every year collecting birds and mammals of the western states for this museum that focused on the evolution of species and subspecies.[62]

The most influential anti-hunting author and artist of the period was former bounty-hunter of wolves, Ernest Thompson Seton. He wrote animal stories based on personal observations, including *Wild Animals I Have Known* (1898) and *Animal Heroes* (1905), both of which were still being reprinted as late as 1966.[63] These stories created a controversy, because he portrayed particular animals as having their own unique behavior. Anyone who keeps dogs, cats, or horses knows that they have distinct personalities, and Seton described particular wild animals in the same way. Theodore Roosevelt and naturalist-author John Burroughs accused him of "nature faking," but Seton produced field notes to validate his claims.[64] The implication of his stories was that hunters and trappers were not killing just "generic" animals, but ones that might be valued as one values a pet.

Seton realized that, with the growth of cities, many boys grow up more or less isolated from nature, and that they need both encouragement and guidance in order to experience and appreciate nature. He organized the League of Woodcraft Indians around 1900, which taught about camping, Indians, and wildlife and he also wrote a book, *Two Little Savages: Being the Adventures of Two Boys Who Lived as Indians and What They Learned* (1903). His ideas were taken over for the Boy Scouts by Robert Baden-Powell, who Seton thought cast them into a militaristic mold. The ideas and activities of Seton and Dan Beard, with some input from Baden-Powell, were organized into the Boy Scouts of America in 1910.[65] The first *Boy Scout Handbook* (1910) included requirements for a merit badge in marksmanship that showed the influence of the NRA's junior marksmanship course, and the 1911 *Handbook* made qualification in the NRA junior marksmanship program a prerequisite for that merit badge.[66] I grew up in the Boy Scouts, and neither hunting nor marksmanship were among our activities in Durham, NC. Archery might have been taught at the summer Scout camp but not rifle-shooting. Robert W. Peterson's history of the Boy Scouts (1984) illustrates archery practice but not gun practice. I became an Eagle Scout but earned a merit badge in neither archery nor marksmanship. While a scout, I read *Boy's Life* with great interest, and I have recently paged through four issues from 1954-55, which confirms my memory: there were ads for air rifles and .22 caliber rifles and ammunition, ads to teach taxidermy by mail, ads for earning an NRA Ranger emblem, and ads for military residential academies, where presumably the use of rifles was taught. One issue had a one-page article on skeet shooting and another issue had a one-page article on $CO_2$ powered pellet guns. In my experience, guns were on the distant periphery of the Boy Scouts, perhaps for safety reasons.

No sooner were game laws written than they led to conflicts. These laws were supported by élite hunters who wanted either to preserve game for long-term sport hunting or to stop the unsustainable killing of birds for plumage for the millinery trade. The laws were designed to restrain men who depended on game to support their families. Modern conservation leads to conflicts between game wardens and poachers. Sometimes these conflicts led to arrests and prosecution of poachers, but at other times it led to shootouts, with people being wounded or killed.[67] An early example was Guy Bradley, a Florida native who had hunted plume birds himself as a boy, but became a dedicated warden for the American Ornithologists Union and Florida Audubon Society in 1902 to enforce the U.S. Lacy Act of 1900 and Florida's bird protection law of 1901. On July 8, 1905 he attempted to arrest the son of Walter Smith and another boy for poaching in Florida Bay near Flamingo, but Smith shot him dead with a rifle and claimed that Bradley had fired his pistol at him. Although it was clear to the sheriff that Bradley's pistol had not been fired, a grand jury would not indict Smith.[68] In 1908, in Swan Valley, Montana, State Game Warden Charles Peyton engaged in a heated argument with a party of off-reservation Indians hunting in Swan Valley, which ended in the deaths of him and four Indians. The circumstances of this tragedy remain controversial.[69]

More recent examples were William Pogue and Conley Elms, Idaho Fish and Game Wardens, who responded to a complaint from a rancher that a poacher was trapping bobcats out of season on the South Fork of the Owyhee River in southwest Idaho near the Nevada and Oregon state lines. On January 5, 1981 they confronted Claude Lafayette Dallas, Jr. on the rim of the canyon and removed the bullets from his visible pistol and did not realize he had another one concealed. They then accompanied him down to his camp by the river and found bobcat skins and possibly told him he was under arrest. Dallas had an anarchistic, survivalist mind set, rather similar to that of Gordon Kahl, whom we meet in chapter 6, but without the Posse Comitatus. He was an outstanding woodsman who knew guns well and had great hostility toward government, especially game wardens. He had been arrested in 1973 as a draft dodger and had vowed he never would be captured again. When he believed they were arresting him, he pulled out his concealed pistol and shot both wardens. For good measure, he shot each in the head with a rifle after they were unconscious. Then he went into hiding, just as Kahl would two years later. He evaded the law for 15 months until someone tipped off the FBI about his location. There was also a shootout, but this time (unlike with Kahl of the Posse Comitatus, whom we meet in chapter 6) no one was killed. Dallas was well liked because he was a hard worker, moderate drinker, and a loyal friend. After a long parade of glowing testimonials at his trial, he was only found guilty of manslaughter by the jury, and although sentenced to thirty years in prison. Aside from the families of Pogue and Elms and law enforcement people, virtually all regional sympathy went to Dallas, not his victims.[70] Dallas was released from prison on February 6, 2005, after serving almost 22 years.

Here is an example of a hunter shooting people (*JT* Oct. 20, 1994):

SENEY, Mich.—A hunter described as a hothead and gun fanatic was killed in a shootout with police Wednesday, a day after he gunned down an off-duty officer and a hunting guide in a fight over bear hunting.

Jack Kidd Jr., 31, had argued with the two men over who could leave a pile of bait at a site in the Michigan's Upper Peninsula.

The three men left, then returned to the site, where Kidd opened fire on their vehicle with an AK-47 assault rifle, police said.

Kidd stole a car at gunpoint after the shooting. When police spotted him Wednesday morning on a highway, Kidd pulled over and began firing, police said. Officers shot back and killed him.

An even worse shooting occurred near Exeland, in northwest Wisconsin. Chai Soua Vang was a 1980 immigrant from Laos who was in the California National Guard for six years. He later moved to St. Paul, MN, where he earned a sharp-shooter ribbon. He began deer hunting in 1992, but on November 21, 2004 he occupied a tree stand when deer hunters to whom it belonged demanded that he leave. He shot dead six hunters and wounded two others. He later claimed that one hunter shot at him before he returned fire, which the wounded hunters denied. Vang was sentenced to six consecutive life terms plus 165 years in prison.[71] Another Hmong hunter, Cha Vang, 30, was killed while hunting in northeast Wisconsin on 6 Jan. 07, by another hunter, James Nichols, 28.[72]

The creation of wildlife refuges and the enforcement of game laws helped prevent the rarity or extinction of some species of birds and mammals, but it was not enough to sustain good hunting for all who bought hunting licenses. What more was needed? A professional forester wanted to find out. Aldo Leopold was the son of Carl Leopold, a prosperous furniture maker in Burlington, IA. The Leopolds lived beside the Mississippi River and were avid hunters.[73] After Leopold obtained a master's degree in forestry from Yale University in 1909, he joined the U.S. Forest Service and became a forester in District 3 National Forests—those in New Mexico and Arizona. He connected with fellow hunters in the area and began eradicating wolves and cougars which competed with hunters for deer. However, once when he and colleagues shot a mother wolf and some of her puppies, his eyes locked onto hers before she died, and he had a jolt of conscience. Leopold's Yale education had not included courses in the fledgling science of ecology, but somehow, watching that wolf die nudged him toward an ecological awareness:[74]

> We reached the old wolf in time to watch a fierce green fire dying in her eyes. I realized then, and have know ever since, that there was something new to me in those eyes—something known only to her and to the mountain. I was young then, and full of trigger-itch; I thought that because fewer wolves meant

more deer, that no wolves would mean hunters' paradise. But
after seeing the green fire die, I sensed that neither the wolf
nor the mountain agreed with such a view.

He realized that killing all the wolves would lessen his wilderness
experience when he hunted.

If not predator control, what was needed to sustain good hunting?
There were both practical and theoretical answers to this question. The
theoretical answers came to Leopold after he left the Forest Service in 1928
and undertook a game survey for the Sporting Arms and Ammunitions
Manufacturers' Institute. He surveyed conditions in the eight upper
Midwest states for two years. He concluded that the secret to maintaining
adequate game populations for hunters depended upon habitat management,
primarily on private land. In 1933 he became America's first professor of
wildlife management at the University of Wisconsin, and he published the
first textbook on the subject. When I took Prof. Fred Barkalow's course
in wildlife management at North Carolina State University in 1958, he
was still using Leopold's *Game Management* (1933) as the course text. At
the practical level, in 1936 conservationists gathered in Washington and
founded the National Wildlife Federation to provide non-governmental
pressure and guidance for legislation to protect wildlife. A crucial result
was the Wildlife Restoration Act of 1937, introduced into Congress by
Senator Key Pittman and Rep. Willis Robertson (thus known as the
Pittman-Robertson Act) that taxed guns and ammunition to assist states
in wildlife restoration, but only given to states that committed all revenue
from hunting and fishing licenses to wildlife programs. Pittman-Robertson
funds went to wildlife research, wildlife management, land acquisition,
and hunter education, while license funds went to running state wildlife
programs and game law enforcement.

The fame of Leopold's *Game Management* was eventually eclipsed by
a collection of essays which he called *A Sand County Almanac*. In 1948 he
had arranged for Oxford University Press to publish it before he died of
a heart attack while fighting a neighbor's forest fire. The book appeared
in 1949 and became the founding document for the land ethic ideology
and movement.[75] It is full of complaints about how Americans abuse their
environment, the remedy of which is to extend the concept of ethics to

include the environment. He addressed the ethics of hunting, but only in the narrow sense of what constitutes sportsmanship—he would have been scornful of anyone who hunted wolves or polar bears from aircraft. He and his family took up bow hunting as being a greater challenge than using guns and it gave game a greater chance to escape.[76] He probably never seriously considered the more fundamental question of whether sport hunting is ethical. He had such great respect for his father and his father's concept of hunting sportsmanship that it would never have occurred to him to even consider anything his father did as possibly unethical.

But he could hardly have been oblivious to the question within society at large. The most powerful single anti-hunting document in American history appeared in 1942—Walt Disney's film, *Bambi*.[77] Walter E. Disney was born in Chicago, but when he was between the ages of 5 and 9, his family lived on a farm, and he remembered those years as the happiest of his childhood. However, he once saw his older brother, Roy, shoot a rabbit and then wring its neck to stop its thrashing. Walt burst into tears and refused to eat the rabbit stew. However fertile Disney's imagination was, he did not dream up the script for *Bambi* from thin air. It is based on a novel by the Austrian author Siegmund Salzmann, who wrote *Bambi: A Forest Life* in 1924, using the pen name Felix Salten. Whittaker Chambers translated it into English in 1928, and Disney's studio began working on the film in 1937. Although the novel is anti-hunting, it is also more fundamentally anti-human in the tradition of Jonathan Swift's last book in *Gulliver's Travels* (1726). Salzmann was, or had been, a hunter himself. When *Bambi* appeared, to great acclaim, the editor of *Outdoor Life*, Raymond J. Brown, denounced the film as "the worst insult ever offered in any form to American sportsmen," and asked that the film carry a disclaimer that it does not portray typical law-abiding American hunters.[78] Disney responded (during World War II) that the film was based on a novel about German hunters. Professional nature writer Donald Culross Peattie also responded in an essay in *Audubon Magazine*, in which he cited evidence from the U.S. Forest Service indicating that some American hunters were as bad as the film indicated.[79] The National Audubon Society, publisher of the magazine, does not oppose legal hunting. A third of a century after Peattie's commentary, "CBS Reports" expressed sentiments similar to his in its *Guns of Autumn*.[80]

The percentage of Americans who hunt has steadily declined since

World War II—about 25 percent of men hunted in 1945, but by 1991 only 7.5 percent of Americans over the age of 15 hunted.[81] A 2008 survey of why former hunters ceased found: lack of free time, %40; family obligations, 35%; work, 34%, and loss of interest, 33%.[82] Both Cartmill (1993) and Herman (2001) discuss possible reasons for the broader decline, to which I can add a few more. Children's stories are often about appealing animals and provide images not easily reconciled with hunting. Every year, Santa has reindeer and Easter has bunnies. The animal rights movement arose during the 1960s when there were parallel movements defending the civil rights of blacks, women, and gays. Leopold's concept of extending ethics to nature may have had some influence on the animal rights advocates, but if so, they took his concept further than he did. The animal rights movement here may have been influenced by a similar movement that started earlier in Britain. Some rural land owners now oppose hunting on their property, either because of negative experiences with hunters or because the owners oppose hunting. As a result, wealthy hunters often belong to hunting clubs that own land, or they can afford to fly to Canada or elsewhere to hunt without interference. The popularity of hunting declined with the increasing popularity of both participatory and spectator sports, the latter being accessible both on location and on TV. Most people prefer watching live animals with binoculars and camera to watching them die from bullet or arrow. In 1996 America had 14 million hunters, whose hunting expenditures were $21 billion, and 63 million wildlife watchers, whose watching expenditures were $29 billion.[83] One can still enjoy the chase and the capture, only one captures images on film instead of carcasses. There are also exciting new sports—kayaking, mountaineering, rock climbing, sky diving, and skiing—which test one's skill, stamina, and courage without killing animals.

However, not many hunters have gone quietly into the night. Many are concerned to maintain the popularity of their sport by recruiting new hunters and by writing defenses of hunting. Two new defenses of hunting that emerged after World War II, critic Marti Kheel called holist and holy.[84] She traces the holist defense to Leopold's land ethic; hunters cull excess animals that would otherwise starve. This argument seems plausible where deer or elk are abundant and their natural predators—wolves, cougars, and Indians—have been eliminated. The holy hunter argument is that hunting is a religious or spiritual experience. A substantial number of books on the desirability of hunting have appeared in recent years, I cite some, both pro[85] and con.[86] Two books by women claim that, although the total of hunters in America is declining, the number of women hunters is actually increasing.[87] Women constitute about ten percent of American hunters. Books defending hunting reassure hunters that there are still strong advocates and arguments on their side, and also reassures non-hunting family members and friends that hunting is still considered by many to be an acceptable sport.

Pro-hunting arguments are based on what it does for the hunter, whereas anti-hunting arguments are based on what it does to animals. This controversy is not entirely academic. Hunting defender James Swan reported that in Kalamazoo, MI, a man was arrested in 1993 under suspicion of having gunned down eight hunters during two years. Swan assumed that whoever shot the hunters was an animal rights activist.[88] On the other hand, he also reports one hunter's remark that if one wants to kill someone, do it in the hunting season because one can claim it was an accident.[89] Hunting is a hazardous activity. Every year a few hunters are seriously wounded or even die during Wisconsin's deer season, from accidental shootings, heart attacks, falling out of trees while waiting for deer, and so on. The same is probably true in many other states with deer hunting seasons. A Wisconsin example: on November 23, 2003, after a hunt in Sheboygan County, Mark A. Weber, 42, was preparing a deer he had killed in a field at night when he thought he saw another deer. He picked up his shotgun and fired. It was instead his hunting companion, William Mundt, 33, whom he mortally wounded. Weber was prosecuted for second-degree reckless homicide and on August 19, 2004 was found not guilty. Mundt's parents then announced that they would sue Weber for wrongful death.[90] Of homicides in America, about 72% are with guns, and a significant proportion of them are with hunting guns. It is reasonable to assume that most of those shot with hunting guns are shot by hunters. For the year 2007 there were 10,129 homicides with guns: 7398 with handguns, 453 with rifles, and 457 with shotguns.

Swan wrote that he enjoys watching animals outside the hunting season, but that hunting is a different, peak experience.[91] Opponents might respond that, in the first place, they have peak experiences from just watching or photographing wildlife, and, in the second place, that some men have had peak experiences by beating, raping, or killing other people or animals, but society has never condoned these practices because of what they do to the actor. If one extends ethics to nature, then one cannot condone hunting just because it provides a peak experience for hunters. The main argument in favor of hunting that non-hunters can acknowledge is that those who buy hunting licenses and pay Pittman-Robertson taxes contribute to maintaining some wildlife habitat and enforcing game laws designed to prevent game species from becoming scarce. Wildlife management since World War II has been a great success. However, even if animal rights advocates acknowledge this, they might nevertheless respond that this success merely corrected a problem which hunters had created in the first place.

What seems noteworthy is that as hunting populations declines, there have been few if any anti-hunting laws passed, aside from ordinances against shooting inside city limits. One reason is that families and friends of hunters are usually supportive of hunting rights. Another reason is that hunting is big business, both from the standpoint of selling hunting and camping equipment (including guns and ammunition) to hunters and providing services for them during hunting season in areas where hunting is popular. By 1992, hunters were spending $10 billion annually, of which $1.4 billion was on weaponry.[92] No one involved in these businesses wants to kill the geese which lay golden eggs, even if the business owners do not hunt. In 1998, one author reported that American hunters killed about 250 million animals a year.[93]

Authors of books for and against hunting are self-appointed spokesmen for their movements, but what are the thoughts of people within these movements? This chapter ends with two letters to the editor of my hometown newspaper, the Racine *Journal Times*. They are quoted in chronological order; the titles were added by an editor:

Don't encourage hunting (December 1, 1995)

I am surprised at your insensitivity in the majority of your readers—the people who do not hunt, find it distasteful, and don't like constant propaganda trying to force us to accept it for something far removed from what it really is. Yet, you actually run a commentary in which we are told to "salute" hunters and treat them like heroes?

You are glamorizing a violent pastime and thereby helping to perpetuate violence in our society. Most hunters do not hunt out of a need for food; they hunt because they like to kill. Why are you encouraging this? We've never heard any bragging about the "clean shot" that dispensed the animal—it's always asinine-grin-and-smirk accounts about how much the terrified animal was run down, hurting, thrashing, struggling to survive—often beaten (in the name of "humaneness" to put it out of its misery, of course!).

You are condoning, encouraging and even "saluting" something that is clearly bully-boy stuff. You have even featured it in your sports section. (Tell us: What is sportsmanlike about an entirely one-sided contest, distinguished only by brutality?)

There are alternatives to population control. Why don't you listen to some of these suggestions and help publicize peaceful, nonviolent solutions instead? You are not being objective, not being balanced or, especially, not being sensitive. Get out of the NRA's pocket and do something to discourage violent tendencies.

Diane L. West


Wisconsin hunting (April 27, 2004)

Wisconsin has and always will be the hunting state. I don't think we should have a 23-day season. The tradition for me has always been the nine-day gun season.

Growing up as a hunter I always looked forward to going up north with my family for the gun season. It always seemed like every year I learned something new.

Now that I'm 34 years of age and been hunting for 22 years, it's time to pass on all the things I've learned over the years of being in the woods. A new wave of kids are wanting to get involved in hunting and I have so much to show and teach them and I love that they are asking me to go hunting.

My son Zachary is one of those kids who is very excited to hunt. Even though my son is only six years old he talks about going with me for those nine days and learning all about the woods and hunting.

Believe me I'm one father who can't wait for those memories to start. For me to pass on the tradition of father and son gun hunting together like my father did for me is what it is all about. The bond you feel is unmatched to anything that I know of.

I guess I'm a little old-fashioned when it comes down to changing something that has been in my life for so long. Feeling like you have to decide what weekend or what week you want to go, just doesn't seem right, or should I say the traditional way I was brought up.

We always knew what day and what time we were leaving and to me that was and still is so exciting. I don't care how young or how old the hunter is they always have that smile on their faces when it came to be that time of year. Please, please keep our deer season the way it has always been.

Brian Nielsen

Nielsen's objection to the 23-day hunt seems to be because it changed a tradition. The importance of family tradition is the theme in William Faulkner's hunting story, "The Bear" (1942). The above two letters illustrate the differences between hunters and animal rights advocates. The former focus on human satisfaction and the latter on animal welfare. Hunters also have two concerns for animal welfare: a quick death when shot and an annual harvest that does not decimate the species.

In the fall of 2006, the World Hunting Association, founded by David Farbman, sponsored a no-kill deer hunt competition for ten hunters. They will shoot tranquilizer darts from bows, guns, and blowguns, and a veterinarian will attend to the deer after they are shot.

Many hunters during the 1900s and beyond became receptive to recruitment by the National Rifle Association (which disapproves of no-kill hunts), partly because of an interest in the guns they use to hunt, and partly perhaps as a defense against the hostility of animal rights advocates or gun control advocates.

It is true that there has been a gradual decline in the number of American hunters; a University of Chicago study found that 36 percent of American men hunted in 1977, but by 2012 there were only 20 percent hunting.[94] But that does not mean hunting is fading away. Wisconsin's deer season in November 2017 lasted only nine days, with over 600,000 hunters and about 200,000 deer killed.[95] Just in time for that hunt, the state legislature passed and the governor signed into law (despite newspaper editorial disapproval), removal of the minimum age of hunters at ten, instead, leaving it up to a parent to decide when to entrust a child with a loaded gun.[96] During this season, seven hunters were shot accidentally, none fatally.

# 4

## MAKING AND SELLING GUNS
## AND AMMUNITION

Guns and ammunition were produced by craftsmen to the end of the 1700s. A gunsmith made one gun at a time, and only prosperous men could afford to own one—about 15 percent in 1765-90, and rising to about 33 percent in 1840-50, when guns were factory-made.[1] The earliest gun merchant in America was Thomas Morton (*d.* 1646), an attorney who settled in Massachusetts Bay in 1625 and gained control of his settlement in 1626, which he named Merry-Mount. He traded guns and ammunition to Indians for furs, which the Plymouth colony had outlawed. When Plymouth was unable to persuade him to stop trading guns, it sent Capt. Myles Standish to arrest him and send him back to England in 1628. He returned to Massachusetts Bay in 1629 and was arrested again and deported again to England in 1630. He was imprisoned for a while but released in 1631. He published *New English Canaan* (1637) about conditions and his experiences in America. Morton's story illustrates a dilemma that was never solved: trading guns to Indians seemed potentially dangerous, but it was profitable and prohibitions were difficult to enforce. Two other persistent gun problems were quality control and contract completion. Thomas Archcraft of South Carolina was America's first (and probably last) defense contractor jailed for poor workmanship and non-fulfillment of contract, in 1672.[2]

James Watt patented his steam engine in 1767 and began manufacturing them in 1775. No relationship between steam engines and gun making existed during the 1700s, but that relationship would become important in the 1800s.

The idea of interchangeable parts originated with Swedish clockmaker Christopher Polhelm in the 1720s, but the first published account of his methods in Swedish was not until 1752.[3] When Jean-Baptiste Vaquette de Gribeauval (1715-89), French Inspector General of Artillery, introduced standardized methods and parts and had rigid inspections, in order to produce the best artillery in Europe by 1765, it seems to have been based upon his experience. He later found a talented gunsmith, Honoré Blanc, who was able to develop comparable methods to manufacture muskets with uniform parts. In 1785 Thomas Jefferson, our ambassador to France, visited Blanc and tried to persuade him to emigrate to America. That failing, Jefferson sent six of his muskets to Philadelphia in 1789 and later interested others, including possibly Eli Whitney, in the idea. However, it took more than Jefferson's introduction of the idea and Blanc's six muskets to transfer that skill to America. Major Louis de Tousard, graduate of the Strasbourg artillery school, immigrated to America for political reasons in 1793, and in 1795 he joined the new U.S. Corps of Artillerists and Engineers. He built forts, modernized the curriculum at West Point, and, at President Washington's behest, wrote *American Artillerist's Companion* (3 volumes, 1809), which emphasized the need for a system of uniformity and regularity, based on science.[4]

The goal of interchangeable parts was too complex for private gunsmiths alone, and it was what raised America's firearms industry from insignificance to world dominance, by instruction and orders from the Federal Government, gained by some gunsmiths working under federal contracts and in cooperation with the two federal arsenals. In 1777 General George Washington had asked General Henry Knox to establish a war arsenal, and he did so at Springfield, MA. Afterwards it was shut down with only a caretaker staff, but was reinforced by Massachusetts militia in January 1787 during Shay's Rebellion.[5] In 1794, President Washington asked Congress to make it active and establish another one at Harpers Ferry, VA (now, WV). The Springfield Armory began craft production of muskets that year, and Harpers Ferry Armory opened in 1798. America was having serious diplomatic and naval conflicts with revolutionary France, and the War Department decided the two federal armories could not make muskets fast enough to meet the Army's needs, and since European countries were at war with each other, the War Department could not buy what it needed abroad. The timing of that national crisis coincided with a personal financial crisis of Massachusetts inventor Eli Whitney (1765-1825), who had failed to make and sell his cotton gin, as his idea for it was easily duplicated by others (Grant 1999). He was friends with Treasury Secretary Oliver Wolcott and got his help to obtain a contract to make 10,000 muskets, patterned after French Model 1795.[6] He claimed he would produce them more rapidly than others could by using machines for forging, rolling, grinding, and polishing, but he never bought any machines with his government advance of $5000, using it instead to pay his debts. What he did do in January 1801 was to take a musket and ten locks to Washington and show government officials that he could attach any of the locks to the musket. This was intended to demonstrate something that he had not actually achieved:[7]

> The story of Eli Whitney and armory production is the story of a man who espoused the two principal ideas that lay behind the system—interchangeability and mechanization—but who never understood, much less developed, its basic principles let alone its complex subtleties.

He had hired some fifty skilled workers but could only deliver the last of his contracted 10,000 muskets in 1809 and, according to Hounshell, probably would not have gotten another contract because of his slowness and the poor quality of his muskets, except that the War of 1812 came along and the Army still needed muskets. Hounshell's harsh judgment of Whitney, quoted above, is neither unique nor universal.[8] Grant cited "The government arms inspector, Captain Decius Wadsworth, a frequent Whitney visitor and friend, [who] claimed that Whitneyville out-performed the Springfield Armory with much less manual labor, and he had nothing but the highest praise for Whitney's ingenuity and integrity."[9] Furthermore, Whitney's armory not only survived him, it flourished until sold to Winchester Repeating Arms Company of New Haven in 1888.

Whitney had also gotten the federal government to set a precedent of advancing funds to contractors to make guns. Another contractor in 1798 was Simeon North, who had been making agricultural tools. He got a contract to make only horse pistols, based on French Model 1777, which he delivered in 1800, and then got a contract to make 1500 more. With each delivery he also got a larger advance on the next contract, which enabled him to steadily expand his facilities and workforce. He and the War Department made history in 1813 when they signed a contract for him to make 20,000 muskets over five years with interchangeable parts. In 1816 he requested an advance of $50,000 in addition to the $30,000 he had already received. The secretary of war then asked the superintendents of the Springfield and Harpers Ferry Arsenals, Roswell Lee and James Stubblefield, to evaluate the request. They found that he had indeed achieved a greater degree of uniformity of parts than any other armory. North got the money and "In his execution of a huge contract for pistols, Simeon North helped set American manufacturing on the road toward mass production."[10] Still, the revolution in industrial production had only begun. It took the mediocre performance of American arms in the War of 1812 to win the support of Congress and the War Department for serious improvements. The U.S. Army created an Ordnance Department under the able leadership of (by now Colonel) Decius Wadsworth, Whitney's friend. In June 1815 Wadsworth called a meeting in New Haven to discuss problems and strategy to achieve production of muskets with interchangeable parts. Whitney was the host, and the other participants included superintendents of the two federal arsenals. The goal was to copy the French musket, and the project was to begin at Harpers Ferry, with both arsenals cooperating on it. Wadsworth assigned Lieutenant Colonel George Bomford (1782-1848) to supervise the armories. Bomford was also a capable officer, and he later succeeded Wadsworth as chief of Ordnance. Superintendent Stubblefield (1780-1855), at Harpers Ferry, was a gunsmith in the craft tradition and not temperamentally or intellectually able to guide the anticipated transformation in production from craft toward uniformity and mass production,[11] but the Hartford meeting had established a policy of close communication between the arsenals, and when Stubblefield lagged, Superintendent Lee at Springfield, stepped successfully into the breech. There were three important developments that the federal armories adopted to make this transition from craft to industry and from tailored parts to uniform parts, and all three originated with private contractors who made guns for the government. One was a set of 63 standard gauges to measure rifle parts which John H. Hall, of Portland, Maine, brought to Harpers Ferry in 1819 in order to make his breech-loading rifle which he had patented in 1811.[12]

Fig. 6. Harpers Ferry.

The second was the milling machine that Simeon North invented about 1816 and was soon used by Hall at Harpers Ferry.[13] Both North and Hall continued to improve production, and the earliest extant milling machine is an improved model from the 1820s used at Whitneyville.[14]

The third development happened in 1818, when a New England arms contractor for the Army, Asa Waters, asked a mechanic, Thomas Blanchard, for advice on turning and grinding the oval breach end of gun barrels. Blanchard realized that it could be done by using the irregular form as a cam. This was an informed guess, because he was familiar with the technical accounts and illustrations in Diderot's great *Encyclopédie* and also with the *Edinburgh Encyclopaedia*'s account of Marc I. Brunel's special block-making machinery to produce wooden rope blocks for the Royal Navy. By 1807 Brunel and his partner were using a series of machines, with each performing a single operation on the block, and they produced 130,000 blocks a year. No one in Britain took Brunel's idea further. Blanchard set up a series of machines to produce not symmetrical products as Brunel did, but irregular shapes. He built a barrel-turning machine for Harpers Ferry in 1818 and in 1819 a gunstock lathe. He continued working as a contractor with the Springfield Armory, and by 1828 he perfected a series of 14 machines which eliminated skilled labor from stock-making.[15]

Meanwhile, Eliphalet Remington (d. 1828) and his son, Eliphalet

Remington, Jr. (1793-1861), founded the Remington Company near Illion Gorge, New York.[16] After Eliphalet, Jr. died, he was succeeded by his sons, Eliphalet III, Philo (1816-1889), and Samuel.[17] Remington had its ups and downs, but continues manufacturing rifles.[18]

As important as these technological advances were the policies and practices which Army Ordnance developed. It carefully monitored expenses both at its own armories and at private armories of contractors, and it frequently performed inspections and wrote detailed reports. When innovations arose at either federal or contract arsenals, they were shared with the other arsenals. For example, Ordnance distributed six sets of rifle gauges to private contractors. Hall achieved the first rifles with interchangeable parts at Harpers Ferry in 1826, and by 1834 North made rifle parts at his armory that were interchangeable with parts from Harpers Ferry. Bomford persisted until all armories, federal and private contractors, achieved the same uniformity with production of Model 1841 percussion rifle and Model 1842 percussion musket.[19] The federal arsenals made important strides when they had capable leadership, and that usually occurred under army superintendents, but Congress was tempted periodically to provide civilian superintendents, since the jobs then became patronage plums.

In 1830, the Harpers Ferry arsenal was lax, compared to the Springfield arsenal, and Bomford sent Thomas Dunn to Harpers Ferry to eliminate "loitering, drinking, gambling, and absenteeism."[20] Dunn was the strict enforcer which Bomford wanted; however, after six months, ex-employee Ebenezer Cox entered Dunn's office and shot him dead. (This may be the earliest workplace assassination recorded for America.) Major Henry Knox Craig replaced Dunn and also enforced the same discipline. In March 1842, Harpers Ferry workers sailed down the Chesapeake and Ohio Canal to appeal to President John Tyler, claiming they had been reduced to "mere machines of labor."[21]. In 1842, James Wolfe Ripley was superintendent of the Springfield Armory, and he enforced the same strict discipline that Army Ordnance wanted. Springfield workers burned him in effigy three times.

Gunpowder production was encouraged in Massachusetts in 1639, but without impressive results until a gunpowder mill was established between Dorchester and Milton in 1675. In 1676 Englishman Edward Randolph concluded that its powder "is as good and strong as the best English powder."[22] That mill continued its production until at least 1749, though it blew up in

1744, "destroying the building and scattering the remains of the workmen upon the hill nearby."[23] The conflict between British troops and Americans at Lexington and Concord on April 19, 1775 was over General Thomas Gage's attempt to confiscate gunpowder in Concord (which was removed before his troops arrived).[24] Shortage of gunpowder was a chronic problem for the Americans throughout the War of Independence. For example, Americans had to retreat at Bunker Hill on June 17 after firing two volleys because they lacked powder for a third volley.[25] States subsidized gunpowder production. The New York Committee of safety also published in 1776 *Essays upon the Making of Salt-Petre and Gun-Powder.*[26] Despite such efforts, imports provided ninety percent of gunpowder used during the war.[27]

After the war, the shift from craft to industry was simpler for gunpowder than for guns, for it centered on one entrepreneur, E. Irénée du Pont (1771-1834).[28] He was the son of a prominent French politician, Pierre Samuel du Pont. As a boy, Irénée became interested in explosives, and he was sent to study and work under Antoine Lavoisier, the leading chemist of the day, who was in charge of French gunpowder production. Lavoisier, however, fell victim to the Reign of Terror in 1794. The du Pont father and son played active but precarious roles in public affairs until October 1799, when it became prudent for their family to immigrate to America. They arrived on January 1, 1800, and Irénée du Pont discovered some months later that American gunpowder production was at best mediocre and often worse. He returned to France to see if he could get help in establishing a gunpowder factory in America. Napoleon's government was eager for America to stop importing British gunpowder and gladly helped. Back in America with his new machines and French powder-men, du Pont chose a location along the Brandywine River four miles north of Wilmington, DE, near a friend's farm. He opened his plant on May 1, 1804. President Jefferson, who had depended on Irénée's father, Pierre Samuel du Pont, to help close the Louisiana Purchase, provided a government contract. Later, during Jefferson's prohibition of trade with Europe, the Du Pont Company flourished, as it would during the War of 1812. Since gunpowder production was hazardous, production facilities were built with three strong stone sides, but with a light wooden front and roof. When accidental explosions occurred, everything and everyone was blown into or across the river. The first large accident was in 1818 and killed forty people. When Irénée du

Pont died suddenly in 1834, company management passed temporarily to a dependable son-in-law, who three years later reorganized it as a partnership among Irénée's seven children.[29] The Du Pont Company was far from being the only American producer of gunpowder. By 1810 it only produced the third highest amount, though the highest in quality, but it remained at the forefront of innovation and modernization, and it was the only early company that survives.[30]

A fascination with pistols began for Samuel Colt (1814-62) at an even earlier age than du Pont's fascination with gunpowder; Sam took one apart at age seven. At age 16 he went to sea on a ship bound to London and Calcutta, and while aboard, in 1831, whittled wooden parts for his model of a revolver.[31] Later he claimed to have been unaware of Elisha Collier's earlier revolver until he returned to England in 1835, but a recent biographer and curator of his gun collection, William Hosley, finds that unlikely.[32] Although Colt had the determination and persistence needed for success, he was also "an abrasive opportunist who lied, cheated, and bluffed his way toward perfecting the 'first practical repeating firearm."[33] It was practicable because Joshua Shaw in 1815 had invented percussion caps, with expendable copper cap filled with fulminate of mercury that exploded when struck by the revolver's hammer.[34] Colt initiated a new phase in gun production with his patented revolver manufactured with private funds and only a hope of government contracts. His first attempt to manufacture his revolver in Paterson, NJ, 1836-42, failed because his knowledge of production was too shallow, the price of revolvers was too high to sell many, and the U.S. Army failed to buy them. He then became a traveling lecturer-showman on laughing gas and attempted unsuccessfully to sell the federal government his system of underwater explosives for harbor protection.

Two groups who did appreciate his early revolvers were U.S. soldiers in Florida and the Texas Rangers; both forces used them effectively to fight Indians. During the Mexican-American War, 1846-48, Texas Rangers fought along side the U.S. Army and convinced the War Department to order 1000 new Colt revolvers. When a national hero, Captain Walker, brought him the order, Colt was unable to find one of his revolvers to use as a model. He and Walker designed a better one than he had previously manufactured, and Colt contracted with Eli Whitney, Jr. to make the parts which Colt's workmen assembled. Although Colt originally opened a factory with private capital, it failed, and he only succeeded when he got a government contract, doubtless with advanced funds. Colt was not a mechanical genius like his plant supervisor, E K. Root, but he had other qualities that made him the most successful gun maker of his time.

He could identify the men and machines he needed, and he could get them to work effectively towards his goals. He could envision what he needed to do to achieve a more efficient factory than had ever existed, and he was a pioneer in advertising. He commissioned renowned artist of the West, George Catlin, to create nine pictures which showed his guns in action, and he may have been the first industrialist to create a market for his products by advertising, packaging, and collecting testimonials. He already had (he claimed) the largest private armory in the world by 1850, and he had just begun to expand his factories. At Britain's Great Exhibition (1851), he won two of the three gold medals for science and engineering for his revolver and his rifle based on his revolver.[35] That Exhibition open European markets to American manufacturers. He built a factory in London in 1852, and he visited the rulers of Russia and Turkey to sell guns. When Britain complained about him selling guns to both sides during the Crimean War, he replied that none of his guns made in London were sold to Russia. He indulged in the fantasy that better guns would end war, and so he called one of his revolvers a "peacemaker." A small group of New England manufacturers armed almost the whole world during 30 years.[36]

Alert though he was, Colt was not always at the forefront of innovation. His revolvers continued firing cap, ball, and powder long after metal cartridges appeared. These cartridges were part of a transformation that began when Walter Hunt invented a lever-action repeating gun, which was further improved by several other inventors, 1849-54, leading to the founding of Volcanic Repeating Arms Co. in 1855 to manufacture lever-action handguns.[37] Inventors Horace Smith (1808-93) and Daniel Baird Wesson (1825-1906) ran the company in Norwich, CT, and shirt factory owner Oliver F. Winchester (1810-80) of New Haven became a major stockholder and a director.[38] Both Smith and Wesson grew up in the gun business. Smith's father was a carpenter at the Federal Arsenal in Springfield, MA, and Wesson as a youth was apprenticed to his brother, a gun smith. When the company president died in 1856, Winchester became principal owner and president. Soon the company went bankrupt and Winchester acquired all assets. Wesson stayed on for a while as manager, but in 1856 he and Smith formed another company bearing their name to make revolvers that fired metallic-cartridges.[39] They patented the cartridges that year and began production of their revolver in 1858. (It would be years before Colt followed their example—perhaps he was reluctant to pay royalties.) Thus, both the Winchester and the Smith and Wesson Companies had their origins in the same antecedent company. After Winchester lost Wesson as plant superintendent, he was fortunate to replace him with inventor B. Tyler Henry, who developed an improved rifle using metal-cased cartridges, the Henry Rifle.

Gun-maker Henry Deringer, Jr. (1786-1868) was to discover what is now called a niche market when he produced a pocket pistol that became identified with his name as a noun (with an additional "r"). However, the derringer only became popular in the 1850s, after his reputation was well established. He was the son of a German immigrant gunsmith who settled in Easton, PA. Henry Jr. was apprenticed to a Richmond gunsmith, not to his father, and afterwards he settled in Philadelphia, where he began making guns by 1806, mainly for the U.S. Army. During the three decades between the War of 1812 (ending in 1815) and the Mexican-American War, he made over 20,000 guns for the Federal Government, including 5000 treaty guns for Indians who President Andrew Jackson ordered moved in the 1830s from Alabama, Georgia, and Mississippi to Oklahoma Territory.[40] Deringer participated in the government-private gun-making partnership that pioneered development of interchangeable parts, leading to mass production. However, Deringer never moved beyond craft production, and he never followed Colt's lead in prominent advertising. Since he sold all the guns he made, there was no need for expensive advertising. Before making his derringers, he made hunting guns and dueling pistols for the non-government market, and his strongest market was in the South, though in the 1850s his derringers sold better in San Francisco than in any other city. There they received national attention following the shooting deaths of U.S. Marshal William R. Richardson on November 17, 1855 and crusading editor of the San Francisco *Bulletin* James King on May 14, 1856. That notoriety was reinforced when New York Congressman Daniel E. Sickles shot dead District of Columbia District Attorney Philip B. Key on May 12, 1859. The most notorious assassination with a derringer was John Wilkes

Booth's of President Lincoln on April 14, 1865. Ironically, the Civil War marked the decline of derringers—partly because the southern market was cut off by the war, and partly because men who might have bought them were issued government guns when they joined the armies of both sides. Since Deringer's guns were still being made by hand when he died, the business was not large. He left it to a son and a daughter. He had never patented his derringer and several gun makers made similar pistols. Colt was still advertising its derringer in its 1888 catalog. By the early 1900s Colt was selling a very small revolver for the same market; such guns were later nick named "Saturday night specials."[41]

The Civil War was both an opportunity and a challenge to gun and ammunition businesses. Before the war, the U.S. Springfield Armory produced about 10,000 rifles a year. By doubling employment and working almost around the clock, production increased to 3000 a month, but at that rate, it would have taken 28 years to equip a million-man army.[42] Virginia's legislature voted to secede from the Union on April 17, 1861, and the next day the Virginia militia marched on the Harpers Ferry Arsenal, defended by 47 Union troops. Union troops set the arsenal afire and fled, but the militia saved most of the machinery and sent it to Richmond, where it was used to make guns for the Confederacy. After the war Harpers Ferry Arsenal was not rebuilt.[43] (The Springfield Arsenal remained active until 1968, when it became a national museum.) Ordnance Chief, General James Ripley had to revive the public-private procurement system that had declined during the 1840s. He calculated that the Springfield Armory made rifles for $13.93, yet the government would have to pay $20 per Springfield model rifle to private armories to make it worth their while. Contracts were typically signed for 50,000, with delivery due on January 1, 1862. No private arsenal met that deadline, because they all besieged the machine tool industry with orders which could not be filled rapidly enough to enable gun makers to meet that date. The contracts had to be extended to May 1, and presumably contractors sent in batches of guns as they were finished. The contracts were very favorable for large, efficient manufacturers, and Remington notified Army Ordnance that it could make a profit at $16 per gun.

Colt's pre-war price of his revolvers for the Federal Government was $25. However, there were complaints when it was discovered that he sold the same model revolver to the British government for $12.50 (presumably revolvers produced in his London factory) and to civilians for $14.50. His production costs were estimated to be between $4 and $9. In 1860, therefore, he reduced his charge to the Federal Government to $20. Remington sold a comparable revolver to the Federal Government for $13.[44] In 1861, Colt responded to wartime demand by expanding his factory with three new buildings. He was the first American to become a millionaire by making guns. When he died in 1862, he not only left his widow well off, he also left his nephew $2 million (which the widow contested). The Colt factory burned in 1864, with a loss valued at $1.5 to $2 million.

There were some arms factories opened because of the promise of $20 paid per rifle, and these factories often were financially marginal operations. For example, New York City Mayor George Opdyke opened a small factory for $97,000 and made rifles at a cost of $18.10, but the remaining $1.90 was used for rent and insurance. His factory burned in the draft riots of July 1863.[45]

The U.S. Army was slow to buy breach-loaders and repeating rifles because of the cost and because Ripley thought they were unnecessary. Winchester manufactured the Henry Rifle for the Union Army by mid-1862. However, the Spencer carbine was sturdier and favored by the Army, which bought 94,000 of them, but only 4600 Colt revolving rifles and 1731 Henrys.[46]

Meanwhile, if one traveled West, one left the Industrial Revolution behind at the frontier. In early 1800s, most of Tennessee was on the frontier. Jonathan Browning (1805-79) was a frontier gunsmith about whom more is known than any other; his tools, equipment, and some of his guns are preserved and displayed at the Browning Firearms Museum. While a farm boy, he hung out at a blacksmith shop and began helping the blacksmith. He also helped a farmer who paid him with an old broken flintlock gun. Browning repaired it and sold it back to the farmer. At the blacksmith shop he learned forging, welding, brazing, tempering, and soldering, and he made his own tools for gun repair. After seeing a gun stamped with the name of a Nashville gunsmith, Samuel Porter, he rode a horse there and offered to work in exchange for lessons on making gun barrels. Porter was so pleased with his work that he paid him a salary and gave him some tools when he left in 1824 after three months. Browning ran his own gun shop in Brushy Fork, TN, 1824-34, then followed family members west to Quincy, IL, on the Mississippi River. He made one or more repeating revolver rifles but found it too demanding for his equipment and skills and instead developed a repeating slide rifle, which was unequaled for reliability among contemporary repeating guns.[47] It was extremely popular until metallic cartridges replaced percussion caps.

In 1840, a Mormon entered Browning's shop with a gun needing repair, and while there, proselytized him for the new religion. In 1842, he sold his property and moved wife and eight children 43 miles north to Nauvoo. The founder of the religion, Joseph Smith, and his brother, Hyrum, were shot dead by a mob on June 25, 1844. Brigham Young took charge of the church and the congregation, and after reading John C. Frémont's published report on Utah (1845), planned a mass migration to what he believed would be their "promised land." In early February 1846 Mormons were forced to flee across the Mississippi, and Browning abandoned his home and shop, but not his equipment. By June they reached the banks of the Missouri, and in July an army officer arrived with a letter from President Polk requesting volunteers for the Mexican-American War. Despite his large family, Browning was among the 500 volunteers, but Young would not let him go. The wagon trains would need his repeating rifles. He reestablished a gun shop in Kanesville, IA, and on September 19, 1849 advertised in its *Frontier Guardian* that he made and sold "revolving rifles and pistols; also slide guns, from 5 to 25 shooters."[48] His repeating guns were popular among migrating Mormons, and sometimes they surprised hostile Indians with the rapidity of their fire.

In 1852, Young finally allowed Browning to follow the Mormon Trail to Ogden, UT. Two years later, he married his second wife, who was the mother of his sons John Moses (1858-1926) and Matthew Sandifer (b. 1859). In 1859 Browning married his third wife, who bore the last seven of his 22 children. He became a successful gunsmith in Ogden, but never again invented new guns. His son, John Moses, occasionally attended school until he was 15, but his main education was learning gun-smithing from his father. Matthew Sandifer greatly admired his older brother and was constantly at his heels. At age ten, John got the urge to invent a gun, and unlike his father, once he started, he continued inventing guns for the rest of his life, becoming "the greatest firearms inventor the world has ever known." (These words are from a plaque in Fabrique Nationale d'Armes Guerre's factory, Liège, Belgium.[49]) John and Matt took his home-made gun out and killed three birds with one shot, and their mother served them for breakfast the next morning.

After the Civil War, however, there was a glut of surplus Spencers, the company failed, and Winchester bought its assets. In contrast to the large number of Spencers available, Winchester had only made 13,000 Henrys. In 1866, Winchester changed the company name to Winchester Repeating Arms Company, and he hired a new factory supervisor, Nelson King. King developed a tube for loading cartridges under the barrel, and Winchester then brought out an improved 1866 model which became "the Gun that Won the West." (The board of directors voted a $5000 bonus to King for his system.) William E. Webb wrote of his Winchester Model 1866 in *Buffalo Land* (1872): "I became very fond of a carbine combining the Henry and King patents. It weighed about seven and one-half pounds, and could be fired rapidly twelve times without replenishing the magazine."[50] Winchester followed Colt's example both in advertisements and in decorating some of his guns with artistic engravings; the Ulrich family engraved Winchesters for 80 years. In 1871 Winchester moved his factory from Bridgeport to New Haven, where it also made ammunition. Display cases which had a lithographed background with cartridges fastened in a decorative pattern were made and sent to distributors and stores. The pattern of the first board, about 1874, was rather simple (fig. 4.23), but they became more complex over time.

No gun maker could ever rest on his laurels, because of the ever-improving competition. The 239 small arms makers of 1860 were reduced to 26 by 1900.[51] Winchester bought as many of them as it could to reduce the competition. Its models 1873 and 1876 helped make Winchester the dominant American maker of lever-action repeating guns, and then the dominant maker in the world. Model 1873 was made for military markets, both home and abroad. Oliver's son, Will, invented a reloading tool for it that was patented in 1874. Of course, sales were not limited to official armies. George Armstrong Custer was surely surprised to discover that many of the Indians he attacked at the Little Big Horn on June 25, 1876 were armed with Henrys, Winchester 1866s, and Winchester 1873s, while his men only had single-shot Springfield carbines.[52] When the Springfield armory tested the 1866 and 1873 models it concluded they were not powerful enough and only performed well within 100 yards—which must have been good enough for Indians. Nevertheless, Winchester responded with Model

1876, which it exhibited at the Philadelphia Centennial Exhibition (beside Colt's exhibit). It was a larger and more powerful version of the '73. Canada bought fifty '76s for the North West Mounted Police, and it was popular out on the prairie but still judged too weak in construction for the army. Gun enthusiast Theodore Roosevelt owned three versions of the 1876—a carbine and two calibers of rifle—and he wrote expertly in the March 1886 issue of *Outing* magazine that the .40-60 caliber Winchester was best for killing deer, antelope, and sheep, and could even be used against elk and bear if that were all one had at the time.[53]

Following in his father's footsteps, John Browning soon became a repairman, and one of his father's customers gave him a badly damaged single-barreled shotgun which John took apart, saved the parts that could be fixed, made new parts where needed, and then assembled a fine, reliable gun. He later felt that that experience marked his transition from boyhood to manhood. In 1878, while repairing a complicated single-shot .22 rifle, he commented to his father that he could make a better one than that. Jonathan responded, "I wish you'd get at it. [54] It had to be simple, because they had no milling machine or any other power tools. It took John less than a year, and he then wrote to a sporting supply house in New York City and asked how to patent a gun. He was put in contact with a patent attorney, who sent him instructions and application form, and on October 7, 1879 got his patent for him. By then, his father had died and he inherited the shop. For a while he expanded the repair business by advertising regionally, but then he decided to build a small gun factory. He had his brothers built a building, and he bought some used equipment, including a steam engine so they could begin using power tools. He taught his brothers gun making, repairing, and selling, and paid modest salaries until he could do better. When they began moving equipment into the new building, Browning realized he did not know how to organize a factory. While wondering what to do, an English gunsmith, Frank Rushton, who had become a Mormon, saw his sign and asked if they needed expert help. Browning hired him immediately, and he stayed for the rest of his life. They began manufacturing Browning's single-shot .22 rifle, which was in great demand because it was both reliable and cheap.

In 1883, a Winchester salesman came across one of the "Browning Bros." Rifles, which he bought used for $15 and sent back to the factory. Within a week, Thomas G. Bennett, vice-president and general manager of Winchester Repeating Arms Company, rode a train to Ogden and offered to buy manufacturing rights to it and first option on any other guns Browning invented. Browning agreed and their business relationship lasted 19 years. As fast as Browning invented new rifles and shotguns, Bennett snapped them up and discontinued the models his guns replaced. In the two years between October 1884 and September 1886, Winchester bought rights to eleven of his newly-invented guns. All told, Winchester bought 44 Browning guns and manufactured ten of them; Bennett bought the others to keep them from competitors. The most popular hunting rifle ever sold was his Winchester Model 1894 Lever Action Repeating Rifle, and his Model 1897 Winchester Shotgun set the standard for all competitors. The last gun Browning sold to Winchester was, like the first one, a single-shot .22 rifle. (Bennett wanted it in order to undersell a Belgian import and drive it from the American market, which it did.)

Another direction in gun design was stimulated by the Civil War— machine guns. The idea first arose in 1663 but was impractical until metal cartridges were available. Wilson Ager built the Union Repeating Gun in 1861, and it was demonstrated to President Lincoln, who urged the head of Army Ordnance, General James W. Ripley, to buy some. He was uninterested but several field commanders tried it out with mixed results. They suggested improvements, but before they could be made in 1862 another machine gun, the Raphael Repeater, appeared and was superior to the Union Repeating Gun, though its accuracy was low. Ripley also resisted buying it, but again, several field commanders tried it out and were more impressed with it than he was. In 1863 he retired after 49 years of service.[55]

If the army was going to accept officially a machine gun, it would take a more persistent salesman and product improver than either of these two machine guns had. That person was Richard Jordan Gatling (1818-1903), a physician who never practiced medicine, who was disturbed by Union soldiers dying in battle or from disease during the Civil War, and in 1861 he began working on a hand-cranked machine gun.[56] He was the son of a farmer-inventor in North Carolina, and the son's gun seemed influenced by the father Jordan Gatling's seed planter and rotary cultivator. Richard, at age 17 had invented a screw propeller, only to find when he went to Washington to patent it that John Ericsson had beat him to it by a month. Richard Gatling's next invention, a rice and wheat planter, was patented and did make money. In the Civil War, U.S. Army Ordnance received so many new inventions to consider that it stopped considering them. Consequently, Gatling's six-barrel machine gun which he patented in November 1862 never received much use in that war. His first model was not very accurate and cost $1500, which seemed expensive at the time. However, he sold two to the *New York Times* which used them to intimidate looters during the draft riots of July 13-16, 1863. Gatling continued to improve his machine gun, and in 1866 the U.S. Army tested an improved model and ordered 100. He asked the Colt factory to make them, and in 1870 he settled near the factory in Hartford. Gatling continued improving his gun for the rest of his life, and he followed Colt's example of going to Europe to sell them.

Gatling was the first of a series of American inventors of machine guns, several of whom started out at the Colt factory. Since the U.S. Army had adopted Gatling's gun, later inventors also went to Europe to sell theirs. Benjamin Berkeley Hotchkiss moved to France in 1867 and opened a factory there to make his. William Gardner, a Union soldier from Ohio, had his hand-cranked version made by Pratt and Whitney in Hartford. (Francis Pratt was himself a very capable gun designer.) Hiram S. Maxim (1840-1916) was an inventor his whole life, but is most remembered for the first fully-automated machine gun. It used the recoil after a bullet was fired to advance the next bullet into firing position. He patented the idea in 1883 and made them in London for a while but later sold the rights to Vickers Company, which made them under its own name during World War I.[57]

In fall 1889, John M. Browning and his brothers were at the weekly shoot of Ogden Rifle Club, and while watching a short friend fire a Browning rifle at a target, he noticed that the blast out of the muzzle caused a clump of weeds ahead of the rifle to bend forward.[58] He instantly realized that wasted energy from gunpowder explosions might be harnessed to power an automatic repeating gun. They hurried back to their factory, and he ran a crude experiment that convinced him that his idea worked. He speculated that they could have a good automatic machine gun in ten years, but he began taking out patents for one in January 1890, and in November he wrote to Colt Patent Arms Company, which made the Gatling machine gun for the U.S. Army, and asked if the company would be interested in making a fully-automatic machine gun. Colt's president invited him to demonstrate it and was overwhelmed by its perfect performance. That initiated a seventy-year relationship between the Browning and Colt companies. Some months later, Colt Co. arranged a demonstration of the gun for U.S. Navy officers, who had the same experience of being overwhelmed by a performance far beyond anything they could have imagined. Colt signed a contract with royalties with Browning, and the gas-operated gun became Colt Model 1895 Automatic Machine Gun which fired over 400 rounds a minute. The Navy became the first customer, with an initial delivery in 1897. Army tests were less satisfactory.[59]

In 1895 Browning patented his first automatic pistol and began work on an automatic shotgun, which some authorities consider his most daring innovation.[60] The best repeating shotgun in the world was his own design which was manufactured by Winchester. An automatic shotgun would compete with it. He took his automatic shotgun to Bennett in March 1899, and Bennett asked Browning to leave it so his engineers could study it. When Bennett had not acted on it by August 1900, Browning became impatient and returned to Connecticut to confront him. He told Bennett that he wanted a substantial fee (that neither man ever disclosed)—as a down payment on royalties. Unlike other gun companies, Winchester had never paid royalties, and Bennett was unwilling to start doing so. Although Winchester continued to manufacture the Browning guns it had on line, that meeting ended the relationship between the two men and their respective companies. Robert L. Wilson, the official historian of the Winchester Repeating Arms Company, acknowledged that Bennett's decision was not in the company's best interest.[61] The automatic shotgun was Browning's most profitable sport gun.[62] Since Fabrique Nationale d'Armes de Guerre, in Liège, Belgium, was already making his automatic pistol, Browning took his automatic shotgun there, and that company was delighted to also contract for royalties to make his automatic shotgun. Later, because of U.S. tariffs on imported guns, Remington bought the rights to make it in America.

Making and selling guns could be very profitable, but it had already become very competitive in the late 1840s and has remained so. To succeed, one needed good products at competitive prices, with smart advertising and sales strategies. Colt fended off some of his competition by having company lawyers take competitors to court for patent infringements, and other gun makers did likewise. The Civil War was a boom time for all, but we have seen that afterwards Sharps went bust. The problem was greater productive capacity than sales. Government reluctance to buy the best rifles in the Civil

War because of cost was replayed in the Spanish-American War (1898). This time Congress was only willing to buy bolt-action Krag-Jorgensen rifles for the regular army of 25,000 men, with volunteers having to use Springfield rifles from the Civil War. Krags used smokeless powder and the old Springfields used black powder which produced smoke.[63]

During the Civil War, the South had had much more difficulty maintaining adequate supplies of gunpowder than the Union,[64] but after the war, there was a glut of powder that created a financial crisis. Veterans on both sides of the war were given their guns, and they were a hypothetical source of gun powder sales that did not materialize.[65] In 1867, gun dealer Marcellus Hartley (1827-1902) bought two small New England cartridge companies, moved to Bridgeport CT and formed United Metallic Cartridge Company (UMC).[66] In the 1870s and '80s there was a flurry of activity, legal at the time, to moderate cut-throat competition in ammunition sales, since that market would continue to exist. In 1872, Henry Du Pont organized the Gunpowder Trade Association, called the Powder Trust.[67] But there was a difference between gunpowder and ammunition. In 1873, UMC was the largest cartridge maker in the world, and Winchester Repeating Arms Company was a significant competitor. They agreed to avoid lawsuits against each other and to determine royalty payments when making each other's products. At some point, Colt and Winchester came to an understanding that the former would cease making long guns and the latter would not make hand guns. By 1881, Du Pont controlled 85% of U.S. black powder production and even bought shares in its greatest competitor, Lafin and Rand. In 1883 the Ammunition Manufacturers Association formed and included UMC, Phoenix Metallic, U.S. Cartridge, and Winchester; they controlled half of U.S. ammunition sales. Meanwhile, the 1873 agreement between UMC and Winchester led to further cooperation in 1888. Remington Arms Company was in receivership, and each company paid $100,000 for half ownership. They ran the company jointly until 1896. However, in 1890 Congress passed the Sherman Antitrust Act, which may have influenced Winchester's sale of its shares to Hartley, head of UMC. Winchester's gun sales increased from 25,000 in 1870 to 300,000 in 1910.

Before World War I, Du Pont sold only five to ten percent of its gunpowder to the military. When war came in August 1914, Britain and France could not make enough gunpowder to meet their needs and turned to Du Pont.

Pierre Du Pont feared that if he financed the expansion of his factories to meet anticipated war needs, the war could end quickly and leave Du Pont in debt when the demand ended. Therefore, he charged $1 per pound, $.50 of which was to pay for plant expansion. The war did not end quickly, and Du Pont supplied forty percent of the powder used by the Allies. In the last three prewar years, Du Pont's profits were 11.57 percent of invested capital, but its war profits were a "truly staggering" tenfold increase. Congress disapproved and in 1916 imposed a 12.5 percent tax on net income from gunpowder sales.[68]

Both Winchester and Remington received a boost from World War I orders, but both also went broke in the 1930s Depression. Apparently, the ammunition business was more secure than the gun business, because Remington was bought by Du Pont and Winchester was bought by the Olin brothers, John and Spencer, to become a division of their Western Cartridge Company. Guns are durable goods, and many owners only want one or two, whereas users of guns are constantly buying ammunition. U.S. military investment in guns and ammunition were quite modest during the Depression.

Although machine guns proved effective for defense in World War I, since both sides had them, that merely led to stalemate on the western front; a new offensive weapon was needed to break through enemy lines. Major John T. Thompson hoped to provide it. During the Spanish-American War he had helped Second Lieutenant John H. Parker get 15 Army Gatling guns to the Cuban front, only to find that they faced Spanish Maxim machine guns with smokeless power. After that war Thompson made the case for modernizing U.S. Army's small arms. He was made head of Army Ordnance's Small Arms Division and developed the Model 1903 Springfield rifle, which "is still regarded by some as the finest bolt-action military rifle ever built."[69] His push also led to the development of Model 1911 Automatic Service Pistol. However, he failed to convince Army Ordnance that an automatic rifle should become a major priority, and therefore he resigned from the Army in November 1914 to become chief consulting engineer for Remington Arms. He designed and built the world's largest rifle factory in Eddystone, Pa to produce Enfield Rifles for the British Army, then built another factory at Bridgeport, CT to produce rifles for Russia.

In his spare time, he worked on his automatic rifle. Neither the Maxim nor the Browning automatic systems were practical for a hand-held automatic rifle. Thompson studied recent gun patents at the U.S.

Patent Office and discovered John B. Blish's blowback automatic system, patented in 1913. Blish had been a naval officer and he had in mind naval artillery, but Thompson though it could work in an automatic rifle. Blish was enthusiastic about the possibility. Thompson was an ideas man, not an engineer, like Colt but with more integrity. But integrity did not prevent him from obtaining financial backing from robber baron Thomas Fortune Ryan. As chief engineer, Thompson hired Theodore H. Eickhoff, who had worked under him at Army Ordnance. To get started, they used the facilities and expertise of Warney and Swasey Company, a large machine tool firm in Cleveland with whom Thompson had dealt while at Army Ordnance. Although he assembled a capable team, it was only in the fall of 1919, a year after World War I ended, that he felt confident enough to demonstrate his "submachine gun" (his term, though it became popularly known as "Tommygun") to American and foreign armed forces. Interest was high, but sales were low, because governments had spent heavily on weapons during the war and were now focused on other needs. In 1919, Congress passed the War Revenue Act to pay off war debts. It included taxes on the sale of guns and ammunition, making it the first federal gun tax.[70]

Fig. 7. John Thompson.

Thompson opened a New York office and brought his son Marcellus (another ex-Army man) into his Auto-Ordnance Company. It soon became clear that the company could not stay in business (and repay Ryan's half-million-dollar investment) selling only to national armed forces. In 1921 the company sold 107 guns to governments—mostly in Latin America—but did a better business with steel and mining companies that had labor troubles. On June 15 Auto-Ordnance made headlines when 495 Tommyguns were discovered in the hold of a ship preparing to sail to Dublin. Marcellus Thompson had expressed an interest in showing the gun to the Irish, and Ryan and Eamon de Valera were friends. Those 495 guns were confiscated, but others did get to Ireland and saw some, but not extensive, use in the Irish war of independence. Auto-Ordnance marketed its gun to police and sheriff departments nationwide, but this did not prove to be a large market either. By 1925 about 3000 tommyguns had been sold. In quest of new customers, one Auto-Ordnance ad showed a cowboy "mowing down" a group of men on horseback with rifles.

Apparently, a company that advertised a gun to end banditry did not anticipate bandits becoming its customers. But criminals began acquiring them by 1924, if not before. Throughout America, tommyguns were available from gun dealers, even in New York City, where sale of handguns was closely monitored. Prohibition of alcoholic beverages became federal law in 1920, and it was effective in many small towns and rural areas, but not in cities. The law created a huge demand for illicit alcoholic beverages which "bootleggers" met. It became a very lucrative business which was peaceful for two or three years. Assassinations among bootleggers began in Chicago in 1924 and a tommygun was first used in one on September 5, 1925. A rival, gunning for Al Capone, pumped 37 bullets into Martin Costello's saloon on February 9, 1926, wounding two men, one seriously. The next day both a police captain and Al Capone placed orders for tommyguns. When Assistant State's Attorney William McSwiggin was machine gunned in a gang shootout on April 27, it made headlines in New York, and John Thompson walked around the Auto-Ordnance office muttering, "What can we do?"[71] Since the murder gun had been tossed from a car at the scene, Marcellus Thompson went to Chicago and told authorities that although the visible serial number had been obliterated, it was also concealed on a part and could be read when the gun was partly disassembled. That enabled him to identify the dealer who had sold it, but that did not lead to an arrest since the dealer claimed not to know who had bought it. The Chicago bootleg war's climax was the Valentine's Day Massacre in 1929. Capone sent four men to kill a rival gang, and they lined up seven men and shot them in the back. Their leader, George "Bugs" Moran, spotted the assassins in time to escape, and instead of killing him they unknowingly executed Dr. Reinhardt H. Schwimmer, an optometrist. Outrage over that massacre led to a police raid on Capone's headquarters and confiscation of financial ledgers which were used five years later to send him to prison for tax evasion.

The use of tommyguns in bootleg conflicts spread to Philadelphia in 1927 and to New York City in 1928. A war continued in New York until Dutch Schultz was killed in 1935 (though Prohibition had ended in December 1933). There was a chronological overlap between the end of Prohibition and the emergence of "Depression desperados," with the latter arising in rural and small-town America. Some of those desperados acquired media fame (and sometimes celebrity): Dillinger, Baby Face Nelson, Pretty Boy Floyd, Bonnie Parker and Clyde Barrow, Machine Gun Kelly, and Ma Barker.[72] They mostly robbed banks, stores, and service stations. Neither bootleggers nor desperados limited their guns to submachine guns, but the latter, and sawed-off shotguns, aroused the most public alarm since bystanders were often wounded or killed and property badly damaged when criminals used these guns. Franklin D. Roosevelt was elected president in 1932 because he promised action rather than patience to cure America's ills. He appointed an attorney general, Homer S. Cummings, who shared his conviction that the federal government needed to enact tough gun controls since many bootleggers and desperados fled in fast cars across state lines after their gun crimes. The National Firearms Act of June 1934 was not as sweeping as Roosevelt and Cummings wanted (thanks to the gun lobby), and it did not even prohibit machine guns, but did impose a high tax on their sale to private persons, which led to their decline as a public hazard.

World War II was a boom time for manufacturers of guns and ammunition. In 1940 the U.S. Military stockpile of gunpowder was too small to meet the needs of a single day of fighting at the 1943 level, and rifle production was so slow it would have taken 50 years to equip the rapidly expanded armed services. Once more, the need was met by expansion of private factories and opening new ones. The government offered gun makers a five-year depreciation tax provision for building new factories, but in return, Congress wanted defense contracts open to public scrutiny and excess taxes imposed.[73]

After the war, war surplus guns were widely available. Aspects of post-war importation of surplus guns are discussed by Henry S. Bloomgarden, *The Gun: A "Biography" of the Gun That Killed John F. Kennedy*.[74] After the war, European countries were eager to sell guns that they no longer needed to Americans, who had both the money and desire to buy them. Those guns often sold here for one third or less of the cost of a comparable new American gun. Surplus rifle imports rose from 4,104 in 1948 to 729,392 in 1965.[75] A dealer's license cost one dollar to the U.S. Treasury. The gun Oswald used to kill Kennedy was a Mannlicher-Carcano bolt-action carbine, called a Carcano, made at the Royal Arms Works in Terni, Italy. Ferdinand Ritter von Mannlicher of Austria had invented the bolt-action mechanism and Salvatore Carcano, comptroller at the Terni Arsenal, had modified it from a single-shot gun into one with a six-shot magazine in 1891. It had served the Italian Army well in both world wars and in Mussolini's imperialistic wars in the 1930s. By 1940, the Terni Arsenal had 7000 men working three shifts night and day to produce 2500 Carcano 91s daily. Each gun was inscribed to indicate the model, time, and place of manufacture, and each had a serial number—Oswald's was C2766, made in 1940.[76]

After the war, Italy had many more Carcano 91s than the government needed. The Terni Arsenal, only slightly damaged during the war, ceased making guns and instead repaired some of those returned there for storage. In 1958 the Italian Ministry of Defense wanted to sell 570,000 of them, and an Italian attorney contacted a Philadelphia attorney he knew to ask if he could find a buyer so they both could earn a commission. The latter found H and D Folsom Arms Company in Yonkers, NY, that was interested. It, in turn, found financing from Adam Consolidated Industries. Their bid against two other American companies was highest—$1,776,000. Upon winning the bid, the two companies also bought 2,608,704 rounds of ammunition, and they chartered a new company in New York State, Crescent Firearms, to handle distributions. Crescent Firearms and Adam Consolidated were both on the sixth floor of a corner office building in New York City, and they used the same telephone number and receptionist, though the address of Crescent was 2 West 37th Street and of Adam Consolidated was 404 Fifth Avenue.

Bloomgarden commented that "their principals [were] all honest and hard-working men," but later he revealed that Crescent Firearms contracted for repairs of these guns in Italy before shipping, worth $38,635.50, which it never paid, driving the repairman into bankruptcy.[77] The rifles and carbines were sent in twelve shipments as they were reconditioned, between spring and September, 1960, and they all arrived at Jersey City by 25 October. They remained in a warehouse until sold to gun dealers. A carton of them which contained carbine C2766 was sent to Klein's Sporting Goods in Chicago in February 1963. Although Klein's had six retail stores, sixty per cent of its gun sales was by parcel post. The company bought a full-page advertisement in the February issue of *American Rifleman*, which included a 6.5 Italian carbine for $12.88, or with a Japanese four power telescopic sight for $19.95. Shipping was $1.50. In March Oswald sent a U.S. Postal Money Order for $21.45 with the order form from the advertisement filled out, using a pseudonym and Dallas postal box 2915 address. Although he had qualified as a sharpshooter while a Marine, when he took out his new gun on April 10 to shoot retired U.S. Army Major General Edwin A. Walker in his home, he missed and realized he needed more practice with it. He had plenty of time to practice before he used it to assassinate President Kennedy on November 21.

Although no new gun laws had been passed after any president was assassinated, in 1968 after both Martin Luther King (on April 4) and Robert F. Kennedy (on June 5) were assassinated, public pressure on Congress for gun control was slightly stronger than that from the NRA to do nothing. It helped that both houses of Congress and the presidency were under Democratic control. There were actually two bills passed into law: Omnibus Crime Control and Safe Streets Act and the Gun Control Act. They sound impressive, but the NRA was able to prevent licensing of owners and registration of their guns. What was achieved was the end of importation of surplus military weapons and other guns not adaptable to sports.[78] Small cheap handguns were prohibited from further imports. Quality controls imposed on foreign guns did not apply in America. Consequently, American companies began manufacturing comparable guns and foreign companies opened American subsidiaries that made similar guns.[79] Senator Thomas Dodd introduced President Johnson's bill to restrict mail-order sales of rifles and shotguns, which the NRA accepted.[80]

The ineffectiveness of these laws can be seen in shooting statistics for the years before and after the laws were passed (ch. 8), but also in the story of the invention and production of a new handgun. Journalist Erik Larson was so moved by the news of a 16-year-old boy's use of it in 1988 to kill one teacher, Karen Farley, and wound another, Sam Marino, that he traced its history from invention in the 1960s to its subsequent production and sale. The gun that by 1988 was named Cobray M-11/9 began in the Los Angeles gun shop of Juan Erquiaga Azicorbe, an ex-Peruvian army officer, who was making illegal small concealable machine guns for anti-Castro Cubans. Gordon Ingram, an engineer at the Police Ordnance Company, visited Erquiaga's shop and saw how to improve the gun's design. Erquiaga immediately hired him as a production engineer. Although some government officials were aware of Erquiaga's project, in 1965 other officials confiscated the guns and Erquiaga fled the country. Ingram then decided to make the gun as both an automatic machine pistol for military use and as a semiautomatic for civilian sales. He had some trouble getting it produced until in 1974 Hollywood featured one in a John Wayne film, *McQ*, about police and drug gangs. After that, the automatic pistol began to be sold to foreign governments, but early in the 1980s when PRB Industries tried to market the semiautomatic to American gun shops, ATF classified it as an illegal machine gun because of the easy conversion of it to an automatic. PRB challenged this ruling in federal court. The judge agreed with the ATF's ruling but allowed PRB to sell as semiautomatics all guns assembled before June 21, 1982. That decision made the gun a best seller before that date. Later, PRB was liquidated and replaced by S.W. Daniel Inc., which made the gun in such a way that it qualified as a semiautomatic unless the owner drilled one hole and bent a piece of metal. S.W. Daniel also sold some parts that could be combined with parts sold by L&M Guns to make an illegal silencer for the Cobray M-11/9. ATF found the joint sales of silencer parts illegal and had officers of both companies prosecuted for violating federal firearms laws. However, the Daniels were only convicted of failing to pay taxes on the sale of two guns, and for this misdemeanor were sentenced to six months probation and a $900 fine. Since they were not found guilty of a felony, they kept their Federal Firearms License.[81] In the early 1980s, Intratec made TEC-9 semiautomatic assault weapons for civilians. It was a favorite of drug lords and was used in a mass murder. In 1994, Congress outlawed it, but Intratec then produced a modified version which evaded the law.[82]

Larson's book shows how some gun makers and sellers have been willing to make and sell products tailored to the desires of criminals. This occured because the legitimate gun market is limited by the fact that guns are durable goods. But convicted criminals had their guns confiscated, and therefore, when released from incarceration, they sought a fresh supply. That sordid story is the subject of Tom Diaz's *Making a Killing: The Business of Guns in America* (1999). The problem was not limited to guns, however. Some ammunition makers and sellers were also willing to cater to criminals by making and marketing "cop killer" bullets. For example, ammunition maker David Keen bragged in 1994 that he would produce a Rhino-Ammo which splinters when it enters a human body and a Black Rhino which penetrates the Kelvar body armor worn by police.[83] These practices have led some cities to sue certain gun makers and sellers.

Most guns that have been used by criminals since World War II are cheap Saturday night specials, which Carol Vinzant's *Lawyers, Guns, and Money* (2005) explored in detail. There were five or six (at different times) low-end gun producers in the Los Angeles area (called "Ring of Fire") that catered to that market. They sent their guns to the South, where gun laws were most permissive. Their guns were bought by gun-runners, who then took them to Washington, Baltimore, Philadelphia, New York, and Boston and sold them on the street. Most guns used in crimes in those cities and others in the North came from one of the Ring of Fire producers. Even those gun makers needed insurance, and Vinzant also explained the sham insurance companies who sold the policies. Whenever one of these companies was sued over one of its guns, both gun maker and insurer were likely to declare bankruptcy, and later reemerge under a different name.

## Gun Shows

Gun shows have become important venues for gun sales. Gun shows have existed at least since World War II, but Joan Burbick (2006) and Stuart Wright (2007) begin their discussions with passage of the Firearms Owners' Protection Act (1986) which reduced or eliminated parts of the Gun Control Act (1968), passed after the Martin Luther King, Jr. and Robert F. Kennedy's assassinations.[84] That rollback of restrictions was, among other things, a gift to gun shows by relaxing restrictions on sales. Consequently, gun shows increased in frequency, attendance, and sales. The National Association of Arms Shows in 1995 estimated there were over 100 shows in America every weekend (5200 annually), with over five million in attendance, spending over $1 billion. A Violence Policy Center study (1996) found that this was also a gift to criminals, in that there were more guns to choose from and less check on purchasers.[85] The abundant guns were also a stimulus to private militias in America and increased shipments of guns from America to rebels abroad. Some astute gun-show organizers became millionaires; attendees paid an admission fee and those selling guns paid $40 - $60 rental per table, with the largest shows having up to 5000 tables.[86]

## Later Developments

The Austrian company, Glock, entered the U.S. market in 1985 and overtook Smith and Wesson, which had supplied American police for decades. There were over a million Glocks in America by 1996.[87] Making and selling guns and accessories in America by 2014 was a $11.7 billion industry.[88] The National Shooting Sports Foundation says the arms industry contributes $33 billion to the U.S. economy and supports about 220,000 jobs. As more Americans move into cities and suburbs, there are fewer hunters. In 2008, rifles and shotguns for hunting constituted about half of gun sales; that number fell to 25% of gun sales by 2014 and is projected to continue falling. *Businessweek* reported that gun sales rose 30% during Obama's first term, and he was called the "Gun Salesman of the Year." In 2012, the Associated Press found that the two largest gun makers, Strum, Ruger and Smith & Wesson's profits rose 86% and 44% respectively.

A favorite gun for mass murders has been semi-automatic assault rifles. As discussed in chapter 9, Congress passed a law outlawing their manufacture and importation in 1994, but the NRA had an amendment attached that it would expire in ten years, and in 2004, the NRA was able to defeat its renewal. The Sturmgewehr was developed in 1944 for the Nazi army, with the rapid-fire of a tommygun and yet it could be aimed like a rifle.[89] Russia's troops suffered most from its use, and after World War II Russia developed its own Avtomat Kalashnikova (AR-15), which it was happy to provide to armies in conflict with the American Army. America's M14 rifle was not competitive against AR-15s, and so the Army in 1957 asked a a gun manufacturer to develop what was named an Armalite Rifle (AR-15). Yet, the generals were reluctant to give up its reliable AR-14 until after 1962 tests had proven its value (President Lincoln had faced a comparable conservative officer corps during the Civil War). Colt marketed it as a "superb hunting partner," and it made 60,500 in 2001, which zoomed to 1.27 million in 2012. By then, Smith & Wesson was selling its own version of assault rifle, which James Holmes used in an Aurora, CO movie theater to kill 12 and wound 58.

Americans reported 300,000 to 400,000 gun crimes a year for 1973-89, according to the Justice Department.[90] In each of those years, the gun industry produced one million to 2.5 million handguns. In 1993 and 1994, gun production increased to about 2.8 million each year, and gun crimes increased to 560,000 to 580,000 a year. Northern states had stricter laws controlling gun sales than southern states, and so more guns were sent to sell in the South than southern buyers would buy. The excess guns were carried north from Florida and Virginia to northern cities, and from Mississippi and Indiana to Chicago.

Since it was difficult to persuade state and national legislatures to pass effective gun laws, those who wanted more gun control also used the courts. The gun industry argued it could not control what people did with their guns. Gun control advocate Tom Diaz is unwilling to accept such a vacuous excuse:[91]

The blizzard of gun violence documented in this book [2013] is not a "gun safety" problem. Nor is it a problem of legal versus illegal guns. It is a gun problem. It is the direct and inevitable consequence of the gun industry's cynical marketing, the proliferation of lethal firepower, and the waves of relaxed state laws—concealed carry, shoot first, shoot anywhere, shoot cops, just shoot, shoot, shoot—that the gun industry's handmaiden, the NRA, has inflicted on the country to promote new markets for the industry.

# Conclusions

Wars occurred frequently in American history, and they focused attention on guns to fight them. Until the 1840s, the problem facing governments and gun smiths was the slow pace of gun production. Production of gunpowder was an even worse problem until the du Ponts immigrated from France in 1800 and built their production facilities. The gun production problem was solved brilliantly during more than two decades following the War of 1812 by the cooperation between government and private gunsmiths, guided by the U.S. Arsenals at Springfield and Harpers Ferry. In the 1850s a new problem emerged—capacity of gun factories to make more guns than the market demanded. Samuel Colt pioneered one solution by using advertisements not just to tout the superiority of his guns, but also to increase desire for guns. After gun companies, notably Winchester, had begun cannibalizing other gun companies, another solution emerged in the 1870s and '80s among both gun and ammunition companies: manufacturers organized cartels to limit competition. However, the Sherman Antitrust Law banned this solution in 1890.

The market for hunting guns has flourished since American independence, and ammunition has been plentiful since the du Ponts arrived. There are three significant civilian markets for handguns: target and animal shooters, criminals, and those who want guns for protection. If guns were kept from criminals, then those fearing criminals would lose much of their motivation to buy guns. Therefore, gun makers and dealers depend on a steady supply of guns for crime in order to sell guns to anyone else except marksmen.

The complex world history of guns has engendered in some white men a general fascination for guns. Publishers have produced books to cater to them. Two examples are: Larry Koller, *The Fireside Book of Guns* (1959), which is designed, with many color illustrations, to make guns seem as American as apple pie; and Englishman Howard Blackmore, *Guns and Rifles of the World* (1965), which is a reference book without color illustrations.

Gun and ammunition production share many of the challenges of other modern industries, but gun production is not really like making washing machines, for the legitimate needs of society, because no one goes out with a new washing machine and kills others, whereas that is just what many murderers have done, and continue to do, with newly bought guns. This is an industry with a serious moral problem which it chooses to ignore.

# 5

# FEAR MONGERING NATIONAL
# RIFLE ASSOCIATION

The National Rifle Association is the single most important impediment to laws that could provide adequate safety for Americans. How did that happen? In 1973, journalist Robert Sherrill called the National Rifle Association "the most effective lobby in Washington," and it has only become more powerful since then.[1] Sherrill commented further about the NRA: "one of the most hilarious and, some think, one of the most dangerous organizations in the country." Although NRA members disagree with his latter comments, it remains a controversial organization. Virtually every issue of *American Rifleman* reeks of defensiveness and hostility toward NRA enemies and fear mongering for its members. Yet, it was not controversial when it began.

In the Civil War, Union forces were twice the size of Confederate forces, and usually the Union Army had up to twice as many men in a battle as the Confederate Army. One could logically expect that the Confederates had twice as many casualties as the Unionists, since there were two Union guns pointed at every Confederate soldier, but in fact, there were 354,000 Confederate casualties compared to 600, 000 Union casualties.[2] One reason for higher Union casualties was that defenders usually had the advantage over invaders, and the Union Armies were mostly the invaders. The two times Robert E. Lee took the war north—Antietam and Gettysburg—were so costly he could not try again. However, newspaper editor William Conant Church (1836-1917), was the son of a minister turned New York newspaper editor,[3] and lawyer George Wood Wingate (1840-1928), who became Union officers (already met in ch. 3), were concerned that

Southern soldiers were better marksmen than Union soldiers, since a higher percentage of southern men lived in rural areas and hunted than did northern men in urban environments.[4] A modern commentator stated that, in reality, southern advantage at marksmanship disappeared ob the battlefield due to the superiority of Union rifles.[5]

During the war, northern leaders were concerned with morale in the armed forces, and Church in 1863 resigned from the army to found the *Army and Navy Journal* and continued editing it until he died.[6] From the start, his editorials urged more rifle practice, and he suggested that Wingate write a manual on it, which Wingate did, in six issues of the *Journal*, 1870-71, and reprinted as a booklet in 1872. It was the first such manual in America. In his research for writing it, Wingate became acquainted with the National Rifle Association of Great Britain, founded in 1859, which in 1860 had established a shooting range at Wimbledon, where it conducted rifle competitions.

In the *Journal* for August 12, 1871 Church claimed that America's National Guard was too slow to reform, and that private enterprise should therefore intervene and take the initiative. Oddly, the 14 men whom he invited (including Wingate) to his Broadway office a week later to found the NRA were mostly those "slow National Guard officers" from New York City and Brooklyn about whom he complained. A constitution and bylaws were written and approved on September 12, and New York State issued the association of fewer than 100 men a charter on November 17, 1871,[7] stating its purpose:[8]

> To promote rifle practice, and for this purpose to provide a suitable range or ranges in the vicinity of New York, and a suitable place for the meetings of the association in the city itself, and to promote the introduction of a system of aiming drill and target firing among the National Guard of New York and the militia of other states.

NRA's Committee on Organization chose as its first president Ambrose E. Burnside, who had a mixed record as a Union Army general, but he had previously invented a breech-loading rifle which he manufactured from 1853 until his business failed in 1858.[9] After the war he was governor of Rhode Island, 1866-69, and he is best remembered for originating the fashion of wearing what are now called "sideburns." He only served as NRA president from November 24, 1871 to July 22, 1872, but that was long enough to persuade the New York State Legislature to allocate $25,000 and the cities of New York and Brooklyn to allocate $5000 each to purchase and equip 70 acres at Creed's Farm on Long Island for a rifle range, named "Creedmore."[10] Church's "private enterprise" concept was elastic enough to allow feeding at the public trough. This was only the beginning of government support for the NRA, first by New York State, and then in 1903 by the Federal Government. The NRA flourished while it received grants of money and guns and ammunition and fell on hard times when the dole declined. Church served as president in 1873-75, and Wingate in 1886-1902; almost all of the early presidents were active or retired Army or National Guard officers.

The NRA's rifle range opened in 1873, and interest in rifle competition increased dramatically when the Americans accepted a challenge match for 1874 from the Irish team that had won a Wimbledon match and anticipated proclaiming themselves world champions after defeating the Americans. It was to be not only a contest between riflemen but also between hand-made European muzzleloaders and American machine-made breechloaders. Both Remington and Sharps companies were glad to manufacture rifles for the occasion. Wingate was in charge of training the American team. It was a very close match, but the Americans won, creating a sensation in America.[11] Ireland wanted another match in Ireland in 1875; the Americans accepted and won that also. And won again in 1876 at Creedmore against the Canadians, Irish, Scotch, and Australians. The Remington and Sharps rifles seemed superior to European rifles.

Since it got off to a good start, and since the NRA is currently wealthy and powerful, one could easily imagine steady growth and prosperity throughout its history. That did not happen for a variety of reasons concerning friction between different governmental bodies at the local, state, and national levels, withdrawal of support by New York State during Gov. Alonzo Cornell's term (1880-82). The NRA held no meetings from 1892 to 1900. In 1890, during its years of hard times, the NRA deeded Creedmore to New York State, and in 1892 it began using the New Jersey State Rifle Association's Sea Girt Range.[12] That lasted until 1907, when the National Matches were transferred permanently to the Ohio Rifle Range at Camp Perry on the shore of Lake Erie about 45 miles east of Toledo. Adjutant General of the Ohio National Guard Ammon B. Chritchfield persuaded the Ohio Legislature to appropriate $25,000 for the site in 1905. At the time, Chritchfield was also (along with James A. Drain) a vice president of NRA, and he served as president in 1936-37.[13]

NRA's revival came in 1900, because the Spanish-American War of 1898 was a wakeup call that rekindled interest in military preparedness.[14] When the NRA Board of Directors met in 1900, it elected an Army general as honorary president and another general as actual president.

President William McKinley, who took us into the Spanish-American War, only survived it for a month before being felled by an assassin's bullet.[15] President Theodore Roosevelt and Secretary of War Elihu Root both wanted military reforms. The NRA was waiting in the wings, and since its president, General Bird Spencer of the National Guard, had the ear of Senators, it did not have to wait long. The War Department Appropriations Bill, which became law in February 1903, established a National Board for the Promotion of Rifle Practice and provided funds for national matches and for transportation of teams of marksmen to those matches from branches of the armed services and the National Guards of states.[16] This law enabled the NRA to become a quasi-governmental organization dedicated to training American riflemen, with access to government rifles and ammunition. Adjutant General of Washington State's National Guard, James A. Drain, organized powerful support for the 1903 bill among other states' adjutant generals. In 1906 he was elected Vice President of NRA; he also purchased *Shooting and Fishing*, changed its name to *Arms and the Man*, became its editor, and it became an unofficial NRA organ. Drain served as president in 1907-10; in 1916, he retired as editor of *Arms and the Man* and sold the magazine to the NRA for one dollar; in 1923 the title changed again to *American Rifleman*. In 1905 Wingate had organized a rifle-shooting program in the New York City schools, and during his presidency Drain expanded it nationally. In 1910, Congress authorized the U.S. Army to give rifles and ammunition to rifle clubs, distributed by the National Board for the Promotion of Rifle Practice. By 1938 the War Department was providing rifles, ammunition, targets, and accessories to some four hundred junior rifle clubs, and the *American Rifleman* announced in 1939 that the NRA had trained 750,000 youths, ages 12-18, during 13 years.[17] Connections to gun clubs enhanced NRA membership growth.

In 1910, after a would-be assassin shot New York City Mayor William

Gaynor, a corner's assistant, George P. Le Brun, convinced the state Legislature to pass a law prohibiting carrying a handgun in the city without a permit (ch. 9). The NRA's apparent disapproval was expressed in Drain's attempt to defeat the bill before the vote with an editorial in *Arms and the Man* (May 1911):[18]

> A warning should be sounded to legislators against passing laws which...seem to make it impossible for a criminal to get a pistol, if the same laws would make it very difficult for an honest man and a good citizen to obtain them. Such laws have the effect of arming the bad man and disarming the good one to the injury of the community.

His decision to comment on handgun legislation as an unofficial spokesman for the NRA (his term as president having ended) was a momentous decision, going well beyond what the charter granted by New York State had envisioned for the association. From this editorial down to the present, all NRA opposition to gun control has been based on fear that a supposed change for the better is actually a change for the worse. The publication of its fears has sold both guns (to combat whatever is feared) and NRA memberships (because the NRA would become the best protector of gun ownership through its legislative lobbying). What gun owners should fear changed from time to time, but the *American Rifleman* was always there to explain the latest—various crooks, communists, gun grabbers, terrorists, tyrants. The NRA did not become the Fear of the Month Club until the early 1920s, but Drain had set the stage.[19] Why did he do it? Perhaps some of the money spent on advertising and lobbying activated Drain's pen. In 1907 the Du Ponts had pressed the NRA to elect Drain president, and if he was cooperative with ammunition makers, he was undoubtedly equally cooperative with gun makers.[20]

Here is the sour comment made on the 1911 situation in the first NRA-sponsored history:[21]

> The [Sullivan] law was the parting gesture of a machine politician in the final plunge of his decline from power. Only months after he introduced the bill [actually, more

than a year after it became law], and hounded by charges of corruption, Sullivan was committed to an institution for the insane. He was killed by a railroad train on September 1, 1913, after escaping from custody.

The second NRA-sponsored history repeats these words verbatim.[22] Neither history provides any background information, leaving the reader with the impression that the Sullivan Law was the misguided act of one wacky politician. It is true that Sullivan spent some time in a sanitarium, because he had a nervous breakdown after his wife's funeral in September, 1912, and two nieces also died, but he was living with his brother when he wandered away and was hit by a train. It was possibly a suicide, but whatever the circumstances were during his last year, and at his death, there is no reason to believe that he was of unsound mind when he shepherded the Sullivan Bill through the New York Senate. Seventh-five thousand people turned out for his funeral.[23] Perhaps NRA historians might have found an excuse to attack Le Brun, if only they had known where the bill really originated. World War I focused American attention on military preparedness. Although President Wilson was reelected in 1916 because he had kept us out of the war, German submarines sinking U.S. ships in 1917 brought us in. Some of the goals of the NRA were embodied in the National Defense Act of 1916. It established Reserve Officer Training Corps (ROTC) in colleges and universities, increased federal support for civilian rifle training, provided for building rifle ranges and making rifles, ammunition, and instructors available. This law defined three classes of militia: National Guard, Naval Militia, and unorganized militia. The last class included all males willing to train in rifle shooting. American participation in the war did not last long enough for all these provisions to develop on a large scale.[24] The Espionage Act of 1917 abridged first amendment rights of free speech, but that was not the amendment that would mobilize the NRA. After the war, NRA received free guns and ammunition, which helped build its membership.[25]

"Not even martial handguns mattered much to the NRA before the 1920s when its remarkable preoccupation with pistol laws recast what had been a military rifle fraternity."[26] Several factors were involved in the change. Cheap handguns had become common after the Civil War, yet they were of such poor quality that they were undependable. In Norwich, CT, 45,000-50,000 were produced a month in 1882.

Among the strongest supporters of gun controls were policemen, and the NRA set out to change that. Captain Edward C. Crossman, an NRA member, developed a revolver marksmanship training program for the Los Angeles Police Department and Commissioner of Police Charles D. Gaither did the same in Baltimore. Gaither had been NRA president, 1913-15.[27] The NRA established its own police marksmanship course in 1925 and its Police Division in 1927. But Midwestern towns tried a different approach which also involved the NRA. Chicago gangsters began driving out to Iowa and robbing small banks in towns with few law officers. The Iowa Bankers Association got sheriffs to deputize and arm townsmen. Almost 4000 volunteers patrolled 781 communities in the first year, and many of these volunteers joined the NRA to obtain cheap government weapons and ammunition. The NRA also arranged for them to practice with National Guards, sheriff deputies, or policemen. In a year, the Iowa Plan reduced bank robberies from 56 to six, and small towns in Illinois and Indiana adopted the plan.[28]

The NRA secured the services of two very capable advocates in the 1920s who dominated its legal activities for several decades. Karl T. Frederick was a New York lawyer, Vice-President of the United States Revolver Association, and a champion pistol marksman. He was also President of the NRA in 1934-36.[29] Frederick realized that the spread of New York's Sullivan Law to other states could only be prevented if there were a weaker alternative. Therefore, he helped draft a "Uniform Firearms Act" for the National Conference of Commissioners of Uniform State Laws of the American Bar Association, which the ABA approved in 1926. Despite the title, however, it only dealt with handguns.[30] Milton A. Reckord (b. 1879) was a general in the National Guard who saw active duty in both world wars. He became Secretary of the NRA in 1926 and later Executive Vice President. In January, 1955, after his retirement, he received an honorary life membership and a medallion with his image and these words on it: "The present stature of the National Rifle Association of America is a direct result of the years in which he was connected with it."[31] Frederick and Reckord were quite effective as lobbyists and as spokesmen before Congressional committees,[32] though North Carolina Congressman

Robert Lee Doughton responded with incredulity to Frederick's claim in 1934 that "automobile owners are...as a class, a much more criminal body, from the standpoint of percentage, than pistol licensees."[33]

As the NRA broadened its programs, its membership increased. In 1918 its membership was only 1223, but it increased to 3500 in 1921, to 22,054 in 1925, to 27,824 in 1929; membership reached 50,000 in the 1930s, 86,000 in 1945, 155,500 in 1946, and over a quarter million in 1947, a half million in 1962, over 900,000 in 1966, 1,200,000 in 1978, 3,500,000 in 1996, and 4.3 million during 2000.[34] The gun industry spent hundreds of thousands of dollars to stop gun laws in the 1920s, while its partner, the NRA, spent little, but reaped the reward from its campaigns of increased membership. As memberships increased, so did revenue from advertisements in *American Rifleman*. Congress was hostile to gun industry lobbying against gun laws, and the NRA gradually took over the active opposition to gun legislation, and it formed its Legislative Division in 1934. Concurrent with growth in membership was growth in the size of NRA facilities. The Federal Government regularly subsidized the National Matches. For example, in 1989 it cost taxpayers $1.4 million.[35] While Spencer was president, the NRA had one employee, a secretary, who had an office in the bank in Passaic, NJ where Spencer was bank president. When Drain became NRA president in 1907, he took the headquarters back to Broadway for a year before moving it to the Woodward Building, two blocks from the White House. In 1939 NRA took over a handsome mansion at 1600 Rhode Island Ave. for its headquarters, but by 1956 it was also renting offices in other buildings. Therefore, it built a new eight-story headquarters adjacent to the old mansion.[36]

The 1934 law was helpful, but did not meet all the needs of law enforcement, and a new bill gradually progressed in Congress. The NRA complained to its members that the proposed bill would only disarm honest citizens, and that gun registration would encourage a dictatorship in America. In 1937, Attorney General Cummings addressed the International Association of Chiefs of Police, telling them that 11,000-12,000 people a year were homicide victims, and that about 70% of them were killed with firearms, compared to 12% in England and 32% in Canada. Reckord and the NRA helped shape a weaker bill than Cummings wanted: "To Regulate Commerce in Firearms," which became the Federal Firearms Act of 1938 to license manufacturers and dealers in guns.[37] It became unlawful to ship arms and ammunition to anyone under indictment for or convicted of a violent crime.

Although the NRA defeated gun laws that might have significantly reduced city shootings, it became concerned about hunting accidents. The NRA collected statistics on hunting accidents from state conservation departments, which had never been analyzed before. A conference on hunting safety was held in 1938 and a safety program was developed, but little implementation occurred before World War II. During the war, millions of men learned to shoot in the armed services, and afterwards there was an increased interest in hunting and target shooting. The NRA presented to state legislatures hunter-safety bills which were passed into law and led to a decline in the accident rates. Target shooting also increased. There were only about a hundred competitive matches in 1945, but they increased to 7,245 by 1982. In 1983, 200,000 shooters competed in matches.[38] The increasing popularity of target shooting and hunting was encouraged by the increasing number of surplus rifles and ammunition made available to the NRA after the war.[39] During the 1960s, it became evident that both left-wing and right-wing extremist individuals and groups were joining or forming NRA clubs in order to receive free government guns and ammunition.[40] In Monroe, NC, World War II Marine veteran Robert F. Williams, who was president of the local NAACP, decided in 1957 to organize the Monroe Rifle Club and obtained NRA affiliation. The purpose was neither hunting nor target shooting, but protection of the Black community. There was no need to mention to the NRA the race of the club members.[41]

Later, the NRA developed several strategies to increase membership, one of which was to attract blacks. In the mid-1980s, it succeeded in attracting Roy Innis, who led the Congress of Racial Equality, and Representative Mike Espy, Democratic congressman from Mississippi.[42] It had more success attracting (white) women and boys. It developed a working relationship with both the Boy Scouts and 4-H Clubs, but also with unaffiliated boys.[43]

For some years after President Kennedy's assassination, the NRA had a rather negative public image, as it was widely blamed for the lax gun laws that had allowed the assassinations of John and Robert Kennedy, Martin

Luther King, Jr., and many others who, for a while, were remembered as unnecessary deaths. For example, in his book on the carbine that Lee Harvey Oswald used to kill President Kennedy, reporter Henry S. Bloomgarden commented: "the NRA had exerted a profound influence on America's singular position as the most violence-prone, gun-oriented nation on earth—a nation with virtually no firearms controls, a nation with more guns than all other countries combined."[44] Senators Edward Kennedy and John Glenn and several Hollywood starts led a counterattack against the NRA's policies on gun laws. While the NRA never relaxed its legal stance, it did try to keep a lower public profile and to cultivate a positive image. It bought land in New Mexico which it called the National Outdoor Center, and it began to focus on backpacking, camping, and other non-gun outdoor activities.[45] But NRA professional leaders were more sensitive to NRA's public image than was the membership. The NRA attracts more Republican than Democratic members of Congress,[46] but one of its strongest supporters in Congress was Democratic Congressman John D. Dingell, Jr. (who succeeded his father as Congressman from Detroit). Dingell, Jr. wrote to his fellow members on the NRA Board of Directors before the 1977 annual convention and urged decisive action to save the NRA from being diverted from its fundamental purpose of preserving gun rights and shooting sports.[47] Flexible accomodationists were voted out of office and hardline leaders were elected instead. This change of direction seemed so momentous that one member wrote a 52-page booklet about it, *Revolt at Cincinnati*.[48] Dingell and his allies saw this as democracy at work. However, Michael Opsitnik, an officer of the California Rifle and Pistol Association, who was ousted in the purge, pointed out that "they can take over a $50-million organization with 625 votes," which was less than half of one percent of eligible voters. Opsitnik thought that "if they call this election by the members, they must have studied politics in Russia."[49]

The new leaders included Harlan Bronson Carter, son of a Texan in the U.S. Border Patrol. When he was 17, his mother suspected some neighboring Mexican boys might know who had stolen the Carter family's car. Carter grabbed his shotgun and went out and demanded that they come with him to be questioned. They refused, 15-year-old Ramón Casiano pulled out a knife, and Carter shot him dead. A jury found Carter guilty of murder without malice aforethought, but on appeal the verdict was overturned on the grounds that the trial judge had failed to instruct the jury adequately on laws of self-defense. The charges were later dropped and Carter went on to become a commissioner of the Immigration and Naturalization Service. He changed the spelling of his first name to "Harlon" and concocted a story about the killing being by another Carter who spelled his first name "Harlan." A *New York Times* reporter exposed his fraud, after which Carter discovered the NRA was quite willing to ignore the incident. His determined personality was what the NRA wanted as an antidote to the previous accomodationists.[50] A pro-NRA historian commented that "Where before 1977 one could say that the National Rifle Association was a sports organization with some interest in legislative activity, it can now be described as a socio-political movement with the superficial appearance of a sports interest group."[51] One of the new leaders, Warren Cassidy, went further and described the NRA as like "one of the great religions of the world."[52] The shift in leadership seemed responsible for the sharp increase in NRA membership from 1,075,293 in 1977 to about 3 million by December 1984. In 1982 the NRA opened its Practical Pistol Shooting Matches—previously restricted to police—to the public and encouraged its members to think of life in America as so dangerous that they needed pistols and marksmanship training to protect themselves, their families, and property.[53]

Is the paranoia that the NRA encourages among its members through its publications sincere or just a tactic? If the latter, one could hardly expect its leaders to admit it in public, but once a leader admitted it in private. In the early 1980s, lawyer Robert Ricker, Assistant General Counsel for the NRA's Institute for Legislative Action, drove to the Capitol in Washington with Carter to deliver a $5000 check to a loyal senator. After a pleasant visit, on the ride back to NRA headquarters, Ricker commented that he was confident that they could win the fight on which they focused at the time. Carter retorted, "if the NRA wins, we are out of a job. Our goal is to maintain controversy in order to raise money."[54] NRA had already learned that its paranoid message attracted white men of limited education, but also politicians and some other members of the middle class.

By the mid-1980s the new leadership decided on five ambitious goals:[55]

1.  **Preemption laws** which reserve to the state legislatures the power to pass all state gun laws.

2. **State constitutional amendments** guaranteeing the right to keep and bear arms both for defense of the state and for personal protection.

3. **Carry permit laws** which require that permits shall be granted to all applicants of good character unless there is a good reason to refuse and place the burden of proof on the issuer not the applicant.

4. **Hunter harassment laws** to prohibit interference with lawful hunting.

5. **Repeal of New York's Sullivan Law** (which was actually done by the Legislature, but Governor Mario Cuomo, like Franklin Roosevelt before him, vetoed it).

The reason it has pushed for state constitutional amendments to guarantee private guns is because the U.S. Supreme Court had not yet affirmed the NRA's interpretation of the Second Amendment as guaranteeing this. To implement these goals the NRA established a large, well-funded lobby, the Institute for Legislative Action, and established a Political Victory Fund to finance its actions. The NRA has been successful in achieving these goals in most states. The reason the NRA is so effective politically is because it is a permanent organization with well-established political contacts, and when it asks its members to contact legislators or appear at public hearings, it can count on a strong response. By the mid-1980s NRA had a staff of 380 and could count on tens of thousands of volunteers.[56] Instead of diversifying their activities as the rejected leaders had planned, the new NRA leadership tried to diversify the NRA's image, publicizing members who were famous public figures or were female or junior members. The pinnacle of its success in this respect was recruiting Charlton Heston, a movie star famous for his role of Moses in *The Ten Commandments*, for vice-president, and then president in 1998-2003.[57] Aside from the anomalous Monroe Rifle Club mentioned above, the NRA is essentially lily-white. A notable exception was Roy Innis, chairman of the Congress of Racial Equality, who was a long time NRA board member.[58] (He thought middle class African Americans needed guns in their homes for protection.) NRA did hire a black lobbyist and displayed his photograph in its latest institutional history, as a public relations ploy.[59] It is unlikely that members of Congress think he was chosen to represent black members of the NRA, but perhaps he could ward off an affirmative action complaint against the NRA. There is a feel-good ad that appeared in *American*

*Rifleman* showing an apparently benevolent Heston smiling with a group of children, one of whom is black.

There were generally adequate funds for the NRA's ambitions, and if not, it could increase membership fees. For example, in 1985, its income was $66,267,400, from the following sources: dues (58%), interest and dividends (8%), advertising (12%), contributions (11%), and other, such as match fees, book sales, etc. (8%). Its disbursements that year were $68,011,800 spent on: publications (27%), membership and promotions (38%), Institute for Legislative Action (16%), general operations (8%), executive and administration (8%), and other (3%). Since it lost $1,893,000 in 1985, it increased the dues for 1986 by 25% to $20. The new dues were expected to generate a surplus in 1986 of $9,000,000. Total NRA assets for 1985 were $80,670,000.[60]

Why is the NRA effective politically? Partly because it has the money needed to be effective, and partly because it has an active organization. For example, in 1981-82 it spent more money communicating with its members than any other organization: $803, 656. In the same year it raised $2 million for its Political Action Committee, which was more than any corporate PAC and more than any union PAC except for the United Auto Workers, which raised the same amount. The Gun Owners of America's PAC that year also spent $900,000 on pro-gun lobbying, compared to Handgun Control's $200,000. In the elections, the NRA's Political Victory Fund spent that year $700,000 on national races, making it the sixth largest contributor among trade PACs. Its money went to friendly candidates for whom NRA money would be a major factor for victory. In 1984, it contributed to 33 Senate candidates and had 80% success. In 1986, passage of the McClure-Volkmer bill was the greatest single success of NRA lobbying until then. It removed most NRA objections to federal gun laws: allowing gun owners to travel throughout America without violating local gun laws, preventing prosecution of accidental gun law violations, and removing NRA objections to the 1968 Federal Firearms Law.[61] But American police were angry that Congress and the Reagan Administration had sided with the NRA on this bill instead of police.[62] In 1996 Congress moved the civilian marksmanship program, which NRA had run since 1903, into private hands without federal funds or surplus guns.[63]

NRA relied upon lobbyists to maintain its legislative clout. A lobbyist who worked his way to the top was Wayne LaPierre (b. 1949), who grew up in Roanoke VA, attended Catholic Sienna College, B.A., and Boston College, M.A., in government.[64] He joined NRA in 1977, after first working for Democrats in the Virginia Legislature. Unlike others at NRA, he was not a "gunman;" instead, he was a shrewd bureaucrat. He fought his way to the top, becoming the executive vice president in 1991 and currently earns an annual salary of $972,000. He has published six NRA propaganda books, beginning with *Guns, Crime, and Freedom* (1994); all of them provide various reasons why private guns are essential to maintaining American freedoms.

In politics, the NRA is quite willing to exaggerate and mislead in order to win. For example, for the 2000 election, the November issue of *American Rifleman* on p. 53 has this headline in large letters: "Al Gore Wants to Ban Guns in America," and that issue also contained two pro-Bush bumper stickers and a guide to voting which was specific for the candidates of the state of the addressee. Here is a sample of Wayne LaPierre's column, "Standing Guard:"[65]

> For those of us who have been fighting non-stop to protect the Second Amendment during the eight long years of Clinton-Gore, the tyranny of an all-powerful single branch of government has become a sharp reality. Its seizure of power has created an attack machine designed to destroy our rights and our very existence as an Association.

In the 2004 presidential campaign, NRA gave $575,270 to Republican and $110,750 to Democratic candidates, and in the second week of September it spent $400,000 on television infomercials that ran in "battleground states" Florida, Georgia, Ohio, Pennsylvania, South Carolina, and Wisconsin.[66] The NRA also had a half-page political ad attacking John Kerry in the Racine *Journal Times* the day before the election (November 1). If it ran that ad in all city newspapers in "battle-ground states," it may have spent more on newspaper ads for president than any other organization. In 2004, anti-Bush groups, such as MoveOn.org, matched or exceeded the expenditures of anti-Kerry groups. The NRA is willing to exaggerate its political effectiveness in post-election bragging, sometimes claiming more credit for victories than it deserved. It may have been decisive in two states against Gore, but was it decisive in any states against Kerry?

There were three books written on gun control before the 1977 NRA revolt and another written after it that portrayed the leadership as fanatical in its opposition to gun control,[67] but in the 1990s there were three books specifically on the NRA and its opposition to gun control laws which react to the hard-line stance that dominated after the revolt. They portray not just fanaticism but also abuse of power: Josh Sugarmann, *National Rifle Association: Money, Firepower & Fear* (1992), Osha G. Davidson, *Under Fire: The NRA and the Battle for Gun Control* (1993), and Jack Anderson, *Inside the NRA: Armed and Dangerous, an Exposé* (1996). They were written for the benefit of ordinary members of the NRA and for society at large. They have been answered (in general) by the NRA's current CEO and chief spokesman, Wayne LaPierre, in his first two books, *Guns, Crime, and Freedom* (1994) and (co-authored with James J. Baker) *Shooting Straight: Telling the Truth about Guns in America* (2002). There was also an hour television program on the NRA and its politics, "Gun Fight: the NRA and Power," hosted by Peter Jennings on ABC TV on October 9, 2000. LaPierre appeared in it claiming that he had not recruited a Republican candidate to run against Michigan Democratic Congressman and NRA member, Bart Stupak, who had broken with the NRA on a Congressional vote in 1999, and had voted in favor of an amendment to a bill for a three-day waiting period before a gun sale at gun shows. In a different interview, Stupak's Republican opponent in the 2000 election, Chuck Yob, assured Jennings that LaPierre had indeed recruited him and backed him with funds that in previous elections went to Stupak. A re-elected Stupak learned that the NRA punishes those who break with it on a single vote. (And the NRA learned that Stupak is a man of integrity who cannot be either intimidated or bought.) More recently, Michael Moore's documentary film, *Bowling for Columbine* (2003), criticized NRA for its opposition to gun control laws and for holding meetings in Denver and East Lansing in the wake of tragic shootings in both areas. The most devastating critique of the NRA, however, is Richard Feldman's insider tell-all *Ricochet: Confessions of a Gun Lobbyist* (2008). The NRA's attack dogs frequently turn on each other, and Feldman's book is payback for the way he was pushed out of his job and without a severance pay he had been promised verbally, but not in writing.

What did the books attacking the NRA complain about? There are too many stories to summarize, and since those books are in public and academic libraries, one example will suffice. In 1978, under Democratic President Carter, the Bureau of Alcohol, Tobacco and Firearms (ATF) announced it would computerize its files to speed up tracking guns. NRA then informed its members that the federal government was taking steps toward gun registration. NRA members responded strongly and negatively to Congress, which denied ATF funds for the project. When Republican Ronald Reagan became president in 1981, NRA leadership concluded that it could persuade him to simply abolish ATF. It invested $80,000 in a propaganda film, *It Can't Happen Here*, in which Democratic Congressman Dingell, Jr. complained, "if I were to select a jack-booted group of fascists who are perhaps as large a danger to American society as I could pick today, I would pick ATF. They are a shame and a disgrace to our country."[68] The film explained highly biased cases of alleged ATF abuse. Nevertheless, the propaganda worked. Getting government off our backs was a favorite line with Reagan, as was shrinking government. Reagan announced a plan to abolish ATF at a meeting of the International Chiefs of Police in September 1981, only to be met with dismay. Police chiefs needed ATF. Therefore, Reagan's Administration developed a compromise: it would abolish ATF (pleasing the NRA) and transfer gun enforcement officers to the Secret Service (pleasing the police). Now it was the NRA's turn to express dismay (privately). ATF had been its favorite whipping boy ever since it began enforcing the 1968 gun control law. If its agents entered the illustrious Secret Service, it would have to tone down its rhetoric. Alarmingly, gun control advocates liked abolishing ATF and transferring its agents to the Secret Service. An embarrassed NRA withdrew its opposition to ATF, which survives to this day.

NRA's important stealth collaboration with the Republican Party in achieving Newt Gingrich's planned Republican takeover of Congress in 1994 involved abandoning Democrats who had supported NRA bills, and it involved learning from its failures in the 1992 election when it had run campaign ads on gun issues.[69] In 1994 it ran ads instead on other Republican issues that had broader appeal. NRA also tried various tactics to evade campaign finance laws and FEC rules in raising and spending money on Congressional campaigns. By the 1990s NRA had outgrown its Washington headquarters, and in 1994 it moved into its present dazzling headquarters in Fairfax, VA. "Though not one D.C. official encouraged NRA to stay, Virginia state and county officials assiduously courted the organization."[70]

When Dingell, Jr. called ATF "a jack-booted group of fascists" in 1981, there was no public outcry. Maybe none but the NRA true believers watched the propaganda video, or if anyone else did, they dismissed his remark as just a politician politicking. Amusingly, however, when in May 1995 chief spokesman LaPierre dusted off Dingell's epithet and used a version in his letter to rouse the faithful to open their pocketbooks, the public learned that he had called ATF "jack-booted thugs," and all hell broke loose. Former President George Bush, Senator Ben Nighthorse Campbell, and General Norman Schwarzkopf all announced an end to their membership in the NRA. Ironically, Congressman Dingell, Jr. resigned his seat on the NRA board of directors (after all, his calling ATF a "jack-booted group of fascists" is not as bad as calling them "thugs," is it?). NRA lost 323,000 members that year.[71] After so much heat, NRA publicly apologized for LaPierre's letter. President Bill Clinton then commented:[72] "If the NRA's apology is sincere, what they ought to do is put their money where their mouth is. They ought to give up the ill-gotten gains from their bogus fund-raising letter..." Clinton suggested that the NRA donate the projected $1 million being raised by it to families of police officers slain in the line of duty. LaPierre was not grateful for the suggestion and replied: "We're the people who helped clean out Congress in 1994 [replacing Democrats with Republicans] and we are going to help clean out your clock in 1996,"[73] meaning to help prevent Clinton's reelection.

Besides being a sports club and gun lobby, the NRA is a fountainhead of American gun culture and ideology, with fresh doses in every issue of *American Rifleman*. NRA members are notorious for their stock of slogans which they repeat at the slightest opportunity. These slogans are presented as truisms and serve to cut off debate. In reality, they are half-truths and have been exposed as such.[74] Here are examples: Guns Don't Kill, People Do; Control Criminals Not Guns; When Guns Are Outlawed, Only Outlaws Will Have Guns; Gun Control Will Leave Citizens Defenseless; Gun Laws Don't Work; Registration Is the First Step toward Confiscation of All Guns; and Americans Have a Constitutional Right to Keep and Bear

Arms. The last of these, referring to the Constitution's Second Amendment, is the most repeated and the most basic.

If we go beyond slogans and propaganda, what are the fundamental beliefs of the NRA concerning guns and public safety? Obviously, I do not speak for the NRA, but here is a list of its basic beliefs as I understand them:

1. Our founding fathers were wise and set fundamental rules in the Constitution that should not be changed very much; the Second Amendment guarantees every law-abiding citizen the right to own guns.

2. NRA is a guardian of American freedoms and provides a guide for patriotism.

3. Citizens must be trusted with guns unless they commit crimes or are mentally incompetent.

4. People can be separated into law-abiding citizens and criminals.

5. Government cannot be trusted to regulate access to guns except in limited ways (e.g., no machine guns, sawed-off shotguns or silencers); any restrictive gun law is a step down a slippery slope toward gun confiscation.

6. Private guns are needed to protect our democracy from both internal and external threats, and to protect ourselves; hypothetical threats would become real without numerous private guns.

7. Licensing gun owners would lead to confiscating guns.

8. Gun rights are virtually absolute and should seldom be abridged.

9. Some gun crimes are the price we pay to maintain our freedom from tyranny.

10. Government should concentrate on controlling criminals, not law-abiding citizens.

11. NRA is competent to judge what is best for America concerning gun laws.

12. Law-abiding NRA members have a right to shoot other Americans if they conclude that whoever is being shot is a serious threat to themselves, others, and possibly to property, even if the perceived threat comes from a government official.

NRA's overall message: fear government more than deranged citizens with deadly guns. Historian Richard Hofstadter traced paranoia in

American politics back to a sermon preached in Massachusetts in 1798, and it has been a part of politics in one form or another ever since.[75]

NRA has been the self-appointed gate keeper of American gun laws since the 1920s. Very few gun laws have slipped by without its approval, and it tries to eliminate or undermine those few that did slip by. For example, it could not stop the 1994 assault gun ban, but it did have a ten-year sunset clause attached, and in 2004 when it was up for renewal, a U.S. Senate bill that included its renewal was defeated, and gun rights lobbying prevented any vote at all on renewal in the House. What is the result of its control of our gun laws? Has this font of wisdom served us well? America has the highest rate of gun ownership and gun crimes of all countries with a stable government. America is safe for guns but dangerous for people. What is wrong with NRA managing our gun laws? Too much mythology and rigidity in NRA ideology and very little empiricism. It is a myth that people can be separated into law-abiding citizens and criminals. Some people can be identified as habitual criminals, but anyone who has been law-abiding for decades can pick up a gun and change his/her category by shooting someone. This transformation happens all the time, and with NRA in charge of gun laws, we are not protected from such people. A good example is church deacon John Patton, 99, who fatally shot his wife, Lillie Bell Patton, 67, for suspected infidelity, in Jasper, FL,[76] but notorious examples are men like James Floyd Davis, 47, who lose their jobs and come back later to the workplace and shoot former fellow workers. In May 1995, he killed three and wounded four others in Asheville, NC.[77] Ralph Catalano of the University of California, Berkeley, found that laid-off men are six times more violent than those who are employed.[78] The desires of "law-abiding gun owners" trump the right of people to have laws to adequately protect public safety.

It was also in 1995 that President George H.W. Bush ended his NRA membership after Wayne LaPierre, following Timothy McVeigh's arrest for bombing the Murrah Federal Building in Oklahoma City, on April 19, called Federal agents "jack-booted thugs...wearing Nazi bucket helmets and black storm trooper uniforms to attack law-abiding citizens."[79] Bush's act precipitated resignations from NRA by some members of Congress.

NRA wants government to concentrate on punishing people who break laws with guns and leave law-abiding gun owners alone. This is a not a very controversial policy as far as it goes, but one cannot punish the dead.

There are many occasions where someone with a gun kills one or more people and then kills himself/herself or has the police do so—most deadly examples being: Charles Whitman shooting 43 and killing 12 in 1966; George Hennard shooting 45 people and killing 23 in 1991; Eric Harris and Dylan Klebold fatally shooting twelve classmates and a teacher and wounding others at Columbine High School on April 20, 1999; Seung-Hui Cho killing 32 and wounding others at Virginia Tech on 16 April 2007;[80] Omar Matten killing 49 and wounding 53 in Orlando; and Stephen Craig Paddock killing 59 and wounding 527 in Las Vegas on 1 October 2017. The Columbine tragedy inspired Michael Moore's documentary film, *Bowling for Columbine*, which is more about the gun problem in America (including the NRA) than specifically about that massacre. Even when a killer is apprehended and punished, that is no consolation to someone the killer killed, or their loved ones. Those killed had rights that should have trumped the rights of gun owners. The NRA philosophy of guns and freedom—private guns protect democracy—is unduly pessimistic. It is at the level of sophistication of the Ernie and Bert routine in the children's television show, "Sesame Street," in which Ernie asks Bert why he has a banana in his ear, and Bert says to keep away alligators. Ernie responds that there are no alligators around here, and Bert triumphantly says, "See, it works!" All other democracies function without the threat of private guns to shoot down democracy's subverters and ours would also. The most basic flaw in the NRA's version of democracy is that it believes it already has all the answers, and those who disagree with it want to rob gun owners of both guns and freedom. In reality, our society, awash with private guns, robs those people who are killed or seriously wounded by private gunners of their freedom to live normal lives. While the NRA protects us from hypothetical dangers that never materialize, real multitudes of people with guns kill thousands of Americans yearly. Democracy does not work adequately if people accept the freedoms and ignore the responsibilities.

All Americans remember the 9/11 attacks in 2001 on the New York Trade Center and the Pentagon by terrorists. Wayne LaPierre published *Shooting Straight: Telling the Truth about Guns* the next year and changed the emphasis of fear from criminals to emphasizing fear of terrorists.[81]

Some scholars consider Miguel de Cervantes' *Don Quixote* (1605-15) the greatest satire and one of the greatest pieces of fiction ever written. Don

Quixote was a delusional knight errant who went forth to save civilization from non-existent threats. He symbolized a delusional aristocracy and royalty that imposed its defective culture on both Spain and its colonies. Spain's failure to heed Cervantes' critique of its priorities resulted in its decline from a major power in Europe. The United States has not produced satire in the league with *Don Quixote*, but Herman Melville's *Moby Dick* (1851) is a notable metaphorical novel, about a fanatical Captain Ahab of a whaling ship who lost a leg during a previous voyage while attempting to kill a great white whale. On a return voyage, his fanaticism caused him to endanger his crew and ship in his second attempt to kill the whale, and as a result, both ship and crew are lost (excepting the narrator of the story). Perhaps Captain Ahab symbolized a fanatical South that held onto slavery despite the fact that it was ruining itself and threatening the Union. The failure of the South to heed Melville's warning resulted in great destruction of life and property in the Civil War. The NRA seems to me to be a kind of blend of Don Quixote and Captain Ahab, having the delusions of the former and the fanaticism of the latter.

Jack Anderson wrote his attack on the NRA leaders under the impression that they did not represent the thinking of NRA's rank and file:[82]

It is inconceivable that many members of the NRA know what the organization is doing and still support it—either that or the NRA has assembled as its membership 3.5 million fanatic-fringe extremists who are wholly out of touch with reality.

Yet, my local NRA sparring partner with whom I have exchanged letters for years (privately and twice on the editorial page of the Racine *Journal Times*) follow the party line very closely. Here is a sample (editor supplied titles):

Toughen gun laws (Sept. 16, 2004)
Thank you for your editorial lamenting the lapse of the assault weapons ban after ten years.

You rightly blamed Senate Republicans for their shameful vote against renewing the ban but you failed to mention that Sen. Russ Feingold voted with them. And Congressman Ryan did nothing to bring this to the floor of the House for debate. You pointed out that Bush did nothing to encourage Congress to renew the ban, but you failed to mention that Senator Kerry has made Bush's inaction an issue in the current presidential campaign.

Unfortunately, you also failed to understand the NRA's strategy in preparing for this lapse. When it could not stop the ban in 1994, it had a sunset clause attached and had the bill worded so as to allow gun makers to evade it. Since the gun makers (who probably suggested the loopholes in the first place) took advantage of the loopholes, the NRA and its Congressional lackeys could then dismiss the bill as ineffective and unworthy of renewal.

A rational response to a weak but needed law is to strengthen it.
Frank N. Egerton
Racine

Good riddance to ban (Sept. 19, 2004)

Frank Egerton's 9/16 letter to the paper praises the Journal Times' 9/14 for lamenting the lapse of the assault weapons ban. I say good riddance!

This law at best was a feel good law that had no measurable effect on violent crime. It banned certain guns for the mainly cosmetic reason that they looked deadly. The banned guns may have had a folding stock, muzzle flash suppressor, bayonet mount or pistol grip. When was the last time you read about someone being killed by a grenade launcher or a bayonet?

It also banned high capacity magazines holding more than ten rounds. Big deal! With semi-automatic weapons, all you have to do to reload is push a button and snap in another clip. It takes about a second. This ban did not reduce the firepower of any weapon.

Egerton says the rational response to a weak but needed law is to strengthen it. He has shown his colors on this subject in previous letters to the editor. His idea of strengthening this law is an outright ban on private ownership of weapons of any kind. He believes that only governments should have weapons. Does he really believe that would reduce violence?

I say a rational response to a weak, feel good law is to forgetaboutit!
David Kristopeit
Racine

Although the *Journal Times* had published previous letters from me on gun control, the above letter is the only one I had written on this law, so Kristopeit's claim about my idea to strengthen it is to ban private ownership of weapons of any kind is his miss-remembered impression of one or more previous letters which had said no such thing. (He and I had exchanged two personal letters on guns, the precise subject(s) of which I do not recall.) Maybe there are other members of the NRA who skip the political diatribes in *American Rifleman* and only read articles on guns and gun activities. After all, Michael Moore, who produced the film, *Bowling for Columbine*, which attacks NRA control over American gun laws, said in the film that he was an NRA member and showed his membership card to former NRA president Charlton Heston. Nevertheless, if Anderson expected his 1996 exposé of the NRA leadership to cause another revolt in the opposite direction from the 1977 revolt, it has not happened and is unlikely to happen. The NRA has developed a rigid ideology, and although grounded in democracy, it seems useful to compare the people trapped in it to the true believers in German Nazism, which lasted a quarter century, and Soviet Communism, which lasted three quarter centuries. Those ideologies were taught to many otherwise intelligent people who were unable to understand society in any other terms—until the defeat of Germany in 1945 and the collapse of the Soviet Union in 1989. Political power supporting defective ideologies makes them seem plausible—until that power ends. There is no way to know how, when, or if the NRA's ideology, which has been building for a century, will ever collapse. NRA endowments are substantial; it is unlikely ever to go broke again.[83]

Who is right about the most dangerous organization in America? Congressman Dingle, Jr. (1981) that it is a fascist ATF or Sherrill that it is a fanatical NRA?[84] The answer depends on whether the threat to America is a hypothetical loss of freedom that would occur if we had strict gun control laws or is it the real loss of 10,000-15,000 lives a year killed with guns (and a comparable number of suicides with guns) that are facilitated by our lax gun laws, which are kept lax by the political power of the NRA?[85]

Some light is thrown on this question by former president and lifelong hunter, Jimmy Carter in his book, *Our Endangered Values: America's Moral Crisis* (2005):[86]

...many of us who participate in outdoor sports are dismayed by some of the more extreme policies of the National Rifle Association (NRA) and by the timidity of public officials who yield to their unreasonable demands. Heavily influenced by the firearms industry, their primary client, the NRA has been able to mislead many gullible people into believing that our weapons are going to be taken away from us.

In addition to assault weapons, the gun lobby protects the ability of criminals and gang members to use ammunition that can penetrate clothing worm by police officers on duty and assures that a known or suspected terrorist is not barred from buying or owning a firearm—including an assault weapon.

The current NRA, aside from being a cash-cow for millionaire executive vice president Wayne LaPierre, exercises its powerful lobby in courts as well as in legislatures. An important achievement was to persuade the Supreme Court justices to vote to reverse the long-standing interpretation of the Second Amendment that emphasized the militia, to emphasize instead personal ownership of guns.[87] It did so by challenging the Washington, DC ban on handguns, passed in 1976, which was the most restrictive gun control law in America. The idea to challenge it came not from the NRA, but from two lawyers, Clark Neily and Steve Simpson, at the conservative Institute for Justice in Washington, in 2002. The NRA thought that the time was premature, but their efforts continued and they added lawyer Robert Levy at Cato Institute to their team. As a defendant, they chose Dick Heller, security guard at a federal building, who lived in a neighborhood where drug deals occurred, and he wanted a gun for protection. Therefore, the NRA hired lawyer Steve Halbrook to file a supportive parallel lawsuit. The D.C. courts dismissed the suits on procedural grounds, but a U.S. Court of Appeals struck down the ban in 2007, and the D.C. mayor appealed to the Supreme Court. Halbrook filed an amicus for the NRA signed by 55 U.S. Senators and 250 House members. In 2007, Justice O'Connor retired and Justice Rehnquist died. President Bush chose NRA approved circuit court judges John Roberts and Samuel Alito as replacements. They ensured NRA's success in *Heller v. United States* in 2008.[88]

The NRA has become a de facto wing of the Republican Party. Conspicuous evidence is its contribution of $30 million to Donald Trump's presidential campaign, more than it ever gave to any previous presidential candidate. In gratitude, he was the first president in over three decades to address its annual meeting, on 28 April 17. His simple message was "You are my friends."[89] And, "The eight-year assault on your Second Amendment freedom has come to a crashing end." The Republican Party was quite willing to accept the NRA's price for collusion: no more gun laws.

When Franklin Roosevelt became President, he reassured the country that concerning the Depression's impact, there was nothing to fear but fear itself. Today, one might say there is nothing to fear except the NRA's fearmongering about government. Yes, Nazis seized a few guns which Jews had in the 1930s, but there is such a glut of private guns in America that it would be ludicrous for any government to attempt to confiscate them. Nor would members of the armed forces or government agencies even try to enforce such a silly idea if any president or other leader ordered them to do so. And, as far as that person becoming a tyrant, when he ordered police and armed forces to destroy our democracy, who thinks they would? Only NRA members with limited education or a tendency to paranoia would even swallow such phony baloney. How long can the NRA cry "wolf" before members realize there is nothing behind the cry? Also, this is a case of the emperor having no clothes! If the NRA is like a major religion, as Cassidy suggested, then LaPierre can be considered its current pope (who is now infallible). Shedding the original NRA goal of being a gun club, becoming instead a gun lobby paid off handsomely for its permanent officers.

Among the many irresponsible and hurtful pronouncements that have come from LaPierre and the NRA, it seems especially noteworthy that it has demonized the U.S. Bureau of Alcohol, Tobacco, and Firearms (ATF). If that unjust attitude did not originate with U.S. Rep. John D. Dingell, Jr., who had a long-time tenure in both Congress and NRA Board of Directors, he gave it much publicity, which showed a strange, irresponsible understanding of his responsibilities in both positions.[90]

# 6

## GUNS IN CRIME

This chapter is divided into six topics: Unorganized crimes, Organized crimes, Mass shootings, Gun shows, Militia/Patriots, and Youth gangs.

### Guns in Unorganized Crime

This is a vast subject, covering more crimes than a total of the crimes covered in all five other topics being discussed. Much violence in America has had a racial aspect, though now there is more intra-racial than inter-racial violence, which is a reversal of the situation during the 1800s and much of the 1900s.[1] Negro lynching is another topic, which is discussed below as a type of mass shooting. This account is limited to prominent examples, which will represent a million less-remembered victims. Many examples are also included below, under Mass Shootings.

Perhaps Puritans were more law-abiding than average settlers. Otherwise, we may assume that guns and unorganized crimes soon followed settlement. Of course, guns in 1600s America were scarce and unreliable, and most victims of shootings were likely native Americans.

### Dueling

Dueling is a category of victims which actually were organized crimes, though spontaneously and temporarily organized between antagonists, and so not organized enough to consider an "organized crime." Most dueling victims were not prominent, but Alexander Hamilton and Andrew Jackson were prominent examples, the former a fatality and the latter a wounded antagonist (ch. 2). Notably, this category of victims was declining in America before the Civil War and disappeared by the end of that war.

## Wild West

Novels, Hollywood films, radio and TV programs give the impression that crime and gun play were rampant in the West during the later 1800s and early 1900s, when municipal, state, and federal governments lacked adequate personnel to police their laws as well as governments did in the East.[2] (I grew up before TV, listening to "The Lone Ranger" on the radio and saw "cowboy movies" on Saturdays.) The level of actual crime in the West was far less than fictional accounts indicated, but there was some such crime, nevertheless. Historical accounts can give the same impression of commonness when collected within covers of books, such as James Horan, *Desperate Men: Revelations from the Sealed Pinkerton Files* (1963), Carl Breihan, *Great Gunfighters of the West* (1977), Harry Drago, *Road Agents and Train Robbers: Half a Century of Western Bandits* (1973), and Paul Trachtman, *The Gunfighters* (1974).[3] After all, Jesse James (1847-82),[4] Billy the Kid (Henry McCarty, 1859-81),[5] and Butch Cassidy (Robert Leroy Parker, 1866-c. 1909) and Sundance Kid (1870-c. 1909)[6] were indeed historical figures who used their guns to impose their wills upon others involved in legal activities, and occasionally there were shootouts, as at the O.K. Corral.[7] Western law men are discussed in chapter 9.

## Prohibition

There is general awareness that prohibition stimulated an organized crime response, with rival gangs at times shooting member of opposing gangs. This topic is discussed below. Less known is the fact that some advocates of prohibition were shot by opponents of prohibition.[8] (Organized crime, of course, supported prohibition.) Between 1874 and 1908, six advocates were killed and 19 were either shot, beaten, or their abode dynamited. This conflict occurred in all regions, but especially in the South and West. Unlike abolitionists (John Brown) and antiabortionists (Michael Griffin, John Salvi), there were no incidents of advocates of prohibition attacking their opponents. However, Carry Nation (1846-1911), who was glad to picket and pray at legal saloons with others in Woman's Christian Temperance Union, was also willing to use an ax to attack illegal bars in dry Kansas. Others joined her in attacking a dozen such bars, prompting some gunfire from the proprietors.

## Assassinations

Assassinations is a category of victims that are relatively few in number, but who are mostly prominent and historically important.[9] President Abraham Lincoln (1865, see ch. 2) was the most prominent victim until President John F. Kennedy (1963) became one. Now, they are co-equal most prominent victims. Presidential victims between Lincoln and Kennedy were James A. Garfield (1881)[10] and William McKinley (1901).[11] Attempts were made to assassinate presidents Andrew Jackson, Theodore Roosevelt, Franklin D. Roosevelt, Harry S. Truman, Gerald Ford, and Ronald Reagan.[12] Also, six governors were assassin's victims,[13] only one of whom died: Huey Long, Jr. (1893-1935),[14] of Louisiana. George Corley Wallace, Jr. (1919-1998) of Alabama was the most recent such surviving victim.[15] Both Long and Wallace were populists, whose persuasive powers led them into demagoguery. Long was an ex-governor, who in 1935 was a senator, who could have been a powerful ally of President Franklin D. Roosevelt, but instead he aspired to defeat Roosevelt in a Democratic primary in 1936. He was assassinated by Dr. Carl Weiss, whose father-in-law, a judge, was being harassed by Long. Wallace, campaigning for president on 15 May 1972, survived Arthur Bremer's shooting him five times; but he became a cripple in a wheelchair.[16] Bremer's motivation was a desire for fame.

Fig. 8. (a) President William McKinley. (b) Governor Huey Long, Jr.

Racism was clearly the motive of Byron de la Beckwith (1920-2001) to assassinate Mississippi NAACP field secretary, Medgar Evers (1925-12 June 63) as he reached the front door of his home.[17] However, a white jury found him not guilty. Evers, a veteran, was buried at Arlington National Cemetery.

John F. Kennedy (1917-22 Nov. 63) was a handsome World War II hero, with a glamorous wife, and he became a wildly popular president.[18] Lee Harvey Oswald's assassination of him in Dallas, Texas was a stunning blow to the country, and a day later, Oswald himself was assassinated,[19] depriving history of whatever might have been learned from him as a prisoner (see below). There have been numerous detailed books postulating one or another reason why Oswald shot Kennedy. There is lots of smoke concerning the Mafia connection, which some authors have explored to find a fire (see below, Organized Crime). And JFK's was not the end of the jolting assassinations during the turbulent '60s.

Fig. 9. Kennedy brothers: Robert, Ted and John.

Malcolm Little (1925-65) grew up in Lansing MI, son of a preacher who died in a racist attack when Malcolm was six. His mother entered a mental institution when he was 13. He later quit school and went to live with a sister in Boston, where he learned to deal in drugs. He served time in prison for burglary, 1946-52, where he converted to the Nation of Islam, founded by Elijah Muhammad, and took the name Malcolm X.[20] He also spent those years reading intensively, educating himself. He was obviously charismatic, because he rose to prominence in the Nation of Islam almost as soon as he left prison. By 1964, he had become dissatisfied with Elijah Muhammad's leadership and made a pilgrimage to Mecca, where he met Muslims of different races and lost his hostility to white men. He returned to America and founded the Organization of Afro-American Unity. His energetic leadership eclipsed Elijah Muhammad as a leader of Black dissidents, and when he gave a speech at Harlem's Audubon Ballroom on 21 Feb. 65, he was assassinated by two members of the New Jersey Nation of Islam.[21] Yet, as a martyr, his influence did not fade away. His autobiography was already in press and appeared in 1965. Like Gandhi, Muhammad X was assassinated by someone within a larger movement,[22] but that was not true of the next Black leader assassinated.

Martin Luther King, Jr. (1929-1968), like Gandhi, stressed "nonviolent coercion."[23] He was the son of a Baptist preacher and became one also. His ministry began in Montgomery, Alabama, as did his civil rights movement. His eloquent speeches made him a national leader of a peaceful struggle for equal rights for Blacks. His leadership attracted worldwide admiration, for which in 1964 he won an honorary doctorate from Yale University and a Nobel Peace Prize. That leadership was also what made him a target in Memphis, 4 April 68, for another racist assassin, James Earl Ray.[24] Ray fled to England before he was captured, extradited, and sentenced to 99 years in prison.

Just two months later, 6 June, Senator Robert F. Kennedy, leading candidate in a Democratic primary race for president, was assassinated after giving a California victory talk by Palestinian settler, Sirhan Sirhan, 24, who wanted to avenge his people for America selling jet planes to Israel. He has been in prison ever since.[25]

By 1980, John Winston Lennon (1940-80) was one of the most famous celebrities in Britain and America.[26] He was leader of the immensely popular musical group, the Beetles, and had also become a peace activist. However, he made one fatal mistake: instead of in peaceful Liverpool or London, he chose to live in risky New York City. In the late afternoon of 8 December1980 he approached his residence on 72nd St., and a 25-year-old security guard of Honolulu, Mark David Chapman, who had earlier obtained his autograph, shot five bullets at his back; one missed and the others were fatal. Chapman, who sought fame, was sent to prison for life and is still there.

Fig. 10. Malcolm X Little, Martin Luther King, Jr.

# Gun Control

On 16 April 74, Nick Shields, 23, was shot dead in San Francisco. Nick's father, Pete Shields, was a Du Pont executive in Wilmington, Delaware. Pete was a Navy Airforce vet from World War II, a waterfowl hunter, a Republican, but not an NRA member.[27] He had no interest in gun control until after his son's death. He began reading and discovered that there had been five presidential commissions on gun violence in the previous decade and listed them in his book, *Guns don't Die—People Do*.[28] However, the recommendations of these commissions had never been passed into law. He agreed with those commissions that America needed more gun laws, for he felt that the level of gun violence nationwide—11,124 gun murders and 250,000 handgun victims in 1974—was what one might expect in war. Japan, with half the population of America, in 1974 had 37 gun murders.

Shields saw that the NRA had organized opposition to gun control, but those favoring gun control had no comparable organization and were therefore ineffective. He founded Handgun Control, Inc. in 1975. To run it, he recruited: a young Ph.D. in psychology, Mark Borinsky, who had been a victim of a holdup; Ed Welles, retired from the CIA; and Georgetown

University graduate, New Yorker Charlie Orasin, who had been an assistant to liberal Republican Senator Jacob K. Jarvis of New York.[29] To raise money to get underway, Shields asked those on his Christmas card list, who all knew of the murder of his son, for donations. After getting started, he then solicited members of this political lobby for $15 each. By 1981, he had 150,000 members (impressive, but not in the NRA's league). That is the American way in politics.

However, "Threatened gun rights leaders likened the gun control group, Handgun Control, Inc., to Nazis and labeled their actions fascist. NRA president Dick Riley called HCI founder Pete Shields' book on gun control a *Mein Kampf* sequel for the gun control movement."[30] Blatant fear mongering, but NRA members lapped it up. Cars should be registered and regulated, but not guns. To counter Shield's book, *Guns don't Die, People Do* (1981), Alan Gottlieb published *The Gun Grabbers* (1986), with a 1.5-page introduction by conservative Republican Senator Steve Symms of Idaho. Its blurb informed readers that Gottlieb was chairman of the Citizens Committee for the Right to Keep and Bear Arms, founder of the Second Amendment Foundation, and publisher of *Gun Week*. His book publisher, Merril Press, had also published his *Gun Rights Fact Book* and *Guns for Women* by Gottlieb and George Flynn. Richard Poe, a later author of similar ilk, wrote a sequel to *Gun Grabbers: The Seven Myths of Gun Control: Reclaiming the Truth about Guns, Crime, and the Second Amendment* (2001).

## Guns in Organized Crime

In the year 2000, The United Nations Convention against Transnational Organized Crime defined organized crime as "structured groups of three or more people acting in concert to commit one or more serious crimes for material benefit."[31] This section is about criminals whose gangs committed many more than one serious crime, with guns. Immigrants from different ethnic heritages have formed gangs in American cities. Members of the Sicilian Mafia periodically fled to America, providing the foundation from which "the American Mafia formed the most influential and cohesive element to the loosely organized national crime syndicate that emerged in the 1930s."[32] Therefore, it is the main ethnic gang discussed here. A biker gang, Hell's Angles, is discussed below. This chapter discusses representative samples of the history of American Mafia, mainly from New York, Chicago, and New Orleans. Virgil Peterson wrote a detailed *The Mob: 200 Years of Organized Crime in New York* (1983). Daniel Waugh wrote a history of the St. Louis gang during the prohibition era.[33] Other organized crime gangs included Jews and Irish by the 1930s,[34] and other ethnicities after World War II.[35] Finally, a brief discussion notes the money and gun trafficking by Mexican drug gangs.

Herbert Asbury (1891-1963) pioneered historical criminology, writing histories of gangs in several cities. His *The Gangs of New York* (1928) surveys gangs and their exploits for about a century. He stated in his introduction that, happily, criminal gangs had disappeared about a decade earlier from New York City—a laughable claim during Prohibition.[36] The gangsters he described were mainly Irish and British. His discussion of the Italian Mafia amounts to only about a page.[37] Considering that he judged Ignazio Lupo to be "one of the most desperate and blood-thirsty criminals this country has ever seen," the Mafia would seem to have been worthy of more discussion. Presumably, his information on the New York Mafia was quite limited in 1928. He stated that Giuseppi Morello was Lupo's lieutenant, whereas the reverse was true. However, Asbury was better informed when he published *The French Quarter: an Informal History of the New Orleans Underworld* (1936) and *Gem of the Prairie: an Informal History of the Chicago Underworld* (1940). His knowledge of the Mafia was far greater than what the public knew before the Kefauver Hearings in 1951, or what J. Edgar Hoover (1895-1972) claimed to know about Mafia before the mob's Apalachin conference was exposed in 1957, forcing his hand.[38] Members of early gangs had pistols, knives, and blackjacks or baseball bats, and in a conflict used whichever one seemed appropriate or convenient, which meant guns in about three-quarters of the time.

Prof. Richard Gambino made a mistake similar to Asbury's in his *Vendetta: A True Story of the Worst Lynching in America* (1977) when he denied the Mafia existed in New Orleans by 1890.[39] It would have been safer to state that he had found no evidence of it being there before 1890. Historian Mike Dash found evidence of the Mafia being in New Orleans by 1875, though Salvatore Marino, who organized it, called it Stoppaglieri.[40] Needless to say, that early presence does not lessen the atrocity about which Gambino wrote: the lynching of 11 Italian men in retaliation for the assassination of Police Chief David Hennessy. Sicilian gangsters began fleeing to America by at least 1875, when Salvatore Marino fled there after evading a murder trial in Sicily.[41] Kidnapper Giuseppe Esposito fled Sicily for New Orleans in 1880, where he started the extortion ring, Black Hand.[42] He was arrested in 1881 and taken back to Sicily, where he received a life sentence in prison.[43] In 1890, New Orleans Police Chief David Hennessy denounced a court verdict against six members of the Provenzano family, claiming that members of the Matranga family had given perjured testimony. Some nights later, Hennessy was assassinated on his way home from work.[44] Before he died, a fellow police officer asked him who did it, and Hennessy replied, "Dagos." (His father had also been an assassinated police officer in New Orleans, when David was 11.) Both Matranga and Provenzano families had motives for killing him. Five gunmen were seen, though not clearly, and later five shotguns were recovered.[45] After the shooting, police stormed into an Italian saloon and arrested all 30 Italians inside. Five of the Italians questioned were charged with murder and held without bail. Mayor Joseph A. Shakspeare was outraged: "Heretofore these scoundrels have confined their murderings among themselves" and got away with it because no one dared testify against them."[46] He urged the City Council to "teach these people a lesson that they will not forget for all time." The Council authorized him to establish a committee to investigate this murder. His Committee of Fifty (with 83 members) was led by two prominent attorneys and was given a budget to establish an office and take testimony. The Committee of Fifty indicted 14 more Italians in addition to the 5 already indicted. At a trial, all accused produced witnesses who claimed they had been with them elsewhere at the time of the murder, and they were acquitted for lack of evidence. Non-Italian citizens were outraged, and the next day's New Orleans *Times Herald* carried an ad from members of the Committee of Fifty urging people to attend a meeting to remedy this failure of justice. All understood that citizens would take things into their own hands when courts were impotent.[47] Mob justice was administered to 11 Italian men, and non-Italian citizens celebrated the lynch mob's actions. There was no effort to hold members of the mob accountable for these murders. The New Orleans branch of the Mafia kept a low profile for a time, but it became the most important Mafia organization in the South, and much later, alleged headquarters for planning the assassinations of the Kennedy brothers and Martin Luther King, Jr.[48]

The other main entry point for Sicilians and other south Italians was New York City, where probably more arrived than in New Orleans, though its organized Mafia developed later.[49] Historian Mike Dash tells the early New York story in *The First Family: The Birth of the American Mafia* (2009). Mafiosi murderer-counterfeiter Giuseppi Morello (1867-1930) fled from Sicily to New York in 1892, not long before the financial crash of 1893, which encouraged some 2000 Sicilians to move to Louisiana, and then some, including Morello, on to Texas, before he returned to New York in early 1897.[50] Morello made four different attempts to earn an honest living, failing in all. By 1900, he was back into counterfeiting, and by 1903, into murder. He was arrested for both but convicted for neither, because anyone testifying against a Mafiosi would be killed, as all knew. Although he had a deformed right hand, his intelligence and ruthlessness overcame this handicap, and he formed America's first organized crime gang with staying power. He had a formidable lieutenant, Ignazio Lupo (1877-1947), who married Morello's sister. A number of American cities acquired a Mafia gang, but New York City was the only city that acquired more than one gang, and it had five (and an attempted sixth family in the 1960s[51]). Morello became boss of the bosses until imprisoned, 1910-20.[52] American Mafia bosses communicated with each other and with Mafia bosses in Sicily, and bosses sometimes held meetings. Morello began by having counterfeiters in Sicily make his America bills, but he soon found that the quality was inadequate for selling them wholesale to other Mafia around America. In 1908, therefore, he kidnapped a skillful Sicilian printer in New York, Antonio Comito, and took him to an isolated farm where he was provided with machinery and supplies to make counterfeit U.S. and Canadian bills.[53] After five months of counterfeiting, Morello's gang took Comito back to New York City, where he was eventually arrested by the U.S. Secret Service as a suspect counterfeiter. He willingly told everything he knew, and his memory was quite remarkable; his testimony filled over 100 typed pages, and when Morello and his gang was arrested, this time the witness was not intimidated into silence. His lengthy account was compelling testimony, and the suspects were found guilty and sentenced to up to ten years in Federal prison. Comito was brave enough to testify because he had been promised a ticket out of America—he eventually settled in South America.[54] Those in Morello's gang not swept into prison fared badly without the boss, as other Mafia families asserted their power. When Morello regained his freedom in 1920, there was no chance he could regain dominance, and he became another boss' lieutenant until assassinated in 1930.[55]

The Black Hand was not a gang, but an extortion scheme.[56] Its perpetrators were of Italian heritage and were often Mafia members. Its perpetrators lived in large cities where Mafia families were. They sent letters to wealthy Italians threatening dire consequences unless a payment was made. If the victim did not respond, other threatening letters followed, and if still no response, then violence followed, even death. Threatening letters were usually sent in the mail, and so the U.S. Government investigated and prosecuted such cases. Black Hand schemes occurred during the first two decades of the 1900s, and U.S. intervention led to their demise by the early 1920s.

Prohibition became the law of the land in 1920 (passed in 1919), and remained so until the 18th Amendment to the Constitution was nullified by the 21st Amendment, in 1933. In 1920, there was a drop in the rate of alcoholism, but then those who could profit from evasion made evasion into a profession, and long before Prohibition ended there was more alcoholic consumption in America than there had been before Prohibition went into effect.[57] General John Thompson developed his machine gun ("Tommy gun"), that could fire a thousand rounds a minute, for use in World War I, but that war ended before it could be used (see ch.5). Not to worry, it was just in time for the Prohibition Wars.[58] There was so much money to be made selling bootleg alcoholic spirits that organized crime greatly expanded in personnel, equipment, and impact.

James "Diamond Jim," or "Big Jim" Colosimo (1878-1920) was the mob boss in Chicago in 1920, and he refused to go into bootlegging. Consequently, his nephew, Johnny Torrio (1882-1957), from New York, had him killed by a New York hit-man, probably Frankie Yale (originally Lole or Uale, 1893-1928).[59] Torrio replaced Colosimo in running brothels and slot machines, to which he added booze.[60] Torrio (called "The Fox") was much smarter than Colosimo; detective Thomas Reppetto credits him with being "the architect of modern organized crime..."[61] Torrio called together other bosses and organized bootleg distribution so that they could avoid conflict among themselves. Torrio's enforcer was a New York thug, Alfonso Capone (1899-1948).[62] Chicago was the big city "most hostile to Prohibition and most openly defiant of the law..."[63] Torrino developed strong ties with Mayor William "Big Bill" Thompson, and there was no struggle with authorities while Thompson reined. Torrio saw that ongoing violence inevitably led to serious trouble for gangsters, and he wanted to preserve the peace. Yet, one of Chicago's Irish gang did not relish Italians telling them what to do, and he negotiated mutually advantageous arrangements with two other Irish gangs. He and Capone organized a city-wide network, the Chicago Syndicate. Despite Torrio's efforts, Chicago experienced 765 gangster murders, 1919-34.[64]

Torrio's arrangements became threatened when the exposed "brazen corruption" of Thompson's administration convinced Mayor Thompson in 1923 not to run for another term. The new mayor was honest, though his police chief was not, and coincidentally a new Federal agent appeared in Chicago who was not only honest, but also active. An Irish gang invaded Torrio's own bootleg turf and even used violence to keep saloon keepers in line. Torrio would not tolerate this, but, disliking violence, he took his wife and mother to Italy for six months, leaving Capone to handle the problem. Capone asked Yale to murder Irish boss Charles Dion "Deany" O'Banion, and he did so on 10 November 24, which started a gang war that lasted five years.[65] In revenge, O'Banion's followers shot Torrio on 24 January 25.[66] Torrio recovered, turned over the Syndicate to Capone, and retired to Italy, then New York City.[67]

The Chicago gang wars culminated in a St. Valentine Day Massacre, 14 February 29, in which Capone's men tricked George "Bugs" Moran's North Side gang into a meeting at which two of Capone's men wore police uniforms and, using machine guns, killed seven.[68] Moran and two others were coming to the meeting but arrived after the massacre and escaped. One escapee was murdered a year later. One of the assassins was Jack "Machine Gun" McGurn, who had previously participated in machine-gunning Frankie Yale.[69] Another assassin that day was Samuel Giancana (1908-75), who later became the Chicago boss.[70] No one was ever prosecuted for the murders. This 1929 massacre created a sensation across America, and the Chicago Crime Commission branded Capone Public Enemy Number One. The Mafia held a national peace conference in Atlantic City in May 1929. Before going to the meeting, Capone personally killed three allegedly traitorous members of his gang. After the meeting, as Capone and bodyguard left Atlantic City, they were arrested for having guns without permits and Capone was sentenced to a year in prison. On 17 October 31, Capone was also sentenced to eleven years in Federal prison for income tax evasion. However, he was paroled on 16 November 39 with mental problems from untreated syphilis. He could no longer lead a gang; his "Outfit" survived his imprisonment, run by a five-man "board of directors."[71] America's most famous gangster had been a boss for about a dozen years.

In New York, bootlegging and other rackets were run to a great extent by Jewish gangster Arnold "the Brain" Rothstein (1882-1928), who was as perceptive as Torrio.[72] However, Rothstein kept his dealings in his head, without leaving a paper trail. He was patron of a series of gangsters—Jewish and Italian—who rose to prominence with his help. He fixed the World Series in 1919, in which the Chicago White Sox were bribed to lose to Cincinnati Reds.[73] He also financed the first liquor shipment during Prohibition from Britain.[74] In the 1920s, it was also his idea to create a national crime syndicate.[75] Yet, Rothstein was also a gambler, and he lost $300,000 in a card game and did not have the money. Rothstein also bet on the 1928 presidential race. Two days before the election, Rothstein was killed, presumably for non-payment of his debt.[76] Had he lived to collect his winnings from betting on Herbert Hoover, he could have paid his debts. A much later confession by one of his associates, George McManus, indicated that there had indeed been an argument over Rothstein's debt, with all involved rather drunk. McManus pulled out a handgun to intimidate him and accidentally shot him in the stomach.[77]

One of his protégés, Meyer Lansky (Maier Suchowjansky, 1902-83), was well positioned to take over Rothstein's rackets. However, Lansky also worked well with other Rothstein New York protégés, Charles "Lucky" Luciano (Salvatore Lucania, 1897-1962),[78] Dutch Schultz (Arthur Flegenheimer, 1902-35), and Frank Costello (Francesco Castiglia, 1891-1973), and Lansky became "among the top three or four mobsters in the country."[79] In 1931 Luciano arranged the murder of bosses Joe Masseria and Salvatore Maranzano, then replaced them; his gang may have included about 500 "boys."[80] New Your nightclubs suffered during the Depression, but Mafia money kept them open.[81] The Mafia supported Fiorello La

Guardia for mayor of New York in 1933, but he was unexpectedly honest and appointed an honest and vigorous police commissioner, who judged Luciano, accurately, as "top gangster." In 1934 Torrio organized Mafia gangs in America into a committee, the Syndicate.[82] This did not mean an end to the killings, but going forward, killing important people required the Syndicate's permission. In 1935 Luciano had Schultz (himself a murderer) and two body guards killed.[83] Thomas E. Dewey had been making Schultz's life so miserable he had requested permission to kill him (permission denied), and with Schultz's death, Dewey turned his attention to Luciano.[84] In the 1930s Dewey held a series of four prosecutorial positions, first as an Assistant U.S. Attorney, then U.S. Attorney, Special State Attorney, and finally New York District Attorney (before becoming New York Governor in 1942). In 1936 Dewey had Luciano and 15 associates indicted for compulsory prostitution, and Luciano received a sentence of 30-50 years.

During World War II, Italy was an American enemy, which provoked conflicting loyalties among Americans of Italian descent. Sabotage and theft at the New York docks seemed attributable to Italians, and Naval Intelligence officers asked Luciano, in Sing Sing Prison, to end such incursions, and he did.[85] Before Anglo-American forces invaded Sicily in July-August 1943, Luciano also sent word to the Sicilian Mafia to assist in the invasion. Since Mussolini had suppressed them for 20 years, they were glad to oblige. One Mafioso, Don Calò, was made an honorary U.S. Army colonel (called "General Mafia" by soldiers); he encouraged Italian soldiers to desert their army. In 1946, Governor Dewey pardoned Luciano, for whatever services he had rendered, and he was deported to Italy, where his Mafia activities continued.[86]

The post-war years were as good for the Mafia as for the rest of the economy.[87] After Luciano went to prison, Costello had taken over his gang and became America's most powerful Mafia boss ("Prime Minister of the Underworld"). Costello ran the national syndicate that had existed informally since the 1930s.[88] Its purpose was occasionally to collaborate on "jobs," but mainly to keep peace among Mafia "families." Yet, killings continued, and perhaps mostly among themselves, though they also killed honorable people who refused to let the Mafia control their lives. In general, there were two causes of Mafia shooting other Mafia members: (1) unacceptable behavior and (2) rivalry between gangs or even within gangs;

it was a dangerous profession, and no one was too valuable to kill. However, one usually had to get permission from the national syndicate to kill an important person, either within or without the Mafia.[89]

In April 1951, the Kansas City mob boss Charles Binaggio and his body guard were gunned down in a Democratic Party club house. That prompted the U.S. Senate to create a committee to investigate organized crime, chaired by Democratic Senator Estes Kefauver.[90] The hearings were televised at a time when daytime TV, until then, had few viewers. The Kefauver Committee's hearings were a sensation because its investigative staff was very astute in collecting information and selecting witnesses to testify. One witness was Costello, who was questioned for three days, demonstrating his nationwide leadership of organized crime. On top of that, he was given a contempt of Congress citation for not revealing his finances, and his Mafia colleagues were dismayed at his poor performance. The Kefauver hearings and its report convinced many Americans that organized crime flourished in America, but FBI head J. Edgar Hoover (1895-1972) remained publicly skeptical.[91] The reason, said an anonymous author ("Michael Milan"), was that Hoover had a private, secret "squad" from 1947 to 1971that was assisted by the Mafia in doing jobs that Hoover would not assign to his official agents.[92] Harry Anslinger, head of the Treasury Department's Bureau of Narcotics knew better than what Hoover claimed and had been quietly collecting information on the Mafia, using undercover agents who infiltrated Mafia gangs. The hearings also convinced leading politicians to stay away from the Mafia.[93] Costello was shot in the head in 1957 by rival boss Vito Genovese's henchman, Vincenzo Gigante, but survived and retired to his estate on Long Island.[94] Genovese (1897-1969) replaced him as family head, but not as prime minister, even though he was the most feared Mafia boss in America.[95] In 1959 Genovese and 14 codefendants went to Federal prison on drug charges, he, for his last decade of life, yet he continued running his Mafia family from there.[96]

Public confirmation of the Kefauver Committee's conclusions about the American Mafia emerged in November 1957, when the national syndicate met at Joseph M. Barbara's estate outside Apalachin, New York, far from the prying eyes of the law. Only it wasn't. Sergeant Edgar D. Crosswell, of the New York State Police, was suspicious of the meeting and brought along three other law officers to investigate. They stopped and interrogated 63 men as they left the meeting, while another 40 or more remained in Barbara's house until after the lawmen had left.[97] Crosswell's report was discussed nationally in the press, and Hoover was embarrassed into establishing an organized crime task force. (He had known about the Mafia all along but had left its members alone because Frank Costello gave him tips on fixed horse races, enabling Hoover to make substantial money at the races.[98]) This fiasco—no charges were served but the men arrested were fingerprinted and photographed—convinced the Mafia to avoid large meetings. In the discussion after Apalachin, it was estimated that there were 24 Mafia families, with about 4000-5000 members and ten times as many associates.[99] About a third of them were in the five New York City families.[100] In 1959 a federal grand jury investigating the Apalachin meeting charged 27 with conspiracy to obstruct justice by perjured testimony, and 20 were convicted and sentenced to prison for three to five years.[101] However, on appeal, these sentences were overturned.

Patrick Joseph Kennedy (1858-1929) was born in Boston to Irish immigrants, and his father died of cholera before Patrick was a year old. His mother had to work to support her three daughters and son. Patrick as a teenager worked as a stevedore on the docks to help support his family. He was a bright, frugal, hard worker, who did not drink. At age 22 he bought his first saloon, and he prospered in the liquor business and was politically well-connected and served in the Massachusetts Senate.[102] He married well, and was wealthy enough to send his son, Joseph Patrick Kennedy (1888-1969), to Boston's best school and to Harvard University.[103] After graduating from Harvard, Joseph was convinced he was as good as the Protestant ruling class. Like his father, Joseph married well and was ambitious for wealth and political power. With his father's assistance and advice, he far exceeded his father in achieving both. The wealth came first. Much later, Mafioso Sam Giancana's brother recalled being told:

> Kennedy was no stranger to Chicago. Mooney [Sam Giancana] had known the scheming Irish bootlegger for over twenty-five years, a relationship that hailed back to the days of Diamond Joe Esposito and Mooney's sugar runs to Boston during Prohibition's heyday. Nor had he forgotten the scrape Kennedy had had with Detroit's Purple gang;

Chicago had bailed the arrogant mick's ass out of a sure hit back then.

Kennedy's ties to the underworld intersected at a hundred points. Besides making a fortune in bootlegging, Kennedy had made a financial killing in Hollywood in the twenties—with the help of persuasive behind-the-scenes New York and Chicago muscle. When Prohibition came to a close, as part of a national agreement between the various bootleggers, Kennedy held on to three of the most lucrative booze distributionships in the country— Gordon's gin, Dewar's, and Haig & Haig—through his company, Somerset Imports.

It was also no secret, according to Mooney, that Joe Kennedy—along with such industrialists as General Motors's founder William Crapo Durant, and John David Rockefeller, Jr.—had been given prior knowledge of the coming stock market crash in 1929. "In fact," Mooney told Chuck [his brother, an author of this quotation] "they *made* it happen. They figured out how they could get even richer. "Shit, old man Kennedy made over a million bucks sellin' the market short before it fell."[104]

While I cannot vouch for the veracity of this mobster's (Sam's) recollections, other sources also mention Joe Kennedy's Prohibition bootlegging.[105] He became rich enough to be a major donor to Franklin Roosevelt's election funds in 1932, which led to his appointment as ambassador to Great Britain (where he became a Nazi sympathizer). His eldest son died a hero in World War II, while his three other sons all became U.S. Senators, with one of them also becoming President of the United States.

When John F. Kennedy (1917-63) ran for president in 1960, Frank Sinatra solicited help from his Mafia friends, first to win the Democratic primary contest in West Virginia, and then, with Frank Sinatra's encouragement, to win the general election against Nixon, depending heavily upon Giancana in Chicago.[106] Sinatra's advice was based upon the assumption that the son thought like the father, which turned out not to be true. Jimmy Hoffa and New Orleans Mafioso Carlos Marcello supported Nixon.[107] President Kennedy appointed his brother Robert F. Kennedy (1935-68) Attorney General, who turned out to be a pit bull who, far from neglecting the Mafia, went after it with all the force of his office.[108] He had a "Get Hoffa" squad of investigators on his staff, and Hoffa wanted him assassinated. Marcello thought killing Robert Kennedy would only bring overwhelming Federal investigation of the Mafia; President Kennedy should be assassinated first.

Currently, the single assassin versus conspiracy plot is ongoing. The argument and evidence for the single assassin case is lawyer Gerald Posner's *Case Closed: Lee Harvey Oswald and the Assassination of JFK* (1993), supplemented by Gus Russo's *Live by the Sword: The Secret War against Castro and the Death of JFK* (1999). An early defense of the conspiracy plot is Dr. David Scheim's *Contract on America: The Mafia Murder of President John E. Kennedy* (1988), then Robert D. Morrow's *First Hand Knowledge: How I Participated in the CIA-Mafia Murder of President Kennedy* (1992), followed by Harrison E. Livingstone's books, including *Killing the Truth: Deceit and Deception in the JFK Case* (1993) and *Killing Kennedy and the Hoax of the Century* (1995), and finally Lamar Waldron and Thom Hartmann's *Legacy of Secrecy: the Long Shadow of the JFK Assassination* (2008). I have no expertise on this extremely complex subject, but my historian's judgment leads me to seriously consider the Mafia conspiracy theory—there is too much evidence of Mafia involvement to dismiss this possibility.

Waldron and Hartmann's 800-page argument is that Carlos Marcello, New Orleans, Santo Trafficante, Jr., Tampa, and Johnny Rosselli, Chicago and Hollywood, undertook arrangements for the assassination, with Marcello in charge. The Mafia was cooperating with the CIA in secret plans for an invasion of Cuba, managed by Robert F. Kennedy who did not know of a Mafia connection, set for 1 December 63. The Mafia strategy was to kill Kennedy before the invasion, which would restrict the investigation because the CIA would not want to expose the Mafia connection to the planned invasion. Marcello had arranged for the assassination of Attorney General Elect of Alabama Albert Patterson before he took office in 1954 without arranging for a patsy, or fall guy, to take the blame, and as a result, there was too much scrutiny of the New Orleans family. When the Mafia arranged the assassination of President Castillo Armas of Guatemala in 1957, a patsy was planned, and the subsequent investigation after the assassination ended when the patsy was killed. A comparable plan was then used to assassinate Kennedy on November 23, 1963. Lee Harvey Oswald was the patsy, and Kennedy was assassinated from the grassy knoll across from the Book Depository where Oswald was located. Marcello expected Oswald to be killed after the assassination. Jack Ruby, who later assassinated Oswald was a long-time Mafia associate, first in Chicago, and later in Dallas. Since Oswald survived Kennedy's assassination, the Mafia had Ruby kill him. Since their strategy had worked for John F. Kennedy, Marcello was willing in 1968 to arrange for the assassination of Martin Luther King, Jr., paid for by white supremacists. James Earl Ray, bank robber and drug smuggler, had shared a prison cell with a contract killer in Missouri's State Penitentiary before Ray escaped. He became a Mafia smuggler of drugs from Montreal into America. The Mafia had its own reasons to assassinate presidential candidate Robert Kennedy in 1968. Sirhan Sirhan might have been a patsy, like Oswald, and Waldron and Hartmann also discussed evidence that Sirhan was not the only shooter.

In 1968 Congress passed and President Nixon signed the Omnibus Crime Control Law, allowing wire-taps on suspected criminals' telephones, and in 1970 it was supplemented with the Racketeering Influenced and Corrupt Organizations Law (RICO). The latter allowed gangsters to be prosecuted for merely being members of outlaw organizations.[109] Brooklyn boss Joseph Bonanno (1905-2002) was deposed, retired to Arizona, and published A Man of Honor: the Autobiography of Joseph Bonanno (1983), in which he discussed the "Commission."[110] U.S. Attorney Rudolph (Rudy) Giuliani found that admission sufficient to convene a grand jury in which Bonanno was given immunity and compelled to discuss the Commission's activities.[111] Bonanno declined and had to spend about 14 months in a Federal prison. Giuliani persisted, and in 1986 a court prosecuted eight men for membership in an unlawful organization, and seven were sent to prison for 100 years.[112]

Mexican drug cartels themselves are beyond the scope of this chapter, but their interactions with Americans is worth scrutiny. The relevance for this chapter is illustrated in Lora Lumpe's "The US Arms Both Sides of Mexico's Drug War," and by M. Wuearker's political cartoon from Politico.[113]

# Mass Shootings

"A mass shooting is an incident of targeted violence carried out by one or more shooters at one or more public or populated locations." Schildkraut and Elsass 2016, 28.[114]

These two scholars of such American atrocities thought they occurred in two waves: first, in 1920s-30s, which were mainly familicides; second, beginning with Charles Whitman's shootings from the Tower of the University of Texas in 1966, and continuing into recent times. The shootings which they survey had no ideological aspects.

As a historian, I wish to consider a much broader problem, in both time and geography. In an earlier period, Euro-Americans pushed their way across North America and used guns to convince Native Americans to make do with much less land than was their custom. Sometimes negotiations sufficed, with Natives accepting some compensations for lands relinquished. However, there were many occasions in which Natives were unconvinced by negotiations and fought for their lands. Those conflicts did not all end with massacres of natives (or in a few cases, massacres of invaders), but a good number of such conflicts did.[115] The examples from California are well documented.[116]

American society was still developing during the 1800s, and several new religious groups were part of the new developments, not all of which lasted. One that did last and even flourish was the Mormon religion, founded by Joseph Smith (1790-1844), a charismatic leader who grew up in upstate New York.[117] Polygamy was part of his teaching, which generated hostility among "gentiles."[118] Smith was arrested at a Mormon settlement in Nauvoo, Illinois, and thrown in jail, from which a mob seized and lynched him. Mormons had moved further west in response to harassment, and the new leader, Brigham Young read an exploration report by Army officer John C. Fremont and decided that the Great Salt Lake region was an isolated oasis where they could live without harassment.[119]

True, but Mormons had not forgotten their harsh treatment by other Americans, and in 1857 some Mormons decided it was payback time. Furthermore, Mormon anger was also increased by Federal efforts to turn their settlement into an official U.S. Territory.[120] A wagon train west had stopped briefly in Salt Lake City to buy supplies. In September, this Francher Party headed southwest to California, but when it reached Mountain Meadows, it was attacked by a force which John D. Lee, one of Young's trusted assistants, had organized of Mormons and neighboring Indians. About 120 settlers surrendered and were slaughtered. Inevitably, Lee and his lieutenants were tried in a Federal Court in 1859, and he was found guilty, and executed. Brigham Young had given no indication of disapproval before Lee and his men were arrested and so was suspected by "gentiles" of having been complicit in planning the massacre. Two books on the massacre by Mormons expressed doubt Young was involved in planning the massacre.[121] William Wise, however, was not a Mormon, and in his book he commented:[122]

> During the 1850's, when the Fancher Train arrived in Utah, conditions were such that no large-scale crime could possibly have been planned and executed without Brigham Young's full knowledge and participation. The Territory was a private kingdom ruled by a single despot whose submissive underlings lived in constant fear of his anger or disapproval...

After the Civil War and Reconstruction, in the South, Whites sometimes perpetrated mass shootings to remind Blacks they needed to remember their place, at the bottom of society (I grew up in North Carolina, where this was obvious to everyone). Between 1865 and 1955, over 5000 Blacks were lynched, mostly in the South.[123] The Ku Klux Klan arose after that war to ensure this.[124] Most members of the Ku Klux Klan seem to have been blue collar workers, who did not wish to compete with Blacks for jobs. There were occasions when Whites were tried for murder, but with no Blacks on juries, no convictions. Anthony Pitch wrote a commendable book with an ambiguous title: *The Last Lynching: How a Gruesome Mass Murder Rocked a Small Georgia Town* (2016). The murder he discussed was of two black couples executed with guns in 1946. My thought was that that was certainly not the last lynching in America. The latest lynching Charles Christian reported was in 1981.[125] In his "Afterword," Pitch explained that this was the last *mass* lynching, of George Dorsey, 30, World War II veteran, and wife Mae, 24, and Roger Malcolm, 25, and his wife, Dorothy. The murderers were never identified.

The actual last lynching, in 1981, was of Michael Donald, age 19, in Mobile, Alabama. Laurence Leamer wrote a book on it, *The Lynching: the Epic Courtroom Battle that Brought Down the Klan* (2016). Leamer commented that "Two decades earlier...it was almost impossible to find a jury in the Deep South that would rule against the Klan."[126] In this case, also, there was an all-white jury. The prosecuting attorney was Morris Dees (b. 1936), founder of the Southern Poverty Law Center. What made this the end of the Klan was that a white jury found six Klan members guilty of the lynching.[127]

Some memory of those earlier atrocities against Indians or Blacks persisted in American consciousness, whether or not any particular later shooter was influenced by that memory.

Schildkraut and Elsass acknowledged mass shootings occurred before 1920s-30s—which they discussed (out of chronical order)—in 1880, 1883, March 1891, April 1891, 1893, and 1898.[128] The April 1891 shooting was likely inspired by the March 1891 shooting, and perhaps the first wave should be considered as actually starting in the 1890s. Maybe the killing of two at a school in 1908 should also be considered part of the 1890s tradition.[129] But that was not the end. In the Carroll County Court House, Hillsville, Virginia, on 14 March 12, Floyd Allen was found guilty in trial, and family members shot the judge, prosecutor, sheriff, and two witnesses.[130] However, it was Floyd Allen who was condemned to death. Michael Newton cited an unidentified home invader in Texas and Louisiana, Jan. 1911-June 1912, who in eleven attacks, killed 49; Newton did not specify how the murders were done, but a gun would have been a likely weapon.[131]

Manuel Fernandez, on 17 January 1913, killed one and wounded seven at a Honolulu school. On 8 August 1919, assistant professor Roger Sprague, Chemistry Dept., University of California (campus not specified), was denied tenure and shot two professors and attempted to shoot a vice-president before being stopped.[132] Schildkraut and Elsass then only provided one example from the 1920s and one from 1930s: in 1922, John Glover shot dead two students at a Valdosta, Georgia school, and was then killed by a mob; on 12 December 1935, Victor Koussow, former employee at New York City hospital and medical school, shot dead two professors and wounded a third before shooting himself. On 6 May 1940, a principal of a junior high school, at a school board meeting in South Pasadena, California, Verling Spencer, shot dead four and wounded two before killing himself. (On evidence provided, these two authors' 1920s-30s wave seems illusionary). At any rate, none of the mass shootings between 1880 and 1930s seemed to establish a definite tradition.

Howard Barton Unruh (1920-2009) distinguished himself at the Battle of the Bulge (Dec. 1944-Jan. 45), but he also kept a diary on the Germans he killed and their appearances.[133] After the war he returned home to Camden, NJ, and lived with his mother. He went to church, studied the Bible, and did target practicing in the basement. He also kept a diary on perceived slights from his neighbors. On the morning of 6 Feb. 49, he took his 9-mm German Lugerand and walked down his block, shooting neighbors, killing 13 and wounding three. Diagnosed a schistophrenic, he spent the rest of his life in prison.

## A. At Educational Institutions

Notice that almost half the examples in the above paragraph were from educational institutions, whereas in general over a third of mass shootings are at such places. One may question mention of two mass bombings in this discussion of mass shootings, but they are noteworthy here because they represented the same mentality: callous disregard for human life. Andrew Philip Kehoe (1872-1927) was a farmer at Bath, Michigan, and treasurer of the school board. Enraged by an increase of his property taxes, on 18 May 27 he bombed his house and barn, killing his wife and livestock, then went to school and bombed that, killing 38 children and six adults. He then bombed his own truck, killing himself, others, and wounding still more.[134] Apparently, he did not stimulate any copy-cat crimes. In 1959, Paul Orgeron used a bomb to kill himself and five others and wounded 19 at a Houston playground.

Charles Joseph Whitman (1941-66) was eldest of three sons of Charles Adolphus Whitman and wife Margaret.[135] C.A. Whitman was raised in an orphanage in Savannah, Georgia, and was a "self-made man" who founded a plumbing business in 1941 that flourished, with Margaret's running his office and tending his finances. He "on many occasions beat my wife, but I loved her."[136] He excused this by apologizing for his "awful temper." To discipline his sons, he used fists, paddles, and belts. C.A. was fascinated with guns and taught his sons to use them as soon as they could hold one, and a photograph shows Charlie as a toddler holding two rifles, one in each hand. He became proficient with guns at an early age.[137] He attracted national attention by becoming the nation's youngest Eagle Scout at age 12, thanks to his father's prodding. He also made the honor roll at school.

To escape his father, he enlisted in the Marines after he turned 18, in 1959. After basic training, he was sent 9 December 1959 to the Guantanamo Naval Base, Cuba, where he earned a Good Conduct Medal, Sharpshooter's Badge, and Expeditionary Medal for Cuban service. He took a competitive exam and won a scholarship to the University of Texas, beginning fall 1961. A friend, Francis Schuck, Jr., in February 1962 introduced him to an attractive freshman, Kathleen Leissner, whom he married on August 17. Before that, he and Schuck were caught after they had illegally killed a deer at night and Charlie paid a $100 fine. From the balcony to Whitman's dorm room, he once commented to Schuck that from the conspicuous University's Tower, "A person could stand off an army from atop it before they got to him," and one could shoot people from its observation deck.[138] A passing thought which Schuck did not take seriously. Without his father's prodding, Charlie did not prepare adequately for his courses; he earned an A in algebra, but otherwise received an F, D, and three Cs. After a year and a half, his scholarship was withdrawn and he returned to Camp Lejeune, where he came to hate the Marines but was still promoted to Lance Corporal. On 26 November 63, he was court martialed for gambling, usury, and unauthorized possession of a non-military pistol, and he was busted back to being a private and sentenced to the base's jail until 25 February 1964.[139] He received an honorable discharge 18 July 65 and became a Marine reservist.

Fig. 11. Charles Whitman

His wife, Kathy, admitted he beat her and she feared him. Back at the University of Texas, she was a student-teacher in spring 1965 and graduated afterwards. Her success seemed to inspire him to also attempt to graduate.[140] She apparently contemplated divorce, and feared he might kill her.[141] None of C.A. Whitman's younger sons wanted anything to do with him, and after they left, his wife contemplated leaving also. With Kathy's support, Charlie began to earn high marks at the University of Texas. On 2 March 66, Charlie convinced his mother to leave his father, and he drove 1,400 miles to pick her up. Kathy persuaded Charlie to seek help from the University psychiatrist, and he told Dr. Heatly of a fantasy he had of climbing the University Tower with a deer rifle and shooting people, and that he had beat his wife twice. Dr. Heatly concluded Charlie was not dangerous but asked him to return in a week, which Charlie never did. However, Charlie took 13 prescription drugs from seven physicians.[142]

"During the summer of 1966 mass murder frequented the news. Truman Capote's *In Cold Blood* ushered in a 'new journalism,' in which "real events were reported with fictional techniques."[143] It became a bestseller. In July, drifter Richard Speck murdered eight of nine nurses (one escaped) with his bare hands. A few days later, he attempted suicide by slashing his wrists. It was called "the crime of the century," but held that title for only 19 days. The observational deck of the University Tower is 231 feet high. Charlie Whitman took summer courses. On July 31, he bought a Bowie knife at a surplus store, picked up Kathy for lunch, which they had with his mother. Later, he "liberated" his mother and wife. Kathy went to sleep in their house and he went to visit his mother around midnight. He apparently strangled her with rubber hose. He returned to his sleeping wife and used the knife to kill her, on August 1. He had stashed away weapons and other equipment for the tower and retrieved that store, but then decided to buy more guns and ammunition.[144] At the Tower's observation deck he probably killed the receptionist the same way he had killed his mother. A family tried to enter the reception area before Charlie had gone outside, and he sprayed them with a sawed-off shotgun.[145] Soon after he began shooting from the observation deck, the bodies were discovered on the stairs to the reception area and police were called. On the ground far below, Whitman killed 12 in addition to three he had killed inside the tower, and he wounded 32 before police killed him.

In their history of school violence, Elizabeth Midlarasky and Helen Klain's earliest cited record is of Whitman's 1966 massacre. The next one discussed involving a gun was a 15-year old boy at a Brooklyn high school in 1992 who argued with two classmates and a few days later brought a gun to school and killed both boys.[146] It seems unlikely that the shooter was aware of Whitman's massacre at a Texas university. They also cite a study which reported that 20% of American students admitted carrying a weapon to school, bringing an estimated 270,000 guns to school daily.[147] With that many guns at schools, one would expect a shooting before 1992. I spoke once with a middle-aged man who had gone to school in a small town, who said he had a good hike daily to and from school, and he took along a handgun to shoot squirrels or rabbits along the way.

On 20 April 1999, Eric Harris and Dylan Klebold took two shotguns, a rifle and a handgun, and other weapons to their small-town high school, Columbine, about ten miles south-west of Denver, and killed 13 (plus themselves at the end) and wounded 21 with guns (plus 3 others).[148] Their goal was more casualties than McVeigh had achieved. They fell short (he had used a massive bomb), but they did cause the worst gun massacre at a school until then. This shooting became a vivid inspiration for subsequent school shooters.

There has been a strong academic response to mass school shootings,[149] 117 of which were reported by Schildkraut and Elsass, 1880-2014, constituting 37% of all mass shootings during that period.[150] Possibly, their tally represented the number of such shootings in which someone died, since Augusto De Venanzi cited a 2010 study by the National School Safety Services that reported 445 school shootings, 2000-10.[151] They cited his study but did not discuss the discrepancy between their tally and his. The 445 figure may include all school shootings, whether or not anyone was hit by a bullet.

Presumably, however, neither tally included shootings at colleges and universities. Charles Whitman, discussed above, began mass shootings at universities in 1966, which might have influenced later shootings at other campuses of higher learning. J.A. Fox and J. Savage counted 14 cases of multiple fatalities at campuses, 1990-2008, in which 70 were wounded.[152]

Professor Lucinda Roy, from England, taught English at Virginia Tech in 2004, when she had South Korean native Seung-Hui Cho (1984-2007) in her poetry class, where he read aloud his poem, with a threating tone. In 2005, another instructor in English asked to have him removed from her class because he intimidated his classmates and her. Roy was then Chair of the English Department, and so she asked him to stop going to that class.[153] She tutored him instead. She realized that he was deeply troubled and wanted a psychiatric counselor to meet with him, but that required him seeking help. She eventually persuaded him to seek help, which was of no help because he was not really interested. He had had counseling in high school. On 16 April 2007 he went to campus with a handgun and killed 32 and wounded 17, before killing himself. He had been inspired by Eric Harris and Dylan Klebold's massacre at Columbine.

In an article on school violence, John Devine noted in 1999 that "firearms-related homicide rate for children less than fifteen years of age in the United States is nearly sixteen times higher than that of the other twenty-five leading industrialized countries of the world combined."[154] Katherine Newman and four collaborators studied *The Social Roots of School Shootings* (2005) and identified five important factors:[155]

1. Shooter's perception of himself as extremely marginal in social worlds that matter;
2. Shooters suffer from psychosocial problems that magnify the impact of marginality;
3. "Cultural scripts"—prescriptions for behavior—must be available to lead the way toward an armed attack;
4. Failure of surveillance systems that are intended to identify troubled teens before their problems become extreme;
5. Gun availability.

A therapist for teenagers, Peter Langman, Ph.D., studied the case histories of ten school shooters and wrote *Why Kids Kill: Inside the Minds of School Shooters* (2009). He acknowledged that there might be other diagnoses for shooters he did not study, but he found his cases fell into three psychological types:[156]

1. **Psychopathic**: narcissistic persons without a conscience; they may get angry when desires are thwarted; they lack empathy and may be sadistic.

2. **Psychotic**: out of touch with reality in certain ways, usually hallucinations and delusions; they may have schizophrenia or schizotypal personality disorder; they lack intimacy and have a sense of isolation.

3. **Traumatized**: as children, beaten or molested; may have grown up with alcoholic or violent adult; may have posttraumatic stress disorder; may feel constantly threatened and may become violent.

Langman's insights are presumably helpful for school therapists who study his case histories. Although causes of school shootings can be complex, conspicuous factors in some of them are bullying,[157] violent video games, and associating with peers who are violence-prone.

The shooting of five high school students by a disturbed fellow student, T.J. Lane, in Chardon, Ohio, on February 27, 2012 deserved the media attention that it received.[158] Three of the students died and a fourth was still hospitalized on February 29. Mass shootings are by now rather frequent; they have occurred at about weekly intervals. The Mass Shooting Tracker found that there were 1,850 of them between Jan. 2013 and 1 Oct. 2017.[159]

These shootings receive a paragraph on page 3A in The Journal Times, Racine WI, and only receive radio and TV coverage in the region where it happened. Everyone deplores the senseless violence, and if the shooter did not take his/her own life, he/she is apprehended and dealt with in our justice system. Some schools have installed metal detectors to keep guns and knives out of school. Sandy Hook Elementary School had locked glass security doors as protection from intruders, but Adam Lanza (1992-2012) blasted through them with a Bushmaster AR-15 assault rifle in 2012, after which in five minutes he killed 20 children and six adults. He had previously killed his mother; after this carnage, he killed himself.[160] In the case of Nikolas Cruz's school shooting on Valentine's Day in Parkland, FL in 2018 that killed 17, there had been warnings of his instability, to which the FBI and others did not respond.

## B. Not at Educational Institutions

Most mass shootings are not at institutions of learning. Schildkraut and Elsass (2016) overlooked the worst mass shooting by Americans ever recorded, which occurred two years after Whitman's, when American soldiers killed between 347 and 504 Vietnamese civilians, at My Lai, on 16 March 68. Only their officer, 2nd Lt. William Law Calley (b. 1943) was found guilty and sentenced to life in prison, soon reduced to 3.5 months of house arrest.[161] Ervin Staub also viewed America as a contributor to mass murder in Cambodia and Latin American countries, and as a complicit bystander to mass murder in Germany (1936), Iraq (1980s to August 1990), and Rwanda (1994).[162]

On 20 August 86, a mail carrier, Patrick Sherrill, who had experienced conflicts at the Edmond, Oklahoma post office, shot dead 14 and wounded 7 others there before committing suicide.[163] From that shooting came the expression, "going postal," referring to shootings where one worked. Mark Ames, who entitled his mediocre survey *Going Postal: Rage, Murder, and Rebellion* (2005), the immediate examples which he cited as being influenced by Sherrill were at workplaces, but none at a post office. On the other hand, when postal carrier DeShaune Stewart, 24, killed two supervisors from the Dublin, Ohio post office on 23 December 17, he may well have been influenced by the expression, "going postal," because such stories persist in the lore of a profession.

Two unfortunate shootouts attracted nation-wide attention, particularly since the second one occurred six months after the first. Former Green Beret Randall Claude (Randy) Weaver and wife Vicki took their family, in August 1983, from Iowa to northern Idaho, at Ruby Ridge near an Aryan Nations compound, where he associated with its leaders, who were being watched by Bureau of Alcohol, Tobacco and Firearms (ATF).[164] He referred to government as ZOG (Zionist Occupational Government). At the 1989 World Aryan Congress, ATF informant Kenneth Fadeley, under cover, persuaded Weaver to sell him two sawed-off shotguns, a federal crime. ATF was not much interested in Weaver, but since he was in a vulnerable situation, ATF attempted to persuade him to spy on Aryan Nations leaders. He refused, and so ATF arrested him for his illegal weapons transaction. He went to court and was given a date for a trial in February 1991, for which he did not appear. Vickie Weaver wrote two defiant letters to U.S. attorneys. She and their three daughters carried guns. After 15 months, ATF had federal marshals send two teams of three agents each to gather intelligence on Weaver. On 21 August 1992, the Weavers' son, Sammy, went out with his dog, and the dog discovered hidden marshals and began barking at them. A marshal shot dead the dog and Sammy shot dead the marshal. A second marshal then shot dead Sammy. The next day, over 100 FBI agents, 26 Idaho national guardsmen, and scores of U.S. Marshalls converged on his cabin. Vickie Weaver was shot dead and a family friend, Kevin Harris, was severely wounded. Nine days later, Weaver surrendered, with his daughters and Harris. On 8 July 1993, Weaver was acquitted of the weapons charge since he was set up by ATF, but convicted of lesser charges and spent 16 months in jail. U.S. Government paid Weaver and his daughters $3.1 million for the deaths of Sammy and Vickie Weaver.

Federal ATF and FBI agents had not done well in the Weaver case, but blame can nevertheless be pinned on Weaver for not cooperating with the government in the first place. In the second conflict, ATF agents performed very badly. Their problem was that they drew an erroneous conclusion based upon very little evidence and then acted upon their misunderstanding.[165] Vernon Howell (1959-93) was born to unwed 15-year-old Bonnie Clark in Houston, and later they lived in Dallas with a man who became his step-father. He dropped out of school in Dallas after grade nine. He developed a strong interest in Christianity. In 1981 he went to join the Branch Davidians at their compound, Mount Carmel, ten miles from Waco. In the 1980s, he struggled for control and won. In 1990, he legally changed his name to David Koresh, with Biblical implications. He became a messiah and became the only man who could have sexual relations with the women there. The Branch Davidians were a harmless religious sect, but Koresh learned from a local gun dealer, Henry McMahon, in 1993 that Congress was going to outlaw assault rifles, and that when that passed, the price of assault rifles would increase significantly at gun shows. Thus, the Branch Davidians could buy them at a current price and sell them later for a much higher amount. The ATF got wind of his purchases and concluded he was head of a militia planning some attack. McMahon called Koresh, told him this while ATF agent Davy Aguilera was beside him. Koresh then invited Aguilera, over the phone to McMahon, to come visit the compound, and Aguilera declined to speak to him or to visit the compound. Possibly Aguilera suspected Koresh would hide whatever incriminating evidence he had before Aguilera arrived. Be that as it may, a Congressional hearing later concluded that refusal had been a fundamental mistake. Meanwhile, Koresh believed, and convinced others to believe, they were acting the script of the Book of Revelations and would be killed at the end.[166]

ATF's Operation Trojan Horse marshaled 80 federal agents in combat gear and weapons on 28 February 93 for an invasion. ATF knew that Koresh had learned of the raid before-hand, but proceeded anyway (so many agents on hand!). The result: a shootout in which 6 Davidians and 4 federal agents were killed. Afterwards, the FBI's Hostage Rescue Team (HRT) went to Waco and a 51-day standoff began. Patriots, including Timothy McVeigh, went to Waco and protested the federal siege. HRT persuaded Davidians to release 28 people from the compound. However, with no further progress, on April 19, a tank breached the defenses and fired canisters of CS (tear) gas inside. Six hours later, fire erupted and 76 Branch Davidians died, including 24 children.

There is a first-hand account of another mass-shooting, by a severely wounded survivor, Gabrielle ("Gabby") Giffords (b. 1970), who was just beginning her third term as a U.S. Congress Representative from Tucson when an assassin, Jared Lee Loughner, 22, shot her and wounded twelve others and killed five.[167] He had attended Pima Community College in 2010 and heard a talk she gave there. Afterwards he asked a nonsensical question: "What is government if words have no meaning?"

She answered as best she could, but he was dissatisfied with her answer and decided to kill her. Meanwhile, his behavior at the college was so strange that it expelled him, and a campus policeman went to his home and read to him and his mother why he was expelled. His father took Jared's shotgun and locked it in the trunk of his car. Jared went to a gun store and paid $560 for a Glock pistol, a bullet magazine, and a box of bullets. Giffords at times held "Congress on Your Corner" meetings with whatever constituents wanted to come and talk. It was at one of these pre-announced meetings that Loughner brought his Glock and his plan of assassination. After firing 33 shots in 15 seconds, he attempted to reload but was overpowered by those who he had not shot and held for the sheriff. Giffords was shot in the head, and her partial recovery was slow and extremely difficult. She attended his court case on 7 Aug. 2012, where he pled guilty and was sentenced to life in prison. About a year after being wounded, she resigned her seat in Congress, and one of her assistants ran successfully to replace her.

White supremacist Dylann Roof, 21, entered a Black church in Charleston SC, 17 June15, and killed nine and wounded three others.[168] His massacre most likely inspired Devin Patrick Kelley, 26, who on 5 Nov. 17 killed 25 and wounded 20 at a church in Sutherland Springs, Texas, near San Antonio.[169]

"The worse mass shooting in modern American history took place at Pulse, a gay nightclub where patrons were enjoying 'Latin Night' and also celebrating Pride Month."[170] That massacre was at Orlando FL, 11 July16, that killed 49 and wounded 53, done by native American Muslim, Omar Mateen (1986-2016). His religion is relevant here, for it was the background for the righteous indignation that motivated his actions. However, his first wife reported that he was "an angry, violent, and controlling man" long before July 16. He died in a shootout with police.

Sadly, Mateen's record of perpetrating America's worse mass shooting lasted little more than a year before wealthy gambler-investor Stephen Craig Paddock, 64, killed 59 and wounded 527 in Las Vegas, on Sunday, 1 October 2017. It imitated Whitman's massacre (1966) in that Paddock was high above his victims, on the 32nd floor of the Mandalay Bay casino-hotel. Paddock was a retired accountant from Mesquite, Nevada, who took 23 guns into his hotel room and police found 19 more at his home, with explosives and thousands of bullets. This became the worse mass shooting in (modern) America.[171] He broke two windows in a corner room on the 32nd floor of the Mandalay Bay Resort and Casino, in Las Vegas, overlooking a plaza where some 22,000 people were seated, listening to a folk concert. He had brought a small arsenal into the room, hidden in luggage. When he had shot all the bullets in one gun, he picked up another and continued shooting. Furthermore, he had added bump stocks to semiautomatic rifles to convert them into automatic machine guns. None of his associates imagined he was capable of this atrocity. He had no difficulty buying the guns in gun stores because he had no previous criminal record. He killed himself before police reached him.

No other stable industrialized country tolerates this level of ongoing violence, excepting Mexico, which has a drug war fueled by American appetite for drugs, and by American guns. Here, there is not even any discussion of doing anything about it because everyone knows that the NRA has become the self-appointed gatekeeper of our gun laws, and its response to every gun crime is to have more guns, not more laws.

## Gun Shows

Where do shooters get their guns? Some, like Stephen Paddock, with no criminal record, buy them in gun stores. Some with criminal records persuade someone without a record to buy for them, a "straw purchase." Some criminals steal one or more guns from the residence of a lawful gun owner.

Another important source of guns for criminals have been gun shows. Gun shows were also important places for militias/Patriots to spread their ideologies and to recruit members. One feature of the McClure-Volker Act (1986) allowed federal gun license holders to sell guns at gun shows in their state.[172] Even though President Reagan had been wounded by John Hinckley in 1981, he nevertheless, a loyal NRA member, signed that act.[173] Gun shows flourished, and in 1995, the National Association of Arms Shows estimated there were over 100 gun shows in America every weekend, or 5,200 a year, with over 5 million people attending the shows yearly, and $1 billion in sales.[174] Yet, passage of the McClure-Volker Act was also followed by an increase in gun violence, which worried the George H.W.

Bush Administration. Despite having campaigned on flexible gun laws, when Bush saw the results, he strengthened his administrative measures on gun control. Bush also wanted to have an active war on drugs, which did not mesh well will flexible gun laws. The ATF estimated that 2 or 3 million military rifles had been sold in America since the Vietnam War ended. This reversal of Bush's policy alarmed those in militias/Patriot groups.

## Guns and Militias/Patriots

One might think that private militias should be discussed in the Organized Crime section, but although militias are organizations, they are not organized to maintain dominance with guns.[175] Militia members often commit crimes with guns as individuals, even if inspired by a militia's ideology, and a gun crime might involve more than one militia members. Militia may be secretive in their deliberations, but their existence is not a secret (though some members may have kept their membership secret). Fear of government confiscating guns of citizens was/is the dominant motivation for militias.

A common, if not universal, claim of militias was the assertion that existing government was not legitimate, and therefore whatever militia one joined constituted legitimate government. They were/are local or regional, and at times they have been fairly numerous. They often published newsletters, with small circulations. The Ku Klux Klan, which arose in the South after the Civil War, was a forerunner of militias. Klan members were armed and they enforced their ideas about the law concerning African Americans to the extent that they could, with guns, nooses, and intimidation. The Klan faded during the late 1800s, as attention turned to Spanish-American War and World War I, but it revived during the 1920s.[176] Lynchings occurred in the South into the 1960s (and occasionally 1970s), and Klan members were commonly involved. Racism was a common characteristic of members of a militia, though usually racist demands were not made explicit in a militia's public image.[177] A different early influence on the movement was the John Birch Society, founded by Robert Welch, former director of National Association of Manufacturers, in 1958, dedicated to anticommunism and an ally of Wisconsin's fanatical anti-communist Senator Joseph McCarthy.[178]

In 1967, a news item in the *New York Times* stated that the stock market had declined because of a "peace scare." That caught the imagination of Victor Navasky and two friends, who persuaded Leonard Lewin to write an ostensibly secret government report which had been leaked to the press, *Report from Iron Mountain on the Possibility and Desirability of Peace*, and they found an editor, at Dial Press, who was willing to go along with the hoax and publish it as a serious book.[179] It was supposedly secret because it "found" that America's economy could not survive in peacetime. The hoaxsters were surprised when a reporter asked the White House if the report was authentic, and the response was no comment. The Johnson Administration did not know if the Kennedy Administration had ordered it. The *New York Times* then ran a front-page story that it was possibly authentic. Navasky commented:

> ...it was more than a hoax; it was a satire, a parody, a provocation. Its acceptance by super-patriots and conspiracy theorists of the far right is roughly akin to the Irish Republican Army considering Jonathan Swift's *A Modest Proposal* proof that eating Irish babies is official British policy.

Unfortunately, Navasky's confession was too little, too late, and unpersuasive to militia members. He published it in June 1995; McVeigh had bombed the Murrah Federal Building in April.

Some militants, including William Potter Gale (1916-88)[180] and Robert De Pugh (1923-2009),[181] thought Birchers were too restrained. Gale founded the California Rangers in 1959, though it did not last beyond the arrest of a key member. De Pugh founded the Minutemen in 1960, advocating armed "civil defense" and outdoor survival training. He criticized Birchers for operating within the political system. His militia promoted gun rights and feared world government. The Minutemen were disrupted by authorities in 1961, when citizens in Shiloh, IL complained of frequent gunfire near a community center. Police discovered a guerrilla group doing tactical exercises. Their many weapons made national news. In November 1966, De Pugh and two other minute men were convicted in Federal Court of violating National Firearms Act by making, possessing, and transferring automatic weapons and silencers, and tax delinquency. Awaiting appeal, they fled to New Mexico, but were captured in 1969 with a large cache of weapons. In 1970, De Pugh was convicted of jumping bond. Seven months later he was convicted of violating federal gun laws and given additional years. The Minutemen dissolved.

That was Gale's opportunity; he established a more lasting and prominent Posse Comitatus in 1970, which synthesized racist Christian Identity beliefs with anticommunism, and vigilantism.[182] He had served under General Douglas MacArthur in World War II, and had achieved the rank of Lieutenant Colonel.[183] His biography is a little bit bizarre. His Jewish father, Charles Grabifker immigrated from Russia in 1894 and settled in North Dakota. He changed his name to Charles Gale and married a Christian, Anglo-American Agnes Potter, and they raised their children as Christians. What was bizarre was that their son William became an anti-Semite. After being discharged, he associated with right-wing conspiracy theorists who convinced him that the federal government was unreliable—despite his experiences while serving competently in that government's army.

Atlanta native William Luther Pierce (1933-2002) earned a B.S. in physics from Rice University (1955), and Ph.D. from University of Colorado (1962), and became an assistant professor of physics at Oregon State University 1962-65. In 1966, he moved to Washington, D.C. to join forces with white racist George Lincoln Rockwell, who was assassinated in 1967. Pierce soon became the leading white racist, neo-Nazi, in America and founded the National Alliance, which published a periodical, *National Vanguard*. In 1978, Pierce published a political novel, *The Turner Diaries* (1978), (under pseudonym Andrew Macdonald), the plot involved government attempted confiscation of guns, with patriots resisting. By 2002 his organization had 1500 members and brought in over 1$ million a year. Pierce is relevant here because his novel became a bible for many militia members.

Timothy McVeigh (1968-2001) viewed the Koresh disaster as a federal declaration of war. His bombing was in revenge for what the Federal Government had done at Ruby Ridge and at Waco, and although neither group fit the usual description of a militia, because one was a single household and the other an isolated commune, their concerns were similar to issues which also concerned militias. He and Terry Nichols were Army veterans who became heavily influenced by the militia culture and attended some meetings without being committed to any particular militia.[184] McVeigh was one of those inspired by Pierce's novel. He was quite familiar with guns, and if that project had required guns, they would have been used. He believed his bombing would precipitate a national uprising against the Federal Government. He would be convicted of bombing Murrah Federal Building in Oklahoma City on 19 April 1995, which killed 168 and injured over 600, using a truck bomb. He was condemned in court on 13 June 97 and executed on 11 June 2001. His biographers called him an *American Terrorist* and *All-American Monster*.[185] His chief lawyer, Stephen Jones had published *Others Unknown: Timothy McVeigh and the Oklahoma City Bombing Conspiracy* [1998], to explain the complexities of the bombing, and after reading Michel and Herbeck's book, Jones reissued his ([2001] with new preface to correct errors taken from their book, due to McVeigh having lied to Michel.)[186]

McVeigh's vain hope of starting a revolution did not die with him, and on 29 March 2010 the FBI arrested nine members of Hutaree, a Christian militia in Ohio, Michigan, and Indiana, who had revived that hope with a planned murder of a police officer followed by a massive bombing at his funeral. That arrest attracted widespread attention.[187]

The new gun control law of 1994 and the Oklahoma City bombing in 1995 provided additional stimuli until by 1996 there were almost 400 militia in America.[188] That did not last long, however, and by 2002 there were only an estimated 42. Obama's election in 2008 boosted the number to about 127 by 2009.[189] By then, Federal agents had uncovered and prevented 75 criminal plots.[190]

## Young Gangs and Guns

Young gangs are under a separate heading from adult crime gangs because young gangs are not organized specifically for crime, though most young gangs had members who collectively engaged in crime at various times. Street gangs were generally younger on average than biker gangs.

## Street Gangs

American youth gangs have been studied extensively.[191] In late 1800s, many immigrants settled in industrializing cities, and from their youth emerged criminal gangs in New York, Boston, Philadelphia, St. Louis, and

Pittsburg.[192] Such gangs roamed neighborhood streets, committed petty property crimes, and fought other gangs. During 1920s, gangs developed symbols of membership and engaged in more serious crimes. Frederic Thrasher initiated gang research in *The Gang: a Study of 1,313 Gangs in Chicago* (1927). Gangs initially arose from spontaneous group activities, and cohesiveness of such groups was strengthened by conflict. Some gang members matured and gained legitimate roles in society, while other members remained engaged in criminal activities. During 1960s, Blacks and Hispanics organized gangs, and availability of cars and guns impacted gang behavior. Prisons became important for recruiting gang members. Most juvenile crimes were caused by gang members.

Malcolm Klein studied *Street Gangs and Street Workers* (1971) and concluded that gang-intervention programs actually enhanced gang attractiveness and thereby promoted violence.[193] Walter Miller conducted the first Federal survey of America's gangs, published in 1977. He estimated there were 760-2700 gangs in six major cities, having 28,000-81,500 members. The Department of Justice subsequently funded five more national surveys, 1975-95, each showing that gang problems had increased and become more geographically wide-spread. In 1993, there were 8,625 gangs known, with 378,807 members, who committed 437,066 known crimes. In 1995, 23,388 youth gangs were known, with a total of 664,906 members, in more cities than had reported serious gang problems than in 1993. However, David Curry and Scott Decker found (1998) that there were fewer gangs in 1997 than there had been in 1996.[194]

# Biker Gangs

Biker gangs arose after World War II. Their memberships are mainly men of Anglo-Saxon and German descent, but there are also Hispanic biker gangs. Otto Friedli organized a gang in 1947 in California, and in 1948 they adopted the name "Hell's Angels," borrowed from fighter pilots during World War II, since members were mostly Air Force veterans.[195] Friedli lost control in 1958 when he was sent to jail, and the presidency went to Ralph (Sonny) Barger, a U.S. Army veteran who had enlisted at age 16, lying about his age.[196] "Barger's foresight, drive, and cunning shaped the Hell's Angels into the fearsome gang it is today."[197] Barger's autobiography provides the details: "With the coke came the guns. Hell's Angels have always been accused of stockpiling guns. Lots of Americans—especially Hell's Angels—love guns. While I was in the Army I was *taught* to love guns." [198] At that time, over 90% of members were veterans. Although some of them had jobs, they made money by making and selling methamphetamine. By 1965, there were four chapters in California and one in Auckland, New Zealand.[199] They allied with hippies because they sold then drugs, for two months; however, when the hippies protested the Vietnam War, Hell's Angels responded angrily, then thought better of it so as not to lose customers.[200] In 1969, the Rolling Stones hired Hell's Angels to keep order at a concert that attracted 250,000. One Angel was offended by a bi-racial couple, and they severely beat the African American male.[201] Hell's Angels built a more productive relationship with the Mafia, though the two kinds of gang are quite different in style, with the Mafia relatively genteel compared to the grubby Angels. However, both want money and power, and "The Angels break legs and kill for the mob in the early 1970s."[202] Their marriage of convenience spread across America.

In early 2000s, two federal agents infiltrated Hell's Angels chapters, in order to bring its members to court. Jay Dobyns infiltrated the Arizona chapter as an undercover ATF agent, and his adventures and findings are discussed by Kerrie Droban, *Running with the Devil* (2007) and in Dobyns' *No Angel: My Harrowing Undercover Journey to the Inner Circle of the Hells Angels* (coauthor, Nils Johnson-Shelton, 2009). Allen Caine infiltrated the San Diego chapter as an undercover agent for DEA, ATF, and the San Diego Sheriff's Department, which he described in *Befriend and Betray* (2008). Both agents were risking their lives, yet both were successful in obtaining enough evidence to try members of those chapters for several crimes. However, Hell's Angles chapters are now spread widely around the world, though it had to fight the Outlaws club to establish its Chicago chapter.[203] Journalist Yves Lavigne's historical survey, *Hell's Angels* (1987), placed some emphasis upon chapters in his native Canada. Photographer Andrew Shaylor published a coffee-table book on the UK members, *Hells Angels Motorcycle Club* (2004), which he imagined is non-judgmental, but viewers are likely to see such lavish coverage as a positive statement. However, none of the portraits give the impression of warm fuzzies. Hell's Angels seemed to use guns even more readily than Mafia members (and often in the Mafia's service).

According to Thomas Barker, *Biker Gangs and Transnational Organized Crime* (2015), 30 or more years ago outlaw motorcycle gangs (OMGs) in America:[204]

> spread their criminal tendrils throughout the world to the extent that some U.S.-based clubs—Hells Angels MC, Outlaws MC, Bandidos MC—now have more chapters outside the United States than within U.S. boundaries.

There were also foreign OMGs that later established U.S. chapters. Barker surveyed five major American OMGs, then their spread to Canada, Australia and New Zealand, Britain (UK), and Europe. He then constructed a chronology of notable OMG crimes from 1968 to 2012.[205]

## Conclusions

This long chapter covers gun crimes from early settlements until recent events. Most such crimes were unorganized—some planned, some not—which for practical reasons are here presented under familiar headings: dueling, wild west, prohibition, and assassinations. Organized crime arose among some immigrants from European countries who settled in a few cities where immigrants landed, and such gangs later spread elsewhere. Prohibition in 1920 provided a stimulating situation for gaining wealth from illicit sale of alcoholic beverages, and guns enabled gangs to defend their turf from rival gangs. That led to well-publicized gang murders, and prohibition doing more harm than good led to its repeal in 1933. Organized crime was not so easily eliminated, so Congress established agencies in the Department of Justice to defend against it. A legendary J. Edgar Hoover, who developed the FBI, however, turned a blind eye to organized crime as long as he could. The Bureau of Alcohol, Tobacco, and Firearms was established later and remained a stepchild in Justice, partly because of NRA hostility.

Mass shootings is a home-grown social pathology in America that had a sporadic beginning. A notable early example was a Mormon massacre in 1857 of the Francher wagon train of about 120 Americans. Two Mormon histories of the Mountain Meadows Massacre argued that Brigham Young, the Mormon governor, would not have known about it in advance. William Wise in his history of the massacre argued that it would not have happened without Young planning it. I find Wise's argument persuasive. Until Charles Whitman climbed a university tower in 1966 and attracted national attention by killing 15 and wounding 32 before police killed him, there had not been a conscious American tradition of mass murders. The My Lie massacre in Vietnam, 1968, might not have been influence by Whitman since it was in a very different context, but it was by Americans. The FBI and ATF had trouble trying to protect against such catastrophes, as seen in their miss-handling of the Ruby Ridge and Waco standoffs in 1993. Timothy McVeigh's blowing up of the Murrah Federal Building in Oklahoma City in 1995 was to avenge the Waco catastrophe and to start a revolution. In most cases, law officers were not available until after a mass shooting, as seen in the Orlando, 2016, and Las Vegas, 2017, massacres.

Local sheriffs arose during the Middle Ages, but city police were first established in London in 1829 and the idea taken up by New York in 1844. A few historical examples of local law officers are briefly sketched, and the modern controversy over White officers shooting Blacks (who may or may not have had guns) is briefly discussed. Gun shows are now common and frequent throughout America, and they provide places where criminals can obtain guns without background checks, and where private militias can spread their propaganda and recruit new members.

The Ku Klux Klan arose after the Civil War in the South to show Blacks that although the Federal Government liberated them, Whites were still in charge of former slave states and that they resisted at their peril. It faded in the late 1800s but arose again in the 1920s. The Klan's example was at least one source of private militias that arose after World War II. Militiamen mistrusted the Federal and sometimes State governments and felt that they needed to join together to prevent confiscation of private guns and a tyrannical government—despite their being no evidence that either possibility has ever been contemplated by anyone in government. A collection of suspicious men who felt that guns were important in their lives led some of them to then use those guns in illegal activities, leading in turn to conflicts with the law, ending sometimes to terms in jails or prisons.

Timothy McVeigh's bombing of a federal building in 1995 was the most extreme example of a destructive militia mentality.

Some young gangs apparently had a similar origin as did adult organized crime gangs, among immigrant boys. Their example in cities may then have prompted boys of different ethnicities developing their own gangs for comradery and mischief. The easy availability of guns made gangs dangerous—for themselves, but also for others caught in the crossfire. Militias were commonly not in cities. Biker gangs arose after World War II, initially among veterans, but over time attracting others. Some biker gangs allied with organized crime gangs. Guns made all such groups more dangerous than they would have been without guns.

A consequence of all this gun crime is that there have been 1.6 million deaths from domestic guns since 1968, compared to 1.3 million Americans killed in all our wars since 1776!

# 7

## GUN VIOLENCE AS ENTERTAINMENT

The same civilization that produces the industrial world's worse peacetime gun violence also produces the world's most violent cultural entertainments involving guns. If these entertainments are harmless cultural artifacts, then it hardly matters. However, if such entertainments incite further gun violence, then we have a cultural pathology that should be changed. The goal of this chapter is to explore: first, the roots of this part of our culture so we can appreciate its scope and momentum; and second, discuss and evaluate arguments that entertainment featuring violence with guns stimulates actual gun violence.

### Early Gun Stories

What is the source of the human impulse to tell violent stories and our fascination to hear them? The earliest development of language, perhaps 100,000 or more years ago, probably dealt with daily transactions among members of foraging bands. Such transactions would have included life-threatening dangers—from other humans, fierce animals, and natural disasters. Eventually, language was also used to tell others about the dangers encountered and which tactics were successful and which were not in dealing with danger. Those listening were eager to hear how the danger was either overcome or not, because some day they might confront a similar danger, and learning from past experiences of others would help them decide how to act. Stories of violence thus played a constructive role in preparing people for real dangers. As society became more complex, professional story tellers emerged who could compellingly tell of famous events that lingered in collective memory. Their stories not only informed but also inspired listeners with a desire to do as well or better than predecessors. By the time these stories were immortalized by being written down, they had become artistic creations. As artistic creations, they took on an additional function of entertainment. Among the examples that come down to us from antiquity, the best known are Homer's *Iliad* and *Odyssey*. Stories about danger could stimulate the same or similar emotions as those being described, even when the dangers described were not actually feared as potentially real by listeners.

How did America develop a major aspect of its culture as pro-violence and possibly antisocial? One critic suggests that: "In the traditional American narrative, violence is envisioned as both a moral imperative and a rite of passage."[1] Richard Slotkin has written a trilogy of hefty volumes to explore this situation in detail. People are susceptible to the influence of myths which "reach out of the past to cripple or strike down the living."[2] Myths have three elements: (1) a protagonist with whom the audience identifies, (2) a universe in which the hero acts, and (3) a narrative of his/her interaction with that universe.[3] Our initial question concerns Slotkin's second element: why has the American universe been so violent?

The answer seems obvious: Euro-Americans fought with Indians; English, French and Spanish settlers fought each other; and after international conflicts diminished, the English fought among themselves as Rebels versus Tories, 1776-83, and as Union versus Confederate soldiers, 1861-65. The frontier struggle with Indians ended in 1890, just as William Cody turned the wild west into entertainment, with real Indians playing either themselves or other Indians in theatrical fights with pretend soldiers or with real veterans and cowboys. And there was violence against Blacks, both while they were slaves and continuing after emancipation. Meanwhile, with the rise of cities came urban crime. In response, police forces were created, and they were somewhat effective against unorganized crime but were unable to suppress organized crime. (The FBI did not even acknowledge organized crime until publicly shamed into doing so in 1957 after the Apalachin raid.) Large-scale organized crime emerged after passage of Prohibition in 1919 but survived the end of Prohibition in 1933 and gained new momentum with the rise of large-scale illicit drug trade after World War II.

So much for Slotkin's second element in myth-making. The protagonists (his first element) were originally the real characters within that violent universe, but narratives of their interaction with that universe (his third element) were never objective documentaries. Euro-American authors had their own perceptions of themselves, their antagonists, and their audience, and their narratives reflected those biases. The dominant bias or framework that Slotkin identified in his first volume is stated in its title: *Regeneration through Violence: The Mythology of the American Frontier, 1600-1860* (1973). Euro-Americans came here to better their lives, and they struggled against climate, Indians, and predatory animals. The main narrative message was that God rewarded virtuous struggle.

Some early English settlers saw their situation as analogous to the Israelites, who fled Egypt and conquered a promised land from heathens, though some participants in Indian wars, such as John Underhill (1638) and Benjamin Church (1716), disapproved of Christians behaving like savages when at war with savages.[4] As British-American civilization developed, new narratives of the regeneration emerged, which is the theme of Slotkin's twelve chronological chapters (out of fourteen chapters). Guns were involved in most of the real conflicts and often figured in the narratives as well. Daniel Boone (1734-1820) was a leading explorer and Indian fighter who migrated westward as civilization advanced, and he became a legend in his lifetime, thanks mainly to John Filson's sketch of his life in a book promoting Kentucky (1786).[5] In addition to being the subject of more or less historical accounts, Boone inspired novelists, especially, James Fenimore Cooper (1789-1851), whose Leatherstocking novels—*The Pioneers* (1823), *The Last of the Mohicans* (1826), *The Prairie* (1827), *The Pathfinder* (1840), and *The Deerslayer* (1841)—were also an American response to Sir Walter Scott's novels about European knights in shinning armor—America's counterpart being Leatherstocking. Gun fights were not only prominent in these five novels but also in other Cooper novels. He was the most important founder of our long tradition of gun-violence fiction. He recycled real gun conflicts from the 1700s and early 1800s into adventure stories, and Americans loved it.[6] Cooper also inspired much of the popular fiction written between the 1840s and 1875.[7] Bellesiles argues from Gerold

Kennedy's biography and source book on William Darby (1981) that Darby's writings from the 1830s were next after Cooper's in importance to elevating the gun to "the cultural icon of the American frontier."[8]

In the 1700s, the Anglo-American frontier extended only to the Mississippi, but the Lewis and Clark Expedition, 1804-06, opened the frontier to the Pacific. Although their expedition experienced only minor Indian conflict and evaded Spanish troops, from the 1840s until 1890 the relentless American push to the Pacific meant there were many conflicts with Indians as well as a war with Mexico. Americans back east took great interest in western events. Highlights before the Civil War were the Texas War of Independence (1836), the U.S.-Mexican War (1846-48), and the California Gold Rush (1849-59). The Texas War of Independence has lasted in national memory (unlike the larger U.S.-Mexican War), and David Crockett and Sam Houston gained legendary status, the former by dieing in battle at the Alamo and the latter by avenging the Alamo. Slotkin's second book of his trilogy, *The Fatal Impact: The Myth of the Frontier in the Age of Industrialization, 1800-1890* (1985), explains that, although Houston was the historically more important figure, the Crockett legend has been more influential, partly because he wrote his own autobiography, and partly because he was a latter-day Daniel Boone figure.[9] Although Slotkin discussed six dime novels based on the U.S.-Mexican War,[10] this war was not assimilated into the myth of a frontier struggle against nature and Indians and never captured the national imagination. In the 1850s, Kit Carson's adventures as a trapper and army guide became fodder for novels.[11] He was another successor to Daniel Boone who was both frontiersman and agent for civilization, and so his story which involved frequent use of guns was absorbed into the national frontier myth.

## War Stories

Another popular purveyor of gun violence in American culture is the war story. Fictional war narratives go back at least to James Fenimore Cooper's *Last of the Mohicans* (1826), set in the French and Indian War. By far, however, the most popular settings for war narratives have been the Civil War and World War II. Of all our wars, the Civil War, in which millions of young men were trained to use guns to shoot their opponents, had the highest number of casualties. Our national anthem, Francis Scott Key's "The Star Spangled Banner" (1814), is a war song from the War of 1812, and the Civil War also stimulated two lasting war songs: "John Brown's Body," and the "Battle Hymn of the Republic;" Julia Ward Howe wrote the latter in 1861 in response to a request for better words to the song's tune. The cultural impact of the war itself was ambiguous. It did end slavery, yet the assassination of Lincoln and the partial failure of Reconstruction prevented acceptance of the war as a great step forward. The best writing about the war by those who experienced it was President Grant's *Personal Memoirs*, which also includes his experience in the U.S.-Mexican War.[12] His memoirs have not had the lasting popularity it deserves, possibly because his presidency was tarnished by the graft of some of his associates. His memoirs do not dwell on the carnage of the war—he was disturbed at the sight of blood and the wounded. Although Edmund Wilson entitled his study of Civil War literature *Patriotic Gore* (1962), none of the writers he discussed evoke the level of bloody gore found in some literature on World Wars I and II and the Vietnam War. Notable later books on wars are: Stephen Crane's *The Red Badge of Courage* (1895), which focused on the Civil War and set the modern pattern of using war as a test of coming of age and manhood; Ernest Hemmingway's *A Farewell to Arms* (1929) about World War I; World War II is the focus of Norman Mailer's *The Naked and the Dead* (1948), Joseph Heller's *Catch-22* (1961), and Kurt Vonnegut's *Slaughterhouse-Five* (1969), all of which exhibit the violence of war while sending a message of its futility and waste. Other fiction and films of lesser merit emphasized war as an adventure.[13] If war stories ever inspire gun violence, it is probably when the books are made into movies. In the Civil War, over half a million men were killed, yet this war is now the focus of hobbyists who read numerous books on its battles and then don costume Civil War uniforms and reenact battles. Hobbyists usually have period guns or modern facsimiles; which are props to enhance a game.

FRANK N. EGERTON

# Western Stories, Illustrations, and Shows

Both the mystic of the gun and the mystique of the West flourished after the Civil War. Both happened because of the mass training of soldiers to handle guns in that war and the continuation of war against Indians, on a smaller scale. Both mystics arose partly because of the American push to conquer the West and partly because writers and artists recorded their versions of what was happening for the benefit of people back east. Of course, Indian Wars were not the only western conflicts. Law enforcement was thin on the land, which led people to carry weapons for protection and for conflict resolution.

During the Civil War, William Quantrill's Raiders on the Kansas frontier included the James brothers, Frank and Jessie,[14] and the Younger brothers, Coleman and Jim, who, after the war, became western train robbers. Their exploits were publicized by authors who were often Confederate sympathizers who admired these outlaws for defying federal authority. Post-war Indian conflicts and frontier cowboys also attracted some authors' attention. After Custer's defeat and death at the Little Big Horn in July 1876, his friend Frederick Whittaker published *A Complete Life of George A. Custer* (1876), turning his life into a Horatio Alger type saga.[15] The far west continued to endure gun fights for the rest of the century, and these fights inspired both histories and fiction. Popular dime novels between 1877 and 1883 included Edward Wheeler's stories of "Deadwood Dick." These stories were unusual in having class conflict as a theme, with Deadwood Dick leading a western miners' union against management and government. He defied the law and got away with it.[16] Critics objected and these novels ceased publication.[17] There were also ostensibly true western outlaw stories. For example, Pat F. Garrett killed Billy the Kid in 1881 and wrote his biography in 1882, claiming to correct errors of earlier biographies, while making fresh errors of his own. Also in 1882 Frank Triplett created a legend with his *Life, Times and Treacherous Death of Jesse James*.[18] Authors of dime novels achieved no literary acclaim, but sold lots of adventure stories with gun fights.[19] Don Russell's biography of Buffalo Bill Cody lists by title nine pages of dime novels written about Cody.[20] Authors of statue such as Mark Twain and Bret Harte also wrote about the wild west.

Fig. 12. Original cover of Pat F. Garrett's An Authentic Life of Billy the Kid (1882).

Historian Richard White complained that "Western myth has preempted history in explaining conflict in the West," and Panela Hass agreed.[21] In fiction, such conflicts tend to be either cowboys versus Indians or two White men having a spontaneous gun duel. The reality was that government was often complicit in or passive about oppression of Indians, Hispanics, Chinese, and Japanese, and that other conflicts were usually between classes or interest groups.

Nevertheless, "Buffalo" Bill Cody (1846-1917) was a real western pioneer who replaced Daniel Boone, David Crockett, and Kit Carson as mythic hero of the frontier in the later 1800s. His own early life was filled with dramatic adventures. He had been a cowboy, Pony Express rider, professional hunter, Civil War soldier, Army scout in Indian country (winning a Medal of Honor), hunting guide, and rancher. Furthermore, guns had been part of his experience on the frontier since he was eleven years old.[22] Wild west shows began with George Catlin's Indian Gallery in 1837 and continued with P.T. Barnum in 1843, and others tried their hand at it from time to time.[23] Edward Judson (pen name "Ned Buntline") met Cody at Fort Sedgwick, CO and was impressed enough to write a novel about him: *Buffalo Bill, the King of Border Men* (1869). He followed it with a serial that ran in the *New York Weekly* entitled "Buffalo Bill's Last Victory." In 1872 Judson persuaded Cody to play himself in a theatrical drama, *The Scouts of the Prairie*, which involved hunting stories and Indian fights and was a hit. In 1882 Cody merged his theatrical experience with the tradition of outdoor western shows and created his immensely successful Wild West show. Although Annie Oakley (borrn Phoebe Ann Mosey, 1860-1926), who joined the show, was a better standing shot, Cody was the champion shooter from a running horse. (Oakley's biography has been written several times,[24] and she is the focus of Irving Berlin's musical, *Annie Get Your Gun* (on stage, 1946, movie, 1950). During the 1800s, only James Fenimore Cooper exerted an influence comparable to Cody's in associating guns with entertainment. And, like Cooper's, Cody's fare was good clean family fun; bring the kids, or Queen Victoria. All those dime novels written about Cody, mentioned above, undoubtedly helped gain and maintain his celebrity status.

Theodore Roosevelt was so enthusiastic about the West that he decided to write a sweeping work on *The Winning of the West* from the Atlantic to the Pacific, and published four volumes, covering from Jamestown to the Lewis and Clark expedition (1804-06), and was mainly devoted to the winning of Kentucky and Ohio by civilization from what he considered to be not-so-noble savages.[25]

The first significant western novel was by a prominent literary figure, Owen Wister, who had, like his friend Roosevelt, gone west as a young man to recover from stress and fell in love with the country.[26] He published collections of his stories on the West before writing *The Virginian: A Horseman of the Plains* (1902), that was an immediate best seller and sold more than 1.5 million copies by 1938. The novel was well illustrated with ten paintings by Frederic Remington and forty-one drawings by Charles M.

Fig. 13. An earlier Remington drawing, of the Wham stagecoach robbery of 1892, drawn from a photograph by Wister of the robbery site, for a story by Wister, "A Pilgrim on the Gila."[27]

Russell, and was dedicated to Roosevelt. The novel was turned into a play, and then in 1929 into a movie. It contained the ingredients of many later imitators: a strong, virtuous cowboy who falls in love with a new school teacher but who has to deal with a cattle rustler before they can marry. When the Virginian and the cattle rustler, Trampas, meet, they both draw their revolvers and fire, but the Virginian is a better shot and kills Trampas.[28] Three good friends—Wister, Remington, and Roosevelt—made very large contributions to developing the mystic of the West. None were fixated on guns, but guns were important accessories in their creations. Charles M. Russell was not part of their "Eastern establishment" (born close to St. Louis), but his Western art was as important as Remington's and portrayed a similar West. Wister transmuted the southern code of the duel into the code of the West, but there was a difference.[30] Western shootouts were spontaneous, and there were no formal seconds to offer the protagonists their weapons. Wister's plot formula for westerns—a strong peaceful man knows how to use violence when threatened by evil—later spread to other violent fiction. The consumer gets to enjoy the violence while feeling that virtue is triumphant. The "western" industry in 1958 produced 10.76% of American fiction and at least 54 films, and in 1959 eight of the top ten shows on television were westerns.[31]

Besides the substantial market for such fiction, there was a large market for true stories about western conflicts involving guns. James D. Horan was one of the authors who catered to this market. He wrote at least 17 books about American conflicts, six of them focused on the western frontier. His *Desperate Men: Revelations from the Sealed Pinkerton Files* appeared in 1949, and an enlarged illustrated edition of 1962 contained fifty stories. Former police commissioner Carl W. Breihan published his much briefer, also illustrated, *Great Gunfighters of the West* in 1962, with a revised and expanded edition in 1977. Harry S. Drago, a popular author of books on the West, published his illustrated *Road Agents and Train Robbers: Half a Century of Western Banditry* in 1973. Some stories from these books later migrated from print to film. The editors of Time-Life Books published a series of well-illustrated volumes on the Old West, one of which is *The Gunfighters*, by Paul Trachtman (1974), with a bibliography of still other books on the subject.[32] Drago and Trachtman's books appeared after the classic western movies were no longer being made. Book catalogs from several western university presses show there is still a good market for books on western conflicts involving guns.

## Urban Stories

Although industrial worker productivity increased steadily, worker benefits increased slowly and were wiped out during economic depressions. Urban crime became a lasting problem, and fighting it became a theme of dime novels. Edgar Allen Poe created classic detective stories in "The Mystery of Marie Roget" (1841), "The Purloined Letter" (1842), and "The Murders of Rue Morgue" (1843).[33] Others soon followed his example. Slotkin argues that the origin of this genre is more complex than stories by Poe.[34] Allen Pinkerton, founder of a detective agency, established the stock formula for detective stories in 1875 by publishing his version of conflicts in which his men had been engaged.[35] The classical formula for detective stories includes situation, setting, characters and their relationships, and pattern of action. The characters include four main roles—victim, criminal, detective, and those threatened by the crime—and the pattern of action has six phases. The detective story became popular when *The New York Weekly* published "The Old Detective's Pupil; or, The Mysterious Crime of

Madison Square" in 1886. Nick Carter, its protagonist, became an industry in 1891 when the Nick Carter Detective Library began. American detective stories were more violent than the famous Sherlock Holmes stories, which English physician Arthur Conan Doyle began publishing in 1887. Doyle began his stories after a murder was committed, and Holmes reported his conclusions to the police. In Nick Carter stories and later American detective stories, the detective carried a gun and violence continued after the detective began investigating. New levels of violence were portrayed in the "hard boiled detective tales" of Dashiell Hammett, Raymond Chandler, Ross Macdonald, and Mickey Spillane during the 1930s-50s.[36] The chief distinctions between the classical and hard-boiled stories is that in the latter, the city is more dangerous, the detective encounters more violence, and he becomes more directly involved in resolving the situation:[37]

> Where the classical detective's role was to use his superior intellect and psychological insight to reveal the hidden guilt that the police seem unable to discover, the hard-boiled detective metes out the just punishment that the law is too mechanical, unwieldy, or corrupt to achieve.

Hard-boiled detective stories eclipsed the classical stories, except for the persisting classical Agatha Christie stories; she was English and her crime novels do not emphasize guns.

## Hunting Stories

Although hunting is, or was, a popular sport, the market for hunting stories is largely confined to hunters. The editors of a book on William Faulkner's story, "The Bear" (1942), assert that "it is one of the great hunting stories in the English language."[38] But what are the other great hunting stories? Hemingway's "Short Happy Life of Francis Macomber." is about a woman who got bored with her husband and "accidentally" killed him on their hunting trip. Besides "The Bear," the only American hunting stories that appear to have attracted a significantly broader audience than hunters were by Theodore Roosevelt, who was a special case. He was already a prominent politician when he published *Hunting Trip of a Ranchman*

(1885), and he became progressively more prominent as he published others until 1914. In the National Edition of his works (20 vols., 1926), the first five volumes contain his nature writings, most of which are about hunting. There is plenty of hunting and killing of animals in Faulkner's "The Bear," but it is primarily a story about coming of age; the hunt is a test of manhood. The majority of Americans accept hunting, but the only successful hunting film is "Bambi," which is anti-hunting. Americans might enjoy reading stories or watching movies about people getting shot, but not about animals getting shot. In that respect, Americans differ from ancient Romans, who enjoyed watching animals being killed as much as they enjoyed watching gladiators or other people being killed in an arena. A passionate few Americans supported dog fights or cock fights when they were legal. Hunting stories popularize guns but seem unlikely to inspire gun violence, though substantial numbers of hunting guns are used to intentionally shoot persons. It seems likely that the shooters usually were owners of the guns.

## Gun Books and Magazines

There is a vast industry that cranks out gun books and magazines. There are far too many such publications to mention here, and I limit this account to those at hand. It is a rather random sample which I collected at public library sales in Kenosha and Racine or bought from mail catalogs of remaindered books. My criteria for purchase was that the books be cheap. I got them all for pennies-on-the-dollar of their original prices. These books can be generally divided into two categories: those that discuss guns and those that discuss gunmen.

Yet, some books discuss both. One example is Robert Elman's *Fired in Anger* (1962); it contains lots of pictures of gunmen and even more pictures of guns. The latter pictures illustrate guns used by gunmen discussed. Some gunmen were heroes, others villains. Elman also included pictures of three assassinations—presidents Lincoln, Garfield, and McKinley. Carl Breihan published *Great Gunfighters of the West* in 1962, though my copy is the revised and expanded 1977 edition, in paperback (price new, $1.50). It included biographical sketches of nine gunslingers, both heroes and villains, with photographs of eight of them and guns they used. A third book that discusses both guns and gunmen is George Virgines' *Saga of the Colt Six-Shooter and the Famous Men Who Used It* (1969). It is not an official history of the Colt Patent Firearms Manufacturing Company, but members of that company assisted Virgines in any ways they could. The photographs of famous gunmen concluded with one of Virgines dressed in western gear, demonstrating the two-gun butterfly spin. Perhaps that feat qualified him to add his photograph to those of the famous men he discussed.

James Horan's *Desperate Men: Revelations from the Sealed Pinkerton Files* (1949, enlarge ed., 1962) contains portraits of both the desperados and law men. Robert Pinkerton II decided to open the detective agency's files to Horan to counter the impressions given by movies, TV shows, books, and magazines that the Jameses, Youngers, and other western bandits were Robin Hoods. Paul Wellman's *Dynasty of Western Outlaws* (1961) has drawings of his rogues gallery in the end papers of his book, a map of places discussed, and a synopsis of what happened at each place, from Columbia, Kentucky to Spearville, Kansas; action drawings decorate the beginning of chapters. Wellman also diagramed the relationships between his gangs of rogues. By far, the best illustrated gunfighter book is by Paul Trachtman, *The Gunfighters* (1974, revised 1977), as it is part of a Time-Life Books set on The Old West. It also has some color illustrations and the best bibliography. The message in these books is that life on the western frontier was precarious because the country was enormous and law enforcement was quite limited.

Books on guns lack a social context; the readers hopefully are responsible citizens. W. H. B. Smith first published his *Book of Pistols and Revolvers* in 1946. My 832-page copy is of the seventh edition, updated by Joseph E. Smith (1968). It contains much technical information on and photographs of all handguns on the market, which was useful for dealers, Parker Ackley was a gunsmith in Utah who wrote a handy *Home Gun Care and Repair* (1969), for anyone brave enough to repair his own gun. Larry Koller's *The Golden Guide to Guns* (1961, updated 1974) is an attractive handbook with flexible cover and many color illustrations of animals and of guns that sold for $2.95 in 1974. The title does not say so, but it is limited to civilian guns. George Nonte's *Firearms Encyclopedia* (1973) is slightly technical, but nevertheless unlikely to scare off gun aficionados. It is well illustrated in black and white, or occasionally in brown in white; an adequate reference work. Major Frederick Myatt compiled *An Illustrated Guide to Rifles and Automatic Weapons* (1981), which is limited to military weapons, though the title does not say so. It was helpful to international arms dealers for showing revolutionary quartermasters what they could buy to arm their rebels. A good number of long-established gun manufacturers have funded company histories. The one I own is a lavish *Winchester: an American Legend*, by R. L. Wilson, who had earlier written other books on Winchester guns and Colt guns. Winchester's rather complex beginning dates back to 1849. Aside from gun magazines (including NRA's *American Rifleman*), there are two American gun annuals published. The *Gun Digest* published in 1966 a *Gun Digest Treasury*, edited by John Amber, with "the best from twenty years," since its founding in 1946. It contains both technical and human interest stories, beginning with an eight-page illustrated article on "The Guns of Lewis and Clark." The *Shooter's Bible* claims to be the "World's Standard Firearms Reference Book. My copy is the 88th one, for 1997. It begins with nine articles in 76 pages, followed by 400 pages on handguns, rifles, shotguns, blackpowder, sights and scopes, ammunition, and ballistics, and ends with twenty pages of references, which includes a "Directory of Manufacturers and Suppliers."

## Newspapers, Magazines, and Radio

Newspapers began in America in 1689, 1690, or 1704, depending on one's definition of a newspaper. Until the 1900s they carried few or no illustrations, had limited circulation, and probably incited few if any copy-cat crimes. Their main early relevance for gun violence was probably in gun advertisements. The earliest ads in the 1700s were mere notices that a given establishment sold and/or repaired guns. Later, gunsmiths advertised their particular guns. We have already seen, for example, Jonathan Browning advertised his guns in the Kanesville, Iowa *Frontier Guardian* on September 19, 1849;[39] he was unlikely the first gunsmith to advertise his own guns. As important as newspapers were for selling guns, Magazines and mail-order catalogs were also important for selling guns. Magazines were additionally important for publishing stories about gun usage. The first two American magazines began in Philadelphia in 1741, one of them published by Benjamin Franklin. Most early magazines had short life spans (Franklin's magazine lasted six months and his rival's three months). The first magazines to emphasize guns were hunting magazines, the first in America being the *American Turf Register and Sporting Magazine*, started in 1829. Several others also appeared before the Civil War, but all were war casualties. In 1872 *Forest and Stream* began and lasted into the 1890s. In 1895 *Northwestern Field and Stream* began and the next year dropped *Northwestern* from its title. *Field and Stream* gun advertisements were not confined to hunting guns, as seen in Fig. 6.8. Now there are numerous gun magazines, the most prominent being *American Rifleman* and *Guns and Ammo*. The early large mail-order catalog companies were Montgomery Ward, founded in 1872 and Sears Roebuck, founded in 1895. Both were greatly helped by the start of rural free delivery in the 1890s and the parcel post system in 1913. The 1908 *Sears Roebuck Catalog* devoted 33 pages to guns, 4.5 pages to ammunition, and 2.5 pages to gun accessories. Currently, a sporting goods company, Gander Mountain, has frequent glossy flyers or folded advertising sheets inserted into my local newspaper which advertise both long guns and handguns.

America's first commercial radio station began broadcasting in 1920, and the first national network was in 1926. Radio programs eventually included both news reports and drama, both of which discussed gun violence. The possibility that such broadcasts might have incited copycat violence seems much less likely than the displays of gun violence in movies and in television programs. I grew up listening to a serialized western, "The Lone Ranger," and to Sam Spade detective stories without thinking about even playing such roles. (But, growing up during World War II, my friends and I did use toy guns to play at being soldiers.) The eclipse of radio drama and news began in the 1950s and was accomplished during the 1960s. Both radio and television are important venues for advertising commercial products, but neither is being used to advertise guns.

# Movies, Television, DVDs and the Internet

There are three main genres of American violent movies: westerns, gangster films, and war films.[40] In 1903, a year after Wister's western novel, Edwin S. Porter, chief of Edison's Manhattan studio, created the first fictional movie, a western, *The Great Train Robbery*, which lasted eleven minutes and ended with a massacre.[41] It was an immediate success and remained the most successful film of any kind for twelve years. It was quickly imitated by the Edison Company, which produced *The Great Bank Robbery*, *The Bold Bank Robbery*, *The Little Train Robbery*, and *The Hold-Up of the Rocky Mountain Express*.[42] And that was just a start. No wonder Slotkin entitled the third volume of his trilogy *Gunfighter Nation: The Myth of the Frontier in Twentieth-Century America* (1992). Most of its 850 pages are devoted to exploring violent movies and television shows, 1903-73, because books and magazines became secondary sources of violent entertainment during that period. Buffalo Bill Cody made the first docudrama in 1911, on the Wounded Knee massacre (1890). He hired Oglala Indians from Pine Ridge who had survived the massacre, and he persuaded the War Department to provide 11,000 troops for the most ambitious movie yet produced. By 1911 he had had many years experience staging pretend battles between Whites and Indians in his Wild West show, including dramatizations of Wounded Knee.

During the 1920s public agitation over movie content and a push for censorship convinced Hollywood producers and directors to establish a voluntary Production Code in 1930 to guide the depictions of guns and violence. However, Hollywood also released *Little Caesar* (1930), *The Public Enemy* (1931), and *Scarface* (1932), all showing tommy-gun murders, which revived public protest. Therefore, in 1934 Hollywood created the Production Code Administration to monitor films before release.[43] In 1966, Hollywood revised its Production Code and in 1968 instituted a Rating Administration to assign to each film a rating of G, M, R, or X—supposedly to reflect changing societal standards,[44] which really meant making films as violent as TV dramas. In 1967, two violent films appeared, *In Cold Blood* and *Bonnie and Clyde*, which under previous guidelines would have had to be modified before release.

Classical western stories, novels, movies, and TV dramas remained an important American "industry" until the 1970s, and reruns of western movies and TV dramas continue down to the present on TV and DVDs. (Neo-western movies lack the same level of gunplay found in classical westerns; two notable examples released in 2006 are *Brokeback Mountain* and *The Three Burials of Melquiades Estrada*.) The end of classic westerns was not due to a loss of interest by producers and directors but by some blend of cultural factors. Violent TV westerns were attacked in Chicago in 1949 and those complaints have continued ever since.[45] The complaints did not kill TV showings of violent westerns, though they did lead to a reduction in the level of TV violence. The demise of westerns is attributed to several cultural developments in the 1970s:[46] real Vietnam War violence was on TV nightly, and this made imaginary violence seem obscene; President Nixon's scandals "undermined the political solemnity inherent in the Western;" the feminist movement discredited the Western's machismo theme; and the ineffective U.S. response to global strife undermined the myth of U.S. invincibility. Or perhaps the decline of the Western "reflects our growing uncertainty about American uniqueness and about the special place of the West in establishing that uniqueness."[47] I suspect that the real civil rights struggle may also have made the imaginary conflicts of western white men seem rather small scale. The demise of the western would be a sign of good judgment if only its place in entertainment were taken by less violent alternatives. However, one student of gangster films thinks westerns faded because gangster movies have greater fire power and greater relevance to modern life.[48] For a while, though, before westerns faded, studios managed to recycle stories from one genre to the other, as Warner Brothers did when it used the same plot in a gangster film, *High Sierra* (1941), a western, *Colorado Territory* (1949), and then again in a gangster film in CinemaScope, *I Died a Thousand Times* (1955). This recycling was possible because both genres are about the "American odyssey."[49]

Although there had been post-Civil War gangs of veterans, such as the James brothers and the Younger gang, the classic gangster film was in response to Prohibition and the Depression. Both westerns and gangster films involve violence and guns, but these genres differ in that westerns focus on strong heroes who used guns reluctantly, to uphold the law, while the protagonists of gangster films are the bad guys. However, they are usually portrayed so sympathetically that the audience sympathizes with them rather than with the stogy law men. This slant arose when gangsters were seen as performing a service many people wanted—selling illicit alcohol during Prohibition and posing as Robin Hoods when they robbed banks during the Depression. The lasting success of gangster films may be due to feelings of hostility among the films' audiences—if members of the audience feel that society is too restrictive or has dealt unfairly with them. Another gangster film authority, Shadoian, thinks that when World War II replaced the Depression, gangsters were forgiven, because their brutal skills suddenly became social assets.[50] This was literally true when the U.S. Government turned to famous Mafia members for advice before the invasion of Sicily and Italy. Perhaps this was something of an excuse for Shadoian, who brushed aside social critics in favor of a functional analysis of gangster films:[51]

> The gangster is a paradigm of the American dream. The gangster film is a vehicle that responds to our wish to have our dreams made visible to us in a form that retains their dreamlike qualities, but contains a narrative that is the living dream of its hero who makes it happen, actualizes it. One can never be entirely certain about the precise analogies between films and dreams, but the condition of presence-in-absence is common to them both. It is our psyche that we watch—displaced, dislocated, alien yet familiar. Our involvement with the gangster rests on our identification with him as the archetypal American dreamer whose actions and behavior involve a living out of the dream common to most everyone who exists in the particular configurations and contradictions of American society, a dream in conflict with the society.

Shadoian's speculative claim makes no sense to me, but two reputable university presses published it.[52]

Director Aric Avelino's film, *American Gun* (2006) deserves credit for an honest, non-sensational portrayal of aspects of our gun dilemma in three different stories. The film moves continuously from one story to another, and one may wonder if these stories will ever connect. They do not. The only message I can see in the film is: here is our problem; think about it.

Documentary films have not been prominent influences on American culture, but two quasi-documentaries are noteworthy. The movie made from Truman Capote's book, *In Cold Blood* (book 1966, film 1967), could be called a docudrama (though the term was coined later). Michael Moore's film, *Bowling for Columbine* (2002) was widely seen and discussed; it is part documentary and part social criticism. Many of the recent movies and TV programs are available on DVDs, and one can play such as often as one wishes. Four television authorities in 1999 discussed violence on TV and public and Congressional concern for its detrimental effects on viewers, especially children.[53] Their articles can be summarized: pressure from public, government, and non-governmental organizations on TV producers to limit violence in programs has led to reluctant voluntary production of rating systems and addition of v-chips to enable parents to block programs from their children's viewing, and to scheduling violent programs after children's bedtime. TV producers cherish violence, because it attracts viewers, and if viewing violence on TV leads some viewers to copycat behavior, that is not the responsibility of the TV industry.[54]

The internet is now a significant competitor of newspapers and even of television in the form of both the world wide web and email. Modern terrorists remind us that this new communications technology can be used to encourage violence. There are ample choices if one Googles "guns" or "gun games," and anti-abortion web sites apparently inspired some anti-abortion assassinations.[55] Anyone seeking violent inspiration on the web can find it.

## Video Games and Gangstra Rap

While westerns faded from the screens in the 1970s, video games were becoming popular. At first, they were not violent, but by the late 1970s some of them were, and by 1998 nearly 80% had aggression or violence as a game objective.[56] Concerns over the violence had led to congressional hearings in 1994, which resulted in development of an industry rating system to warn parents about violent video games.[57] The ineffectiveness of the system is illustrated by Eric Harris and Dylan Klebold, who were obsessed by violent video games; their favorite was *Doom*.[58] On April 20, 1999 they massacred their classmates at Columbine High School in Littleton, Colorado. The most notorious video game, published by Traffic Games, is entitled *Grand*

*Theft Auto,* in which one can shoot someone and take his car. In November 2004, around the forty-first anniversary of the assassination of President Kennedy, Traffic Games released a new game, *JFK: Reloaded,* in which the player can vicariously try his luck at killing the president.[59] In April 2005, a downloadable game was published: "Super Columbine Massacre RPG!"[60] The U.S. Army uses video games to overcome soldiers' inhibition to shoot someone.[61] On 28 June 11, the U.S. Supreme Court, in a 7-2 vote, struck down a California law banning the sale of violent video games to minors. Seven justices felt that there was not enough evidence of the harmful effects of such games on children. Conservative columnist Cal Thomas asked: "Why does the state consider it injurious for minors to take alcohol into their stomachs and nicotine into their lungs, but not harmful for them to absorb the most violent images into their minds?" Thomas wondered if the justices knew that games like *Mortal Kombat* allowed children "to emulate school shooting sprees or virtually carry out assassinations, decapitations, rape, torture and ever other unimaginable horror one human being can inflict upon another."[62]

Hip hop was invented in the 1970s in South Bronx to counteract Black gang violence. However, by 1986 this led to gangstra rap, which emphasized violence and guns. Rapper KRS-One's song, "My 9-mm Goes Bang," is about a drug dealer who shoots his rivals. KRS-One and Scott La Rock posed on the album cover with guns, bullet belts, and grenades. In 1988 KRS-One commented in *Spin* magazine that "This violence, it's everday to the kid in the ghetto. No big deal."[63] But it was a big deal to Delores Tucker, chair of the National Political Congress of Black Women, who told a congressional panel in 1994 that "the record industry is out of control. If it has to be regulated, so be it."[64] Time Warner Inc. divested its shares in Interscope Records, which produced many gangstra rap albums. Yet, no effective action was taken before leading gangstra rappers Tupac Shakur (1996) and Biggie Smalls (1997) were shot dead.[65] Two years before his murder, on November 30, 1994, Tupac Shakur had been shot five times during a robbery in New York. the CEO of Death Row Records, Gangstra rap CEO Marion "Suge" Knight, was sent to prison (1996) for engaging in the kind of violence gangstra rap describes.[66] In 2005, Irv "Gotti" Lorenzo, CEO of a hip hop recording company, Murder Inc., was arrested by the FBI for laundering more than $1 million in drug profits.[67] 50 Cent Jackson made a film about his rise from gangbanger to stardom, *Get Rich or Die Tryin*, that was released in 2005. In November, he said he was saddened to hear that Shelton Flowers was shot three times after seeing his movie, "But you know, these weren't kids. This was a 30-year old man who had a dispute with three other guys."[68] *Milwaukee Journal Sentinel* columnist Eugene Kane urged (13 Nov 05) all Wisconsin legislators who thought a concealed carry gun bill should become law to see 50 Cent Jackson's film. At first, gangstra rap's only social message was: this is how it is in the Black ghetto—no moral drawn. However, in June 2006, when Ice Cube—one of the founders of gangstra rap—released his first album in six years, it contained a more explicit message: this is how it should be. After all these shootings, he had a change of heart.[69]

When national Black leader Rev. Al Sharpton addressed the National Association of Black Journalists in summer 2006, he made national headlines by urging Black youths to turn their back on the culture gangstra rap portrays and instead to become active in politics.[70] Disillusioned hip-hop fan Lonnae O'Neal Parker goes even further by condemning hip-hop, the source of gangstra rap, as now having a trend toward "more violence, more misogyny, more materialism" than when she was young.[71]

## Political Myths Old and New

America's fascination with frontier violence has been catered to not only in fiction but also in politics. Three Republican presidents—Theodore Roosevelt, Ronald Reagan, and George W. Bush—cultivated the image of themselves as cowboys on western ranches, and all three indulged in imperialistic conflicts. By the time of Reagan and George W. Bush, the frontier myth was defunct as a classical film genre, but no matter. It worked for Reagan but backfired for Bush. Slotkin suggests that we construct a broader national myth:[72]

> There is no reason why a myth of national solidarity and progress should not be claimed and used by Americans who envision the nation as polyglot, multicultural, and egalitarian, and whose concept of "progress" is not defined by the imperatives of the commercial corporation or the preferences of a managerial or proprietary elite.

In other words, let us get beyond being manipulated by an anti-humane tradition.

## Satire

The alternative to simulated gratuitous violence as entertainment is non-violent entertainment, of which plenty is available. The trick is to convince those who want violence in their entertainment to choose an alternative. One possibility, that is little developed in America, is satire. As far as the gun culture is concerned, the only poetic example of satire known to me is Tom Lehrer's "Hunting Song" (1952):

I always will remember,
Twas a year ago November,
I went out to hunt some deer
On a morning bright and clear.
I went and shot the maximum the game laws would allow
Two game wardens, seven hunters, and a cow.

Surely Lars von Trier's *Dogville* (2003) is satire, but with what message? A sweet young lady escapes from her city gangster family to live with apparently wholesome small-town Americans, only to discover they are easily corrupted when they learn there is a reward for her return. In the end, disillusioned, she asks her father to shoot them all with his machine gun.

Is Jean Shepherd's *A Christmas Story* (2003) satire? Not at first glance—just a comedy to read or watch on video at the Christmas season. However, it can also be seen as a gentle spoof of overly cautious or overly liberal parents who think Red Ryder BB guns are too dangerous for boys to own. Whether satire or not, it provides free publicity for BB guns as possible Christmas gifts for boys.

A Milwaukee columnist, Joel McNally, writes satirical comic commentaries that are published weekly in Wisconsin newspapers. Once a year he targets deer hunters, and occasionally he writes a column on other gun issues. The NRA provides ample ammunition for satire, but aside from McNally, the only creative artists who seem to use it are political cartoonists. After Democratic Governor Jim Doyle vetoed a concealed gun carry bill passed by a Republican legislature, the NRA in early 2004 attempted to intimidate Democratic legislators into helping provide the two-thirds majority needed to over-ride his veto. McNally wrote a column entitled "The Pop-Guns of the NRA," in which he pointed out that only 27% of Wisconsin residents favored the bill and concluded:[73]

> Let the NRA campaign against every Democrat who voted against concealed carry. When the overwhelming majority that opposes concealed carry re-elects those politicians, the bullies of the NRA finally would be revealed for what they are—posturing pipsqueaks with pop-guns.

McNally's derision seems rather sedate compared to the contempt portrayed in Carlson's political cartoon, "Override," published in the *Milwaukee Journal Sentinel*. (The Democrats held firm, supporting their governor.)

## Violent Cultural Products Versus Violent Behavior

That our popular culture is violence ridden is obvious. But does it stimulate violent behavior? Those who produce violence-laden entertainment usually deny a connection and often point to the prevalence of guns as the real cause, even though their products are heavily dependent on simulated gun violence. While their products may provide harmless thrills for many, they may also provide inspiration for a very few people to commit violent acts—very often with guns. If this latter possibly is real, then our cultural products with imaginary gun violence are far from harmless. Two ways in which researchers have determined such influences are illustrated by the researches of Leonard Eron and of Loren Coleman. Eron interviewed 835 third graders in a New York county and found a correlation between the number of violent TV programs watched and degree of aggressive behavior at school. He re-interviewed them again in 1971 and 1980 and found those who were aggressive third graders continued to have behavioral problems as they grew up.[74] Coleman sought out examples of violent crimes that were copycat crimes of stories real or fictional told on TV or in films; his work is discussed below.

The main consumers of TV violence are males aged 18-34, followed by females aged 18-34. This audience is highly valued by advertisers, which is why there are so many programs depicting violence.[75] This is the same age group that causes most violence in society. There is an extensive literature on the influence of media violence on children, which finds that children exposed to media violence show more aggression than children without such exposure.[76] What about teenagers and adults? Florida State University Professor of Communications W. James Potter, who researches media violence, cautiously concludes that "when violence permeates the media year after year...the mean of society is likely to move gradually in the antisocial direction."[77] Criminologist Nicole Rafter, who teaches "Crime Films and Society" at Northeastern University, argues that "so far as we know at the moment, movies do not cause crime; their power to influence behavior is apparently limited to nudging crime-prone individuals in directions they are already headed."[78] But more recently, social worker Loren Coleman has synthesized much evidence that violent entertainment does indeed encourage violent behavior in *The Copycat Effect: How the Media and Popular Culture Trigger the Mayhem in Tomorrow's Headlines* (2004). His book—which is not limited to influences on children— deserves our attention, and some of its arguments are summarized here.

In 1774, Johann Wolfgang Goethe, Germany's foremost author, published a novella, *The Sorrows of Young Werther*, about a young man who fell in love with a young woman already engaged to another man. Werther finally decided that he did not want to live without her and shot himself. The book became a best seller, and so many young men followed this fictional example with real suicides that the book was banned in Germany, Denmark, and Italy.[79] In 1888, after a series of murders and mutilations of London prostitutes, newspapers dubbed the unknown killer "Jack the Ripper." Although a contemporary researcher, Jean-Gabriel de Tarde, pointed out that the newspaper stories seemed to have a "suggestive effect" of inspiring rape-murders beyond the London area, that did not inhibit J.F. Brewer from publishing a contemporary Jack-the-Ripper novel, *The Curse of Mitre Square*, nor did it prevent 38 Jack the Ripper movies and TV programs, 1917-2001. Some of this publicity apparently inspired truck driver Peter Sutcliffe to become the "Yorkshire Ripper," who stabbed and mutilated 20 women, 1975-81, before being apprehended.[80] Copycat suicides in the late 1700s and copycat murders in the late 1800s in Europe were insufficient warnings to inhibit the pervasive dissemination in America during the 1900s of stories, true and fictional, about gun violence. After all, Japanese teenage boys play video games as violent as those American teenage boys play, but this does not lead to gun violence in Japan (where there are very few private guns). Furthermore, the American experience of newspapers and television stations was that "happy stories don't sell," and therefore, "if it bleeds, it leads."[81]

In 1962 Ford Clark published a novel, *Open Square*, about a psychotic student who climbed a tower at a Midwestern university and shot students and faculty below with a high-powered rifle. There are striking similarities between the book's plot and details with the real massacre of people in Austin from the University of Texas Tower on August 1, 1966 by Charles J. Whitman. We do not know whether Whitman read the novel, but the similarities were itemized in the *Austin American-Statesman* on August 5, and an anonymous caller threatened the author's life if he ever came from Iowa to Texas.[82] The fact that this massacre was possibly a copycat crime did not stop Hollywood from making the movie *The Deadly Tower* (1975), though the University of Texas would not rent its tower for use in it (the producers rented the Louisiana State Capitol instead). There were also two songs written about Whitman and his massacre. Although Mark James Essex's murder of ten and wounding of thirteen from the roof of a New Orleans Howard Johnson's Motor Lodge on December 31, 1972 was triggered by the deaths of two Black students in a shootout with deputies at Southern University, memory of publicity about Whitman's massacre may also have influenced Essex.[83]

Release of the Vietnam War film, *The Deer Hunter* (12 Dec. 78) inspired scores of suicides.[84]

Did Oliver Stone's *Natural Born Killers* (1995) start out as satire, as he claimed? If so, it was too similar to the genre he satirized to be taken as satire. It became a film appreciated by devotees of violence.[85] It inspired Benjamin Darras, 18, and Sarah Edmondson, 19, to go on a killing spree. One victim was Bill Savage, friend of lawyer-author John Grisham, who characterized Stone's film as "a horrific movie that glamorized casual mayhem and bloodlust." Grisham suggested that if families of victims sue the directors and distributors of such films as defective products, it would motivate them to choose more responsible subjects for films. A suit was mounted but was thrown out of court in March 2001. Stone noted a similarity between his film and Stanley Kubrick's *A Clockwork Orange* (1971), which Kubrick pulled from distribution after copycat killings (Stone disapproved of pulling it).

A rash of post office shootings (eventually called "going postal") across America, 1983-98, is a special case. Although there is obviously a copycat effect here, that is not the whole story. During that period there were many Vietnam veterans who had U.S. Postal Service jobs, either as supervisors or as workers, and both their military training with guns and the stress of their former military service may have influenced some of their behavior. Furthermore, the media influence was news reporting, not literary recreations.[86] However, in 2003 the Fox network promoted a coming episode of *Mad TV* about two postal workers waving guns and customers cowering in fear. The U.S. Postal Service responded on December 10, saying this program would be offensive and insulting, and it asked its 750,000 workers to complain to the Fox Entertainment Group. Fox responded that *Mad TV* was "an equal opportunity offender."[87] Although the U.S. Postal Service announced in 1998 that it had improved screening of employees and increased post office security, the carnage continues. On January 30, 2006 former postal worker Jennifer Sanmarco, on medical leave for psychiatric problems, returned to a mail-processing center in Coleta, California and shot dead six workers and herself.[88]

The post office shootings may well have inspired other workplace shootings in the late 1980s and 1990s at brokerage firms, warehouses, assembly lines, and construction places. Most shooters were suicidal and either killed themselves or were killed by police. When Joseph Wesbecker shot to death seven fellow workers and then himself on September 14, 1989, he left behind at home a *Newsweek* article (17 Jan. 89) about Patrick Purdy's use of an AK-47 assault rifle to kill five students (and wounding 35, plus a teacher) at a Stockton, California school and then killed himself. Wesbecker followed Purdy's example and bought an AK-47 to use in his massacre.[89] The early school massacres by Purdy and other outsiders (non-students) seem to have been inspired by Laurie Wasserman Dann's school shootings at Winnetka, Illinois on May 20, 1988.[90] George Hennard, in 1991, watched a video about James Huberty killing 21 people at a California

McDonald's in 1984 before he drove his truck into Luby's Cafeteria in Killen, Texas and killed 23 and wounded 20 before killing himself.[91] Coleman describes many other examples of workplace copycat murders and suicides. Although these criminals acted out their own psychoses, earlier examples inspired and guided them.

Timothy McVeigh's bombing of the Murrah Federal Building in Oklahoma City in 1995 was not a gun crime, but it deserves mention here because it was inspired by a novel, *The Turner Diaries* (1978), by Nazi William Pierce, under pseudonym Andrew Macdonald (Levitas 2002:291).

A series of insider school shootings (by students) seen to have been inspired initially by Stephen King's novel, *Rage* (1977), about a student shooting a teacher. King's audience, as he admitted, is primarily adolescent.[92] Coleman describes four examples of real student shootings at schools, 1982-1996.[93] Finally, in 1999 King asked his publisher to recall the copies from stores and stop selling it. He said he regretted writing it, but that was a little late—school copycat killings continued, reaching a climax on April 20, 1999, when Eric Harris and Dylan Klebold at Columbine High School killed 12 students and a teacher and wounded 23 others before killing themselves.[94] In addition to King's novel, the later shootings were clearly inspired by the news reports of earlier school shootings. News accounts of Columbine continue to inspire copycats despite proactive school programs and policies. Since schools and police are aware of this danger, some copycat crimes have been prevented. A recent example occurred in Green Bay, WI, where two high school boys, age 17, and a former student at their school, age 18, were apprehended with their weaponry before they struck.[95] However, there are other examples in which high school shootings did occur, including Hillsborough, NC and Montreal, Canada in September 2006, and Tacoma WA in Jan. 07.[96]

In 1983, Paladin Press, of Boulder, CO published a 130-page book, *Hit Man: A Technical Manual for Independent Contractors.* James E. Perry followed 27 of the book's suggestions when he killed a mother, her disabled son, and his nurse. He shot the women between the eyes and unplugged the boy's respirator. In 1993, the victims' families sued the publisher for damages.[97]

A vampire cult swept across America as a result of three influences: (1) a game, *Vampire: The Masquerade*, with a half-million copies sold, 1991-96;

(2) Anne Rice novels, including *Queen of the Damned*, and (3) the movie, *Interview with the Vampire* (1994). In December 1996, five teenagers in Eustis FL, who frequently played "Vampire: The Masquerade" and also drank blood, beat to death Richard and Naoma Wendorf, parents of one member of the group, and then they fled to Baton Rouge LA in the Wendorf car before being apprehended. A spokesman for the game's publisher, White Wolf Inc. of Atlanta, doubted that there was any connection between playing the game and the murder.[98]

In 2003, in Fayette, AL, 20-year-old Devin Moore shot dead three policemen, and when apprehended, he told other police that "Life is a video game; everybody has to die sometime." At his trial, defense lawyer Jim Standridge blamed the killings on Moore's fascination with the video game *Grand Theft Auto*. Moore pleaded not guilty by reason of mental defect, but a jury found his guilty of capital murder.[99]

The constant dead-end sameness of TV gun crime entertainment is summarized by critic Amanda Petrusich on 1 Jan. 18:[100]

> There may be no genre of television easier to parody than true crime. The style is formulaic by design: an atrocity is followed by an investigation, a left turn, a revelation, *fin.* Think "America's Most wanted," or "Dateline." Fictionalized vaariations of the idea, in which a crime is committeed, sscrutinized, and solved within the hour, are called procidurals for good reason. The accoutrements (plasltic evidence bags, grainy security footage, an incriminating fibre tweezed from a corpse) are consistent from episode to episode, and the action unfolds in the same way each time.

America can do better by not depending on gun violence as entertainment.

## Conclusions

American culture that features guns began with testimonials about conflicts between colonists and Indians, or between English colonists and French or Spanish colonists. Such accounts fit the hypothetical model explained in the second paragraph of this chapter: acquainting others with the nature of prevailing dangers. After the American War of Independence, those dangers declined, and those early accounts became grist for James Fenimore Cooper's novels about early American conflicts. His novels became models for later writers who could find more recent conflicts to discuss, either as history or as fiction. Frontiersmen, especially Daniel Boone, David Crockett, Kit Carson, and Buffalo Bill Cody, functioned as both imperial Americans and as medieval knights and were both heroes of adventure stories and models for aspiring American heroes.

Newspapers reported western conflicts for eastern readers, but with few illustrations during the 1800s. Magazines, however, contained stories of adventure, using guns, and magazines were more often illustrated than newspapers. Most war stories provide an opportunity to absorb stories of gun violence while feeling patriotic. Stories about the folly of war seem to have less impact on society as a whole than do the war stories that provide narratives of adventurous conflict. Westerns provide a sense of freedom and adventure, with guns being the protectors of freedom; the good guys win. Urban stories are somewhat sinister; police are often portrayed as unimaginative and only partly able to protect society from crime. Criminals have been glamorized since Prohibition in the 1920s. Private detectives with guns usually save the day.

Hunting is now a minor pastime, about which there is disagreement in our society. Hunting stories, whether true or fictional, usually attract only hunters and do not appear to be an important source of entertainment for the general public or of encouragement of violence against humans.

Newspapers, magazines, and radio all attract a wide audience, though readership of newspapers has declined as the popularity of television and the internet has increased. Newspapers, magazines, radio, and the internet all publish accounts of real gun violence, and magazines and radio also have been sources of fiction on gun violence, though television dramas have usurped this role from radio since the 1960s. Movies and television drama (and reruns on videos and DVDs) presently are our most compelling sources of stories involving gun violence, both true and fictional. For decades, movies were accompanied by "news reels," but this function has moved to television.

Video games are the most vivid and brutal sources of violent gun entertainment, consumed primarily by young males, ages about 8 to 30. Gangstra rap arose among young Black males, and young Blacks remain its main audience. It emphasizes gun violence in Black neighborhoods, often without passing moral judgment, and some of it seems to condone rough treatment of women.

Does America's preoccupation with guns in its cultural products have significant influence on our being the country in peacetime with the highest rate of gun crime? Scholars, judges, and juries answer yes. Assuming we do not want a violent society, we have a serious pathology in our cultural expressions. In remote antiquity, stories of real violence had survival value, telling others about dangers they might also face, but now stories of violence are often counterproductive by encouraging similar behavior from members of an audience who are alienated.

# 8

## GUNS, POLITICS AND PARANOIA

The politics of guns in America is astonishing. This country is very diverse in its peoples and their outlook. Yet, on this issue a gun subculture has imposed its views upon our legal system. If this was merely a recreational issue, the rest of us could say: "Oh well, let them do their thing, it is not our business." Unfortunately, guns are a life-and-death issue, which concerns us all, even if we choose to ignore it, because chances of law-abiding citizens getting shot in America are far greater than in any other advanced nation not at war. And that situation is an aspect of our politics, which has become paranoid. How did that happen?

### Background

Aspects of the conflict between colonies and British government during the 1770s still lingers in our collective memory. Britain won the French and Indian War (Seven Years War in Europe) in 1763, but went into debt doing so. It sought to raise money to help pay the debt by taxing its American colonies, which benefited from the victory. The 13 colonies responded, "No taxation without representation." Brits might have resolved that by adding 13 Americans to its Parliament. However, it responded with anger at the presumption of colonies standing up to its protector with ingratitude. It imposed taxes without granting representation.

Americans resisted the taxes, and so Britain tried to find a tax that did not incite anger. The Boston Massacre was a small conflict in 1770 between a Boston mob and soldiers who fired and killed five civilians. John

Adams and Josiah Quincy defended the soldiers in court and obtained acquittals. The Boston Tea Party in 1773 was a later incident in America's tax resistance in which Bostonians pretended to be Indians and boarded tea ships and dumped 342 chests of tea into the harbor rather than pay a tea tax. In 1774 a ship attempted to unload tea in New York and met a similar response. A British response was to order the quartering of troops in taverns and dwellings. A colonial response to that was the meeting of the First Continental Congress (1774), which advised colonists to obtain guns and form their own militias.

Small conflicts continued, as did unsuccessful efforts to resolve them. A confrontation between 70 militia men (Minute Men) and British infantry occurred in Lexington and Concord in 1775 and resulted in an initial victory by the infantry. Eight Americans were killed and ten wounded. However, the British infantry then had to march back to Charlestown, near Boston, and as it did so, other militia men arrived to harass them. Almost 4000 Americans fought that April 19, with 93 dead, wounded or missing. Britain suffered 73 dead, 174 wounded, and 26 missing. America's War of Independence had begun (not a "revolution" as that term was later understood, as a rebellion of lower classes against upper classes).

Britain was fighting a foreign war and Americans were fighting for their homeland, with help from France. Americans and French isolated Cornwallis at Yorktown, Virginia in 1781, and he was forced to surrender before help arrived, which effectively ended the war, though peace treaties were not signed until January 1783. Articles of Confederation had been adequate for wartime cooperation among allied colonies, but afterwards that organization proved inadequate for states. A Constitutional Convention met in May 1787 to patch up the Articles, but soon realized a new organization was needed for 13 united states. In September, the Continental Congress received the new Constitution and sent copies to each state for ratification. Delaware ratified on December 7, and other states did so throughout 1788, while North Carolina did not until 1789, and Rhode Island not until 1790.

Heated discussions had occurred between those who saw the need for a strong central government, the Federalists, and their opponents who placed their confidence in state governments. States had suggested amendments, and the U.S. House of Representatives sent 12 amendments to the states to ratify, 10 of which became the Bill of Rights. Of concern here is the Second Amendment:

A well-regulated militia being necessary to the security of a free state, the right of the people to bear arms shall not be infringed.

It reads as if it was a compromise between two different points of view. The dominant concern at the time was fear that the Federal Government would bully states, as Britain had bullied the colonies. There was little, if any, worry about the right of individuals to be armed, simply because the states had no arms, and each local militia expected its members to have their own muskets and ammunition. After a while, Americans lost their fear of Federal Government bullying states, because the people came to believe they had responsive governments at the local, state, and national levels. [1]

That confidence began to weaken as Congress debated whether slavery could be extended to new territories and states. That potential conflict was averted by admitting to statehood alternately free and slave states. In 1820 there were 11 free and 11 slave states, and a concern arose when Maine was to be admitted as a free state and Missouri as a slave state. Missouri was carved out of the enormous Louisiana Purchase of 1803 from France, and northern Congressmen feared that Missouri's admission might later be interpreted as allowing slavery in the rest of the Louisiana Purchase when territories within that region applied for statehood. Senator Jesse B. Thomas of Illinois introduced an amendment to the bill of admissions specifying that slavery would not be allowed north of a line of latitude 36 degrees 30'. That amendment passed and Maine and Missouri became states.

In 1831, two events would have increased slave owners' concerns: Nat Turner's revolt in Virginia and William Lloyd Garrison founded his antislavery newspaper, *Liberation*. Two potential slave revolts had already been suppressed in Richmond (1800) and Charleston (1820) before Nat Turner's. He began by murdering his own master, who had treated him well. He led five other slaves to neighboring plantations. They killed 55 whites at several plantations and added slaves to their ranks until there were 60 of them. Whites then overpowered them and hung over 40, including Turner.[2]

There were at least fifty black abolitionist societies in the North by

1830, and so Garrison was pouring oil on a smoldering fire when he began publishing *Liberation*. He not only wanted to free slaves, he also wanted to give them full citizenship. Northern antislavery societies included women as well as men, though women did not have the vote. Not to worry, by 1837, Garrison began advocating women's rights. Abolitionists began to move into politics, and in 1854 Whigs, Free-Soilers, and antislavery Democrats met at Ripon, Wisconsin and founded the Republican Party to carry their message to the country. Its first presidential candidate, explorer Colonel John C. Frémont, in 1856, lost, but in 1860, it nominated anti-slavery candidate Abraham Lincoln. The free Northerners outnumbered the slave advocates of the South and won the election.

The U.S. Constitution does not say that once a state joined the Union, it could never leave. Southern states feared Lincoln's presumed agenda and wanted out. A South Carolina convention met on 20 December 1860 and voted to dissolve the state's bond with the United States. A complication was that defensive forts scattered around the South were Federal facilities. On December 30, state troops seized the U.S. Arsenal at Charleston. Lincoln made reassuring speeches before his inauguration, and after becoming president, he notified South Carolina that he was sending provisions to the Fort Sumter garrison. South Carolina demanded that the garrison surrender, and on April 12, after its commander, Major Anderson, declined to do so, Southern shore artillery began firing on the fort. After 34 hours of that, Anderson surrendered and the Civil War began.

The Civil War was the most-costly of all America's wars in casualties, since Americans were lost on both sides of the conflict. Union dead were 359,528, wounded 275,175; Confederate dead, 258,000, wounded, over 100,000. Just as that colossal tragedy was ending, John Wilkes Booth assassinated President Abraham Lincoln, April 14, 1865.[3] Booth was shot dead 12 days later.

War casualty statistics were interesting, because Union armies were larger than Confederate armies, yet the Union suffered the most casualties. Part of the explanation could be that the Union armies were more aggressive than Confederate armies, and aggressors might suffer more casualties than defensive armies which often had fortified positions. However, that might not be the whole story. The North had more and larger cities than the South, which meant that most southern young men lived in rural environments, where they likely grew up hunting in winter and whenever else they were not needed in agriculture. More northern young men grew up in urban environments, where they did not learn to hunt and handle guns. As explained above, chapter 5, such thoughts prompted William Church and George Wingate to organize the National Rifle Association in New York City in 1871.

If America had fought no more wars, the NRA might not have lasted, but not to worry, a succession of conflicts, from Indian wars in the West to World War I, kept the NRA's concern for marksmanship relevant and the organization active (excepting a hiatus during the 1890s), with shooting contests between Americans and English-speaking foreign countries. Laws against carrying concealed handguns had begun in Kentucky in 1813 and later spread to other states, but that was not a concern of the NRA in its early decades.

What became a concern to Americans was the fact that Booth's assassination of Lincoln set an example for later assassins. (An attempt on Andrew Jackson's life in 1835 had left no lasting memory in national consciousness.) On July 2, 1881, Charles J. Guiteau shot President Games A. Garfield, who died on September 19, and Guiteau was hanged in 1882.[4] Assassination of two presidents 16 years apart did not lead to any new initiative to protect presidents, because Congress would not appropriate the money needed.[5] The Secret Service had been established in the Treasury Department in 1865, to apprehend counterfeiters of U.S. paper money. It proved to be successful, and in 1870, when Congress sent a resolution to President Grant

On 6 September 1901 Leon Czolgosz shot President William McKinley, who died on September 14.[6] The Secret Service had been created in 1865 to suppress dissemination of counterfeit money. After McKinley's assassination it acquired a second responsibility, to protect the president and vice-president. More comprehensive gun control laws were not enacted. The Secret Service did not save former President Theodore Roosevelt (1858-1919), running for a third term, from being shot by John Schrank in Milwaukee on October 14, 1912.[7] Fortunately, the bullet hit Roosevelt's folded speech and metal glasses case in a pocket and did not penetrate far into his chest, thus preventing his death or serious wounding. Attempts continued against future presidents: Franklin Roosevelt, 1933,

Harry Truman, 1950, John F. Kennedy in 1963 (successful), Gerald Ford, 1975, twice, and Ronald Reagan (wounded), 1981. None of these attempts led to new gun laws.

By 1898, Americans were annoyed by Spanish control of Cuba, which coincided with the sentiments of many Cubans. After a Havana riot of Jan. 12, gunboat diplomacy seemed appropriate, and the U.S. battleship *Maine* was sent to Havana harbor, ostensibly to protect American lives and property. On Feb. 15, an explosion sank the *Maine*, with the loss of 260 lives. Some Americans blamed Spain, but a naval court of inquiry concluded the explosion had been caused by a submarine mine of unknown origin, and a chief engineer in the Navy, George W. Melville, suggested it had probably been caused by an internal explosion of the magazine, ignited by a spontaneous explosion of the coal fuel. Spain accepted demands by the U.S. government, but Congress was not interested in wasting this opportunity, and President William McKinley yielded to Congressional demands and asked for a military intervention. Congress demanded freedom for Cuba and withdrawal of Spanish troops. Spain broke off diplomatic relations with the United States on April 21, and the United States imposed a blockade on Havana harbor on April 22. On April 24, Spain declared war on the United States, and on April 25, Congress declared war on Spain.[8] Relevant here, state militia were inept,[9] which prompted a bored Vice President Theodore Roosevelt to raise his own force for action in the U.S. Army, the famous "Rough Riders."[10] Although that imperialistic war only lasted four months and was not much of a strain on America, Filipinos wanted their freedom and fought America unsuccessfully for three years, resulting in 200,000 Filipino and 5000 American casualties. These American actions increased confidence in resolving political disagreements with guns. (The Boer War in South Africa and the Boxer Rebellion in China also occurred during that time.)

The Battle of Blair Mountain in 1921 was a unique event in American history. There have been a good number of conflicts between labor unions and industry management, but this one differed in magnitude from all others.[11] It occurred in the coal fields of West Virginia, where miners labored under miserable conditions for little pay. The United Mine Workers Union was formed in 1890 by merger of two previous labor organizations, but it had little power until the mid-1930s with President Franklin Roosevelt's New Deal. On 20 May 1912 a conflict arose between coal miners who wanted to be represented by UMW and private Baldwin-Fells detectives representing mine owners. Three townsmen and seven agents died in a shootout that became known as the Matewan Massacre. On 26 Jan. 21, Sheriff Sid Hatfield was tried for killing Albert Fells, and acquitted. On 1 Aug. 21, Hatfield was supposed to be tried for dynamiting a coal tipple, but as he and a colleague climbed the steps to the court house, they were gunned down by Baldwin-Fells detectives, who were never held accountable. The Battle of Blair Mountain began on Aug. 29 and lasted until Federal troops arrived on Sept. 3. The government lost about 30 men and the miners lost 50-100. Because West Virginia National Guard and Federal troops allied with the mine owners, the miners lost the battle, but the conflict publicized their miserable plight.

## The NRA's Fearsome Ideology

In 1911, after the attempted assassination of New York City's mayor, New York State Legislature passed the Sullivan Law, requiring registration of handguns, which annoyed NRA, which received funds from the War Department to run its shooting contests, and it did not protest publicly, though it grumbled to its members.[12] New York City policemen were strict enforcers of this law as a means to keep illegal guns out of the city.

The 18th Amendment to the U.S. Constitution, prohibiting manufacturing or sale of alcoholic beverages, became law on 16 January 20.[13] It failed to prevent alcoholic consumption and was repealed by the 21st Amendment (1933). However, for a dozen years gangsters who made and sold bootleg alcoholic beverages flourished, and fought over which gang controlled particular territories. Guns used were sometimes "tommyguns," portable machine guns. Congress did ban shipment of guns through the mails to individuals in 1927, but not shipment by other carriers of freight.[14] Finally, Congress was prodded into considering a gun control law in 1934, the National Firearms Act (NFA). The bill proposed by the Justice Department was much stronger than what got through Congress (it did outlaw tommyguns), for this time NRA protested loudly, and urged its members to write their Congressional delegation.[15] In 1937, the Justice Department proposed adding handguns to the 1934 law, and the Federal

Firearms Act (FFA, 1937) was another compromise with NRA.[16] It became the responsibility of the Treasury Department to enforce both acts

After World War II, with the development of a cold war between the United States and the Soviet Union, a general fear arose, not limited to NRA members. What was somewhat limited to NRA was the notion that private citizens could resist a Soviet invasion with guns in their homes. Some members of the John Birch Society, founded in1958, shared this belief, as did right-winged militias, which began to emerge in late 1950s.[17] There were fellow travelers having that ideology in a militia movement, and gun shows have been important means of disseminating this fear. When the Cold War began to wind down, that fear needed to be transferred elsewhere. One possibility was fear of the UN invading America with black helicopters, but that was difficult to develop into an ongoing and wide-spread fear. Much better was to transfer that fear to the American Federal Government.

The NRA may seem to be the originator of an ongoing paranoid mind-set, based upon its preaching fear. However, J. Edgar Hoover (1895-1972) discovered fear's effects before the NRA took it up.[18] He was director of the FBI from the mid-1920s (originally with a slightly different name) until his death. He was deeply prejudiced and imposed his paranoia upon the FBI. He was suspicious of any group that did not conform to his concept of true Americans, including communists, Blacks, and liberals. He viewed critiques of government or mainstream society as communist-inspired and had his agents harass those, such as Martin Luther King, Jr, who did so. He believed activist Blacks and liberals were closet communists, and communists were to be feared above all others. The goal of his fearmongering was to gain power and glory for himself and his agency. Hoover approved of Don Whitehead's *The FBI Story: a Report to the People* (1956), since Hoover wrote a Foreword for it. However, Ronald Kessler's *The Bureau: The Secret History of the FBI* (2002) would have been, like his recent biographies, Hoover's nightmare if known to him, because it exposed his prejudices and unlawful acts and policies.

An ideological understanding of NRA, Birchers, and militia depends on an awareness of their version of American political history, beginning with the Constitution in the later 1700s. When it went to the states for confirmation, there was fear that that federal government might assume the role the British government had played with the colonies before the War of Independence. A Bill of Rights was needed to reassure against that possibility. State militia seemed to be a way to counter that possibility, insured by the Second Amendment. In practice, however, the Federal Government showed no tendency to behave as British government had, and so interest in state militias declined. They had performed poorly during the War of Independence, because of a lack of uniform equipment, training, and command, but perhaps under a new government that could be corrected, but not in time for the War of 1812. That did happen in 1903, when state militias were transformed into the National Guard. NRA discussed neither state militias nor National Guard in its fearmongering—complexity which might confuse members.

At some point, the NRA developed possibly its strongest two arguments against gun laws and registration: slippery slope (one law leads to more and eventually to private gun confiscation) and, second and more complex (after World War II), the Nazi confiscation of guns from German Jews in 1938, followed later by the death camps. The NRA argument: if it happened there, it could happen here. That is a powerful argument for NRA members and others who lack a historian's ability to see its flaws. The German democracy had only existed since World War I, and Germany was in a severe depression in the 1930s, for which Hitler seemed to have had solutions. America already had democracy during the colonial period, which is why colonies were unwilling to be taxed without representation in Parliament. The severest test of American democracy was the Civil War, a great trauma, but followed by recovery, not further descent into chaos, such as Hitler brought to Germany. America's democracy is the oldest in the world, and its traditions were too soundly established to be overthrown by NRA's self-serving fearful hypothetical scenario. Private guns do not prevent government takeover by a dictator, as a dictator would need the American police and armed services to do so, and would they take orders to destroy their own democracy? Americans experience with democracy made this a vanishingly small possibility, but NRA members with limited education, or with advanced education and paranoia, were easily persuaded otherwise.

Akin to these arguments are pro-gun bumper stickers, such as "control criminals, not guns." The NRA has encouraged their use, but Joan Burbick attributed their origin to the Young Americans for Freedom in 1974.[19] Pete Shields responded to seven of these bumper stickers, explaining why they are untrue.[20]

Might the NRA's (recent) five million members be sophisticated enough to wonder why America's armed services, not to mention the National Guard, would become sheep if a tyrant decided to take over America— even if there were no private guns? Service members could still access military guns. Instead, it is NRA members who have become sheep, sending in annual dues to ensure the continued existence of democracy! And, afraid that any new gun law would lead to American enslavement. Gullibility seems characteristic of NRA members.

Although the NRA's main supporters have limited education and are willing to accept advice from its leadership, it does have members with higher education. Are they taken in by the same propaganda? Some, no doubt, are, but a large portion of the latter are either in elected office or aspiring to an elected office, and being an NRA member is part of their qualifications for office. Few Republicans who are not members get elected, and some few Democrats from "red states" take out the same electoral insurance, including Rep. John Dingle, Jr., of Michigan and Senator Joe Manchin of West Virginia.

U.S. Rep. Jim Sensenbrenner, Menomonee Falls, WI, who represents such a comfortable Republican suburb that he has not even needed NRA campaign funds for quite a while, stuck his neck out in mid-September 2006 by attacking Mayor Tom Barrett, Milwaukee, who objected to a bill that Sensenbrenner, chairman of the House Judiciary Committee, had reported favorably out of committee—a bill to restrict the power of the Bureau of Alcohol, Tobacco, and Firearms to revoke licenses of gun stores that were not vigilant in ensuring that criminals did not buy guns. Sensenbrenner called Barrett a "crybaby" who presided over a city rapidly becoming the murder capital of America. The *Milwaukee Journal Sentinel* came to Barrett's defense by publishing statistics which showed that, of cities with over 100,000, Milwaukee ranked tenth in its murder rate.[21] An editorial in the same 15 September issue stated: "Irascible. Cantankerous. Crusty. Crotchety. All words used to describe Rep. Jim Sensenbrenner (R-Wis.) over the years. Let us now add another: Graceless." One of the paper's editorial writers, Gregory Stanford, wrote two weeks later: "when the NRA points to what appears in its paranoid vision to be a problem, the sound you hear next is that of a stampede of lawmakers coming to the rescue."

# Fighting the Wrong Domestic War

## By Frank N. Egerton, about 2005

Murder is no big deal! What's important is out right to own guns, so that when you want to blow someone away, you can! Try it, you'll like it! This, of course, is not what we preach, but it is what we practice. If murder were a big deal, we would not waste billions of dollars fighting rather harmless marijuana while we tolerate up to 15,000 gun murders a year, with feeble efforts to stop them.

We have a self-destructive society that persists because those perpetuating our gun culture are seldom its victims. The perpetuators include a very profitable gun lobby that disseminates a bogus ideology that equates guns and freedom, a gun industry that is legally immune to the consequences of its murderous products, an entertainment industry preoccupied with gun violence, and politicians either bought off or intimidated by the gun lobby.

Senator Feingold (D-WI) ducked an NRA attack in 2004 when he was running for reelection by voting not to renew the Clinton Administration's 1994 ban on selling assault rifles. He claimed assault rifles were no problem. When American gunmen proved him wrong—most recently along the Wisconsin-Minnesota border with the murder of three teenage swimmers—he remained silent.

"Try it, you'll like it!" This is the message of our entertainment industry that produces video games in which participants can "blow away" cops. It produces movies and TV shows that recycle real violence as entertainment. These games, films, and shows are aimed at 14 to 30-year-olds, who are the most likely citizens to pull real triggers in gun crimes.

Gun violence is a well-established American tradition. Massacres are often aimed at random victims, such as the Virginia Tech students and faculty, but recently aimed at those who oppose our gun culture—Unitarians in Knoxville and a Democratic Party chairman in Little Rock. When such massacres are added to our ordinary street shootings—Ahattola T. Feemster being Racine's latest—one sees that America today is no safer than in the old Wild West.

Meanwhile, legislative bodies continue to vote vast sums for a "war on drugs," and law enforcement finds it easier to destroy marijuana that does less harm than tobacco than to get guns off our streets. Our drug war is too visible, and our gun war is almost invisible.

# Counteractions: Gun Control

On 16 April 74, Nick Shields, 23, was shot dead in San Francisco. Nick's father, Pete Shields (age 69 in 1993), was a Du Pont executive in Wilmington, DE. Pete was a Navy Airforce vet from World War II, a waterfowl hunter, a Republican, but not an NRA member.[22] He had no interest in gun control until after his son's death. He began reading and discovered that there had been five presidential commissions on gun violence in the previous decade and listed them in his book, *Guns don't Die—People Do*.[23] However, the recommendations of these commissions had never been passed into law. He agreed with those commissions that America needed more gun laws, for he felt that the level of gun violence nationwide—11,124 gun murders and 250,000 handgun victims in 1974—was what one might expect in war. Japan, with half the population of America, in 1974 had 37 gun murders.

Shields saw that the NRA had organized opposition to gun control, but those favoring gun control had no comparable organization and were therefore ineffective. Mark Borinsky, when a graduate student, had suffered the trauma of being held up by three men with a gun. He had founded, in 1974, a National Council to Control Handguns, in Washington, but he had a new job and could not devote full time to it. Shields received a year's leave from Du Pont Company[24] in 1975 to help Borinsky's organization get started. His leave of absence became early retirement in 1976, and the organization was renamed Handgun Control, Inc. (HCI). To run it, he recruited Ed Welles, retired from the CIA; and Georgetown University graduate, New Yorker Charlie Orasin, who had been an assistant to liberal Republican Senator Jacob K. Jarvis of New York.[25] To raise money to get underway, Shields asked those on his Christmas card list, who all knew of the murder of his son, for donations. After getting started, he then solicited members of this political lobby for $15 each. By 1981, he had 150,000 members (impressive, but not in the NRA's league). That is the American way in politics.

However, "Threatened gun rights leaders likened the gun control group, Handgun Control, Inc., to Nazis and labeled their actions fascist. NRA president Dick Riley called HCI founder Pete Shield's book on gun control a *Mein Kampf* sequel for the gun control movement."[26] Blatant fear mongering, but NRA members lapped it up. Cars should be registered and regulated, but not guns. To counter Shield's book, *Guns don't Die, People Do* (1981), Alan Gottlieb published *The Gun Grabbers* (1986), with a 1.5-page introduction by conservative Republican Senator Steve Symms of Idaho. Its blurb informed readers that Gottlieb was chairman of the Citizens Committee for the Right to Keep and Bear Arms, founder of the Second Amendment Foundation, and publisher of *Gun Week*. His book publisher, Merril Press, had also published his *Gun Rights Fact Book* and *Guns for Women* by Gottlieb and George Flynn. Richard Poe, a later author of similar ilk, wrote a sequel to *Gun Grabbers*, *The Seven Myths of Gun Control: Reclaiming the Truth about Guns, Crime, and the Second Amendment* (2001).

There has been an obvious pattern to passage of gun-control bills: an awful incident propelled public interest, which for a while overcame NRA's absolutist policy against any gun laws, though without getting all the control advocates wanted. Lee Harvey Oswald's assassination of President John F. Kennedy on 22 November 1963 (with a rifle) was such an event,[27] but it threw the country into turmoil, and later there was conflict in Congress about what the bill should include. A bill was voted on in a Senate committee on 4 April 1968 and was defeated. Rev. Martin Luther King, Jr. was assassinated about an hour later by James Earl Ray.[28] Nevertheless, Senator Thomas J. Dodd had to delete rifles and shotguns from the bill to bring it to the Senate floor, and when Senator Edward Kennedy attempted to restore rifles and shotguns to the bill, it was voted down. On June 5, his other brother, Senator Robert F. Kennedy was shot dead by Sirhan Sirhan.[29] On the same day, Congress passed the first gun bill in 30 years (to the day). Many Americans blamed the NRA for the lax gun laws that enabled these assassins to wreak their havoc.

There were two attempts to assassinate President Gerald Ford, and he sent Congress a handgun control bill in 1975, which went nowhere. Nevertheless, in 1976 when he ran for re-election, he announced opposition to further gun laws, in order to have the NRA endorse him—its first presidential endorsement, but not its last.[30] Jimmy Carter, in a primary contest in Florida against George Wallace, mentioned his support for further handgun laws. Pete Shields gushed: Carter was a Southerner, retired military officer, hunter, businessman, conservative, and victorious against Ford.[31] Shields commented, it was almost too good to be true, which turned out to be correct.

Senator Edward Kennedy (D-MA) who was a strong supporter of handgun control—having lost two brothers to assassins with handguns—was Chairman of the House Judiciary Committee, and a Senate bill could be shepherded through the House by Congressman Peter Rodino (D-NJ). In supporting a bill, Shields would mention that he was father of a young man killed with a handgun. He gave his first ever political speech before a sympathetic audience at his church in Wilmington, DE. The Justice Department wrote a draft for this bill and sent it to the White House, but its introduction kept being postponed month by month. Finally, in 1978, the pro-bill lobby was told it would become part of a comprehensive crime bill. Since that bill also kept being postponed, HCI decided to prod the Treasury Department to increase its registration requirements for gun makers and dealers, and by March three new regulations were under discussion: 1. Have manufacturer put a unique serial number on each gun so it could be traced, 2. Require prompt reporting of thefts and losses, and 3. Track movement of handguns through commercial channels from manufacturer to sale and send the data to Treasury Department. Working on this project was James Fetherstone, who proved to be quite knowledgeable. However, that was as far as this project went, because Fetherstone left Treasury and was hired as a general counsel by the NRA.[32] Then, Congress asked Treasury Assistant Secretary for Enforcement Richard Davis what it would cost to implement the proposed three new regulations, and he replied $4.2 million. Congress then lowered by $4.2 million the budget of the Bureau of Alcohol, Tobacco and Firearms for the coming year![33] NRA lobbyist Neal Knox commented that this was part of President Carter's education.

For NRA's education, HCI produced a slide show, turned later into a TV film, *The American Handgun War*, which included a photograph of Nick Shields' body on a San Francisco sidewalk after he had been shot. Both *Parade* magazine and *60 Minutes* had feature stories on Pete Shields in Sept. 77.[34] A week later *60 Minutes* had another report on the work of HCI. In response to these stories, parents of other children killed with handguns contacted Pete Shields and asked what they could do to further the cause of handgun control. He summarized the tragic stories of seven such losses in *Guns Don't Die—People Do* (1981). One victim was raped, then shot; another was shot during a robbery; still another story was by a woman who had been a victim of an attempted rape, who had been left permanently paralyzed, and so on. Shields' book concluded with accounts of HCI's political fights, resulting in the defeat of a congressman and changes in the attitude of other members of Congress toward gun control. His book appeared soon after folksong genius John Lennon (1980), President Reagan, his press secretary, Jim Brady, and two lawmen (1981) had all been shot, Lennon fatally.

Both Jim (1940-2014) and Sarah Brady (1942-2015) held several positions with Republicans in Washington before Jim, Reagan, and two lawmen were shot in 1981. Reagan recovered from his wounds,[35] but Jim Brady was left seriously impaired.[36] In 1985, Sarah heard on a news cast that NRA was pushing in Congress for passage of a Republican-supported McClure-Volkmer bill that would undo the 1968 gun control act—which angered her.[37] To her, the 1968 act seemed so modest in its achievements that she could not imagine anyone wanting to undo it. She immediately called NRA's headquarters in Washington and said, "I am going to make it my life's ambition to try to put you out of business."[38]

She also called HCI and asked if she could help defeat McClure-Volkmer, and its new president, Charles Orasin, said yes. He asked her to write a letter and send it to all members of the Senate. When the Senate voted on that bill, she was shocked to see only 17 senators vote against it, while 83 voted for it. She fought against its passage in the House, and although it passed, she saw that strong lobbying did mean that the version that passed was watered down from what had been introduced in the House.[39] American police had sometimes cooperated with NRA, but that ended when NRA championed McClure-Volkmer, since police opposed it. Working in HCI, she decided that Shields was its heart and soul, and Orasin its brain.

The next cause she fought for at HCI was to ban armor-piercing bullets, which production NRA also defended, further alienating America's police. NRA lost that battle in 1986, as also its opposition to the requirement that handguns contain enough metal to register in metal detectors at airports. Orasin decided HCI should also develop gun legislation to be introduced into Congress. Would-be assassin Hinkley had bought the Saturday night special which he used to shoot Reagan and three other victims in Washington in a Dallas pawnshop for $29, gave an address no longer current, and showed an old Texas driver's license to indicate he lived in Texas. That perfunctory level of record keeping was inadequate. The Brady Bill was written to improve that system. As a sponsor, they tried Rep.

Morris Udall (D-AZ). He was a liberal in a state that was very conservative on gun control. With them sitting in front of him, he called Police Chief Peter Ronstadt in Tucson, explained what the bill would require, and asked his opinion. Ronstadt responded that he had no objections to it, but doubted it would accomplish much.[40] Udall was relieved to have a reasonable reason to decline their request, and HCI leaders were humiliated by their not having done sufficient homework before approaching Udall. They later found sponsors of a modified bill: Rep Edward Feigham (D-OH) and Sen. Howard Metzenbaum (R-OH). Metzenbaum was considered the most liberal Republican in the Senate, yet his support in Ohio was rock-solid.

NRA would have enough money to buy plenty of TV ads, and HCI could not come anywhere close to matching that. It had to depend mainly upon press conferences and news stories. However, HCI began with an ad showing a photograph of Pete Shields with a headline: "A bullet from a Saturday-night special shattered my life." Orasin appealed to HCI's most generous donors for enough money to place the ad in the *Washington Post*, where it raised enough money to run it in other large city papers. At this point in her autobiography, Sarah Brady declared that she and Jim both supported the Second Amendment to the Constitution.[41] However, she also thought that if Jefferson, Adams, and Franklin were alive in modern times, the amendment's language would have been different to reflect the different circumstances existing recently verses in the early Republic, and she speculated on how it might have been different.

Sarah Brady was a volunteer at HCI in 1985-88, but Orasin saw that she needed to help support her family. He suggested that she give speeches around the country, and HCI could pay her for doing so. Her first ever talk was given at her mother's garden club meeting a year after Jim was shot, discussing their life since then. Later, Sen. Bill Roth (R-DE), who had once been Jim's boss, called and said that Wilmington College wanted to give Jim an honorary doctorate and have her give the commencement speech.[42] One of Jim's friends was a speech coach, and she had him give her some advice. Her next speech was before the National Republican Women's Federation at its convention in Phoenix. That experience taught her she did not like being away over night from Jim and their son, Scott, and so she tried to fly to a speech destination, speak, and return home the same day.

She agreed to give a speech in winter in New Hampshire, "the heart of gun country." It snowed the day of the speech but she still managed to get there on time. Unfortunately, only two town residents came out in the snow, but as she was adjusting to a small audience, two busloads of NRA members (about 150) came marching in.[43] Although she was apprehensive, they were all polite during speech and questioning, though no one smiled. Later, she testified before a House Judiciary Committee and was grateful not to have any hostile questions asked. An invitation to participate in a debate at Harvard University intimidated her, but she was relieved not to suffer any embarrassment. Still, she decided not to participate in future debates.

Reagan was shot on 30 March 81, little more than two months after becoming president. He was a life member of NRA, but the advantages which NRA expected to come with his presidency never materialized. He was not an opponent with whom HCI had to contend. Mollie Dickenson wrote *Thumbs Up: the Life and Courageous Comeback of White House Press Secretary Jim Brady* (William Morrow, 1987), and both Bradys accompanied her on book publicity tours.

HCI realized that if it could get explicit support from police, that would be a strong asset, so it established a law-enforcement division, that included Jane Clarenbach, who had previously worked with law enforcement and knew relevant organizations and effective approaches. Sarah Brady also became involved, and spoke at the Fraternal Order of Police's national convention in Mobile, AL. Clarenbach accompanied her. Brady mentioned that her father's career had been in law enforcement. After her speech a poll indicated that almost all of them supported the Brady Bill.[44] HCI also sought support at meetings of many large organizations in America.

Like the NRA, HCI started a state legislative division, which frequently lobbied in opposition to NRA lobbies. HCI helped Maryland in 1988 plan a referendum to ban sales of Saturday-night specials, which was successful—the first state to do so. However, fighting against NRA initiatives to have state legislatures pass preemption laws which prevent individual cities from passing gun laws without legislative consent and against concealed carry laws failed.

Sarah and other HCI women still found time to lobby on Capitol Hill, especially in 1988, keeping their message factual, not emotional. Their reward would be an occasional persuasion of a congressman to change an upcoming vote in their favor. They won that year—thanks to support from

Sen. Nancy Kassebaum (R-KS)—the struggle to require all handguns to contain enough metal to trip airport detectors when sent through them. One of four who voted against this bill in the House was Rep. Dick Cheney (R-WY). They also began work on an assault gun ban that took several years of preparation.[45] Sen. Edward Kennedy (D-MA) could be counted on for strong support on every gun control bill. In June 88, Rep. Ed Feighan (D-OH) introduced the Brady Bill as an amendment to the Omnibus Drug Initiative Act, before the House Judiciary Committee. The Committee approved the amendment and the bill was sent to the full House. These lobbyists were unsure of its fate there, and they contacted as many Congressmen as possible. Since Brady had met the Cheneys at the home of a mutual friend, she even called his office, but he did not return her call. They did not get a definitive vote in the House, however, because Rep. Bill McCollum (R-FL) introduced an amendment to substitute a possible instant background check for their proposed five-day wait between gun purchase and pickup, to allow ATF to check buyer's background. McCollum proposed Treasury Department study his alternative, and many House members were glad to vote for that delay.[46]

HCI was disappointed, but persevered. They lobbied for two more years, not just in Congress, but also giving speeches and news interviews. Law enforcement organizations were overwhelmingly supportive. They developed a Law Enforcement Steering Committee to make sure they kept that support. HCI's board chairman, Pete Shields, had had prostate cancer and wanted to retire. He asked Sarah to take over as chairman. In a new 101st Congress, the chair of the Crime Subcommittee was Rep. Chuck Schumer (D-NY [now, Senator]) was very supportive, but the Judiciary Committee was chaired by Jack Brooks (D-TX), who was a Democrat, but in a western state and supported NRA's priorities, as did the new Speaker of the House, Tom Foley (D-WA), also from a western state. George H.W. Bush, Reagan's Vice-President and Republican candidate to replace him in 1988, had spoken words of encouragement to the Bradys at Reagan's last Super Bowl party. Sarah then thought the new president of whichever party won would be supportive of HCI.[47]

Both Sarah and Jim Brady had grown up as moderate Republicans, and Sarah had become apprehensive in 1985 when ideologs began dominating the party. In 1988 when the Brady bill had come before the House, it was not a partisan issue. In 1989, President Bush banned importation of assault weapons.[48] That infuriated NRA, and Bush never supported the Brady bill. In 1989, eight years after being shot, Jim testified before a Congressional committee, and subsequently they toured the country giving joint speeches to build support for the Brady bill. Students at the University of Nevada, Las Vegas, invited them to speak, and publicized their appearance before hand. Almost 2000 attended the event, in a gymnasium. Students were very supportive, but NRA had bused in members from California, who were silent when Jim spoke, but when Sarah spoke, they were constantly shouting, "Liar, liar!" CNN showed their speeches and the disruptions on TV.[49] Their hosts began sending audiences through metal-detectors beforehand, and at one location a man with a gun was caught. Later, she realized that the rude hecklers actually helped her cause.

By 1990, HCI thought its lobbying had possibly convinced enough Congressmen to pass the Brady bill, but Foley would not allow a vote on it. That only increased press coverage of HCI's struggle with Foley. HCI placed ads in large-city newspapers on this. He, in turn, received NRA pressure not to yield. By January 1991, Foley had had enough negative publicity and agreed to let the Brady bill have a vote, without his endorsement. He scheduled it for debate in May. Yet, there was still the proposed instant background check to consider. The difficulty was that the federal data against which the check would be made did not yet exist. Chuck Schumer assumed responsibility of shepherding the bill. One strategy was to have opponents also vote against the instant check amendment. On 8 May 91, the Brady bill passed in the House, 239 to 186.[50] Senate majority leader George Mitchell (D-ME) attempted to mediate a compromise bill between HCI and NRA, but although HCI was willing to compromise, NRA was not. Mitchell added to it a federal grant to each state to update its records on those who could not buy guns so that at some future time, an instant background check would be possible. That was good enough for Kansas senator and NRA loyalist Bob Dole. The Brady bill was added to a general crime bill, which on July 11 passed the Senate 71 to 26.[51] However, after the reconciliation between the House and Senate bills, it passed the House, but in the Senate, a vote to end debate failed, and it was stalled for almost a year. Mitchell thought he might get a vote if the Brady bill was debated separately from the general crime bill, but Bush indicated he would only sign if it were part of the crime bill.

In a presidential election year, 1992, Sarah Brady decided to oppose Bush's re-election, as a private citizen. NRA had already endorsed Reagan when he first ran for president, and later, Bush; now she made a de facto HCI endorsement of Clinton. The Clinton Campaign asked her to speak in Florida, a toss- up state. In Miami she met Janet Reno and a police chief from Fort Pierce. Clinton's victory seemed to clear the way for passage of the Brady bill. Neither Foley nor Brooks would provide support in the House, but in 1993 Attorney General Reno provided support from the Clinton administration. Schumer was a champion in the House. By then, Jim Brady had recovered enough to campaign separately from Sarah, accompanied by a nurse. That was a morale booster for both Jim and Sarah, as was Clinton's signing the Brady bill on November 30, with both Bradys and other HCI members present at the White House for the occasion.[52] It went into effect in 1994.

HCI's next agenda was an assault weapons ban, which had been incubating while the main focus was the Brady bill. Meanwhile the demented Colin Ferguson had entered a commuter train from New York City on 7 December 93 with a Ruger 9mm gun, which he had bought in California, and began shooting passengers.[53] He shot 25 commuters, six of whom died before he needed to exchange an empty for a filled bullet magazine, and he was overpowered. One of the wounded, Tom McDermott, 50, and a widow of a fatal victim, Carolyn McCarthy, whose only son was among the wounded, became gun-control activists, focused on assault guns.[54] McDermott was a lawyer and McCarthy a nurse; they interacted with other victims and family of victims, instead of with HCI. In spring 1994, when McCarthy traveled to Capitol Hill, she discovered her own Republican Congressman would not support her efforts, and in 1996, she ran as a Democrat against him and won that seat and served in the House from 1997 to 2015.

During past Congresses, both Senators Metzenbaum (R-OH) and Dennis DeConcini (D-AZ) had introduced bills banning assault rifles which went nowhere. In 1994, Sen. Dianne Feinstein (D-CA), advised by HCI lobbyists and borrowing from both Metzenbaum's and DeConcini's bills, named 19 kinds of assault guns to prohibit, and any handguns, rifles, or shotguns that had specific features also prohibited. This became part of Clinton's crime bill, which he signed on 13 September 1994.[55] That did not end the matter, because the gun industry designed new guns that could evade prohibitions in the law. In 1998, Clinton ordered ATF to prohibit imports of 58 models of semi-automatic guns not used for hunting.[56]

The HCI staff after two victories, developed grandiose plans for what it might achieve, but 1994 was also the year in which the Republicans, under Newt Gingrich, took over Congress. The Bradys, therefore, turned their attention to state legislatures and referendums. They also assisted the Center to Prevent Handgun Violence in its educational programs. Jim Brady had regained his health enough to become active at fund-raising.[57] They opposed NRA's push to have all states legalize concealed carry of handguns. NRA, with much greater resources, won this one. On the other hand, after a Florida mother lost a child when his friend found a handgun, she was able, with HCI assistance, to convince her state legislature to pass a Child Accident Prevention law, making parents liable when a child found a gun and shot it. After Florida passed it, at least 14 other states did also.[58] In 1996, when Rep. Dick Durban (D-IL) decided to run for the Senate; his opponent accepted FRA funds, and the Bradys gladly endorsed Durban, who won by a landslide.[59] In 1997, in a five-to four decision, the Supreme Court struck down the mandatory background check in the Brady Law, but left in tack its mandatory waiting period between purchase date and pickup.[60] Five years after the Brady Law went into effect, the waiting period changed automatically to an instant check system.

Probably the most controversial book ever published on gun control was by economist John R. Lott, Jr., *More Guns Less Crime: Understanding Crime and Gun Control Laws* (University of Chicago, 1998, ed. 2, 2000, ed. 3, 2010). NRA was delighted with it, and pro-gun partisans leaped to its support. Pro-control partisans were not convinced. Lott, Ph.D., is not a criminologist, and other scholars found much to dispute. Even the third edition did not satisfy his critics. Tom Diaz in 2013 characterized Lott as a "Perennial pro-gun activist" who was "a virtual factory of much-criticized and regularly debunked pro-gun academic 'studies.'"[61] And Distinguished Service Professor Robert J. Spitzer, SUNY-Cortland, who has published several books on gun control, commented in 2015 on Lott's third edition: "others who have analyzed his data have concluded that it not only does not support his more-guns-less-crime thesis but in fact reveals opposite trends."[62] Spitzer also complained: "Lott has engaged in a series of problematic behaviors, including making up a fictional person who extolled his work on the Internet (using the name "Mary Rosh"), referring to study findings that he could not produce, and other problems." Lott, however, was unwilling to let Diaz and Spitzer have the last words; in 2016, he published *The War on Guns: Arming Yourself Against Gun Control Lies.*

In 1999, Sarah Brady retired from chairman of HCI, and so did its president. The latter was replaced by Mike Barnes, a former Maryland congressman. Soon afterwards, HCI's board changed its name to Brady Campaign to Prevent Gun Violence, in recognition of the campaigning of both Sarah and Jim, with him being also a reminder of the effects of gun violence.[63] They both continued to speak wherever the Campaign wanted them to go. They also returned to Washington for the Million Mom March on 14 May 2000, to urge more gun control laws.

There was a shooting at the Los Angeles Jewish Community Center on 10 August 99, with three children and two adults wounded. Donna Dees-Thomases in New Jersey watched TV reporting on it and became angry. She persuaded six others from the New York area to join her in holding a news conference announcing their intent to organize a Million Mom March on Mother's Day, 14 May 2000, in Washington, D.C., to protest the lax gun control laws in America. About 750,000 women, men, and older children did march as planned in Washington, and in other cities there were about 250.000 marchers. The women who organized it transformed it into an organization to hold annual marches. In 2001, New Jersey's MMM got its legislature to pass a law requiring all new handguns have childproof safety features. In 2002 MMM persuaded H. R. Block to cancel its plan to donate money to NRA for every member who had his tax return prepared at one of its offices. In 2005, Illinois MMM persuaded its legislature to close the gun show loophole that had allowed gun sales without background check. In 2007, MMM had seven state legislatures push for laws to ensure that mental health records were uploaded to the National Instant Check System for gun purchases.

In 2000, Missouri's Democratic former governor, Mel Carnahan, decided to run against John Ashcroft for Senate. The Bradys were friends with the Carnahans and also felt that Republican Ashcroft was far too conservative for Missouri. They gladly pitched in, but Carnahan died in a small plane crash heading for a political rally. However, the current governor announced that if Carnahan won the race, he would name Mel's wife, Jean, to fill that seat.[64] The Carnahans did win, but Ashcroft still went to Washington, as President George W. Bush's Attorney General. The Bradys did not win many of their battles. They supported in a Virginia Senate race Democrat Chuck Robb, who had been a strong supporter of gun control. NRA supported former Virginia Governor George Allen, who won that contest.

The gun control debate reached a stalemate, in which all the arguments which either side proposed were countered by equally plausible refutations by the other side. That was nicely illustrated by two collections of pro and con arguments published in 2000 and 2006.[65] Professor James Jacobs, New York University, argued in *Can Gun Control Work?* (2002) that interpretation of the Second Amendment as guaranteeing an individual's right to own a gun for protection would promote more rational gun policies. In 2008, Jacobs' position became law, in the Supreme Court's decision in *Heller v. District of Columbia.* Lawyer Dennis Henigan became vice president for law and policy at the Brady Center to Prevent Gun Violence, and he founded its Legal Action Project. After 20 years tenure, he wrote *Lethal Logic: Exploding the Myths that Paralyze American Gun Policy* (2009). He pointed out that the same decision in favor of Heller listed gun laws not affected by its decision to allow citizens to own guns for protection.[66] The NRA hoped to maximize the breadth of the decision, but Henigan disputed NRA's interpretation of the ruling.

On 14 Dec. 2017, the fifth anniversary of the Sandy Hook Elementary School shooting, a National Interfaith Clergy Witness gathering occurred outside the NRA headquarters in Fairfax, VA, attracting about 500 participants who remembered 20 students and 6 educators murdered there, while also attacking the lobbying, greed, and lack of humanity of the NRA. The massacre of 17 people at the Marjory Stoneman Douglas High School in Parkland, FL occurred on Valentine's Day, 2018; surviving students gathered a week later at the Florida Capitol to protest legislative inaction, despite there being 239 school shootings in the United States since Sandy Hook in which 438 people were shot, killing 138.[67] They demanded new laws which would ensure that Douglas High was the last school shooting. Earlier government inaction became such an embarrassment that both President Donald Trump and Florida Governor Rick Scott proposed new legislation to ensure schools safety from guns, and the Florida Legislature actually passed a bill raising age for purchase of all guns to 21, and a ban on assault guns.

Corporations that had been giving NRA members discounts suddenly backed away from those agreements, as they felt the heat of opposition to NRA. High school students confronted law makers and President Trump and asked them to stop accepting NRA political money. Students also asked Congress to lift restrictions on gun crime data, so CDC can carry out studies relating to gun safety. On March 14, a month after the Parkland massacre, and on April 20, 19 years after the Columbine massacre, high school students all over America marched to demand that laws be passed to prevent further massacres.[68]

The NRA has not, however, been a shrinking violet. It managed a few counter-protests, though with considerably less public impact than the student marches.[69]

# 9

## Laws: Making America Safe for Guns and Dangerous for People, including Law Enforcers

The United States is the best run large democracy in the world. It functions as well as we imperfect Americans should reasonably expect. A diverse nation, some ethnic and racial groups have shown hostility toward others with different backgrounds, looks, and standards. The rich and powerful have always thought they know best, and have used their wealth and power to exert influence over government disproportionate to their numbers. Competition in business and commerce is often stiff, producing winners and losers. Some citizens willfully disobey laws, because of self-interest or a belief that certain laws are improper. Our socio-political problems are challenging enough to keep us busy, as in other democracies, but our democracy has an additional burden of a tradition of violence, frequently leading to gunfire toward others. Law enactment has been very erratic and inadequate, and law enforcement, therefore, is no picnic.

### Law Enactment

The first gun law among English settlers was enacted by the Virginia General Assembly in 1619.[1] It outlawed providing Indians with guns or powder, under penalty of death. Other colonies later followed Virginia's lead. However, those laws were ineffective, because trading guns and powder to Indians was very profitable. The situation became complicated when Dutch colonists armed their Indian allies. Should English New York colonists just watch without doing likewise?

In 1624, all men in Jamestown had guns, but not all guns performed reliably, and in time, the rate of gun ownership declined, because as numbers of settlers increased and numbers of Indians decreased, a need for guns as protection also declined. Colonial governments, and later state governments, expected militiamen to bring their own guns to drills, since governments lacked guns. By early 1800s, gun ownership was about 40% of households, with wealthier citizens owning more than poorer citizens. That was before mass production, when each gun was made individually by a gunsmith, and there were no standardized parts to replace damaged parts. Inventor Eli Whitney (see chapter 4) grasped a European idea of interchangeable parts and "Sometime between 1801 and 1807 his system came to fruition."[2] He obtained a government contract to manufacture 10,000 muskets, but it took him 11 years to finish. Presumably, they had interchangeable parts and so were more easily fixed when damaged. The federal government also had two arsenals which made guns, at Springfield, Massachusetts and Harper's Ferry, (now) West Virginia, but their importance declined as private manufacturing increased efficiency and production.

After the War of 1812, state militia deteriorated and gun ownership declined.[3] Fear of a tyrannical federal government had faded away. There were numerous manufacturers of guns in the early decades of the 1800s, but four gradually emerged as the largest and most permanent: Colt, Winchester, Smith and Wesson, and Remington. Assembly-line production increased rate of gun manufacturing and standardized parts, but these companies had to invest in machines to make and assemble the parts and in skilled workers to operate them, and they came to depend upon government contracts to stay in business. When the U.S. Government did not need all the guns they produced, representatives of the companies sold their wares in Europe and elsewhere (Haag 2016:35-40). This situation changed as civil war began to seem likely.

Gun control legislation began in western states, where honest men who wanted guns had rifles or shotguns and criminals had handguns. Therefore, the early laws were against carrying concealed weapons, starting in Kentucky in 1813, and spreading to Indiana and Arkansas before influencing two eastern states, Georgia and finally Virginia in 1838. After the Civil War, several southern states passed laws to prevent freed Blacks from getting handguns. Their earliest efforts were negated by the Fourteenth Amendment to the Constitution, but then they passed other restrictive laws that were only enforced against Blacks.[4]

Although not gun legislation, the Militia or Dick Act (1903) is nevertheless relevant to this history. President Theodore Roosevelt emerged from the Spanish-American War with awareness of the inadequacies of the state militia for meeting modern needs. Secretary of War (now, Defense) was a Wall Street lawyer, Elihu Root, appointed by President McKinley, who agreed with Roosevelt, and the U.S. Army worked with Rep. Charles W. Dick (R-Ohio) to provide a National Guard to replace the antiquated state militia, which could be called up for service by either state or national government.[5] States readily accepted the change, because the federal government was funding the National Guard, whereas the states had never provided adequate funds for the state militia which had existed without federal input.

Until the turn of the century, guns in cities were commonly viewed as an annoyance, not a serious problem. Both gentlemen and criminals began carrying concealed handguns in New York before the Civil War, and in 1863 when draft rioters stole guns from gun stores and used them, the U.S. Army and some police also used guns.[6] An ordnance of 1866 merely made it a misdemeanor to fire a gun in the city. In 1877 another ordnance required a permit to carry a handgun, but it was poorly enforced.[7] Attitudes began to change at the turn of the century. Newspaper editors, judges, and police officials all wanted stricter controls, but in 1905 the Board of Aldermen merely increased the penalty for carrying a gun without a permit. New York's district attorney, William T. Jerome, then tried to get the state legislature to control guns—unsuccessfully. However, in 1910 attitudes changed after a disgruntled former city employee, James Gallagher, shot Mayor William J. Gaynor at a public ceremony; although he survived, his recovery was slow and painful. And this was not an isolated gun assault: New York "seemed in the grip of a crime wave of unprecedented proportions."[8] In the Progressive Era, New York reformers often set an example for the nation. The Corner's Assistant in New York City, George P. Le Brun, was an active reformer who concluded that restriction of handguns in the city would reduce violent deaths by a third, and he persuaded civic leaders to back his proposal to license gun buyers and carriers. City leaders in turn convinced State Senator Timothy D. Sullivan, the city's most popular politician (and a Tammany boss), to introduce into the State Senate Le Brun's bill (which became Sullivan's bill). It had strong New York City support and ineffective opposition from pistol makers, who nevertheless spent $30,000 on the attempt, according to Le Brun.[9] The NRA would have opposed it, but its historian complained that the Sullivan bill passed before opposition could be marshaled.[10] It passed the Senate 35 to 5 and the Assembly 123 to 7, and Governor John A. Dix signed it into law on May 29, 1911. The Sullivan Law was the strictest gun law in America, which pleased the New York police since it enabled them to arrest suspected criminals who possessed guns but not permits for them.[11] The New York State Legislature's response to technical complaints about its gun law was to amend the law, more than forty times, not to repeal it. New York State hoped its gun law would inspire similar laws in other states, and it did so in Arkansas, Hawaii, Michigan, Missouri, New Jersey, North Carolina, and Oregon.[12] Before 1870, police were usually unarmed, but after 1870 New York Police began to arm themselves with guns confiscated from criminals. By the 1890s, they began target practice, and in 1920 they were allowed to wear handguns on a belt.

During the 1920s, fear of armed urban Blacks, southern Europeans, and criminals led to a revival of the handgun control issue. Violent crime increased sharply after World War I. In the early 1920s National Police Conference and American Bar Association passed resolutions favoring gun control, and a National Crime Commission (NCC) was established in 1925 to encourage handgun control and to oppose organized crime. NCC formed a Joint Committee on Firearms Legislation and met with representatives from gun manufacturers and the NRA in hopes of drafting a handgun bill they would accept. The effort failed, and when the NCC had its bill introduced in the New York Legislature, that also failed. There were some state laws passed against carrying concealed weapons, but excepting a federal law against shipping pistols through the mails except to officers of police or military (1927),[13] the gun manufacturers allied with the NRA defeated gun control laws.[14]

Despite the fact that three American presidents had been assassinated in office and attempts had been made on the lives of two others, there were no federal gun laws of any significance on February 15, 1933, when an unemployed bricklayer, Guiseppe Zangara, bought a revolver for $8 in a Miami pawnshop and used it in a failed attempt to assassinate President-elect Franklin D. Roosevelt. Zangara had not had time to practice marksmanship, and he hit five others but not Roosevelt. Mayor Anton Cermak of Chicago died of his wounds on March 6 and Zangara went to the electric chair.[15] Roosevelt already wanted to increase restrictions of national gun laws (as governor of New York State, he had vetoed the legislature's bill to repeal the Sullivan Law). Attorney General Homer Cummings and his staff prepared a series of anti-crime bills in 1933, including a National Firearms Act that went before Congressional Committees in April and May 1934. The NRA's Executive Vice-president, retired Brigadier General Milton A. Reckord, whom one senator called "the most influential man in this country in opposition to firearms legislation," alerted NRA members that he considered the National Firearms Act a bad bill, and they flooded the House and Senate committees with angry letters and telegrams.[16] Reckord had no objection to strict controls of machineguns, sawed-off shotguns, and silencers, and they were the main things regulated in the Act which Roosevelt signed into law.[17] It identified three categories of weapons whose manufacture, sale, and subsequent transfer were taxed and monitored: 1. sawed-off rifles and shotguns; 2. Destructive devices and silencers; 3. fully automatic guns.[18] It was the first of a handful of gun laws passed during sixty years.[19]

In 1935, the Senate Committee on Crime estimated that there were 15-20 million handguns in the USA, and the committee sought to regulate their further manufacture and distribution. The Federal Firearms Act (1938) established a fee-required system of licenses for manufacturers, importers, and dealers, with enforcement in the Department of Treasury. It also established categories of individuals who were "unfit to possess firearms." A former head of the Bureau of Alcohol, Tobacco, and Firearms, William Vizzard, complained that the 1938 Federal Firearms Act (NFA) "proved to be a symbolic effort, with little practical effectiveness."[20]

In 1957, importation of foreign rifles and handguns seemed to the Secretary of Treasury to be creating a problem, and he imposed new rules on gun sales: (1) serialization of all guns, (2) federal records kept by gun dealers to be kept permanently (later changed to ten years); (3) .22-caliber rifles were exempted from the serializations required.[21] It has proven ineffectual in asserting even minimal federal controls over interstate commerce in ordinary handguns, shotguns, and rifles.[22]

Although there were other worthy attempts to restrict guns, no significant laws were passed again at any level of government until 1968. The NRA, ever vigilant, urged weakening existing laws wherever it could. In 1958 Senator John F. Kennedy introduced a modest bill to prohibit importation of foreign surplus guns, but the NRA objected. It only agreed to prohibit the return of U.S. arms sent abroad as foreign assistance. The bill that passed on June 23 allowed the importation of the Italian rifle that killed Kennedy five years later. The Carcano rifle Lee Harvey Oswald bought was advertised in the *American Rifleman*. The day before he shot President Kennedy, the NRA had this amendment inserted into an Arms Control and Disarmament Act:[23]

Nothing contained in this act shall be construed to authorize any policy or action by any Government agency which would interfere with, restrict, or prohibit the acquisition, possession, or use of firearms by an individual for the lawful purpose of personal defense, sport, recreation, education, or training.

The amendment was accepted by Congress and the law passed the day after Kennedy's funeral.

Meanwhile, the Senate Commerce Committee was stalling Senator Thomas Dodd's bill, co-sponsored by Senators Birch Bayh, Sam Ervin, Hiram Fong, and Estes Kefauver—all, like Dodd, Democrats—to limit the mail-order gun business as a way to reduce juvenile delinquency. Dodd chaired the Senate's Subcommittee on Juvenile Delinquency which had achieved passage of its bill outlawing switch-blade knives in 1961. Before writing its gun bill, the Subcommittee had obtained the input of U.S. police chiefs and commissioners, psychiatrists, psychologists, and criminologists, who wanted broader coverage in the National Firearms Act. The subcommittee drafted and passed a bill to require mail-order handgun purchasers to submit a notarized statement certifying that the purchaser was at least 18 years old and lacked a serious criminal record. In August 1963 the bill went to the Senate Commerce Committee where it slumbered. Shotguns and rifles had been omitted from coverage from fear that the NRA would cause its defeat. President Kennedy was assassinated on November 22, 1963, and since Oswald did it with a rifle, Dodd felt it was appropriate and safe to include all firearms, not just handguns, in his bill. The NRA reluctantly agreed in public, but then made it clear to its members that the bill went too far. Many other Americans thought it did not go far enough. Oswald had purchased his rifle using a coupon from *American Rifleman*, and he filled it out using a false name.[24] Democratic Senator Warren Magnuson polled members of the Senate Commerce Committee and announced that no hearings on the bill were needed, and it would be sent to the Senate for a vote. A few days later, the Committee announced that there would be hearings on it after all. Senator Magnuson had forgotten to poll the NRA, which not only opposed inclusion of rifles and shotguns, but really opposed *any* bill being passed. Magnuson announced that he opposed shifting responsibility for gun control from states to the federal government, and when the hearings convened, he was seldom present. The bill never made it out of committee. Senator Dodd, however, reintroduced the bill in subsequent sessions of Congress, and it finally received a vote in the Senate Judiciary Committee on April 4, 1968 and was defeated. About an hour later, James Earl Ray assassinated Martin Luther King, Jr. with a rifle. Despite that fact, the next day Senator Dodd deleted rifles and shotguns from the bill in order to get it to the Senate floor. Reporter Richard Harris published a long article on this struggle in the April 20 issue of *The New Yorker*. Readers may have judged his account a devastating indictment of the NRA's tactics, but it seems unlikely that NRA members noticed, there being little if any overlap in readership between that élite magazine and *American Rifleman* (and which magazine do you think had/has the higher readership in Congress?). On May 16 Senator Edward Kennedy moved to restore coverage in the Senate bill of rifles and shotguns; his amendment was defeated 53 to 29.[25] By then, Senator Robert F. Kennedy was campaigning for the Democratic presidential nomination and stressing the need for tighter gun controls. On June 5, at 12:15 am, he was assassinated by Sirhan B. Sirhan, with a pistol. On that same day, Congress finally passed the first major gun bill in thirty years (to the day), but without coverage of rifles and shot guns. It banned gun sales by mail and across state lines and raised the minimum age for buying guns to 21.[26] It banned import of low-quality "non-sporting" handguns, but not their manufacture in America. Roehm Gesellschaft had made most of the imported Saturday night specials imported before 1968, and it found that it could still sell them by only importing the parts and have them assembled in America. (There were actually two bills passed in 1968: Gun Control Act, and Crime Control and Safe Streets Act.[27]) ATF head Vizzard did not think these acts very effective, because of the compromises necessary to get them passed. He was impressed, however, by its impact at the ATF, which, in 1968-72 "doubled its law enforcement force, while refocusing its mission from alcohol to firearms."[28]

The force of circumstances was too strong for the NRA. Its later historian, Rodengen, entitled his chapter on the years 1967-69 "NRA's Darkest Days."[29] NRA deeply resented the neutrality of 141 members of the House who did not vote.[30] It took the NRA almost two decades to reverse some of the "damage" it perceived in the Gun Control Act of 1968.

In 1972, the Nixon Administration raised enforcement of Federal gun laws from being under the IRS to an independent Bureau of Alcohol, Tobacco, and Firearms, still in the Treasury Department.[31] At that time, it focused its attention upon felons who obtained guns—which was not controversial.[32] Its head, Rex Davis, planned to use computers for gun crime traces, but he was blocked by NRA, which objected to government keeping track of gun owners.[33] A Treasury official complained about Davis provoking the NRA.

In 1974, both the National Coalition to Ban Handguns and the National Council to Control Handguns were founded, and in reaction, NRA created in 1975 its Institute for Legislative Action (NRA-ILA) to lobby federal and state legislative bodies.[34] In 1984, Congress passed a bill which NRA supported: Armed Career Criminal Act, that punished criminals without adding new gun regulations.[35]

In 1980, Stuart Speiser had published *Lawsuits*, which argued that gun dealers who sold guns catering to criminals could be sued.[36] A Foundation for Handgun Education held a convention on gun company lawsuits in 1982.[37] In early 1980s, over 60 lawsuits were filed against gun makers and/or dealers on various grounds, with most cases being dismissed by courts. However, a successful suit was filed by grocery store clerk Olen J. Kelley, who was held up five times and shot the last time. He sued Rohm Gesellschaft in *Kelley v. RG Industries* (1985), and the Maryland Supreme Court declared that "the manufacturer or marketer of a Saturday Night Special knows or ought to know that the chief use of the product is for criminal activity."[38] NRA lobbied the Maryland Legislature to pass a law against this complaint, but instead, it established a Handgun Roster Board to determine which guns could be sold in Maryland. Windle Turley and James E. Rooks published a textbook, *Firearms Litigation: Law, Science and Practice* (2 vols., 1988).[39]

In 1986, the NRA lobbied Congress to roll back some restrictions in the Gun Control Act of 1968. The 1986 Law Enforcement Officers Protection Act was called McClure-Volker Act, for its sponsors, Republican Senator James McClure of Idaho and Democratic Representative Harold Volker of Missouri. It: (1) allowed federal gun license holders to sell guns at gun shows in their state; (2) allowed individuals not federally licenses as gun dealers to sell guns as a hobby; (3) reduced records kept by federally licensed gun dealers; (4) restricted authority of ATF to conduct inspections of premises of federally licensed gun dealers; and (5) expanded federal program to allow rehabilitated felons to have guns.[40] In 1988, the Undetectable Firearms Act passed, which prohibited, with few exceptions, manufacture, important, sale, shipment, delivery, possession, transfer, or receipt of guns with less than 3.7 oz. of metal content, to enable metal detectors at airports to detect them.

Most gun laws are passed at the state and local levels, and NRA kept lobbyists in state capitols. Its Florida lobbyist, 1970s to 2016, was Marion Hammer. She is credited with a law for concealed-carry permits in 1987 that became a standard for other states. In 1988, she started the NRA's youth program on gun safety, Eddie Eagle. More controversially, in 2005, she promoted a stand your ground law. According to English common law, which became the source of many American laws, one is obligated to retreat from a violent confrontation if one can do so safely.[41] Whether that law applied to the age of guns in America became the issue in *Brown v. United States* before the U.S. Supreme Court in 1921. Supreme Court Justice Oliver Wendell Holmes, Jr. decided it did not and he carried the Court's vote.[42] That was a precedent for federal courts, but state courts handled cases that never made it to the Supreme Court, and a state law was needed. Hammer's reward was to become the first woman president of the NRA, 1995 to 1998.[43] In 2010, NRA paid her a $190,000 consulting fee and the Unified Sportsmen of Florida paid her a salary of $100,000. Wayne LaPierre was not the only one at NRA to become wealthy. A recent commentator stated: "At 78, she is nearing four decades as the most influential gun lobbyist in the United States."[44]

In January 1989, Patrick Purdy, 24, a drifter, brought an AK-47 assault rifle to the Cleveland Elementary School, Stockton, CA, and killed 5 children and wounded 33 people, then shot himself.[45] In response, President George W. Bush banned importation of some assault rifles. In 1993, President Bill Clinton broadened this ban.

A maniac, Colin Ferguson, with a handgun equipped with a gun magazine holding 15 bullets, on a commuter train out of New York City on 7 Dec. 1993, in three minutes killed 6 and wounded 19.[46] Ferguson was a middle-class Black from Jamaica (almost all mass shooters are White men). Vietnam vet and lawyer Tom McDermott, 50, a former court prosecutor, was one of the wounded, who later attempted, unsuccessfully, to persuade the state legislature to ban gun magazines that carry 15 bullets, and only allow magazines with 10 bullets. He concluded that the NRA would do or say anything to further its goals.[47] NRA also defeated a proposed Great Neck, Long Island, town ordinance to ban gun stores by arguing that bakeries were more dangerous.[48] Yet, the train massacre did have an impact on Congress, which passed Senator Dianne Feinstein's Assault Weapons Ban in 1994, to ban manufacture of 19 assault guns.[49] The best the NRA could do was to attach a ten-year expiration date to it. As it had hoped, in 2004 it was able to block the ban's renewal.

A non-denominational church sponsored a gathering of Ferguson's victims and their families, and McDermott urged them to stay in touch for joint legal actions. He called Republican Congressman Davy Levy, who supported the NRA's opposition to the assault weapons ban and was not eager to meet with Ferguson's victims.[50] McDermott told him if he did not meet with them, the victims would picket his house. Levy agreed to meet with them at the non-denominational church, where he explained his opposition to the assault weapons ban. McDermott and other victims explained why they supported that bill and eventually he changed his mind and voted for the bill, as did all the other Long Island Congressmen.[51]

Building upon that success, McDermott's victims group traveled to Albany, where the State Legislature was discussing a stricter assault weapons ban then the federal ban. McDermott's group merely wanted to limit bullet clips to ten bullets. When the Senate majority leader was evasive, McDermott's son and his classmates went door to door and sat at malls and got 22,000 signatures on a petition to the Legislature, which astonished the majority leader.[52] As usual, NRA trotted out its argument on German Nazis and Jewish gun confiscations as a warning to Americans.

In May 1994, when Congress passed the assault weapons ban (passed in the House by a vote of 216-214), the bill also finally included McDermott's limit on gun magazines to ten bullets. If McVeigh had not bombed the Murrah Federal Building in 1995, the ban might not have lasted more than a year.[53] That atrocity, however, assured it ten-year enforcement before expiring in 2004, when NRA prevented its renewal. Tim Dickinson published mass shootings data on kills July 2012 to June 2016 with assault rifles, with a total of 124.[54] NRA can certainly claim that it helped make those deaths possible.

McDermott's group succeeded in 2000 in having the New York Legislature pass an assault ban, which remained in effect in 2004 when the national ban expired.[55] McDermott realized that the legislative process was slow and provided modest gains which were not always permanent. His group also tried its luck with the courts. McDermott and 14 other victims of the 1993 commuter train rampage decided to sue both Ruger, that made the gun Ferguson used, and the Olin Corporation, that made Black Talon bullets with which Ferguson shot victims.[56] However, their case was thrown out. McDermott, therefore, decided in 1997 to become one of the lawyers in another case that seemed more likely to succeed, *Hamilton v. Accutek et al.*, which had 48 defendants who were victims of several shootings, suing gun makers, distributors, and dealers, and had survived a court motion to dismiss. Its historian devoted 40 pages to its ins and outs, and in 1999, the verdict favored the plaintiffs, though only one of them received an award, of $4 million.[57] Yet, it was a challenged victory, because a higher court ruled the verdict could only stand if plaintiffs showed that specific dealers played a disproportionate role in supplying criminals with guns. However, that challenge could be met, because ATF had already, in 2000, compiled data showing that 1.2% of dealers sold 57% of crime guns traced.

NRA's most notable legislative achievement was the Supreme Court decision in *Heller v. District of Columbia* (2008), which accepted the NRA's argument (chap. 5) that the Second Amendment guaranteed the right of citizens to have private guns.[58] That reversed a long-standing Supreme Court tradition which had emphasized state militia's rights, not private rights. (Incidentally, NRA had always ignored state militias.) The initiative for change came, not from NRA, but from three lawyers at Washington area libertarian think tanks—Clark Neily and Steve Simpson at the new Institute for Justice (founded 1991) and Robert Levy at the Cato Institute.[59] However, once the crusade was under way, NRA support was crucial for success. Justice John Paul Stevens was a dissenter in the decision, and he later explained why he thought it was a band decision.[60]

Adequate gun laws are blocked by gun rights advocates, guided by NRA's phony baloney propaganda and by other gun rights groups. Professor Robert Spitzer devoted his latest book (2015) to exposing such propaganda for what it is. However, Abigail Kohn, *Shooters: Myths and Realities of America's Gun Culture* (2004), before Gabrielle Giffords and Mark Kelly's book, argued that our gun culture is not going away and that both advocates and opponents of gun control need to adopt new approaches in order to reduce our gun violence. She recommended that both sides relinquish contempt for the other side in order for both to explore different strategies. Whatever works is commendable. She did not suggest that gun advocates assume any burden of guilt for gun mayhem. William Briggs, *How America Got Its Guns: a History of the Gun Violence Crisis* (2017) is topically rather than chronologically organized, though it does include historical information. His perspective is similar to Kohn's, yet he goes further by suggesting what each side of the conflict needs to do.

In 2012, one could wonder if we had made any progress curbing gun violence after George Zimmerman killed unarmed Trevon Martin in Florida, 26 Feb., and was acquitted by a jury after Zimmerman pled self-defense; and after James Eagan Holmes on July 20 killed 12 and wounded 70 in a movie theater in Colorado; and after Adam Lanza on 14 Dec. in Connecticut killed his mother, then went to Sandy Hook Elementary School and killed 20 children and six adults. And one could also wonder why these shootings in addition to those occurring every day of every year were not enough to lead to more comprehensive gun laws.

Such envisioned debates are based upon the assumption that relevant data is accessible to all. Unfortunately, that is not the case. Thomas Diaz explained:[61]

> Given the pestilential effect guns have on America, it is little short of incredible that the gun industry and its relentless lobby have succeeded in preventing the federal government from collecting, organizing, analyzing, and—most of all—releasing detailed data about guns and gun death, injury, and crime in America. What data exists is scattered over several different federal agencies in collections that are more often than not inconsistent, incomplete, and incompatible with each other. Information that might shed light on, for example, what makes and models of guns are used in crimes, and how frequently, is locked up tight. Laws slipped through Congress by lawmakers friendly to the gun industry's agenda bar the release of data—even to members of Congress—that was once freely available and routinely released to the public.

As explained in chapter 5, since Congress was hostile to direct lobbying by gun manufacturers, they turn over vast sums to the NRA to lobby for them.

Since the Sandy Hook Elementary School massacre in 2012, there had been 239 other school shootings in the United States by the time that Nikolas Cruz killed 17 on Valentine's Day, 2018, in which 438 were shot nationwide and 138 of them killed.[62] Students from the 3000 at Marjory Stoneman Douglas High School in Parkland, Florida, and parents, then began to protest Congress' unwillingness to pass effective gun control laws to prevent more such shootings. However, their voices were influential upon the Florida Legislature, that defied NRA and passed a bill raising the age at which one can buy a rifle to 21, to match the age at which one could buy a handgun, and a Republican governor signed it on 9 March 18.

A study published in a March 2018 *JAMA Internal Medicine* showed that both homicides and suicides are fewer in states with strict gun laws and are more in states without strict gun laws.[63]

## Law Enforcement

In antiquity, a constable system of law enforcement arose, but constables had very little, if any, training, and were probably paid accordingly, and the most that could be said was it was possibly better than nothing.[64] Armies could be called upon when needed. New York was one of the main ports for emigrants from Europe, and from 1718 to 1775, Britain sent up to 50,000 convicts to its American colonies.[65] Not surprisingly, by the 1830s, New York, with over 400,000 residents, was prone to riots from whatever might anger a crowd. Constables were unable to suppress riots, so they were supported by a city militia when one could be deployed. However, militia were little trained and only slightly more effective than constables.

In 1789, a few months after President Washington assumed office, Congress passed the Federal Judiciary Act which empowered the Supreme Court and the federal judicial system, to establish the United States Marshal Service to implement and enforce judicial decisions.[66] Washington appointed the first 13 marshals, the very first one being Nathaniel Ramsay, heroic veteran of the Battle of Monmouth Court House.[67] Simultaneously, the Bill of Rights was being voted upon by the states, which would establish state militias. In 1794, after Secretary of Treasury Alexander Hamilton, imposed an excise tax on domestic spirits, the U.S. Marshal from Philadelphia, David Lenox, rode out to serve summons on 75 distillers who had refused to pay; he failed to collect.[68] After five months of Whiskey Rebellion, he returned with a 13,000-man force made up of four state militia, to end rebellion and collect tax.

Sheriffs were law officers in medieval Britain and Europe. In 1829, Sir Robert Peel obtained from Parliament permission to establish metropolitan police in London, and soon elsewhere.[69] Peel's innovation spread to New York City in 1845,[70] and soon afterwards to Philadelphia, Boston, and Chicago. Craig Uchida's 1997 essay on history of American policing provided citations to histories of policing in New York, Boston, St. Louis, Denver, Washington, DC, Richmond, and Detroit, and also to studies on aspects of policing.[71] Bruce Chadwick, *Law and Disorder: the Chaotic Birth of the NYPD* (2017), provided a few details about New York's founding legislature for 1845: constables were replaced by 900 policemen, who were organized into a new bureaucracy and police court.[72]

Professors Louis Radelet and David Carter, in *Police and the Community* observed:[73]

> In their attitudes and values...police officers tend to mirror the socioeconomic, cultural, ethnic, occupational, and educational characteristics of the strata of society in which they are reared. Thus, if a high proportion of officers come from lower-middle- or upper-lower-class backgrounds, having had blue-collar working parents, Indo-European ethnic traits, and the like, it follows that what they say and do as officers will reflect the attitudes and values of that background.

On the western frontier, however, Anglo-American lawmen also had to adapt to the conditions which they faced. Four examples illustrate their challenges: James Butler "Wild Bill" Hickok (1837-76),[74] Pat Garrett (1850-1908),[75] John Henry "Doc" Holliday (1851-87),[76] and William "Bat" Masterson (1853-1921).[77] One example will suffice here.

Hickok was born into an abolitionist family in an Illinois town, now named Prairie Grove. In 1856, he moved to Kansas, where he joined Free State Army defending against pro-slavery frontiersmen in a conflict called "Bleeding Kansas." In 1858 he became a constable in Monticello, and in 1861, he became employed by an express station at Rock Creek, Nebraska, where he participated in a shootout in which three men were killed. That incident became an exaggerated story in *Harper's New Monthly Magazine* (Feb. 1867), with him as hero. During the Civil War, he was a civilian scout for the Union Army, becoming known as "Wild Bill." In 1865, he killed a man in a duel. Later, he became a deputy U.S. marshal and army scout at Fort Riley, Kansas. In 1869, and again in 1871, he had gun fights in which he first killed two men, later one man. In 1871, he became marshal in Abilene, Kansas, but in 1876 he moved on to a gold-mining town, Deadwood, in Dakota Territory, where he was shot in the back during a poker game.

Americans became concerned that Booth's assassination of Lincoln set an example for later assassins. (An attempt on Andrew Jackson's life in 1835 had left no lasting memory in national consciousness.) The Secret Service had been established in the Treasury Department in 1865, to apprehend counterfeiters of U.S. paper money. It proved to be successful, and in 1870, when Congress sent a resolution to President Grant condemning the Ku Klux Klan, his attorney general in 1871 sent eight Secret Service agents to six southern states, and during three years they watched Klan activities and arrested almost a thousand of them, who were prosecuted for illegal actions, and many sent to prison.[78]

Despite that success, the Secret Service fell upon hard times, 1874-90, due to Washington politics and a competition for funds from Congress.[79] On July 2, 1881, Charles J. Guiteau shot President Games A. Garfield, who died on September 19, and Guiteau was hanged in 1882.[80] Assassination of two presidents 16 years apart did not lead to any new initiative to protect presidents, because Congress would not appropriate the money needed.[81] In spring 1894, two agents in Colorado reported to Washington threats heard against President Grover Cleveland.[82] Director William P. Hazen responded by assigning two agents to guard the White House. That summer, Cleveland's family went on vacation along the Massachusetts coast before he could join them, and Mrs. Cleveland heard of a plot to kidnap them, so she requested that the Secret Service send three agents to protect them. Hazen did so, and the same agents guarded Cleveland's family again in summer 1895—both times with Cleveland's approval. That protection, therefore was also extended to the next president, William McKinley, until an audit exposed Hazen's initiative. He was then demoted for exceeding his authority.[83]

On 6 September 1901 Leon Czolgosz shot President William McKinley, who died on September 14.[84] The Secret Service had been created in 1865 to suppress dissemination of counterfeit money. After McKinley's assassination it acquired a second responsibility, to protect the president and vice-president. More comprehensive gun control laws were not enacted. The Secret Service did not save former President Theodore Roosevelt (1858-1919), running for a third term, from being shot by John Schrank in Milwaukee on October 14, 1912.[85] Fortunately, the bullet hit Roosevelt's folded campaign speech and metal glasses case in a pocket and did not penetrate far into his chest, thus preventing his death or serious wounding. Attempts continued against future presidents: Franklin Roosevelt, 1933, Harry Truman, 1950, John F. Kennedy in 1963 (successful), Gerald Ford,

1975, twice, and Ronald Reagan (wounded), 1981. None of these attempts led to new gun laws.

The Department of Justice had no law enforcement service before 1908, and when it needed investigations, it had, since 1871, borrowed agents from Treasury's Secret Service. In 1908, Congress passed an act to stop Justice from borrowing Secret Service agents, and President Roosevelt asked the Attorney General to establish his own investigative service.[86] Attorney General Charles Bonaparte did, hiring 34 agents. In 1909, the next Attorney General, George Wickersham, name the service Bureau of Investigation. By 1910, it had grown to 64 agents and 9 support staff. However, in 1914, when the German ambassador and his agents began espionage and sabotage of U.S. munitions production and shipping to Britain and France, the Bureau of Investigation was too unsophisticated to realize the source of sabotages.[87] Even a warning from British Intelligence seemed to have caused no significant response. The Bureau of Investigation became suspicious, however, when a German agent, using an assumed name attempted to buy 300,000 rifles. When a German spy left a briefcase briefly unguarded where a Secret Service agent could open it, he saw espionage papers inside. Soon afterwards, Bureau of Investigation learned of German documents at the Swiss Consulate in New York City. Bureau agents broke into the consulate, stole the documents from the boxes, which were sealed again, and they left without leaving any noticeable evidence of the action. On 31 Jan. 17, German submarines began sinking American cargo ships without warning, and President Woodrow Wilson placed the Bureau in charge of enforcing a proclamation on enemy aliens. The Bureau assigned 300 agents to the task.

J. Edgar Hoover (1895-72) was a native of Washington, D.C. He became fifth head of the Bureau in 1924, and his political skills at self-promotion and Bureau promotion soon made him and his FBI national icons.[88] Unfortunately, he came to believe that he had a right to impose his concept of good American values upon those who had differing values. Furthermore, he could intimidate members of Congress, who gave him what he wanted, and their only question was, "what else do you want?" He found it convenient to deny the existence of the Mafia until 14 November 57, when a New York State Policeman, Edgar Croswell, noticed a stream of limousines converging on Joseph Barbara's house outside Appalachin, NY.

Croswell already knew that Barbara had been arrested for two murders in Pennsylvania, though convicted of neither. Croswell called for help, and he and other patrolmen at roadblocks determined the identities of 63 other Mafia leaders.[89] Hoover was embarrassed at this exposure and had to establish an organized crime force to study its activities. (Fortunately for Hoover, Don Whitehead's *The FBI's Story* had appeared in 1956.) At Congressional hearings and in the news media, complaints about the FBI became widely known, but that did not stop Hoover from harassing those he considered unpatriotic, including Rev. Martin Luther King, Jr., who won a Nobel Prize before being assassinated in 1968. (Where were FBI agents when King needed them?) By 1970, Hoover was still head of the FBI, but his image was tarnished, and William Turner's *Hoover's FBI: the Men and the Myth* began to describe his puffery and abuse. With the passage of time, Ronald Kessler could lay out that history in greater detail, the positive as well as the negative.[90] During the Trump Administration, the FBI came under Republican fire in response to its investigation of Russian collusion in Trump's 2016 presidential campaign.[91]

Parents of Eliot Ness (1903-1957) were Norwegian immigrants who ran a Chicago bakery.[92] He graduated from University of Chicago in 1925 and returned there to earn an M.A. degree in criminology in 1927, then joined the U.S. Department of Justice and sought to arrest violators of prohibition laws. He saw that some lawmen were corrupt, but he carefully selected eleven assistants who were not, who became known as "untouchables." Ness decided to publicize his work and notified the press about pending raids. He became a hero for pursuing organized crime, and after Al Capone had seven gangster rivals massacred on Valentine's Day, 1929, Ness was involved in arresting him for tax evasion, and Capone went to prison. After undermining organized crime in Chicago, in 1935 Ness was hired by the mayor of Cleveland and then undermined organized crime there. During World War II, he worked in the Defense Department and retired after the war. In 1951, he began drinking heavily and often was not able to work. He died virtually broke, of a heart attack, and left his wife only debts. His lasting fame came from his autobiography, coauthored by Oscar Fraley, *The Untouchables* (1957), published in his last year (at Fraley's initiative), and which later inspired a TV series. Due to publicity from that series, the cover of his autobiography, in a later paperback reprint, stated, "over 2 million copies sold."

Rare, but important sources of information on organized crime for law enforcement are confessions from former members of such enterprises. The earliest and most famous example was by Joseph Valachi (1903-71), who, in October 1963, created another sensation similar to the 1951 Kefauver hearings by testifying before the McClellan Senate Crime Committee, on television.[93] Valachi was a loyal member of Cosa Nostra (Mafia) in New York for over 30 years before going to prison, and he remained loyal until he became aware that he was marked for murder by mob boss Vito Genovese, Valachi's cell mate.[94] In 1962 he beat to death a fellow prisoner whom he mistakenly thought was going to murder him. Valachi's testimony before a Senate committee may have been in part to avoid a death sentence for murder. Valachi's testimony was not dull. Attorney General Robert Kennedy thought that Valachi had provided the "biggest single intelligence breakthrough yet, in combating organized crime and racketeering in the United States."[95] Valachi explained that the mob did not call itself Mafia, but rather Cosa Nostra.[96] He was spared a death sentence but did die in prison, from a heart attack. However, he did live to see his *Papers* become the basis of a book by Peter Mass.[97]

The dust jacket of James Lardner's biography of detective David Durk (1936-2012) commented that "he ranked low on the traditional measures of qualification for the police department—he was not blue collar, Irish, or Italian, and none of his relatives were cops."[98] It could have added that he was also a graduate from Amherst College and had attended Columbia Law School. From such an unconventional background, he caused trouble. He joined the New York Police in 1963 and soon saw that some police accepted bribes from drug dealers and were engaged in graft and extortion, which was condoned by other officers, who turned a blind eye to it. He and fellow officer Frank Serpico went to the press with their complaints of police corruption in the late 1960s and early '70s, leading to major reforms.

As long as local law enforcers performed their duty as expected—maintaining peace and apprehending violators of laws—they were, by and large, taken for granted.[99] Radelet and Carter identified seven potential conflicts between law enforcers and citizens within their district: excessive force, corruption, rudeness, authoritarianism, politics, responding to public needs, and public paradox.[100] Most relevant here is excessive force. (The public paradox is reconciling freedoms with law-and-order.)

A unique mob informant was Robert Cooley (b. 1942), son and grandson of Chicago police officers, who went to Loyola University, but also became a police officer himself at age 20, before graduating.[101] In 1970 he became a licensed attorney, though he was already involved in gambling. As his gambling debts grew, and his clients were mobsters, he became a conduit of bribes to judges, law makers, and law enforcers. However, in 1986 he decided to flip and began wearing hidden recorders for the FBI. That meant he also had to be a witness against them at trials. During the 1990s, his evidence sent 24 men to prison—judges, mobsters, politicians, and law enforcers. That meant he also had to spend the rest of his life in unknown locations in a witness-protection program.

When law enforcers are in the news, it is most commonly about a shooting that in retrospect seemed to some of the public to have been unnecessary—mostly of Black men. A basic problem that goes unmentioned is that law officers fear for their own lives because so many Blacks have guns and are quite willing to use them against police when it seems to them to be warranted. A related dilemma is that some shooters decide to take revenge by assassinating law officers who are not involved in a conflict, because they represent their profession. Both problems would end if Black men decided to relinquish their guns. (I doubt my suggestion will cause a stamped of them to do so!) The use of lethal force is a dilemma for law officers, who will be scrutinized for their decision: was it justified? As Chris McNab explained in *Deadly Force* (2009), even when those investigators conclude it was, that does not necessarily end the matter. Supporters of the person shot are unlikely to be satisfied with an innocent judgment: was it biased? And if the judgment is that it was not justified, the officer is likely to lose his job, and he may even be prosecuted for a crime. Books which discuss both sides of the conflict are: Larry McShane, *Cops under Fire: the Reign of Terror against Hero Cops* (1999); Jill Nelson, editor, *Police Brutality: an Anthology* (2000), and at a local level, Marilynn Johnson, *Street Justice: a History of Police Violence in New York City* (2003). What can be said here is, the habit of some police departments of selling confiscated guns to the public is counterproductive; some of such guns were sold to criminals and used to commit new crimes.[102]

Daryl Francis Gates (1926-2010) grew up in Highland Park, in northeast Los Angeles. By his own testimony, he was "a quiet little kid, really shy."[103] But he did not remain shy. His father taught him to box, and at age 15 he announced he would become a professional fighter. In a way, he did, for after graduating from high school he joined the Navy and saw action in the Pacific during World War II. Afterwards, he married and attended Pasadena City College for two years, then switched to University of Southern California and finished his studies after joining the Los Angeles Police Department. In 1949 he became chauffeur for Chief William Parker (d. 1966), which was a valuable opportunity to learn professional insights and details of administration. He worked hard to pass exams to become a sergeant, later, lieutenant, and still later, Parker promoted him to captain and made him his executive officer responsible for intelligence. He was an inspector when the Watts riots occurred, 11-16 Aug. 65, in response to a minor traffic stop, but that was only a spark to ignite smoldering resentment of police racial brutality. During the riot, Gates realized that LAPD's training on how to handle a crowd of rioters did not apply to what they now faced—snipers in houses.[104] He was assisted by other officers in developing the first Special Weapons and Tactics (SWAT) police unit.[105] Joe Domanick explained:

> These warrior assault units were armed with MP5 9mm submachine guns, Cold CAR-15 5.56mm assault rifles with double banana-clip magazines, Benelli 121-M-1 semiautomataic shotguns, scoped bolt-action sniper rifles, flash-bang devices, and other advanced weaponry. The SWAT model spread quickly across the country.[106]

He became deputy chief in 1968, shortly before Senator Robert F. Kennedy was assassinated (5 June 68) after winning California's presidential primary. Gates believed that police would have prevented the assassination, but Kennedy did not want them present.[107] Gates became chief on 28 March 78.

On 4 March 1991, before boarding a plane in Washington, D.C., for L.A., Gates phoned LAPD and was told everything was fine. When he entered his official car late that night, his driver said, "I've got some real bad news for you, Chief."[108] He then heard that four of his officers had been videotaped beating a Black man on the ground 56 times earlier that night, and that the film was all over TV channels. Rodney G. King, 25, had served time for armed robbery and been paroled three months earlier. Two California Highway Patrol were chasing him at a high speed, and after he left the freeway and ran four red lights, he was chased by LAPD in both squad cars and a helicopter. After leading his car, King was uncooperative, and so shot with a taser gun, with no apparent effect, since he charged an officer. What happened next was not pretty, and Gates, in horror, watched the film over and over. The four officers were indicted for use of excessive force.[109] It led to calls for his resignation, and the *Los Angeles Times* ran a headline: MAYOR'S OFFICE SEEN DIRECTING OUSTER EFFORT.[110] Gates responded: "I am going to stay because eighty-three hundred police officers want me to stay..."[111] And left unsaid, LAPD was the dominant institution in L. A.[112]

Those four officers stood trial in 1992, and aside from one minor guilty verdict against Laurence Powell, the jury found them not guilty on 29 April 1992.[113] Gates had been on LAPD during the Watts Riot, 11-16 June 65, precipitated by an attempted arrest of a drunk driver in Watts. It resulted in $40 million in damages in L.A. Surely, with his SWAT team, Gates would be prepared if L.A. ever faced another such riot? Well, no. The Rodney King riot, 29 April-4 May 1992, caused $1 billion in damages, and LAPD's 8300 officers were unable to suppress it. The governor called out 2000 National Guard, then it was still necessary to call in the 1st Marine Division and 7th Infantry Division. Gates' excuse "on national TV was a rambling mix of contradictions, factual distortions, and denial."[114] Gates retired on 28 June 92.

Gina Gallo was a member of the Chicago Police, 1982-98, then published her memoirs.[115] Her father was a 30-year veteran of the same force. She did not anticipate following in his footsteps, but she heard of his experiences, almost daily as a child. In college, she had studied to be a psychotherapist, then discovered her salary was quite modest. A friend told her about the benefits package of police, and told her she could go from her 23 weeks at the Police Academy into the Police Department Counseling Center, and she was convinced. However, after graduating from the Academy, despite her qualifications, she did not go to the Counseling Center, but was assigned to a beat just like the other graduates, with "gangs, whores, and hustlers."[116] When she wrote a ticket to a man who had "connections," as he warned her. When she returned to the station, she was chewed out by a superior, who already knew of the ticket before she arrived. He ended by saying:[117]

> I'll give you this break this time because you're new and don't know your ass from a hole in the ground. Don't let it ever happen, or I'll bury you in the projects on foot patrol for the rest of your career.

Learning about police culture turned out to be important. On the beat, she also learned she was a cop, not a social worker. A car swerved into her patrol car and Gallo wound up in a hospital; her partner told her not to stay there long, because she was still a recruit and a woman.[118] Later, she chased a Black man in a ghetto, who had wounded his woman with a knife, and as he fled from Gallo, he pulled out a handgun, and so she fired and killed him with her gun.[119] Her book described her struggles during 16 years, which ended after she and her rooky partner answered a disturbance call in another ghetto, from a mother about her 19-year-old son.[120] While talking with the mother, the son came up behind her and began hitting her with a baseball bat. Her partner apparently fled while she was yelling for him to shoot the son. The son took her gun and was leaving the apartment, when he was shot dead and she awoke in a hospital.

By 2006, there were 17,535 names engraved on the walls of the National Law Enforcement Officers Memorial, of officers killed since 1792.[121] Over 56,000 officers are assaulted each year, with over 16,000 significant injuries.

The National Instant Criminal Background Check System (NICS) reported that the record number of checks in a single day for buying guns was 203,086 in 2017, up from the previous record of 185,713 in 2016. Might that reflect greater confidence in Obama's presidency than in Trump's?

Fig. 14. These men have blood on their hands—call them. Alex Lubben &
Jessica Corbett. *The Nation* (Oct. 2016).
"This article was first published by The Nation magazine and is reprinted
here with permission."

## Conclusions

History of U.S. gun laws can be divided into two parts: before 1911
and after 1911. Before, there was a miscellany of laws since 1619. Ever since
1911, when New York State passed a gun law requiring a permit to carry
one in New York City, NRA has sought to prevent new gun laws, and ever
since victims of gun violence began suing gun manufacturers, distributors,
and dealers, NRA has sought to foreclose that possibility with new laws
to protect the gun industry, making America safe for guns, but dangerous

for people. Its efforts have succeeded much more than they have failed. Gun laws have passed only after some attention-getting gun crime, but not always even then. NRA has at times had Congress add a ten-year expiration to some laws that passed, and NRA usually succeeded in having attempts to renew such laws defeated.

Law officers have existed in civilization since antiquity, with constables depending on common sense and receiving little, if any, pay. Additional support came from armies, if needed. Sheriffs became part of law enforcement by the Middle Ages. Constables, sheriffs, and armies were continued through succeeding ages, and militia were added along the way. By 1829, when London had grown beyond the effectiveness of that system, Sir Robert Peel persuaded the British Parliament to fund a city police force. It succeeded, and in 1845 that level of law enforcement was introduced into New York City, and from there to other American cities.

The new Federal Government found a need for a federal force to enforce decisions of federal courts, and so a U.S. Marshal Service was founded in 1789 and continues until the present. However, the U.S. Constitution's Bill of Rights was being voted on by the states at the same time, which established state militias. In 1794, the Marshals were too few to ensure implementation of federal tax laws, and four state militia were called upon for assistance.

# 10

## Costs of Gun Violence

Gun violence costs America $100 billion a year, according to two professors of public policy.[1] That enormous sum would be better spent on social programs to minimize or eliminate violence. Professors Philip Cook and Jens Ludwig devote a book to explaining how they determined this figure and suggesting ways to mitigate the carnage. They admit, however, that there is no way to measure the pain and suffering of gunshot victims and to people connected to victims.

Their statistics are important, but it is easier to appreciate particular examples. The *Milwaukee Journal Sentinel* published a series of four articles (Nov. 2006) on gun violence in its medium-sized city of half a million. These articles focused on gunshot victims who were not killed. The first article described the "lifeline" medical system that responds to gunshot victims.[2] Each year in Milwaukee there are about 100 gun homicides and about 600 people wounded. The many police, ambulance drivers, paramedics, nurses, x-ray and other technicians, and doctors who assist the wounded save almost 90 per cent of those treated. Cell phones help save some lives by decreasing the time between shootings and the arrival of paramedics. Most of the wounded receive only a few lines of attention in newspapers.

The usual process is for police and ambulance to arrive where the victim is. Police study the crime circumstances and paramedics assess the wounds and prepare victims for the ambulance race to a hospital emergency room. Along the way, morphine and/or blood may be administered and there is intervention to stop or slow the loss of blood. By the time the ambulance arrives, a team of doctors and nurses are usually preparing to handle the victim. X-rays are taken and then surgery is likely to end bleeding and repair organs and tissue. Victims stay in the hospital until they are well enough to leave, though some leave earlier and may suffer medical consequences for doing so. Police may interview a victim who is in the hospital about what happened and the shooter's identity.

A second major effect is the "wounds that never heal," both physical and psychological.[3] The authors describe the shattered lives of three young Black shooting victims. Seventy-six per cent of Milwaukee gunshot victims are Black. Judea Mack was shot in the leg when she was ten years old by a stranger, looking for someone else. She was 16 when the authors interviewed her. She has a limp and a loss of confidence kept alive by gunshots that still ring out in her neighborhood. After the shooting, post-traumatic stress caused her hair to fall out, though it later grew back. Before the shooting, she was very sociable, but afterwards she remains alone much of her time. She wants to go to college far from Milwaukee, in Tennessee.

Greg Rogers was a senior at Juneau High School. While walking home from school on December 1, 2005 he was shot twice in the face by a gunman he had never seen before. The shots paralyzed the left side of his tongue and damaged a vocal cord before lodging in the back of his neck where they remain. Before, he had a strong voice, but now he can barely be heard. One bullet hit his carotid artery and he was in danger of bleeding to death, but paramedics rushed him to Children's Hospital, where his life was saved and he remained unconscious for three days. Previously, he had been active in football, wrestling, track, and roller-skating, but now he can do none of these. He hopes to work on cars or to become a carpenter.

Bruce Jones, age 18, is the son of a "drug kingpin." At age 14, he shot at someone and was sent to a reformatory school for three years. On June 30, 2005 a young boy told Bruce that an older teenager was picking on him. Bruce slapped the 19-year-old in the face, and the bully left. But later, he ambushed Bruce with a semi-automatic gun having a 17-shot magazine of 9 mm bullets. He fired all 17 at Bruce and hit him with four, leaving him mostly paralyzed from his waist down. He may be able to walk with braces and crutches or a rolling walker, but a wheelchair is easier. His Medicaid bills are tens of thousands a year. He may live into his 60s or 70s.

There are substantial costs to the taxpayer of gun crimes in hospitals, jails, and courts.[4] In 2005, the average cost for the 236 gunshot victims treated at Froedtert Hospital was $38,172, not including physician fees and rehabilitation. Most victims are uninsured. The most-costly wounds are paralyzing ones, which includes broken bones and the danger of deadly diseases. Paraplegics and quadriplegics are at risk for diabetes, cancer, heart disease, and osteoporosis. In Milwaukee, a typical shooting costs additionally $3000 for police investigation, $1200 for paramedics, $1500 for police if they go to court, $4200 for prosecutors and staff if it becomes a criminal court case, and $27,600 if an offender is sent to prison.

Besides these financial statistics, two examples give only their first names. Tony, 43, was a large man who was shot in his side on July 14. He would seem to be the more serious case, but a CAT scan indicated the bullet had missed any organs, hitting only muscle and fat. He went home that night, with the bullet still in his side, yet his hospital cost was $8,700, not including doctor fee. James, 45, was shot in a car on Sept. 9, and the other man in the car was shot dead. James was wounded in a knee, arm, and an eye—none life threatening. However, he suffered complications in the hospital and had to stay 48 days, until Oct. 20, with hospital costs of $277,000, of which Medicare paid $36,000. Medicade and Milwaukee County also paid smaller portions of the bill. Our authors explain that "losses on all those cases are factored into the rates the hospital must charge private insurers."

The fourth article is on the city's response to gun casualties.[5] Froedtert Hospital was treating 34% more gunshot victims in 2006 than in 2005, and Children's Hospital was treating 38% more. The Police Dept. was studying ways to better deploy its police to respond to the problem. Mayor Tom Barret responded by adding funds for 40 additional police officers and by asking the state legislature for stricter gun laws. Prof. Stephen Hargarten, Medical College of Wisconsin, urged that gun violence be tackled the way car crashes were in the 1960s, by improving technology—making guns only usable by authorized owners—and to use tougher measures to limit access to guns. These two suggestions might be possible if guns were no more a political issue than cars are.

Another way to appreciate the cost of gun is to envision historical consequences of our assassinations. President Lincoln had the character and vision to have made the best of reconstruction, which would have been in many ways much better than the muddle-along that the country actually endured. The same was probably also true of President Kennedy. He inherited the Bay of Pigs invasion into Cuba, which was a disaster, but he learned from his mistakes and compensated with his diplomatic handling of the Cuban missile crisis. He conveyed optimism to the country, cut short by an assassin. The same can be said of his brother, Senator Robert F. Kennedy, who seems a good bet to have also become president had his career not ended in the same way. Malcolm X and Martin Luther King, Jr. were contrasting leaders of America's Blacks, and both provided much needed encouragement to that still-disadvantaged portion of our people. Malcolm X's career was ended by a Black rival's follower, and King's by a White racist.

Still another way to appreciate the costs of our gun violence is to contemplate the all-to-numerous mass murders, which could only have occurred with guns. There have now been so many of them that we generally only recall the most horrific, whether in schools—Columbine, Sandy Hook, Parkland—or in public gatherings—an Orlando nightclub, a Las Vegas concert. All those massacred were citizens who deserved to lead their lives as they wished, without them being ended by a deranged executioner.

Or just contemplate this: 1.6 million Americans have died from domestic gunfire since 1968. As Gabby Giffords said, "Enough!"

Fig. 15. We are doing something about this gun violence.
Robert Ariail. Oct. 2017.

# Appendix: Quantitative Estimates

Professors Cook and Ludwig estimated that in 2000 the cost of gunshot injuries was about $5-10 billion a year of their total estimate that gun violence costs society about $100 billion a year.[6] Costs do vary over time, but there are a number of different factors which influence costs, which make prediction of trends difficult. Katherine Fowler and collaborators commented in 2015: "More than 32,000 persons die and over 67,000 persons are injured by firearms each year."[7] However, they also found that "rates of firearm violence declined significantly," from 1993 to 1999. However, "while unintentional firearm deaths continued to decline from 2000 to 2012, firearm suicides increased and nonfatal firearm assaults increased to their highest level since 1995." Too complicated to make predictions.

For 2015, Faiz Gani, Joseph Sakran, and Joseph Canner found that there were 36,252 deaths from guns—homicides and suicides.[8] Guns were the third leading cause of injury-related deaths in America, after poisonings and car accidents. Further, fatal and non-fatal gun injuries cost over $700 million in annual inpatient costs between 2006 and 2014 and an annual cost of $174 billion related to lost work, health care, criminal justice, and decreased quality of life in 2010. Gani et al. also registered two complaints: "Efforts to reduce firearm-related injuries have been limited as a result of the politicized environment surrounding gun violence." and "Despite the high clinical and financial burden associated with firearm-related injuries, resources allocated to prevent them remain low."[9]

Sarabeth Spitzer and collaborators published a more precise figure for average yearly medical cost for 2006-14, of $734.6 million.[10] Medicade paid a third of it and patients paid a quarter. However, Spitzer et al. added that "These figures substantially underestimate true health care costs."

# CONCLUSIONS

Each chapter has a conclusion, and here is my synthesis.

Guns were among the most conspicuous and dramatic advantages which enabled Europeans to take this continent from sparsely settled American Indians, who had only bows and arrows and spears. Yet, English and Dutch settlers very early began trading guns to Indians and sometimes hired Indians to hunt game for European settlers. The French and Spanish were less eager to trade guns to Indians but were nudged into doing so by their English competitors. Anglo-Americans more or less continuously fought Indians, French, and Spanish soldiers, and then fought the mother country in a War of Independence (1775-81) and the War of 1812 (1812-15).

13 independent states united to write a Constitution (1787), which then needed each state's ratification. There was much to like in what had been written, but having recently overthrown British domination, there was some concern among the states that in the future, the Federal Government might become tempted to play a role similar to that of Britain and tyrannize the states. Twelve states had ratified it by August, 1788, but several states urged it be amended to lay to address those fears. That concern was laid to rest by the U.S. House of Representatives, which offered the states twelve possible amendments on 9 Sept. 1790, ten of which had been accepted by the states by Dec. 22. Those ten amendments became the Bill of Rights on 15 Dec. 1791.

The Second Amendment concerned a guarantee that each state could maintain its own armed militia, with members having their own guns. The state militias performed rather poorly in the War of 1812, and by then, fears of the Federal Government had dissipated, followed by dissipation of interest in state militia. Nevertheless, that concern about a possible Federal Government dominating states arose again in 1861, when slave-holding southern states wanted to succeed from the Union. A new President, Abraham Lincoln, disapproved, and a Civil War was fought over that issue, and the Confederate States' Army surrounded to the U.S. Army, some two weeks after Lincoln's assassination, on 18 April 65. That war had barely ended before Americans spread West and precipitated the final Indian wars which ended in 1890, soon followed by the Spanish-American War and World Wars I and II. American men in cities who might never have picked up a gun were trained to use guns while in the armed services and felt comfortable using them after their tours of duty. Guns had been used to shoot deer and turkey for food soon after European settlers arrived in America.

Colonial gunsmiths were usually blacksmiths who made and repaired guns. During the War of Independence, General Washington learned that dependence on purchase of foreign guns was risky, and President Washington concluded that the United States needed arsenals to make guns for its army, and established two. The prominence of guns in American history did not in itself produce a gun culture. Pamela Haag (2015) argued that developing a gun culture was a deliberate strategy of gun manufacturers, in order to increase gun sales to private individuals. David Cole (2016) suspected that she had given too much credit to a single source. I agree. American wars, tradition, and fiction—in books, films, TV, and video games—played major roles in creating that culture. Additionally, action fiction provided a model of solving problems with violence and guns.

The gun lobby, especially the NRA, takes the position that its responsibility is to protect gun freedom, and that public safety is the business of government. This is a shirking of civic responsibility by members of the gun lobby. Public safety is a responsibility of all competent citizens, and when laws and policies which the NRA advocates endanger public safety, NRA leaders have advocated policies counterproductive for all Americans. Assuming that Wayne LaPierre believes his own propaganda, he may be compared to Benjamin Rush (1745-1813). Rush was the most prominent physician of his time, signer of the Declaration of Independence, who nevertheless advocated two medical remedies now known as harmful: bleeding and purging.[1] Americans should ask NRA members to face up to their civic responsibility as citizens. NRA arguments for the necessity of private guns are absolute, and so fallacious. There are hundreds of millions of private guns in America, and no political leaders are stupid enough to think they could all be seized, if any such leaders ever had such a silly thought. And, if there ever were an American who aspired to become a tyrant (which I doubt), he would need to depend upon police and armed forces to undermine their own democracy, and no members of these services would carry out such an order. The Republican Party has become partners with NRA, accepting its demand for no new gun laws in exchange for its money and endorsements.

I do not advocate government seizure of private guns (which would be impossible). I do advocate Americans seeing that our gun culture is counter-productive to achieving a peaceful society, and seeing that maintaining a gun culture is not worth the tradeoff.

There are, in my judgment, two major and one minor impediments to diminishing gun violence in our society: major ones are NRA propaganda and violent fiction of all sorts; minor impediment is the ability of the mentally ill to obtain guns. NRA propagandist Wayne LaPierre's validly attacks Hollywood for its production of violent films, and the ability of the mentally ill to obtain guns as important factors in causing a violent society. Yet, his motive was to shift all blame to those factors, and thereby evade any blame of NRA's gun lobby as being the most important factor, which includes Stand Your Ground laws.

From watching Sesame Street with my children when they were young, I remember one exchange between Ernie and Bert. Bert appeared with a banana in his ear, and Ernie asked why. Bert: it keeps alligators away. Ernie: but we do not have any alligators. Bert: see, it works! NRA propaganda is similar to Bert's logic: privately owned guns are essential to keeping our government from oppressing us. See, we have private guns and government is not oppressing us! That is a decisive argument for naive NRA members, who are willing to take political guidance from NRA.

If the United States was the only nation on Earth, it might be difficult to challenge that logic. However, it is not the only one: Australia, Japan, United Kingdom, France, Germany, Italy, and others, do not have oppressive governments and private gun ownership is very low in these countries. There is nothing more sinister about America's government than in these other countries, and there is no realistic argument that private guns are any more essential in America than in those countries to prevent government oppression. However, NRA's 1977 decision to make its original orientation toward target shooting and hunting a minor consideration in favor of NRA being America's premier gun lobby paid off handsomely for its officers, since NRA propaganda was very persuasive to its members.

At the time of government sieges at Ruby Ridge in 1992 and Waco in 1993, gun rights advocates accused the FBI and ATF of excessive force and tyranny. These agencies are able to concentrate agents at troubled hot spots when needed, but that is a long way from being able to tyrannize the country. As Firmin DeBrabander commented,[2] there is no conflict with the federal government when it seeks to regulate food protection or worker safety. The above mentioned two tragedies occurred because the people in these places were guided by a defiant ideology when confronted by regulatory government agents. The same was true when the Citizens for Constitutional Freedoms seized the Malheur National Wildlife Refuge on January 2, 2016. Both sides, however, seemed to have learned from the previous confrontations, and this ended peacefully on February 11, though at the end, one leader was shot dead trying to resist arrest.

Perhaps NRA's greatest achievement was brain-washing five million members into believing their freedom is in danger without their private guns. In fairness to its members, most have limited education, and they do not so readily see through this ridiculous claim as citizens with college/university degrees. Still, the fact that the NRA can for decades yell "wolf" and "the sky is falling" and still pull it off with a straight face is remarkable. The existence of state militia, which in 1903 became the National Guard, has never been part of the NRA's narrative. That would require a complicated argument; better keep it simple.

The conclusion of this professor-historian (emeritus) is that our gun culture had its uses in establishing American civilization, as slavery did, but we came to recognize (after a bloody civil war) that slavery was a gigantic mistake, and now I think it time to realize that our gun culture was a similarly gigantic mistake, though of a different kind, and we need to do what we can to minimize its horrible impacts and move on to a more positive development of a humane civilization.

# ESCAPING OUR
# GUNCRAZY CULTURE

First, and foremost, no American government is ever going to confiscate the guns of "law-abiding citizens!" It is a completely impractical project, and no American government would ever be so foolish as to try. Yet, that government might do so is the panic button that the NRA pushes constantly to extract dues from its 5 million members and also to prevent all legislative bodies from passing important gun legislation. How many times can NRA shout "wolf" before the faithful catch on to the scam? Members, it is time to recognize "the emperor has no clothes."

The NRA's general argument is that we have enough gun laws and we only need more law-abiding citizens carrying guns for their protection. This argument is self-serving and very pessimistic. Presumably, if all us law-abiding citizens with guns shoot all the bad guys with guns, then we can have a peaceful society. There is no real evidence that this could ever happen.

The alternative for which I argue is more complex than this, and more realistic. The NRA is part of the problem, not the solution. Its propaganda-lobbying machine is the most effective in America and has not led to a less violent society. Should not its political influence produce some discernable positive results? And should we not hold the NRA responsible for depriving America of adequate gun laws?

Slavery was one enormous blunder, initially accepted by America and its Constitution. Our guncrazy culture is another enormous blunder accepted by our democracy, and protected by the Supreme Court's 2008 interpretation of the Second Amendment. It took a civil war to rid America of slavery. Another civil war will not happen. Yet, this blunder is only slightly less tragic than slavery was. A third enormous blunder was the production of cigarettes. That happened long before physicians discovered that smoking leads to serious diseases and shortened lifespans. A U.S. Surgeon General's report in 1964 announced the link between smoking and health, and by 2015, almost all of the middle class had ceased smoking. Why the working class has not done so is a mystery. One blue-collar worker commented to me: "No point in living if you cannot enjoy life!" Yet, America is not so inflexible that it cannot change for the better.

My suggestions:

1. End violent fiction in novels, films, TV, and video-games. This can be done by the public abandoning this anti-social genre. It deserves the same fate as Roman gladiator fighting, into the dustbin of history. We should develop more positive forms of fiction instead. (Censorship would not succeed.)

2. Counter NRA propaganda. There is presently no prospect that our Constitution's 2$^{nd}$ Amendment could be repealed or modified. However, America does not have to be limited by that Amendment. Critics have pointed out that NRA rhetoric about insurrection to counter tyranny is un-American, in that it sets up those who lost an election (to Obama) as the true patriots who will return America to the "proper" way.

3. Most people who have handguns do so for protection of their homes. Ironically, however, if such handguns are ever used to shoot anyone, it is likely to be a resident. A safer alternative protection would be a barking dog.

4. Stop manufacturing and importing handguns and assault rifles and ammunition for both, since these products are public hazards. We have a well-established tradition of banning hazardous products. Two well-known examples are asbestos and thalidomide. Asbestos was a fine building material, if only its dust did not cause lung cancer, and thalidomide was a really great sedative for morning sickness in pregnant women, but babies born to women who had taken it had stunted limbs. There has never been strong opposition to banning such hazardous products. The most hazardous products currently manufactured in America are handguns and ammunition for them. Guns kill many, many times more Americans than did asbestos or did thalidomide stunt newborns. There is already a precedent:

"cop-killing bullets" which can penetrate police armored vests have been outlawed. Yet, in a case against handguns, there would be a determined opposition to ending manufacture and importation of handguns and ammunition for them from both manufacturers and the gun lobby. There is no likelihood government would ever seize handguns and ammunition already owned.

America's legal response to cigarettes and alcohol has been less black-and-white than with asbestos, because both of these substances are less dangerous in small amounts compared to large amounts leading to addiction, and one is only harming oneself if used in large amounts. However, the intent of handguns is to shoot someone other than the shooter, though many handgun owners also use them to commit suicide every year.

5. Encourage hunters to switch from guns to binoculars and cameras when they go into natural environments for recreation.

6. The gun-show, and any other, loopholes in gun registration must be closed with background checks on potential buyers. (Ideally, gun shows themselves could fade away.) Have waiting period for all guns between purchase and acquisition of a handgun.

7. Guns of lawful owners could circulate indefinitely, but whenever a gun is used in a crime, it should be rendered permanently useless as a weapon.

8. Not controversial is a finding by Patrick Sharkey and associates at New York University (2017) that an increase in community organizations and organized activities reduced crimes of all kinds, in such communities.

9. Finally, we must wake up to the enormity of gun casualties in America and counter past ineffective responses with action! America needs a radical political movement that goes beyond the existing anti-gun lobby's quest for reasonable gun laws. It should, however, include people in those lobbies and also those who oppose hunting, and oppose violent fiction, without being limited to them. It should oppose further US military involvements in other countries and lobby for peaceful resolution to conflicts. The 2nd Amendment should not define the bounds of our gun

laws. What should define that boundary is whatever is needed to insure public safety. It likely would require working around the $2^{nd}$ Amendment. This movement could publicize antigun-violence measures that work in other democracies. Guncrazy Abolitionists is a name that could be used by such an organization. Being in my 80s, it is unrealistic for me to lead it, but if others step forward to lead, I will gladly support it. If such a group is organized, there can be no illusion of rapid progress. A comparable case, perhaps, is the women's suffrage movement, that began its campaign for the vote in 1848, and only achieved ratification of the $19^{th}$ Amendment to the Constitution in 1920.

10. Stop NRA's ability to make the Bureau of Alcohol, Tobacco, and Firearms into the step-child of the Federal Government.

11. Over a million Americans have been killed by private guns, and several millions more wounded, some permanently debilitated. Put in a comparative perspective, "More people are killed with guns in the United States in a typical week than in all of western Europe in a year."[1] We need a peaceable society, which cannot be achieved with our existing gun culture. Let's go beyond it!

# FURTHER READING

## GENERAL BACKGROUND

To make sense of America's gun culture, guides to American history are invaluable. I have used Richard Morris & Jeffrey Morris, eds, *Encyclopedia of American History* (1976), Stanley Kutler, ed., *Dictionary of American History* (10 vols., 2003), John Garraty & Mark Carnes, eds., *American National Biography* (24 vols., 1999), John Faragher *et al.*, *Out of Many: a History of the American People* (2000). There are two encyclopedias of American violence, perhaps inspired by Ted Gurr, ed. *Violence in America* (2 vols., 1989), which is similar but on a smaller scale: broadest in scope is Lester Kurtz, ed., *Encyclopedia of Violence, Peace, and Conflict* (3 vols., 1999); however, more relevant to my topics, and so used here, is Ronald Gottesman, ed. *Violence in America: an Encyclopedia* (3 vols., 1999). Richard Hofstadter &Michael Wallace edited *American Violence: a Documentary History* (1970).

American wars, during which many men learned to shoot, have played an important role in developing our gun culture. The six works I used, in alphabetical order are: Fred Anderson & Andrew Cayton, *The Dominion of War: Empire and Liberty in North America, 1500-2000* (2005) is in chronological order, with illustrations and maps, but is thematic and focused upon seven leaders. *The Rockets' Red Glare: When America Goes to War, Two Hundred Years* (1990) is historian Richard Barnet's eleventh book and is an interpretive history, without illustrations or maps. John Keegan was a British military historian, whose *Fields of Battle: The Wars for North America* (1996) is his survey of American warfare,1600-1890, plus a chapter on American air war, with illustrations and a few maps.

Robert Leckie, *The Wars of America* (1981) is encyclopedic, with maps. Geoffrey Perret, *A Country Made by War: from the Revolution to Vietnam—the Story of America's Rise to Power* (1989) is a detailed history, with maps. David Skaggs and Robert Browning III compiled *In Defense of the Republic: Readings in American Military History* (1991), articles previously published, encompassing 1676-1986. *American Wars and Heroes: Revolutionary War through Vietnam* (1984), which Stanley Ulanoff adapted from U.S. Army's *American Military History*, has maps and illustrations.

There is a rich and varied literature on Native Americans. Arrell Morgan Gibson, *The American Indian: Prehistory to the Present* (1980) is a comprehensive textbook, well-illustrated, with maps. To call these four books "coffee-table books" trivializes their texts, yet they otherwise fit that description; in chronological order: William Brandon, *The American Heritage Book of Indians* (1982); David Thomas et al., *The Native Americans: an Illustrated History* (1993); Alvin Joseph, Jr., *500 Nations: an Illustrated History of North American Indians* (1994); Frederick Hoxie, ed., *Encyclopedia of North American Indians* (1996). Three atlases document boundaries of Indian lands: Carl Waldman, *Atlas of the North American Indian* (1985), Paul Pruch, *Atlas of American Indian Affairs* (1990), and National Geographic, Anton Treuer, *Atlas of Indian Nations* (2013).

After the Civil War, warfare moved West into Indian territories beyond the Mississippi, and many books survey Indian Wars. John Tebbel & Keith Jennison's *The American Indian Wars* (1960) discusses wars in chronological order from Jamestown to Wounded Knee. Robert Utley and Wilcomb Washburn's *The American Heritage History of the Indian Wars* (1977) has five chapters on eastern wars and six on western wars. Jerry Keenan, *Encyclopedia of American Indian Wars, 1492-1890* (1997) discusses wars, battles, and people.

## 1. From Conquest to Independence

Organized geographically, James Wilson's *The Earth Shall Weep: a History of Native America* (1998) is a good survey of the time period covered in this chapter and beyond. Slightly older and organized chronologically is Arrell Morgan Gibson, *The American Indian: Prehistory to the Present*

(1980). Jerry Keenan, *Encyclopedia of American Indian Wars, 1492-1890* (1997) is organized topically, in alphabetical order according to names of people, places, and wars. Ted Morgan's *Wilderness Dawn: the Settling of the North American Continent* (1993) also discussed Indians, but emphasizing European settlers. On background for 1600s, Carl Sauer, *Seventeenth Century North America* (1980). Ian Steele, *Warpaths: Invasions of North America* (1994) encompasses the period 1513-1765). Canada had less conflict with Indians than did the United States, reflected in Arthur Ray's *I Have Lived Here since the World Began: an Illustrated History of Canada's Native People* (1996).

The French and Indian War has had at least American histories, with each having unique features: Edward Hamilton, *The French and Indian Wars* (1962, xiii +318 pp.) has still-useful maps; Albert Marrin, *Struggle for a Continent: the French and Indian Wars, 1690-1760* (1987, vi + 218 pp.) is well illustrated; Fred Anderson, *The War that Made America: a Short History of the French and Indian war* (xxv + 293 pp.) is well illustrated, some in color and helpful maps; William Nester, *The First Global War: Britain, France, and the Fate of North America* (2000, 308 pp.) has a strict chronological organization, year by year, gives some attention of foreign wars; Walter Borneman, *French and Indian War: Deciding the Fate of North America* (2006, xxiv + 360 pp.) has good illustrations, maps, and bibliography.

The War of Independence is well known and documented. Prof. Robert Middlekauff's *The Glorious Cause: the American Revolution, 1763-1789* (2005) is a major synthesis, as was Prof. Page Smith's *A New Age Now Begins* (2 vols., 1976). Two illustrated popular histories are Thomas Fleming, *Liberty! The American Revolution* (1997), and a smaller, older, Bart McDowell, *The Revolutionary War: America's Fight for Freedom* (1967). Ernest Dupuy and Trevor Dupuy wrote *The Compact History of the Revolutionary War* (1963), with many maps. Encyclopedic are: Mark Boatner, *Encyclopedia of the American Revolution* (1974) and Henry Commager and Richard Morris, eds., *The Spirit of 'Seventy-six: the Story of the American Revolution as Told by Participants* (1967).

# 2. From Second Amendment to Civil War and Indian Wars

On American and Canadian Indians, see sources for chapter 1. On the Whiskey, Shay, and Fries rebellions, see: William Hogeland, *The Whiskey Rebellion: George Washington, Alexander Hamilton and the Frontier Rebels Who Challenged America's Newfound Sovereignty* (2006) showed this rebellion was more important than a footnote of history, with three maps and bibliography; Leland Baldwin earlier summarized the course and significance of this rebellion (2003). Robert Gross edited the most recent scholarship, *In Debt to Shays: the Bicentennial of an Agrarian Rebellion* (1993). W.W.H. Davis wrote *The Fries Rebellion, 1798-99: an Armed Resistance to the House Tax Law* (1899, 1969).

On the Second Amendment to the Constitution: Adam Winkler, *Gunfight: The Battle over the Right to Bear Arms in America.* (2011) is a history of the *District of Columbia v. Heller* Supreme Court case, by a supporter of victorious Heller. Robert Sptizer disagreed in *Guns Across America: Reconciling Gun Rules and Rights* (2015).

The War of 1812 has only recently attracted much general interest, but it is significant in American history. Aside from Theodore Roosevelt's *The Naval War of 1812* (1882), there are two recent histories, their titles interpreting authors' perspectives: Walter Borneman, *1812: the War that Forged a Nation* (2004) and Alan Taylor, *The Civil War of 1812: American Citizens, British Subjects, Irish Rebels, and Indian Allies* (2010). Michael Wala wrote a summary, "War of 1812" (2003). There are two collections of contemporary comments on the war, from Canada and the United States: Arthur Bowler's *The War of 1812* (1973) is a slender volume of newspaper articles from Canada (vi + 89 pages); Donald Hickey's *The War of 1812: Writings from America's Second War of Independence* (2013) is a much longer volume of writings from both sides of the conflict (xxx + 892 pages).

Mexican-American War has also been previously neglected, and that is also being remedied. Earlier historians wrote small, well-illustrated books, which presumably was what the market could bear. Three examples are: Otis Singletary, *The Mexican War* (1960), with maps and illustrations; Fairfax Downey, *Texas and the War with Mexico* (1961), which is very well illustrated, including numerous ones in color, and advertised as in the

American Heritage Junior Library, but in fact is worth anyone's time; Irving Werstein, *The War with Mexico* (1965), which is also very well illustrated (though none in color). Later histories are much more detailed with few or no illustrations: Brian DeLay, *War of a Thousand Deserts: Indian Raids and the U.S.-Mexican War* (20080; Robert Merry, *A Country of Vast Designs: James K. Polk, the Mexican War, and the Conquest of the American Continent* (2009); Amy Greenberg, *A Wicked War: Polk, Clay, Lincoln, and the 1846 U.S. Invasion of Mexico* (2012); and Peter Guardino, *The Dead March: a History of the Mexican-American War* (2017). There is also a detailed biography of Polk: Walter Borneman, *Polk: the Man Who Transformed the Presidency and America* (2009), with illustrations and maps.

Slavery as a controversy that precipitated America's greatest gun violence is not the focus of books on America's slavery controversy, but abolitionism provided the background for the determined opposition on both sides. These studies illustrate that bitterness: Alice Adams, *The Neglected Period of Anti-Slavery in America, 1808-1831* (1973 [1908]), Herbert Aptheker, *American Negro Slave Revolts* (1943), Gilbert Barnes, *The Anti-Slavery Impulse* (1964 [1933]), Curry, *The Abolitionists* (1965), Louis Filler, *The Crusade Against Slavery, 1830-1860* (1960), Robert Fogel & Stanley, *Time on the Cross: the Economics of American Negro Slavery* (1974), George Frederickson, *William Lloyd Garrison* (1968), Warren Howard, *American Slavers and the Federal Law, 1837-1862* (1963), Henry Mayer, *All on Fire: William Lloyd Garrison and the Abolition of Slavery* (1998), and William Pease & Jane Pease, *The Antislavery Argument* (1965).

By contrast with the Mexican-American War, the Civil War has enormously interested both scholars and general public. Two basic references are David Heidler, Jeanne Heidler & David Coles, *Encyclopedia of American Civil War: a Political, Social, and Military History* (2002) and Mark Mayo Boatner III, *The Civil War Dictionary* (1959). The most detailed history is Allan Nevins, *Ordeal of the Union* (8 vols., 1947-71). However, Shelby Foote's three large volumes, *The Civil War, a Narrative* (1958-74), runs a close second. That war was so popular that Bruce Catton was not inhibited by those two works in progress and wrote his three-volume *The Centennial History of the Civil War* (1961-65). Page Smith wrote a lengthy *Trial by Fire: a People's History of the Civil War and Reconstruction* (1982), and later James McPherson wrote a slightly more concise *Battle Cry of Freedom: the*

Civil War Era (1988). Fletcher Pratt collected illustrations from that era, published with commentary, Civil War in Pictures (1955).

These books on Indian wars in the West are in chronological order of publication: Ralph Andrist, Long Death: the Last Days of the Plains Indians (1964), with illustrations and maps; Dee Brown, Bury My Heart at Wounded Knee: an Indian History of the American West (1970), well-illustrated; Stephen Longstreet, War Cries on Horseback: the Story of the Indian Wars of the Great Plains (1970), well-illustrated; S.L.A. Marshall, Crimsoned Prairie: the Wars between the United States and the Plains Indians during the Winning of the West (1972), well-illustrated, maps; Editors, Time-Life Books, War for the Plains (1994), well-illustrated, maps. Carl Waldman, Atlas of the North American Indian (2009) has a long chapter on Indian wars, which includes minor Canadian conflicts during the 1800s. Warfare was a major theme in Dee Brown, Bury My Heart at Wounded Knee: an Indian History of the American West (1970), covering 1861-90.

Numerous books discuss "Custer's Last Stand," among them: artist William Reusswig studied closely aspects of it to illustrate and discuss A Picture Report of the Custer Fight (1967); Evan Connell, Son of the Morning Star (1984), with a good bibliography; James Welch, Killing Custer: the Battle of the Little Bighorn and the Fate of the Plains Indians (1994) emphasized the Indian experience; Herman Viola, Little Bighorn (2000).

Conflicts in the West between Euro-Americans were also problems while civilization was being established. Harry Drago's Road Agents and Train Robbers: Half a Century of Western Banditry (1973) has notes and bibliography. Paul Trachtman's The Gunfighters (1974) has a broader, more detailed, focus on context than Drago's book. Trachtman provided a bibliography. Carl Breihan's Great Gunfighters of the West (1977) is narrowest in scope and no references. All three books have illustrations, yet Trachtman provided far more of them than either Drago or Breihan.

## 3. Shooting Animals and Targets

### Pro-hunting

Hunting and the American Imagination, by Daniel Herman (2001) is a pro-hunting historical survey of attitudes toward hunting, 1600-1900. John Reiger's *American Sportsmen and the Origins of Conservation* (ed. 3, 2001) defends hunters as important conservationists, mid-1800s-mid-1900s. Retired wildlife biologist Jim Posewitz provided a briefer pro-hunting discussion in *Inherit the Hunt: A Journey into the Heart of American Hunting* (1999), beginning with earliest Paleo-Indians and coming down to recent times. Nicolas W. Proctor's *Bathed in Blood: Hunting and Mastery in the Old South* (2002) is the latest of several books on hunting and southern culture. Jan E. Dizard wrote two defenses of hunting: *Going Wild: Hunting, Animal Rights, and the Contested Meaning of Nature* (ed. 2, 1999) and *Mortal Stakes: Hunters and Hunting in Contemporary America* (2003) and is also senior editor of *Guns in America: A Reader* (1999), which includes rather little on either hunting or target shooting. Earlier, J. Swan wrote *In Defense of Hunting* (1996), which shows some fear of anti-hunters. Catlin Kelly explored all aspects of her subject, *Blown Away: American Women and Guns* (2004); concerning hunting, she is content to quote the comments of various female hunters. Stephen M. Miller compiled *Early American Waterfowling, 1700s-1930* (1986), a collection of writings and illustrations arranged under seven thematic headings. Theodore Roosevelt has attracted a number of biographers. Substantial recent biographies are: H.W. Brands, *T.R.: the Last Romantic* (1997), Douglas Brinkley, *The Wilderness Warrior: Theodore Roosevelt* (2009), David McCullough, *Mornings on Horseback* (1981), and Edmund Morris, *The Rise of Theodore Roosevelt* (1979), *Theodore Rex* (2002), *Colonel Roosevelt* (2011).

## Anti-Hunting

*A View to a Death in the Morning: Hunting and Nature through History*, by Matt Cartmill (1993), covers the entire sweep of history from "killer apes" to recent times, emphasizing America, from an anti-hunting perspective.

Michael a. Bellesiles (2003, 305-348) provides a less favorable perspective on hunting, 1820s-50s, than Rieger (2001) and Posewitz (1999). Marc Reisner's *Game Wars: The Undercover Pursuit of Wildlife Poachers* (1991) shows that not all hunters are law-abiding. Chapters 4-5 in Carol J. Adams & Josephine Donovan, eds, *Animals and Women* (1995) have an anti-hunting perspective. M. Scully, *Dominion: The Power of Man, the Suffering of Animals* (2002) includes a discussion of the ethics of hunting.

## Wildlife Management

Thomas Dunlap, *Saving America's Wildlife* (1988) is a history of wildlife management, 1880-1985.

Keir Sterling wrote the only biography of Merriam: *Last of the Naturalists: the Career of C. Hart Merriam* (1977). Stefan Bechtel, *Mr. Hornaday's War: How a Peculiar Victorian Zookeeper Waged a Lonely Crusade for Wildlife* (2012). Curt Meine wrote the definitive biography of Leopold: *Aldo Leopold: His Life and Work* (1988). Leopold's *Game Management* (1933) is an important source.

## Shooting Targets

Shooting targets has not generated opposition, as far as I am aware. There are many biographies of William F. Cody, Annie Oakley, and Theodore Roosevelt. I have used Robert A. Carter, *Buffalo Bill Cody: The Man Behind the Legend* (2000), Glenda Riley, *The Life and Legacy of Annie Oakley* (1994), and H.W. Brands, *T.R.: The Last Romantic* (1997), and also see the articles on them in the *Dictionary of American Biography* (1999). Abigale Kohn, *Shooters* (2004) has both notes and bibliography. Gerry Souter, *American Shooter: a Personal History of Gun Culture in the United States* (2012) is broader in scope than Kohn's *Shooters*, but emphasizes target shooting, with illustrations, notes, and brief bibliography (but not citing Kohn's *Shooters*.

## Sources

Jan Dizard et al., *Guns in America* (1999) had a discussion of hunting mainly in Michael Bellesiles, "The Origins of Gun Culture in the United

States, 1760-1865," and also included Russell Gilmore, "'Another Branch of Manly Sport': American Rifle Games, 1840-1900." *Hunting and the American Imagination*, by Daniel Herman (2001) is a pro-hunting survey historical survey of attitudes toward hunting, 1600-1900. John Reiger's *American Sportsmen and the Origins of Conservation* (ed. 3, 2001) defends hunters as important conservationists, mid-1800s-mid-1900s. Retired wildlife biologist Jim Posewitz provides a briefer pro-hunting discussion in *Inherit the Hunt: A Journey into the Heart of American Hunting* (1999), beginning with earliest Paleo-Indians and coming down to recent times. Nicolas W. Proctor's *Bathed in Blood: Hunting and Mastery in the Old South* (2002) is the latest of several books on hunting and southern culture. *A View to a Death in the Morning: Hunting and Nature through History*, by Matt Cartmill (1993), covers the entire sweep of history from "killer apes" to recent times, emphasizing America, from an anti-hunting perspective. Michael a. Bellesiles (2003, 305-348) provides a less favorable perspective on hunting, 1820s-50s, than Rieger and Posewitz. Marc Reisner's *Game Wars: The Undercover Pursuit of Wildlife Poachers* (1991) shows that not all hunters are law-abiding.

There are many biographies of William F. Cody, Annie Oakley, and Theodore Roosevelt. I have used Robert A. Carter, *Buffalo Bill Cody: The Man Behind the Legend* (2000), Glenda Riley, *The Life and Legacy of Annie Oakley* (1994), and H.W. Brands, *T.R.: The Last Romantic* (1997), and also see the articles on them in the *Dictionary of American Biography* (1999). Stephen M. Miller has compiled *Early American Waterfowling, 1700s-1930* (1986), a collection of writings and illustrations arranged under seven thematic headings

Jan E. Dizard has written two defenses of hunting: *Going Wild: Hunting, Animal Rights, and the Contested Meaning of Nature* (ed. 2, 1999) and *Mortal Stakes: Hunters and Hunting in Contemporary America* (2003). Earlier, J. Swan wrote *In Defense of Hunting* (1996), which shows some fear of anti-hunters. Catlin Kelly explores all aspects of her subject, *Blown Away: American Women and Guns* (2004); concerning hunting, she is content to quote the comments of various female hunters. Chapters 4-5 in Carol J. Adams & Josephine Donovan, eds, *Animals and Women* (1995) have an anti-hunting perspective. M. Scully, *Dominion: The Power of Man, the Suffering of Animals* (2002) includes a discussion of the ethics of hunting.

# 4. Making and Selling Guns and Ammunition

Harold L. Peterson edited *Encyclopedia of Firearms* (1964, new edition, ed., by Ian V. Hogg, 1992). Hogg summarized some of its information in a brief survey, *The Story of the Gun from Matchlock to M16* (1996). However, the latter book, which is the text for a television series, omits the substantial American literature on the important history of the development of interchangeable parts and also lacks notes and bibliography. An earlier, briefer work is George C. Nonte, Jr., *Firearms Encyclopedia* (1973).

Howard L. Blackmore's *Guns and Rifles of the World* (1965) is a large earlier treatment of the subject, with many black-and-white illustrations and bibliography. An equivalent work is W.H.B. Smith's *Book of Pistols and Revolvers* (ed. 7, 1968). Larry Koller's *The Fireside Book of Guns* (1959) is an informal history of guns in America, with many colored illustrations. Lee Kennett and James L. Anderson devoted a useful chapter of *The Gun in America: The Origins of a National Dilemma* (1975) to gun making and American attitudes toward it. A. Merwyn Carey has compiled an informative alphabetical *American Firearms Makers: When, Where, and What They Made from the Colonial Period to the End of the Nineteenth Century* (1953).

M.L. Brown has written a well-illustrated encyclopedic treatment of *Firearms in Colonial America: The Impact on History and Technology, 1492-1792* (1980), which includes discussions and illustrations on gun making. There are two concise introductions to the American system of manufactures, which grew out of the partnership between two federal arsenals and private gun contractors, 1798-1850. David A. Hounshell tells the story within that broader context in *From the American System to Mass Production, 1800-1932* (1984, 15-65). Merritt Roe Smith's chapter, "Army Ordnance and the 'American system' of Manufacturing, 1815-1861," in the book he edited, *Military Enterprise and Technological Change: Perspectives on the American Experience* (1985, 39-86) draws upon his earlier *Harpers Ferry Armory and the New Technology* (1977), which began in 1794 and was narrower in scope than his 1985 chapter. The other federal armory, at Springfield, is emphasized in Felicia J. Deyrup's *Arms Makers of the Connecticut Valley: A Regional Study of the Economic Development of the Small Arms Industry, 1798-1870* (1948), since there are more records from it than there are from private armories. Her book is supplemented and updated by Merrill Lindsay, *The New England Gun: The First Two Hundred Years* (1975). Positive estimates of Eli Whitney's contributions to gun manufacturing is Carolyn Cooper and Merrill Lindsay's *Eli Whitney and the Whitney Armory* (1980) & Ellsworth Grant's biographical article on him (1999). William H. Hallahan argues, in *Misfire: The History of How America's Small Arms Have Failed Our Military* (1994), that these achievements were seldom adequate. Chapter 7 of Michael A. Bellesiles, *Arming America* (ed. 2, 2003) is a good, well-documented survey of gun making, 1790s-1850s.

Colt's achievements are ably discussed and illustrated by William Hosley, *Colt: the Making of a Legend* (1996). George Virgines, *Saga of the Colt Six-Shooter and the Famous Men Who Used it* (1969) only begins in 1873 and is mainly about use in 1900s. Winchester began rifle and carbine manufacturing shortly later, and his factory's history is well told and illustrated by Robert L. Wilson, *Winchester: an American Legend* (1991). Wilson is also author of at least twenty other gun books. James Norris contributed a positive biographical article on Oliver F. Winchester (1999). Alden Hatch wrote what is clearly an institutional history, *Remington Arms in American History* (1956) that had to have been based on Remington archives, though there is nothing at all in it about documentation. It is illustrated. K.D. Kirkland's *Remington* is sort of a condensed and updated version of Hatch's, with numerous illustrations, many in color. Dean K. Boorman, like Wilson, has authored several books on gun makers. His *The History of Smith & Wesson Firearms* (2002) is typical, with many illustrations, a fairly brief text, and a brief bibliography of more substantial works on the company: Roy McHenry and Walter Roper, *Smith & Wesson Hand Guns* (1944, 2013) and Roy Jinks, *History of Smith &L Wesson* (1977) is. John Browning and Curt Gentry have written a fine biography of Browning's father, *John M. Browning, American Gunmaker: An Illustrated Biography of the Man and His Guns* (ed. 2, 1994). K.D. Kirkland has published three slender volumes under the general title, *America's Premier Gunmakers*, which are on Colt, Remington, and Winchester.

There is a substantial literature on the history of machine guns. George M. Chinn wrote a definitive 4-volume *The Machine Gun: History, Evolution, and Development of Manual, Automatic and Airborne Repeating Weapons* (1951), but briefer and more recent studies followed. C.J. Chivers' vaguely titled *The Gun* (2010) devoted a third to machine guns and two-thirds to assault rifles.

William J. Helmer's *The Gun That Made the Twenties Roar* (1969) is a history of the Thompson Submachine Gun and of the people who made it and used it. Written for a popular audience, it is nevertheless thorough, well documented and well-illustrated. Paul Wahl and Donald R. Toppel's *The Gatling Gun* (1971) is very well illustrated and takes the story into the 1960s; it also illustrates and describes some of its competitors. Julia Keller wrote a dual biography of a man and his gun: *Mr. Gatling's Terrible Marvel: the Gun that Changed Everything and the Misunderstood Genius Who Invented It* (2008). Since Hiram Maxim was a prolific inventor, Arthur Hawkey's *The Amazing Hiram Maxim* (2001) discusses and illustrates but does not emphasize his machine guns. John Ellis' *The Social History of the Machine Gun* (1975) is brief but well-illustrated and emphasizes the period before 1918. David A. Armstrong's *Bullets and Bureaucrats: The Machine Gun and the United States Army, 1861-1916* (1982) is a scholarly exploration of the Army's slow acceptance of machine guns. Anthony Smith's *Machine Gun: The Story of the Men and the Weapon That Changed the Face of War* (2002) is readable, illustrated, up-to-date, with a few minor errors (such as the claim that Jonathan Browning trained at Colt's factory). Its emphasis is also on the period before 1918.

Tom Diaz's *Making a Killing: The Business of Guns in America* (1999) discusses the modern manufacture, promotion, and sale of guns to both criminals and the civilians who fear criminals. Pamela Haag more recently wrote a historical survey covering the 1800s and the early decades of the 1900s, *The Gunning of America: Business and the Making of American Gun Culture* (2016). Stuart D. Brandes' *Warhogs: A History of War Profits in America* (1997) is a well-informed survey of commercial supplying of our armed services during wars from 1607 to 1945. It includes, but is not limited to, small arms. These general surveys are supplemented by particular examples found in Henry S. Bloomgarden's *The Gun: A "Biography" of the Gun That Killed John F. Kennedy* (1975) and Erik Larson's *Lethal Passage: How the Travels of a Single Handgun Expose the Roots of America's Gun Crisis* (1994).

There are three good books on the history of gunpowder and ammunition: Arthur P. Van Gelder and Hugh Schlatter's *History of the Explosives Industry in America* (1927), and Zilg's history of the Du Ponts and their businesses, with emphasis on sharp practices and abuse of power (1974), and Jack Kelly, *Gunpowder: A History of the Explosive That Changed the World* (2994). Hogg (1996) also has a chapter on ammunition.

## 5. Fear Mongering National Rifle Association

Although neither of its own histories—Trefethen's *Americans and their Guns* (1967), Rodengen's *NRA: An American Legend* (2004)— is documented, both are well illustrated, and between them they reveal various changes that have occurred during 37 years. There are also two well-documented, pro-NRA histories by historians: Gilmore's doctoral dissertation, *Crack Shots and Patriots* (1974), which traces its development from founding in 1871 until 1929, and Leddy's *Magnum Force Lobby* (1987), which focuses on its fight against gun controls. LaPierre's two books— *Guns, Crime, and Freedom* (1994) and *Shooting Straight* (co-authored with Baker, 2002)—provide NRA's current arguments against gun controls.

Le Fave's doctoral dissertation, *The Will to Arm* (1970), is a well-documented critical history of the NRA from 1871 until 1970. It places the organization's internal history within a broad cultural context. Three books published in the 1990s provide more recent valuable insights into the workings of the NRA and its fanatical opposition to gun controls. Sugarmann's *National Rifle Association* (1992) and Davidson's *Under Fire* (1993) are documented, and Sugarmann also provides seven photographs of leading NRA figures. Anderson's *Inside the NRA: Armed and Dangerous* (1996) is briefer and without documentation except for two lists of members of Congress who received NRA political funds. In 2000s, two: Peter Brown & Daniel Abel, *Outgunned: Up Against the NRA; the First Complete Insider Account of the Battle over Gun Control* (2002); and Gabrielle Giffords & Mark Kelly, *Enough: Our Fight to Keep America Safe from Gun Violence* (2014) is powerful first-hand testimony with many complaints on NRA (but lacking illustrations, references, or index).

Several books on gun control criticize the NRA, including Bakal, *The Right to Bear Arms* (1968), Bloomgarden, *Gun: A "Biography" of the Gun that Killed John F. Kennedy* (1975), Sherrill, *The Saturday Night Special and Other Guns* (1973), Shields, *Guns Don't Die—People Do* (1981), and DeConde, *Gun Violence in America: The Struggle for Control* (2001). The best book on the current NRA is Richard Feldman's kiss-and-tell *Ricochet* (2008)—his revenge for it ostracizing him for cooperating with the Clinton Administration. Congresswoman Gabrielle Giffords, who was severely wounded in an assassination attempt, and her astronaut husband, Mark

Kelly, wrote *Enough: Our Fight to Keep America Safe from Gun Violence* (2014), devoted over three chapters to a critique of the NRA. There is also an ongoing critique of the NRA by the organization Stop the NRA, which it publicizes at its website: www.stopthenra.com.

The history of the change by the Supreme Court in its interpretation of the Second Amendment from an emphasis on militia to an emphasis on personal gun rights is told in some detail by Marcia Coyle, *The Roberts Court: the Struggle for the Constitution* (2013, 123-196). David Cole, *Engines of Liberty: the Power of Citizen Activists to Make Constitutional Law* (2016, 95-148) did likewise, in less detail and using many sources different from those Coyle used (yet, omitting her book!).

## 6. Guns in Crime

Crime has been a popular subject for both authors and the public—witness the endless series of TV serials on criminals and law officers. There are even popular encyclopedias: Carl Sifakis, *The Encyclopedia of American Crime* (1982, xxix + 802 pp.) is a large book with topical index. Robert Elman, *Fired in Anger: the Personal Handguns of American Heroes and Villains* (1962), which is broader in scope than its title indicates, and is historically organized; on the other hand, Jay Robert Nash, *Bloodletters and Badmen: a Narrative Encyclopedia of American Criminals from the Pilgrims to the Present* (1973) is organized alphabetically, not historically. Organized crime is the most popular crime topic, and there are comprehensive works on that also. Gus Tyler compiled *Organized Crime in America: a Book of Readings* (1973), 51readings, 1927 to 1960, as a by-product of a study sponsored by the Center for the Study of Democratic Institutions. It lacks illustrations and is aimed at an academic audience. Paul Lunde wrote a very different book, *Organized Crime: an Inside Guide to the World's Most Successful Industry* (2004), world-wide scope, organized into chapters on different groups, very well illustrated, with many in color, for the public.

Unorganized crimes are so numerous that they are nevertheless discussed under organized topics. Assassinations is an important topic. A Federal Government report by James Kirkham et al., *Assassination and Political Violence* (1969) was topically organized, such as presidential, gubernatorial, senatorial and so on. Similarly, Richard Hofstadter & Michael Wallace, *American Violence: a Documentary History* (1970) included a topic, "Assassinations, Terrorism, Political Murders." Political assassinations were the subject of two surveys: James Clarke, *American Assassins: The Darker Side of Politics* (1982), which included unsuccessful attempts; and Edmund Lindop, *Assassinations that Shook America* (1992); both included portraits and documentation.

Blacks have been targets of gun violence since the Civil War and rise of Ku Klux Klan. John Hope Franklin & Alfred Moss, *From Slavery to Freedom* (ed. 7, 1994) is a broad textbook history; August Meier & Elliott Rudwick, *From Plantation to Ghetto* (ed. 2, 1970) is a briefer history; Charles Christian, *Black Saga: the African American Experience* (1995) is a reference work organized by years, from before 1492 to 1993. Thomas Frazier compiled *Afro-American History: Primary Sources* (1970), and John Hope Franklin and Isidore Starr compiled *The Negro in the Twentieth Century: a Reader on the Struggle for Civil Rights* (1967). There have been many assassinations of Blacks, most conspicuously Martin Luther King, Jr., on whom there are a number of books. Biographies are by Taylor Branch, whose three volumes on *America in the King Years* (1988, 1999, 2007) is definitive, David Lewis, *King: a Biography* (1978) is more concise, and Stephen Oats, *Let the Trumpet Sound* (1982) is intermediate in length between the other two. Narrower in scope, but not brief, is David Garrow, *Bearing the Cross: Martin Luther King, Jr., and the Southern Christian Leadership Conference* (1986), and two books on his assassination: Gerold Frank, *An American Death* (1972) and Gerald Posner, *Killing the Dream: James Earl Ray and the Assassination of Martin Luther King, Jr.* (1998). Although he is much less well known, there are almost as many books on Malcolm X as on King; however, they are thematic books on his legacy rather than biographies.

On the other hand, there are numerous books on John F. Kennedy's assassination and relatively fewer biographies. Among the latter, I cite Theodore Sorensen, *Kennedy* (1965) and two on parts of his life: Nigel Hamilton, *J. F. K.: Reckless Youth* (1992) and Richard Reeves, *President Kennedy* (1993). Discussion of books on his assassination are in chapter six.

There are many books on organized crime and its dominant criminals. Stephen Fox, *Blood and Power: Organized Crime in Twentieth-Century America* (1989, 512) extends from Prohibition in 1920 until the war on drugs into the 1980s, discussing the similarities between a war on alcohol and a war on drugs. Virgil Peterson, *The Mob: 200 Years of Organized Crime in New York* 1983) is a detailed history with reference notes and illustrations. Gus Tyler, *Organized Crime in America: a Book of Readings* (1962, xvi + 421 pages) was assembled in relation to Senator Estes Kefauver's hearings on organized crime. The FBI's file on criminals in organized crime was published as *Mafia: the Government's Secret File on Organized Crime* (2009, xlv + 843 pages). Jo Smith, *A complete History of the Mafia* (2003) is a large picture book. Richard Hammer compiled *Playboy's Illustrated History of Organized Crime* (1975) from articles in *Playboy* magazine, 1973-74. The longest biographies are of Al Capone: Laurence Bergreen, *Capone: the Man and the Era* (1994, 701 pp.); Robert Schoenberg, *Mr. Capone* (1992, 480 pp.).

There are nine surveys of militias, without extensive overlap in topics discussed: James Coats, *Armed and Dangerous: the Rise of the Survivalist Right* (1985, x + 294 pages), emphasized the early 1980s; James Gibson, *Warrior Dreams: Paramilitary Culture in Post-Vietnam America* (1994, viii + 357 pages), Neil Hamilton, *Militias in America: a Reference Handbook* (1996, 235 pages), began with colonial militia; Kathy Marks, *Faces of Right Wing Extremism* (1996, 238 pages); David Neiwert, *Alt-America: the Rise of the Radical Right in the Age of Trump* (2018, 464 pages; Kenneth Stern, *A Force upon the Plain* (1996, 303 pages) began with the Ku Klux Klan and ends with Timothy McVeigh's bombing (1995); Joel Dyer, *Harvest of Rage: Why the Oklahoma City is only the Beginning* (1997, x + 292 pages); Robert Snow, *The Militia Threat: Terrorists Among Us* (1999, x + 266 pages); Daniel Levitas, *The Terrorist Next Door* (2002, 520 pages), began with the career of William Gale (1916-88) and ended in 2001. John George and Laird Wilcox, *Nazis, Communists, Klansmen, and Others on the Fringe* (1992, 523 pages) surveyed both left-wing (almost 100 pages) and right-wing (over 200 pages) groups. All surveys have good documentation; Levitas' book is illustrated.

There is an extensive literature on the Ku Klux Klan: David Chalmers, *Hooded Americanism: the First Century of the Ku Klux Klan, 1865-1965* (1965) is chronologically broad; other studies focus upon the 1920s: Charles Alexander, *The Ku Klux Klan in the Southwest* (1965), Kathleen Blee, *Women of the Klan: Racism and Gender in the 1920s* (1991); Nancy MacLean, *Behind the Mask of Chivalry: the Making of the Second Ku Klux Klan* (1994); and Linda Gordon, *The Second Coming of the KKK: the Ku*

*Klux Klan and the American Political Tradition* (2017). Later Klan history is put into a broader context by John George and Laird Wilcox, *Nazis, Communists, Klansmen, and Others on the Fringe* (1992) and by Brent Smith, *Terrorism in America: Pipe Bombs and Pipe Dreams* (1994).

Mass murder has become an important scholarly subject recently. Two professors at Northeastern University, Jack Levin and James Alan Fox, collaborated on *Mass Murder: America's Growing Menace* (1991). The Editors of Time-Life Books published *Mass Murderers* (1993) for the public, well-illustrated, on 21 murderers. Fox has continued to focus upon this subject in a number of publications, recently, with Jack Levin, *Extreme Killing: Understanding Serial and Mass Murder* (2014). Most recently, Jaclyn Schildkraut and Jaymi Elsass wrote a scholarly *Mass Schootings: Media, Myths, and Realities* (2017), which is quite useful, despite gaps in coverage.

Juanita Brooks' *Mountain Meadows Massacre* (1950) has never gone out of print since the 1962 edition appeared, and recent reprintings have addenda by Jan Shipps. Will Bagley's *Blood of the Prophets: Brigham Young and the Massacre at Mountain Meadows* (2002) is a definitive survey. Three Mormon authors, Ronald W. Walker et al. have also written a more recent account, *Massacre at Mountain Meadows: an American Tragedy* (2008).

On "going postal," see Mark Ames, *Going Postal: Rage, Murder, and Rebellion from Reagan's Workplaces to Clinton's Columbine and Beyond* (2005) and Don Lasseter, *Going Postal: Madness and Murder in America's Post Offices* (1997).

On school shootings: John Devine, "Schools: Overview" (1999) is a good summary of knowledge until then, with bibliography; Bryan J. Grapes, ed., *School Violence* (2000) reprinted articles arranged topically, with a general bibliography; Katherine S. Newman et al., *Rampage: The Social Roots of School Shootings* (2004) is a substantial discussion, with key traits of shooters; Kimberly A. McCabe & Gregory M. Martin, *School Violence, the Media, and Criminal Justice Responses* (2005) focused upon specific aspects of the problem; Peter Langman, *Why Kids Kill: Inside the Minds of School Schooters* (2009) offers key psychological traits of shooters; two later studies emphasized the danger from bullying: Katherine Klein, *The Bully Society: School Shootings and the Crisis of Bullying in American School* (2012); and Charles Derber & Yale Magrass, *Bully Nation: How the American Establishment Creates a Bullying Society* (2016).

Tom Hayden, *Street Wars: Gangs and the Future of Violence* (2004) focused upon the situation in Los Angeles, with reference notes. Thomas Barker's *Biker Gangs and Organized Crime* (2007) provided references at the end of his ten chapters. Kerrie Droban told the story of ATF and Hells Angels in *Running with the Devil: the True Story of the ATF's Infiltration of the Hells Angels* (2007). The *Journal of Gang Research* has been published since 1994 by the National Gang Crime Research Center.

## 7. Gun Violence as Entertainment

On the history of American media, see Michael Emery and Edwin Emery's *The Press and America: An Interpretive History of the Mass Media* (edition 6, 1988) and Frank L. Mott, *American Journalism: A History of Newspapers in the United States through 250 years, 1690 to 1940* (1941).

Richard Slotkin's trilogy of books analyzing our violent culture— *Regeneration through Violence* (1973), *The Fatal Impact* (1985), and *Gunfighter Nation* (1992)—provide a chronological portrait of our use of gun violence as a theme for entertainment from the early 1600s to the 1980s. *Violence in America: an Encyclopedia* (3 vols., Gottesman 1999) contains several articles on relevant topics: Kimberly R. Gladman, "Literature: Pulp Fiction" (volume 2, 270-274), Craig J. Inciardi, "Music: Popular" (volume 2, 420-423), Sara L. Knox, "Literature: Popular Fiction" (volume 2, 266-270), Robert Shulman, "Literature: Fiction" (volume 2, 262-266), Brian Zimmerman, "Video Games" (volume 3, 374-376). Violent video games are also discussed by Kaveri Subrahmanyam and others, "New Forms of Electronic Media," pp. 73-99, in *Handbook of Children and the Media* (Singer and Singer, eds., 2001).

On William F. Cody and Annie Oakley, see sources for chapter 3. On Cody's Wild West show, see Louis S. Warren, *Buffalo Bill's America: William Cody and the Wild West Show* (2005).

Darwin Payne has written a detailed and well-illustrated biography, *Owen Wister: Chronicler of the West, Gentleman of the East* (1985), and Wister himself wrote: *Roosevelt: The Story of a Friendship* (1930). Wister's friendship with Remington is chronicled in their correspondence, which is well edited by Ben Merchant Vorpahl (1972). On Remington, see Peggy Samuels and Harold Samuels, *Frederic Remington: A Biography* (1982). G.

Edward White has made a study of this trio: *The Eastern Establishment and the Western Experience: The West of Frederic Remington, Theodore Roosevelt, and Owen Wister* (1968). On Charles M. Russell, see John Taliaferro, *Charles M. Russell: The Life and Legend of America's Cowboy Artist* (1996), Brian W. Dippie, ed., *Charlie Russell Roundup: Essays on America's Favorite Cowboy* (1999) and Austin Russell, *C. M. R.: Charles M. Russell: Cowboy Artist* (1956). There is a comprehensive chapter on "The Imagined West" in Richard White's history of the West, *"It's Your Misfortune and None of My Own"* (1991, ch. 21).

There are literary/film scholars who analyze violent fiction and movies from the standpoint of their artistic merits. They tend to either ignore or minimize the social problem which such creations pose for society. Two examples are: Jack Shadoian, *Dreams and Dead Ends: The American Gangster Film* (1977, edition 2, 2003) and John McCarty, *Bullets over Hollywood: The American Gangster Picture from the Silents to "The Sopranos"* (2004). Nicole Rafter, *Shots in the Mirror: Crime Films and Society* (2000), does discuss crime films as a cause of crime, but minimizes its importance, arguing that causes of crime are complex and that movies are only one of several factors. James B. Twitchell, *Preposterous Violence: Fables of Aggression in Modern Culture* (1989), does discuss the concern over violent entertainment leading to aggression, but his response is that teenage boys seem to crave preposterous violence as part of the maturation process, and all the fear about its bad influence has not stopped them from consuming it.

Communications professor W. James Potter's *On Media Violence* (1999) provides a comprehensive survey from the standpoint of his discipline, with cautious negative conclusions. Social worker Loren Coleman's main concern in *The Copycat Effect* (2004) is with the effect of the news media in encouraging later suicides by sensationalized reportage of earlier suicides, but he also provides ample examples of copycat gun violence being stimulated by both reportage and fictional simulations of violence.

# 8. Guns, Politics, and Paranoia

Early American history had a lasting influence on American attitudes toward guns and what guns symbolize, especially the War of Independence from Britain and the Second Amendment to the Constitution. Those developments have been fashioned into a paranoid narrative about private guns being our insurance against a tyrannical Federal Government. The NRA is the main founder and guardian of this tradition, beginning mainly after World War II. Works cited above for chapters 1,2, and 5 are, therefore, also relevant here.

In addition, numerous books on gun control combat this paranoia—some listed here alphabetically: Carl Bakal, *No Right to Bear Arms* (1968); Henry Bloomgarden, *The Gun: a "Biography" of the Gun that Killed John F. Kennedy* (1975); Sarah Brady, *A Good Fight* (2002); Alexander DeConde, *Gun Violence in America: the Struggle for Control* (2001); Gabrielle Giffords & Mark Kelly, *Enough: Our Fight to Keep America Safe from Gun Violence* (2014); Dennis Henigan, *Lethal Logic: Exploding the Myths that Paralyze American Gun Policy* (2009); James Jacobs, *Can Gun Control Work?* (2002); Erik Larson, *Lethal Passage: How the Travels of a Single Handgun Expose the Roots of America's Gun Crisis* (1994); Robert Sherrill, *The Saturday Night Special, with other Guns with Which Americans Won the West, Protected Bootleg Franchises, Slew Wildlife, Robbed Countless Banks Shot Husbands Purposely and by Mistake and Killed Presidents—Together with the Debate Over Continuing Same* (1973); Pete Shields, *Guns Don't Die—People Do* (1981); William Vizzard, *Shots in the Dark: the Policy Politics, and Symbolism of Gun Control* (2000).

Books opposing gun control include: Glen Beck et al., *Control: Exposing the Truth about Guns* (2013); Alan Gottlieb, *The Gun Grabbers* (1994); Richard Poe, *The Seven Myths of Gun Control: Reclaiming the Truth about Guns, Crime, and the Second Amendment* (2001); John Lott, Jr., *More Guns, Less Crime: Understanding Crime and Gun Control Laws* (1998), *The War on Guns: Arming Yourself Against Gun Control Lies* (2016); and books by Wayne LaPierre, such as *Guns, Crime, and Freedom* (1994), *Shooting Straight: Telling the Truth about Guns in America* (2002).

Some authors who covered the debate between the two sides include: Maggi Aitkens, *Should We Have Gun Control?* (1992); William Briggs,

*How America Got Its Guns: a History of the Gun Violence Crisis* (2017); John Bruce & Clyde Wilcox, *The Changing Politics of Gun Control* (1998); Ted Gottfried, *Gun Control: Public Safety and the Right to Bear Arms* (1993); Gary Kleck & Don Kates, *Armed: New Perspectives on Gun Control* (2001); Abigail Kohn, *Shooters: Myths and Realities of America's Gun Cultures* (2004); Elaine Landau, *Armed America: the Status of Gun Control* (1991).

## 9: Laws: Making America Safe for Guns and Dangerous for People, including Law Enforcers

The most important foundation for American gun laws is the Second Amendment to the Constitution. In 2008, the U.S. Supreme Court interpreted it as providing lawful citizens a right to own a gun for protection. Lawyer Dennis Henigan, *Lethal Logic: Exploding the Myths that Paralyze American Gun Policy* (2009) and Professor Michael Waldman, *The Second Amendment: a Biography* (2014), discussed the implications of that new interpretation.

The history of America's gun laws is discussed in books on gun control, cited above. Carl Bakal discussed gun laws in his *No Right to Bear Arms* (1968), which also included appendices summarizing federal (1930s) and state gun laws, with a discussion of the 1968 federal law added to his introduction.

Law enforcement at the federal level is discussed in histories of federal law enforcement agencies. First was the U. S. Marshal Service, whose history was surveyed by Frederick Calhoun, *The Lawmen: United States Marshals and Their Deputies, 1789 to 1989* (1990); Robert Sabbag wrote an informal history: *Too Tough to Die: Down and Dangerous with the U.S. Marshals* (1992). The second federal agency was the Secret Service, whose history was written by veteran crime historian Philip Melanson, *The Secret Service: the Hidden History of an Enigmatic Agency* (2002). The third federal agency was the FBI, whose history was covered in two surveys—Don Whitehead, *The FBI Story: a Report to the American People* (1956), who wrote what Hoover, its head, wanted, and Ronald Kessler, *The Bureau: the Secret History of the FBI* (2002), which caused Hoover to turn over in his grave. Kessler provided notes and a bibliography. A briefer, earlier, *No Left Turn* (1975), by former FBI agent Joseph L. Schott, is a tell-all that described Hoover's quirks and prejudices.

The Bureau of Alcohol, Tobacco, and Firearms' history was told simultaneous by two long-time Bureau veterans: James Moore, *Very Special Agents: the Inside Story of America's Most Controversial Law Enforcement Agency—the Bureau of Alcohol, Tobacco, and Firearms* (1997, edition 2, 2001) and William Vizzard, *In the Crossfire: a Political History of the Bureau of Alcohol, Tobacco, and Firearms* (1997). They tell two very different histories: Vizzard wrote a bureaucratic-political history, and Moore wrote a chronicle of experiences of agents in the field (which he had been). Kerrie Droban told of one ATF operation in *Running with the Devil: the True Story of the ATF's Infiltration of the Hells Angels* (2007).

American police history was surveyed in Robert Wadman and William Allison's concise *To Protect and Serve: a History of Police in America* (2004), an illustrated, well-documented textbook. Narrower in scope are James Richardson, *Urban Police in the United States* (1974), Eric Monkkonen, *Police in Urban America, 1860-1920* (1981), and Peter Scharf & Arnold Binder, *The Badge and the Bullet* (1983). Bruce Chadwick focused upon New York's lead in developing American police in *Law and Disorder: the Chaotic Birth of the NYPD* (2017). Police veteran James Lardner wrote of a reformer of New York police in *Crusader: the Hell-Raising Police Career of Detective David Durk* (1996), and Marilynn Johnson described a later aspect of that history in her *Street Justice: a History of Police Violence in New York City* (2003). Joe Domanick wrote a critical *To Protect and to Serve: the LAPD's Century of War in the City of Dreams* (1994), half of it on the time of Chief Gates.

There are three substantial biographies of J. Edgar Hoover: Curt Gentry, *J. Edgar Hoover: the Man and the Secrets* (1991); Richard Powers, *Secrecy and Power: The Life of J. Edgar Hoover* (1987); and Anthony Summers, *Official and Confidential: the Secret Life of J. Edgar Hoover* (1993). There are three briefer biographies of Eliot Ness: Paul Heimel, *Eliot Ness: the Real Story* (1997), Douglas Perry, *Eliot Ness: the Rise and Fall of an American Hero* (2014), and Kenneth Tucker, *Eliot Ness and the Untouchables: the Historical Reality and the Film and Television Depictions* (2011). Daryl Gates told of his own career as head of the Los Angeles Police in *Chief: My Life in the LAPD* (1992). Domanick provided an independent view of that period. Gina Gallo told of her experiences in *Armed and Dangerous: Memoirs of a Chicago Policewoman* (2001).

## 10. Costs of Gun Violence

Philip J. Cook and Jens Ludwig's *Gun Violence: The Real Costs* (Oxford U.P., 2000) is a careful survey of different kinds of costs that society pays for gun violence. There is also a useful collection of articles on the medical costs of gun violence in the June 14, 1995 issue of *JAMA: The Journal of the American Medical Association*. The four articles by Diedrich & Fauber on gun violence in Milwaukee (*MJS* Nov 06) are rich in detail and are well illustrated with photos and graphs.

# ABBREVIATIONS

| | |
|---|---|
| *ANB* | *American National Biography,* 1999 |
| *DAH* | *Dictionary of American History,* ed. 3, 2003 |
| ed(s). | editor(s.) |
| Ed(s.) | Editor(s.) |
| *J.* | *Journal* |
| *JT* | Racine *Journal Times* |
| *MJS* | Milwaukee *Journal Sentinel* |
| NY | New York |
| *NYT* | *New York Times* |
| *ODNB* | *Oxford Dictionary of National Biography,* 2004 |
| P. | Press. |
| U. | University |

# ENDNOTES

## I. FROM CONQUEST TO INDEPENDENCE

1 Gibson 1980, 95.
2 Gibson 1980, 116-138.
3 Morgan 1993, 71-217, Taylor 2001, 23-464, Wilson 1998, 16-225.
4 Taylor 2001, 39-45.
5 Riley 1995, 266-269, Roberts 2004, Waldrep & Bellesiles 2006:54-61, Weber 1992, 14-141.
6 Weber 1992, 186.
7 Eccles 1972, 9-10, Steele 1994, 25-36, Weber 1992, 60-63.
8 Fischer 2008, 260-270, Leckie 1981, 3-5.
9 Fischer 2008, 276-279.
10 Gibson 1980, 140-160.
11 Eccles 1972, 45-46.
12 Brown 1980, 75-78, 119-124, 178-199, Calloway 2003, 225, Eccles 1983, 53-55, Kennett & Anderson 1975, 51-56, Steele 1994, 59-79, Taylor 2001, 101-112.
13 Brown 1980, 42-48, 73-75, 112-119, 166-178, Weber 1992, 227-228.
14 De Conde 2001, 11-15.
15 Prall 1972:318.
16 Prall 1972:320; see also 274-275.
17 Prall 1972:318.
18 Brown 1970:13.
19 Gibson 1980, 184-216, Longstreet 1970, Tebbel & Jennison 1960, Utley and Washburn 1985.
20 Miller 2000.
21 Van Alstyne 1960, 10.
22 Milton 2000, 262-303, Steele 1994, 37-58.
23 Brown 1980, 98-99, 151-158, 366-371, De Conde 2001, 19-20.
24 Keenan 1997, 176-178, Steele 1994, 43-49, Taylor 2001, 124-136.
25 Emerson 1999.

26  Cramer 2006, 43.

27  Murphy 2004.

28  Hofstadter & Wallace 1971, 47-48, Starkey 1998, 57-82.

29  Keenan 1997, 165-167, Steele 1994, 89-93, Waldrep & Bellesiles 2006, 45-48.

30  Keenan 1997, 165-167, Purcell & Purcell 2000, 188-189, Steele 1994, 80-109.

31  Leckie 1981, 8-13, Schultz & Tougias 1999, 25-27, Steele 1994, 97-109, Wilson 1998, 95-96.

32  Keenan 1997, 117-120, 167-168, Leach 1958, Lepore 1998, Slotkin & Folsom 1978, Purcel & Purcell 2000, 26-27, 134-135, Schultz & Tougias 1999, Taylor 2001, 194-202.

33  Webb 1984.

34  Cramer 2006, 47, Hofstadter & Wallace 1970, 52-56.

35  Starkey 1998, 23-24.

36  Ray 1996.

37  De Condi 2001, 19-21.

38  Headley 1873 (2000), 8-9, Hofstadter & Wallace, 1970, 187-189.

39  Specific: Anderson 2005, Borneman 2006, Hamilton 1962, Marrin 1987; in broader context: Starkey 1998, 57-82 Tebbel & Jennison 1960, 53-82, Utley & Washburn 1977, 70-105.

40  Anderson 2005, 25-34, Borneman 2006, 14-16.

41  Page 1976, I, 123-127.

42  Borneman 2006, 31.

43  Borneman 2006, 38, Page 1976, I, 124-125.

44  Anderson 2005, 70-71, Borneman 2006, 53-56, Hamilton 1962, 154-157, Leckie 1981, 38-80, Page 1976, I, 126.

45  Faragher et al. 2000, 137-141.

46  Keenan 1997, 173-175, Parkman 1991, 343-917, Smith 1976, I, 166, White 1991:269-314.

47  Commager 1963, I:61-62.

48  Morgan & Morgan 1962.

49  Fulton 1981b, Barrow 1981.

50  Smith 1976, I, 317-318.

51  Reproduced in color in Faragher et al. 2000, 149.

52  Smith 1976, I, 373-382.

53  Willison 1969, 266-267.

54  Smith 1976, I, 475-470.

55  Smith 1976, I, 483-484.

56  Eccles 1972, 45-46, Middlekauff 2005, 272-279, Perret 1989, 4-10, Smith 1976, I, 488-489. Figures given here are from Faragher et al. 2000, 154. Cramer 2006, 100, cites British troops as 1800 and militiamen as 3763.

57  Starkey 1998, 39-42.

58  Cramer 2006, 94-139.
59  Cramer 2006, 100-139.
60  De Condi 2001, 28.
61  Whitridge 1965, 59.
62  Perret 1989, 22-26.
63  Middlekauff 2005, 373-391, Perret 1989, 40-43, Smith 1976, II, 891-907.
64  Boatner 1974, 400, Page 1976, II, 944.
65  Whitridge 1965, 84.
66  Middlekauff 2005, 453-468, Wickwire & Wickwire 1971.
67  Davis 1969, 47-62, 109-139, Leckie 1981, 198-200, 209-215, Middlekauff 2005, 481-492, 579-602, Page 1976, II, 1693.
68  Smith 1976, II, 1725-45.
69  Calloway 1995, Tebbel & Jennison 1960, 109-130, Utley & Washburn 1977, 222-229.
70  Gibson 1980, 252-253.
71  DeConde 2001, 25.

## 2.  From Second Amendment to Civil War and Indian Wars

1   Commager 1963, I:100-103 (Declaration of Independence), 111-116 (Articles of Confederation), Jensen 1940, 1950, 18-27, Smith 1980, 1-22, Wood 1969, 354-363.
2   On England's Bill of Rights, see above, ch. 1. For Virginia's Bill of Rights, see Commager 1963, I:103-104.
3   Jensen 1950, 31-36.
4   De Condi 2001, 30.
5   Morris 1965:110-111.
6   Derfner 2003, Morris 1965, 115-116, Middlekauff 2005, 621, Onuf 1999, Smith 1980, 23-37, Stock 1999, Wood 1969, 412-413.
7   De Condi 2001, 31, Middlekauff 2005, 640-641.
8   Middlekauff 2005, 642-668.
9   Berkin 2002, Van Doren 1948.
10  Commager 1963, 138-145, Smith 1980, 50-94.
11  Lynch 1999.
12  June 1788, quoted from De Condi 2001, 33.
13  Commager 1863, 146, Amar 1998.
14  Berkin 2015, Cornell 2000, Cornell & Kozuskanich 2013, Waldman 2014.
15  Cole 2016, 95-148, Winkler 2011.
16  Kohn 1976, Uviller & Merkel 2002, 59, 65, 67, Waldman 2014, 13-14.

17  Perret1989, 558.

18  Anderson & Cayton 2005, xiv, also Longstreet 1970, Tebbel and Jennison 1960, Utley and Washburn 1985.

19  Perret1989, 82.

20  Gibson 1980, 266. Wood 2009, 129-133.

21  Anderson &Cayton 2005, 192.

22  Anderson & Cayton 2005, 192-193, Gibson 1980, 66-67, Hogeland 2006, Perret 1989, 83-84, Wood 2009, 129-130.

23  De Condi 2001, 39.

24  Kohn 1976, reprint in 1991, 79.

25  Gibson 1980, 267, Wood 2009, 130-131.

26  Anderson & Cayton 2005, 194-195, Gibson 1980, 267, Perret 1989, 85-87, Wilson 1998, 154, Wood 2009, 131-132.

27  DeConde 2001, 40-41, Smith 1980, 227-234.

28  Morris 1965, 126, Stock 1999, Wood 2009, 196-197, 415-418.

29  Anderson & Cayton 2005, 197-202, Baldwin 2003, Hogeland 2006, Perret 1989, 87-88, Wood 2009, 106-197.

30  Davis 1899, Wood 2009, 265.

31  Perret 1989, 89.

32  Beach 1986, 1-2, 16-22.

33  Perret 1989, 90.

34  Perret 1989, 90-91.

35  Baird 1999, Freeman 2001, Wyatt-Brown 1999; also, ch. 6.

36  Chernow 2006, DeConde 2001, 45, Elman 1962, 58-67, Fleming 1999, Freeman 2001, 159-198, Sedgwick 2015, Smith 1980, 498-509, Wood 2009, 382-385.

37  Taylor 2010, 10.

38  Wood 2009, 659; also Hickey 2001, Leckie 1981, 219-313, Perret 1989, 107-134, Wala 2003.

39  Wood 2009, 660-661.

40  Barnet 1990, 64, Taylor 2010, 128.

41  Gibson 1980, 288-289.

42  Remini 2001, 62-80, Wilson 1998, 156.

43  Wood 2009, 695-696.

44  Borneman 2004, 303-304.

45  Perret 1989.

46  Elman 1962, 68-78, Remini 1977, 38-39.

47  Remini 1977, 82-84.

48  Remini 1977, 136-143.

49  Remini 1977, 181-185.

50  Smith 1980, 644-653.

51  Remini 2001, 101, 120.

52  Remini 2001, 131.
53  Wilson 1998, 156-157.
54  Smith 1980, 662-668.
55  Remini 2001, 133-134, 137-138.
56  Anderson and Cayton 2005:240
57  Perret 1989:135.
58  Jahoda 75, Remini 2001, 226-238.
59  Gibson 1980, 307-309; much of this bill is quoted by Jahoda 1975, 39-41.
60  Remini 2001, 255-257, Strickland 1999.
61  Waldman 1985, 118-120, Wilson 1998, 264.
62  Perret 1989:136.
63  Perret 1989:137.
64  Clarke 1982, 195-198.
65  Michener 1990, 65-86.
66  Davis 1998.
67  Downey 1961, 38-657, Werstein 1965, 22-52.
68  Borneman 2004, 150-151, Michener 1990, 54-56.
69  De Bruhl 1993.
70  Borneman 2008.
71  Guardino 2017.
72  Anderson & Cayton 2005:283.
73  Perret 1989:168.
74  Perret 1989:171.
75  Gibson 1980, 350.
76  Mackey 1999, Stegner 1964.
77  Bushman 1999.
78  Aptheker 1943, Frank 1999, Hunt 1999.
79  Adams 1973, Barnes 1964, Curry 1965, Filler 1960, Frederickson 1963, Mayer 1998, Pease & Pease 1965.
80  Finkelman 1995.
81  Howard 1963.
82  Reynolds 2005.
83  Boatner 1959, Catton 1961-65, Foote 1958-74, Heidler, Heidler & Coles 2002, McPherson 1988, Nevins 1947-71, Pratt 1955.
84  Faragher et al. 2000, 453.
85  Roberts 1999e.
86  Fogel & Engerman 1974.
87  Clarke 1982, 19-39, Elman 1962:148-163, Goodrich 2005, Kauffman 2004, Lindop 1992, 12-31, Nash 1973, 72-77.
88  Clarke 1982, 198-214, Lindop 1992, 32-44.
89  Clarke 1982, 39-62, Lindop 1992, 45-56.

90  Toy 1989.
91  Tebbel & Jennison 1960, 235.
92  Keenan 191997, 141-144, Lewis 1994, 16-59
93  Brown 1970, 86-94, Gibson 1980, 386-387, Keenan 1997, 199-201, Lewis 1994, 77-89, Longstreet 1970, 115-124, Marshall 1972, 36-42, McMurtry 2005, 55, Schultz 1990, Tebbel & Jennison 1960, 235-258, Utley & Washburn 1977, 234-235.
94  McMurtry 2005, 30.
95  Ware 1960, 380-310.
96  Brown 1962, 1970, 131-135, Gibson 1980, 413.
97  Ambrose 2000 is one of numerous books on that railroad.
98  Gibson 1980, 416-417, Keenan 1997, 195-197, McMurtry 2005, 123, Waldman 1985, 157, Welch & Stekler 1994, 115-122.
99  Connell 1984, Reusswig 1967, Welch & Stekler 1994. Also: Brown 1970, 276-278, Keenan 1997, 123-126, Lewis 1994, 130-173, Longstreet 1970, 218-233, Utley 1973, 259-262, Waldman 1985, 157, Wilson 1998, 281-282,
100 Brown 1970, 439-445, Gibson 1980, 477-481, Keenan 1997, 252-253, McMurtry 2005, 135-160, Wilson 1998, 403-405.
101 Waldman 1985, 160; Ray 1996, 106-109, 197-199.

## 3. Shooting Animals and Targets

1   Hummel 1994, 1999.
2   Kheel 1995.
3   Flannery 2001.
4   Krech 1999.
5   Dunlap 1988, 5.
6   Herman 2001, 20-21, Matthiessen 1959, 281.
7   Meyers and Pritchard 1998.
8   Bedini 1990, 96-97.
9   Miller 1988.
10  Burroughs 1961, Cutright 1969.
11  Cantwell 1961, Doughty 1975, 34-36, Egerton 2004.
12  Wilson 1832, vol. 1, 380.
13  Snyder 2004.
14  Van Valen 1981.
15  Based on his journal entry for June 28, 1820; Evans 1997, 110.
16  Doughty 1975, 37-39.
17  Audubon 1999, 375.
18  Harris 1951, 28-38.

19  Audubon 1999, 552.
20  Herman 2001, 173-181, Reiger 2001, 36-40.
21  Herman 2001, 130-131.
22  Daumas 1979, 416-421, Nonte 1973, Stebbins 1958, 1-13.
23  Daumas 1979, 401, 728.
24  Green 1956, 103-168, Kranzberg & Pursell 1967, 40-41.
25  Blackmore 1972, 251.
26  Hosley 1996, 66.
27  Illustrated in Hosley 1996.
28  Gilmore 1992, 94.
29  Gilmore 1974, 14-15.
30  Hosley 1996, 72-73.
31  Trefethen 1967, 23-26.
32  Reiger 2001, 57-60.
33  Proctor 2002, 170.
34  Carter 2000, 156-159.
35  Haines 1970, 174, 192, Lott 2002:164.
36  Rosa 1985, 86-87.
37  Isenberg 2000, Matthiessen 1959, 147-152.
38  Matthiessen 1959, 158-161, Schorger 1955.
39  Alsop 2002, 38-41.
40  Bigelow 1954.
41  Rodengen 2004, 12-28, Trefethen 1967, 30-66.
42  Burke 1973, Warren 2005.
43  Riley 1994, 1999.
44  Carter 2000, 250.
45  Blackstone 1986, Carter 2000, Havighurst 1954, Yost 1979.
46  Herman 2001,
47  Cutright 1956, Wiley 1955.
48  Roosevelt 1905.
49  Doughty 1975, 92-115, Graham 1971, Welker 1955, 157-212, Reiger 2001.
50  Graham 1990, Trefethen 1975.
51  Clepper 1968, 31.
52  Dunlap 1988, ch. 3, Sterling 1977.
53  Olsen 1971.
54  Egerton 1973, Dunlap 1988, 40.
55  Egerton 2007.
56  Callenbach 1996, 54-55.
57  Quoted by Cartmill 1993, 143.
58  Quoted by Cartmill 1993, 143-145.
59  Johnson 1923, 388.

60  Roosevelt 1905, 272.
61  Quoted by Lutts 1990, 113.
62  Stein 2001.
63  See also Wiley 1954.
64  Dunlap 1988, 22-28, Keller 1984, 139-160.
65  Keller 1984, 164-173.
66  Rodengen 2004, 58, Trefethen 967, 174-175.
67  Neme 2009, Poten 1991, Reisner 1991, Tobias 1998, Warren 1997.
68  Graham 1990, 49-59, Line 1999, 22, 33, 38, 223, McIver 2003.
69  Walter 1985.
70  Olsen 1985.
71  *Newsweek* 6 Dec. 04, *MJS* 22 July 06.
72  *JT* 9 Jan 07.
73  Meine1988.
74  Leopold 1949, 130.
75  Nash 1989.
76  Mech 2002.
77  Cartmill 1993, 162-185.
78  Quoted in Cartmill, 1993, 178.
79  Peattie 1942, 266-268.
80  Mitchell 1978, 10.
81  Swan 1995, 2-3; see also Tuttle 2006.
82  Marshall 2009.
83  U.S. Fish and Wildlife Service, "Quick Facts."
84  Kheel 1995, 95-104.
85  Including Dizard 1999, 2003, Mitchell 1980, Petersen 1996, 2000, Posewitz
    1999, Swan 1995.
86  Including Amory 1974, Caras 1970, Regenstein 1975, Scully 2002.
87  Stange 1997, Stange and Oyster 2000.
88  Swan 1995, 10.
89  Swan 1995, 19-20.
90  *MJS* Aug. 20, 04.
91  Swan 1995, 33-35.
92  Farnham 1992, 80.
93  Tobias 1998:5.
94  Giffords & Kelly 2014, 41.
95  Editors, *JT*, 17 Nov. 17.
96  Editors, *JT*, 9 Nov. 17.

## 4. Making and Selling Guns and Ammunition

1   Bellesiles 1996, 19.
2   Haag 2016:10.
2   Brandes 1997:17, Hounshell 1984, 25-32.
3   Woodbury 1960, 243.
4   Hounshell 1984.
5   Hallahan 1994, 20-22.
6   Cooper & Lindsay 1980, 14.
7   Hounshell 1984, 31.
8   Woodbury 1960; Haag 2016:12-20.
9   Grant 1999, 299.
10  Hounshell 1984, 29; see also Smith 1980.
11  Portrait in M.Smith 1977, 144; Hallahan 1994, 52-53.
12  Smith 1985, 61-63.
13  Rolt 1965, 157.
14  Battison 1973.
15  fig.6., Hounshell 1984, 35-38.
16  Kirkland 2012, 7-8.
17  Carstensen 1999.
18  Hatch 1956, Kirkland 2012.
19  Smith 1985, 61-63.
20  Haas 2016, 23.
21  Hass 2016, 23.
22  Quoted by Van Gelder & Schlatter 1927, 35.
23  ibid., 36.
24  Kelly 2004, 153-159.
25  Kelly 2004, 159-160.
26  ibid., 55.
27  ibid., 66, Addington 1994,
28  Van Gelder & Schlatter 1927, 176, Williams 1999.
29  Williams 1999.
30  Van Gelder & Schlatter 1927, 85, 174-218; Kelly 2004, 171-180; Zilg 1974.
31  Photo of three of his wooden parts is in Hosley 1996, 13.
32  Hosley 1996, 13-14, 47; Gordon 1999; Haag 2016: see index.
33  Hosley 1996, 18.
34  Perret 1989, 192.
35  Perret 1989, 194, Haas 2016, 39-40.
36  Haag 2016, 40.
37  Haag 2016, 32-33.
38  Norris 1999.

39  McHenry & Roper 2013 reprint of 1944.

40  Johada 1975, Wallace 1993.

41  Sherrill 1973, 99-105.

42  Brandes 1997, 83.

43  Mc Pherson 1988, 279.

44  Carstensen 1999.

45  Brandes 1997, 85-86.

46  Wilson 1991, 14.

47  Browning & Gentry 1994, 10, with photos and descriptions, 225-226.

48  Browning & Gentry 1994, 1.

49  Browning & Gentry 1994, vii.

50  Quoted in Wilson 1991, 27-32.

51  Haas 2016, 164-165.

52  Wilson 1991, 32, 51.

53  Quoted in Wilson 1991, 71.

54  Browning & Gentry 1994, 59.

55  Armstrong 1982, 15-26.

56  Parker 1999, Sterling 1999.

57  Smith 2002.

58  Browning & Gentry 1994, 143.

59  Armstrong 1982, 77-78.

60  Browning & Gentry 1994, 134.

61  Wilson 1991, 228-229.

62  Browning & Gentry 1994, 135.

63  Brandes 1997, 115-116.

64  Kelly 2004, 197-215.

65  Haag 2016, 110.

66  Haag 2016, 111.

67  Kelly 2004, 220-223.

68  Brandes 1997, 115-116.

69  Helmer 1969, 5.

70  Diaz 1999, 21.

71  Helyer 1969, 85.

72  Block 1999, Paschel 1999, Peters 1999, Shucard 1999.

73  Brandes 1997, 259-260.

74  Bloomgarden 1975, paperback 1976.

75  Bloomgarden 1976, 49.

76  Bloomgarden 1976, 85.

77  Bloomgarden 1976, 40, 97.

78  Jacobs 2002, 23-26.

79  Diaz 1999, 21-22.

80   Giffords & Kelly 2014, 98-99.

81   Larson 1994, 79.

82   Diaz 1999, 22-23.

83   MJ 28 Dec 94.

84   Burbick 2006, 106-107, Wright 2007, 115-116.

85   Wright 2007, 116-117.

86   Burbick 2006, 127-129.

87   Giffords & Kelly 2014, 56.

88   Giffords & Kelly 2014, 161-162.

89   Dickinson 2016.

90   Figures in Vinzant 2005, 104.

91   Diaz 2013, 220.

## 5. Fear Mongering National Rifle Association

1    Sherrill 1973, 194.

2    Addington 1994, 68.

3    Bigelow 1952:4-16.

4    Bigelow 1952, Rodengen 2002, 14-21, Trefethen 1967, 21-23, Vinzant 2005, 56-60.

5    Gilmore 1992, note 4.

6    Trefethen 1967, 30-31.

7    Bigelow 1952, 184-186.

8    Rodengen 2002, 19.

9    Rable 1999.

10   Gilmore 1974, 52-56, Rodengen 2002, 18-21, Trefethen 1967, 34-41.

11   Gilmore 1974, 58-63, Rodengen 2002, 22-29, Trefethen 1967, 54-66.

12   Gilmore 1974, 91-134, Rodengen 2002, 30-39, Trefethen 1967, 67-114, Vinzant 2005, 61-64.

13   Rodengen 2002, 46-47 + photo, Trefethen 1967, 137-140 + photo.

14   Feldman 2008, 37, Gilmore 1974, 137, LeFave 1970, 29-32.

15   Lindop 1992, 45-56.

16   Gilmore 1974, 154-156, LeFave 1970, 31-36, Rodengen 2002, 41-43, Trefethen 1967, 128-129.

17   LeFave 1970, 76-77.

18   Drain 1911, 129; quoted from Leddy 1987, 83.

19   Gilmore 1974, 246-247.

20   Zilg 1974, 112, cites Chicago *Chronicle*, 2 Jan. 07.

21   Trefethen 1967, 290.

22 Without acknowledgement: Rodengen 2002, 58; Rodengen has a general acknowledgment of his use of Trefethen's book, p. xi, but that is not a license for unacknowledged quotations.
23 Baldwin 1999, Czitrom, 1991.
24 LeFave 1970, 45-48.
25 Trefethen 1967, 191.
26 Gilmore 1974, 223.
27 Trefethen 1967, 214-215.
28 Gilmore 1974, 251-253.
29 Rodengen 2002, *passim*, Trefethen 1967, *passim* & portrait p.233.
30 LeFave 1970, 105-106.
31 Rodengen 2002, 83, 124-125 + photo p. 86, Trefethen 1967, *passim* + photo p.215.
32 LeFave 1970, 68-71.
33 Quoted in Sugarmann 1992, 28.
34 Rodengen 2002, 115, 267.
35 Sugarmann 1992, 107.
36 Rodengen 2002, 127-128, Trefethen 1967, 238, 268.
37 Feldman 2008, 37-38, LeFave 1970, 137-143.
38 Leddy 1987, 72-73.
39 Sugarmann 1992, 110.
40 Bakal 1968, 140-141.
41 Pascoe 1999, 401.
42 Sugarmann, 1992, 160-161, Trefethen 1967, 250-258.
43 Rodengen 2002, 116-117, 157-159, Sugarmann 1992, 148-157,Trefethen 1967, 173-175.
44 Bloomgarden 1976, 51.
45 Leddy 1987, 91-94.
46 Dahl 2002.
47 Leddy 1987, 100.
48 Tartaro 1981; also, Rodengen 2002, 172-185.
49 Quoted in Shields 1981, 121.
50 Davidson 1993, 31-41, Sugarmann 1992, 45-57 *et passim* + photo 2 at p.132.
51 Leddy 1987, 102.
52 Quoted in Davidson 1993, 44, Giffords & Kelly 2014, 125.
53 Leddy 1987, 103, Woods 2018.
54 From a Ricker speech in Milwaukee, 19 May 06.
55 Leddy 1987, 105-106, 136.
56 Leddy 1987, 115-123.
57 Rodengen 2002, 258-260, 283-284, Raymond 2006, 260-271.
58 Feldman 2008, 6 et passim.

59  Rodengen 2002, 175.
60  NRA Annual Report for 1985, cited from Leddy 1987, 132.
61  Leddy 1987, 132-135.
62  Davidson 1993, 108, Sugarmann 1992, 187-191.
63  Vinzant 2005, 79.
64  Giffords & Kelly 2014, 104-106.
65  LaPierre 2000, p. 15.
66  Frederic J. Frommer, *JT* 9 Sept. 04.
67  Bakal 1968, Bloomgarden 1975, 76, Sherrill 1973, Shields 1981.
68  Davidson 1993, 50, Sugarmann 1992, 123.
69  Dreyfuss 1995.
70  Rodengen 2002, 245.
71  Anderson 1996, 16, 159.
72  *MJS* 21 May 95.
73  *MJS* 21 May 95.
74  Henigan 2009, Shields 1981, 122-128.
75  Hofstadter 1965, 9.
76  *MJS* 4 Feb 9.
77  *JT* 18 May 95.
78  *JT* 17 Aug 94.
79  Anderson 1996, 115-120.
80  Cullen 2009, Lavergne 1997.
81  LaPierre & Baker 2002, 1-19.
82  Anderson 1996, 15.
83  Rodengen 2002, 292-295.
84  Sherrill 1973, 194.
85  Woods 2018,
86  Carter 2005, 12-13.
87  Cole 2016, 132-139, Coyle 2013, 199-278.
88  Winkler 2011.
89  Zornick 2017:13.
90  Giffords & Kelly 2014, 178-179.

## 6. GUNS IN CRIME

1  Harris 1999, Hawkins 1999, 3-5.
2  Rothman 1999.
3  Roberts 1999b.
4  Fellman 1999, Stiles 2002.
5  Roberts 1999a, Tuska 1983.

6   Peters 1999a.
7   DeArment 1999, McGrath 1989, Roberts 1999a, b, d.
8   Hamm 1999b.
9   Editors of Time-Life Books 1994, Hofstadter & Wallace 1970, 407-441, Kirkham et al., 1969, Lindop 1992.
10  Hofstadter & Wallace 1970, 412-415, Kirkham 1969, 52-54, Lindop 1992, 32-44.
11  Kirkham et al. 1969, 54-56, Lindop 1992, 45-56.
12  Kirkham et al. 1969, 49-50, 56-61.
13  Kirkham et al. 1969, 23-26.
14  Hair 1996, Lindop 1992, 57-68, Powell 1999, White 2006.
15  Sesher 1994.
16  Schoenebaum 1979, 652-655.
17  Christian 1995, 417, Hofstadter & Wallace 1970, 434-436.
18  Hamilton 1992, Reeves 1992, Sorensen 1965.
19  Reynolds 1999.
20  Christian 1995, 421-422, 427, Cone 1999b, Faragher et al. 2000, 868-869, Frazier 1970, 455-467, Waldschmidt-Nelson, 2012.
21  Frazier 1970, 455-467, Hofstadter & Wallace 1970, 437-479.
22  Cone 1991.
23  Branch 1989, 1999, 2007, Christian 1993, 414, 427, Cone 1999a, Frank 1972, Garrow 1986, Lewis 1978, Oates 1982, Posner 1998, Waldschmidt-Nelson 2012.
24  Cone 1991.
25  Clarke 1999, Hofstadter & Wallace 1970, 439-441, Moldea 1995, Matthews 2017.
26  Coleman 1992, Jones 1999.
27  Shields 1981, 25-26.
28  1981, 27.
29  Shields 1981, 95.
30  Wright 2007, 123.
31  Lunde 2007, 8.
32  Reppetto 2004, x
33  Waugh 2007.
34  Cohen 1998, Lacey 1991.
35  Friedman 2000, Kleinkecht 1996.
36  Peterson 1983, 133-158.
37  Asbury 1928, 248-249.
38  Fabianic 1999, Gentry 1991, 452-255, Kessler 2002, 101-103, Power 1987, 332-333, Reppetto 2004, 255-266, 269, Summers 1993, 246-247.
39  Gambino 1977, 60.

40 Dash 2009, 74.
41 Dash 2009, 74, Mannion 2003, 22-227.
42 Smith 2003, 25-26.
43 Reppetto 2004, 7-10.
44 Asbury 1936, 406-423, Dash 2009, 72-79, Reppetto 2004, 1-2, 9-17, Sondern 1972, 79-82.
45 Gambino 1977, 16.
46 Gambino 1977, 144-145.
47 Dash 2009, 79-80, Gambino 1977, 77-87.
48 Waldron & Hartmann 2008.
49 Asbury 1928, Peterson 1983.
50 Dash 2009, 61-65, Peterson 1983, 127, Reppetto 2004, 24-26, Smith 2003, 29-31.
51 Cook 1972, 106-107, Diapoulos & Linakis 1976.
52 Dash 2009, xvii, 135-143; photograph facing 226.
53 Dash 2009, 158-175.
54 Dash 2009, 207-224.
55 Dash 2009, 277-288.
56 Horn 2008, Peterson 1983, 108-109.
57 Behr 1996, Kobler 1973. Ken Burns' documentary, *Prohibition* (2011), pretty much follows Behr. Reppetto 2004, 91-94.
58 Haller 1989, Helmer 1969, Lunde 2004, 149.
59 Asbury 1940, 312-317, Helmer & Mattix 1998, 12, 25, 45, 50, Reppetto 2004, 73.
60 Asbury 1940, 317-318, 324-331, Messick & Goldblatt 1972, 19-26, 58-61, Reppetto 2004, 54-74, portraits of both follow 144, Smith 2003, 46-47.
61 Reppetto 2004, 269, Mc Phaul 1970, 24-26, Smith 2003, 49-50.
62 Asbury 1940, 318-321, Bergreen 1994, Helmer & Mattix 1998, 7-9, Schoenberg 1992.
63 Reppetto 2004, 94.
64 Helmer & Mattix 1998, 289-304.
65 Bergreen 1994, 134-135, Helmer & Mattix 1998, 21-22, Schoenberg 1992, 118.
66 Helmer & Mattix 1998, 25, Mc Phaul 1970, 14-22, Reppetto 2004, 101.
67 In Tyler 1962, 155-168.
68 Bergreen 1994, 305-314, Helmer & Mattix 1998, 118-123, Kelleher 1997, 112, Lunde 2004, 140-141, Schoenberg 1992, 207-229, Smith 2003, 48-52.
69 Helmer & Mattix, 1998, 45, 50, Lunde2004, 138-139, Reppetto 2004, 106.
70 Giancana and Giancana 1992, 50-51.
71 Lunde 2004, 146.
72 Peterson 1983, 125-127, Pietrusza 2003, 209-219. I have been unable to see Tosches 2005.
73 Pietrusza 2003, 153-156, Smith 2003, 61-64.

74  Pietrusza 2003, 317, Reppetto 2004, 104.
75  Lunde 2004, 148-150.
76  Pietrusza 2003, 278-280, Reppetto 2004, 110.
77  Pietrusza 2003, 348-349.
78  Banks 1999.
79  Reppetto 2006, 5.
80  Helmer & Mattix 1998, 37, Reppetto 2004, 132-147, Smith 2003, 66-71.
81  Reppetto 2004, 145.
82  In Tyler 1962, 214-224.
83  Reppetto 2004, 169-171.
84  Lunde 2004, 152, Reppetto 2004, 162-176.
85  Smith 2003, 91-92.
86  Reppetto 2004, 179.
87  Reppetto 2004, 234-250.
88  Cressey 1972, Reppetto 2004, 150-151, 161, -217-221.
89  Salerno & Tompkins 1972b.
90  Reppetto 2004, 255-267.
91  Kessler 2002, 101-106, Reppetto 2006, 33, Summers 1993, 228-231.
92  Milan 1989.
93  In Tyler 1962, 10-15.
94  Davis1993, 67-71, Reppetto 2004, 216-233.
95  Prial 1972, 163.
96  Frasca 1959, 209, Lunde 2004, 156, Reppetto 2004, 271.
97  In Tyler 1962, 19-37, Salerno & Tompkins 1972a.
98  Gentry 1991, 452-455, Giancana & Giancana 1992, 255-256, Powers 1987, 332-333, Summers 1993, 226-228.
99  Reppetto 2006, 18.
100 Maas 1968, 39.
101 Reppetto 2006, 27.
102 Collier & Horowitz 1984, 23-27, Klein 2003, 71-72.
103 Collier & Horowitz 1984, 34-36, Klein, 91-92.
104 Giancana & Giancana 1992, 227.
105 Behr 1996, 133, 249, Mannion 2003, 102-103.
106 Brashler 1977, 194-196, Gentry 1991, 472, Giancana & Giancana 1992, 268-269.
107 Waldron & Hartmann 2008, 46.
108 Matthews 2017, Waldron & Hartmann 2008, 6.
109 Reppettto 2006, 96-97.
110 Bonanno 1983, 159-160.
111 Reppetto 2006, 219.
112 Lavigne 1987, 130, Reppetto 2006, 223.

113 Lumpe 1997, Wuerker's cartoon is reproduced from CASC/RCPJ *Newletter* Sept.-Oct. 2011. See also Bellí 2012.

114 McCabe & Martin 2005, 50 had a similar definition; Editors of Time-Life Books 1992, 5, focused upon murderer rather than the results: "people who kill several victims in a single short and bloody episode [are] mass killers."

115 Adams et al. 1994, Brown 1962, 1970, Cook 1943, Longstreet 1970, Marshall 1972, Roberts 1999e, Staub 1999, 322, Tebbel and Jennison 1960.

116 Cook 1943, Madley 2016.

117 Bushman 1999.

118 Mackey 1999.

119 Stegner 1964, 40.

120 Furniss 1960.

121 Brooks 1962, Walker et al. 2008.

122 Wise 1975, 175-176; also, Denton 2003.

123 Staub 1999, 322-323.

124 Leamer 2016, Tolnay & Beck 1995.

125 Christian 1995, 487.

126 Leamer 2016, 267.

127 Leamer 2016, 300.

128 Schildkraut & Elsass 2016, 30.

129 Schildkraut & Elsass 2016, 31.

130 Schildkraut & Elsass 2016:32.

131 Newton 1999, 329.

132 Ibid., Fernandez, 32, Sprague, 33, Glover, 32, Koussow, 33, Spencer 32.

133 Brash et al. 1992, 58-59, Everitt 1999, Kelleher 1997, 6.

134 Newman 1999, 331, Schildkraut & Elsass 2016:31-32.

135 Lavergne 1997.

136 Lavergne 1997, 2.

137 Lavergne 1997, 5

138 Lavergne 1997, 23.

139 Lavergne 1997, 26-29

140 Lavergne 1997, 51.

141 Lavergne 1997, 59.

142 Lavergne 1997, 74.

143 Lavergne 1997, 77.

144 Lavergne 1997, 116.

145 Lavergne 1997,132-133.

146 Midlarsky & Klain 2005, 46.

147 They cite Crews & Counts 1997.

148 Cullen 2009.

149 Schildkraut & Elsass 2016, 14-17 cited 16 such studies, by my count. Here are four I have consulted: Denmark et al. 2005, Hunnicutt 2006, McCabe & Martin 2005, Newman et al. 2004.

150 Schildkraut & Elsass 2016, 60.

151 De Venanzi 2012, 262.

152 Fox & Savage 2009.

153 Roy 2009.

154 Devine 1999, 99-100.

155 Newman et al. 2005, 229-230.

156 Langman 2009, 21-126.

157 Derber & Magrass 2016, Klein 2012.

158 Schildkraut and Elsass 2016, 92.

159 Christian Science Monitor Weekly 109, no. 48 (16 Oct. 2017), 9.

160 Giffords & Kelly 2014, 107-108.

161 Fitzgerald 1972, 370-373, Hansom 1999, Staub 1999, 323.

162 Staub 1999, 324-325.

163 Ames 2005, 79, Brash et al. 1992, 66-67, Schildkraut & Elsass 2016, 36.

164 Hamm 1999c, Levitas 2002:301-304, Stern 1996, 19-33, Vizzard 1997, 127-130, Wright 2007:139-148.

165 Gallagher 1999, Hamm 1999d, Lewis 1994, Tabor 1994, Tabor & Gallagher 1995, Vizzard 1997, 155-188, Wright 1994, 1995, 2007:152-164.

166 Tabor 1994, 17.

167 Giffords & Kelly 2014, 47-78.

168 Schildkraut & Elsass 2016, 150.

169 Wikipedia.

170 Editorial, The Nation 4-11, 2016.

171 Elliott et al. 2017.

172 Wright 2007, 115-116.

173 Reagan 1990, 262-263, Wills 1987, 210-211.

174 Wright 2007, 116.

175 Snow 1999, Stern 1997, 1999.

176 Alexander 1965, Blee 1991, MacLean 1994, Marks 1996, 43-55, 207-210, Moore 1999, Toy 1989.

177 Ridgeway 1990.

178 Marks 1996, 39-40, 206, Wright 2007, 54.

179 Navasky 1995.

180 Coates 1987, index, Levitas 2002, index, Marks 1996, index.

181 Beckemeier 2008, Marks 1996, 40-42.

182 Wright 2007, 58-61.

183 Corcoran 1990, 31-32, Levitas 2002, 1-24.

184 Stickney 1996, 129-169, Wright 2007:4-7.

185 Hamm 1999a, Michel & Herbeck 2001, Stickney 1996.

186 Michel & Herbeck 2001.

187 Associated Press 2010, Gellman 2010, Gray 2010, Hosenball & Isikoff 2010, Housenholder & Williams 2010, Jurgensmeyer 2010, Thomas & Conant 2010, Warikoo 2010, Williams & Barrett 2010.

188 Hosenball & Isikoff 2010.

189 Gellman 2010, 28.

190 Southern Poverty Law Center 2009.

191 For example: Covey et al. 1992, Decker & Van Winkle 1996, Huff 2002.

192 Decker & Curry 1999, 6, Decker & Van Winkle 1996.

193 Decker & Curry 1999, 7.

194 Curry & Decker 1998.

195 Lavigne 1987, 23-24, 26-27.

196 Lavigne 1987, 30.

197 Lavigne 1987, 33.

198 Barger with Zimmerman and Zimmerman 2000, 173.

199 Lavigne 1987, 35.

200 Lavigne 1987, 36-38.

201 Lavigne 1987, 39-40.

202 Lavigne 1987, 126.

203 Petersen 2007.

204 Baker 2015, 1.

205 Baker 2015, 220-224.

## 7. Gun Violence as Entertainment

1 Shulman 1999:262.

2 Slotkin 1973, 5.

3 Slotkin 1973, 8.

4 Slotkin 1973, 38, 55.

5 Slotkin 1973, 268-274.

6 Knox 1999, 267, Shulman 1999, 262, Slotkin 1973, 484-507, 1985, 81-106.

7 Slotkin 1985, 200-207, 1992, 127.

8 Bellesiles 2003, 344-346.

9 Slotkin 1985, 162-173.

10 Slotkin 1985, 192-198.

11 Slotkin 1985, 200-207.

12 Grant 1885-86, republished in one vol., 1990.

13 Shulman 1999, 263.

14 Fellman 1999.

15  Slotkin 1985, 502-503.
16  Slotkin 1992, 127-128, 143-146.
17  Denning 1987.
18  Slotkin 1992, 136-137.
19  Knox 1999, 267.
20  Russell 1960, 494-503.
21  White 1991, 328; Haas 2016, 186-194.
22  Carter 2000, 31; Haas 2016, 192-194, Yost 1979.
23  Carter 2000, 235-238.
24  Examples: Havinghurst 1954, Riley 1994.
25  Roosevelt 1889-96.
26  Payne 1985.
27  Vorpahl 1972, 111.
28  Cawelti 1999, 59-64.
29  Wister 1902, 415.
30  Shulman (1999:263.
31  Cawelti 1999, 1.
32  Trachtman 1974, revised edition 1977.
33  Cawelti 1976, 80.
34  James 2011, 17-18, Slotkin 1992, 139, 687, n.40.
35  Slotkin 1992, 139-143.
36  Knox 1999, 268.
37  Cawelti 1976, 143.
38  Utley, Bloom & Kinney 1964, 3.
39  B & G 1991, 1.
40  Prince 2000a, Slotkin 1992.
41  Prince 2000b, 2.
42  Slotkin 1992, 231.
43  Prince 2000b, 2-3.
44  Prince 2000b, 6.
45  MacDonald 1987, 89-93.
46  MacDonald 1987, 117.
47  Cawelti 1999, 6.
48  McCarty 2004, 1.
49  McCarty 2004, 3.
50  Shadoian 2003, xi.
51  Shadoian 2003, 4.
52  MIT in 1977, Oxford in 2003.
53  Cook 1999, Cooper 1999, LaMay 1999, Simon 1999.
54  Herzog 1999.
55  See "anti-abortion violence" on the web.

56  Dietz 1998, cited in Subrahmanyam et al 2001, 85.

57  Zimmerman 1999, 375.

58  Cullen 2009, 134, 137, Grossman & Degaetano 1999, 77.

59  *Newsweek* 29 Nov. 04, p.9.

60  Mummold 2007.

61  Zimmerman 1999, 375-376.

62  Thomas 2011.

63  Ro 1998, 26.

64  Inciardi 1999, 423.

65  Coker 2003, Sullivan 2002.

66  Ro 1998.

67  Michael Weissenstein, AP, in *JT* 27 Jan. 05.

68  *JT* 12 Nov. 05.

69  Sandy Cohen, AP Entertainment, in *JT* 4 June 06.

70  Cliff Brunt, AP, in *JT* 9 Aug. 06.

71  *MJS* 30 Oct 06.

72  Slotkin 1992, 658.

73  *Shepherd Express*, 12-18 Feb. 04.

74  Eron 1963, 1992 & Eron & Husesmann 1984, 1999.

75  Hamilton 1998, 3.

76  e.g., Bushman & Huesmann 2001, Comstock & Paik 1991, Eron & Gunther 1994, Eron & Huesmann 1999, National Television Violence Study 1996-97, Paik & Comstock 1994.

77  Potter 1999, 25.

78  Rafter 2000, 69.

79  Coleman 2004, 2.

80  Coleman 2004, 135-137.

81  Coleman 2004, pp.6-7.

82  Lavergne 1997, 275-276.

83  Coleman 2004, 21-23.

84  Coleman 2004, 226-227.

85  Bok 1998, 83-84, Coleman 2004, 224-225.

86  Coleman 2004, 149-160, Ames 2005.

87  Quoted in Coleman 2004, 162.

88  *JT*, 1 & 2 Feb. 06.

89  Coleman p.163.

90  chapter 1, Egginton 1991, Brash et al. 1992, Davidson 1993, 3-19.

91  Coleman 2004, 163.

92  Twitchell 1989, 103.

93  Coleman 2004, 168-169.

94  Coleman 2004, 170-176, Cullen 2009.

95  *MJS* 15 Sept. 06, *JT* 17 & 18 Sept. 06.
96  *USA Today* 1 Sept. 06, *JT* & *MJS* 15 Sept. 06, *MJS* 4 Jan. 07.
97  *JT* 23 July 93.
98  Ted Bridis, AP, in *MJS* 8 Dec. 96.
99  *JT* 10 Aug 05.
100 Petruisch 2018, 74.

## 8.  Guns, Politics and Paranoia

1   Cooper 1997, 1-22, Uviller and Merkel 2002, 109-124.
2   Smith 1981, 592-596.
3   Donald 1995:596-598, Goodrich 2005, Kauffman 2004, Lindop 1992, 12-31.
4   Lindrop 1992:32-44.
5   Melanson 2002, 24-27.
6   Lindrop 1992:45-56.
7   O'Toole 2012.
8   Doughty et al. 1996, 243-248, Leckie 1981, 546-566, Ulanoff 1984, 202-219.
9   Cooper 1997, 98, Uviller and Merkel 2002, 133.
10  Brands 1997:321-363, Brinkley 2009, 31-336, Morris 1979, 615-661, Powell 2006, 47-63.
11  Shogan 2004.
12  Cole 2016, 100, Rodengen 2002, 58, Trefethen 1967, 290-291, Vinzant 2005, 64, Vizzard 2000, 87-88.
13  Bain 1978, Behr 1996, Kobler 1973, Okrent 2010.
14  Vizzard 2000, 89.
15  Anderson 1996, 23-24, Cole 2016, 28-32, Sugarmann 1992, 27-33, Vinzant 2005, 65, Vizzard 2000, 89-90.
16  Vizzard 2000, 90-91.
17  Levitas 2002, 3-4.
18  Gentry 1991, Powers 1987, Summers 1993.
19  2006, 98.
20  1981, 122-128.
21  Romell 2006.
22  Shields 1981, 25-26.
23  1981, 27.
24  Shields 1981, 22-23.
25  Shields 1981, 95.
26  Wright 2007, 123.
27  Lindop 1992, 69-89.
28  Lindop 1992, 90-111.

29  Lindop 1992, 112-134.
30  Shields 1981, 106.
31  Shields 1981, 107.
32  Shields 1981, 114.
33  Shields 1981, 115, Vizzard 2000, 117.
34  Shields 1981, 133.
35  Reagan 1990, 259-264
36  Brady 2002, 53-69.
37  Brady 2002, 93.
38  Brady 2002, 94.
39  Brady 2002, 97.
40  Brady 2002, 101.
41  Brady 2002, 103-104.
42  Brady 2002, 107.
43  Brady 2002, 112.
44  Brady 2002, 118.
45  Brady 2002, 121.
46  Brady 2002, 123, Vizzard 2000, 134.
47  Brady 2002, 126.
48  Brady 2002, 132.
49  Brady 2002, 138.
50  Brady 2002, 145.
51  Brady 2002, 147-48.
52  Brady 2002, 158, Vizzaard 2000, 136.
53  Vinzant 2005, 1-5, 18.
54  Brady 2002, 163, Vinzant 2005, 44-45.
55  Brady 2002, 164, Vizzard 2000, 141.
56  Vizzard 2000, 144.
57  Brady 2002, 166.
58  Brady 2002, 167.
59  Brady 2002, 177-178.
60  Brady 2002, 180.
61  Diaz 2013, 43.
62  Spitzer 2015, 241.
63  Brady 2002, 198.
64  Brady 2002, 221-222.
65  Roleff 2000, Haerens 2006.
66  Henigan 2009, 204-205.
67  *New York Times* statistics.
68  Zornick 2018.
69  Woods 2018.

## 9. LAWS: MAKING AMERICA SAFE FOR GUNS AND DANGEROUS FOR PEOPLE, INCLUDING LAW ENFORCERS

1   Spitzer 2015, 29.
2   Grant 1999, 299.
3   Spitzer 2015:36.
4   Kates 1979, 10-15.
5   Cooper 1997, 108-109, Uviller & Merkel 2002, 32, 132.
6   Headley 1873 (& 2004), 153, 159-160.
7   Kennett & Anderson 1975, 168-186.
8   Kennett & Anderson 1975, 173, Rodengen 2002, 83-86, Trefethen 1967, 213-215.
9   Baldwin 1999, Czitron 1991.
10  Trefethen 1967, 290, Rodengen 2002:58.
11  Bakal 1968, 150-154.
12  Kates 1979, 15.
13  Kennett & Anderson 1975, 199-201, Trefethen 1967:291.
14  Gilmore 1974, 243-245.
15  The possibility that Cermak was the intended victim is refuted by Gottfried 1962, 318-323; see also Erlebacher 1999, Schlesinger 1957, 464-466.
16  Kennett & Anderson 1975, 206, Rodengen 2002, 96-97, Trefethen 1967, 293.
17  Kennett & Anderson 1975, 210-211.
18  Reed 1999, 67.
19  Reed 1999, 67-68.
20  Vizzard 1997, 28, 2000, 90.
21  Shields 1981, 77.
22  Vizzard 2000, 93.
23  Bakal 1968, 147.
24  Bakal 1968, 147, 185-190.
25  Bakal 1968, iii.
26  Vinzant 2005, 66.
27  Reed 1999, 67, Vizzard 1997, 29-31, 2000, 93-105.
28  Vizzard 1997, 37.
29  Rodengen 2002, 147.
30  Rodengen 2002, 153.
31  Moore 2001, 147, Vizzard 1997, 11.
32  Vizzard 2000, 106-119.
33  Vinzant 2005, 107.
34  Cole 2016, 102-103, Rodengen 2002, 163-164.
35  Reed 1999, 67.
36  Cited from Vinzant 2005, 93.

37  Vinzant 2005, 93.
38  Quoted in Vinzant 2005, 94.
39  Cited from Vinzant 2005, 213, n. 15: Colorado Springs, Shepard's/McGraw-Hill.
40  Wright 2007:115-116.
41  Brown 1991.
42  Brown 1991, 30-35.
43  Cole 2016, 105. Rodengen 2002, 279.
44  Spies 2018, 24.
45  Giffords and Kelly 2014, 126, Schildkraut and Elsass 2016, 36.
46  Vinziant 2005, 5.
47  Vinzant 2005, 56.
48  Vinzant 2005, 47-49.
49  Giffords and Kelly 2014, 128.
50  Vinzant 2005, 36-37.
51  Vinzant 2005, 43.
52  Vinzant 2005, 46-47.
53  Vinzant 2005, 77-78.
54  Dickinson 2016.
55  Vinzant 2005, 74.
56  Vinzant 2005, 95-97.
57  Vinzant 2005, 99-140.
58  Cornell & Kozuskanich 2013, Waldman 2014, 119-133, Winkler 2011.
59  Coyle 2013, 123-137, 141-148.
60  Stevens 2014, 125-133.
61  Diaz 2013, 170.
62  *New York Times* statistics.
63  Healy, for Tribune News Service, in *JT* 11 March 18.
64  Chadwick 2017, 3-15.
65  Wadman & Allison 2004, 3.
66  Calhoun 1989, Sabbag1992, 39.
67  Calhoun 1989, 11-12.
68  Calhoun 1989, 28-34, Sabbag 1992, 41.
69  Radelet & Carter 1994, 8-10.
70  Uchida 1997, 23.
71  Uchida 1997, 18.
72  Chadwick 2017, 193-195.
73  Radalet & Carter 1994, 11.
74  DeArment 1999a.
75  Ketz 1999.
76  DeArment 1999b.
77  Roberts 1999c.

78  Melanson 2002, 20.

79  Melanson 2002, 21-23.

80  Lindrop 1992:32-44.

81  Melanson 2002, 24-27.

82  Melanson 2002, 24.

83  Melanson 2002, 24-25.

84  Lindrop 1992:45-56.

85  O'Toole 2012.

86  Kessler 2002, 9-10, Whitehead 1956, 20-21.

87  Whitehead 1956, 27-32.

88  Gentry 1991, Powers 1987, Summers 1993.

89  Kessler 2002, 102-103.

90  Kessler 2002, Turner 1970.

91  Tucker & Gurman 2018.

92  Perry 2014, Ryan 1999, Tucker 2011.

93  Reppetto 2004, 139-140, 2006, 12-14, Smith 2003, 81.

94  Mass 1968, 27-28.

95  Maas 1968, 9; see also 58.

96  Mass 1968, 10, 36.

97  Mass 1968.

98  Lardner 1996, blurb.

99  Kempton 1970 reviewed four relevant books.

100 Radelet & Carter 1994, 40-46.

101 Cooley 2004.

102 Bellisle 2018.

103 Gates 1992, 5.

104 Gates 1992, 91-92.

105 Gates 1992, 109-116.

106 Domanick 1994, 207, Hayden 2004, 91.

107 Gates 1992, 148.

108 Gates 1992, 2.

109 Domanick 1994, 403-419, Gates 1992, 321.

110 Gates 1992, 322.

111 Gates 1992, 331.

112 Domanick 1994, 6-7.

113 Domanick 1994, 419.

114 Domanick 1994, 426.

115 Gallo 2001.

116 Gallo 2001, 79.

117 Gallo 2001, 48-49.

118 Gallo 2001, 68.

119 Gallo 2001, 71-74.
120 Gallo 2001, 330-332.
121 McNab 2009, 10.


## 10. Costs of Gun Violence

1    Cook & Ludwig 2000, 117.
2    Fauber & Diedrich, *MJS* 12 Nov. 06.
3    Diedrich & Fauber, *MJS* 13 Nov.06.
4    Diedrich & Fauber, *MJS* 14 Nov.06.
5    Diedrich & Fauber, *MJS* 15 Nov 06.
6    Cook & Ludwig 2000, ix.
7    Fowler et al. 2015:1.
8    Gani et al. 2017, 1729.
9    Gani et al. 2017, 1731, 1736.
10   Spitzer et al. 2017, 770.


## Conclusions

1    Bordley & Harvey 1976, 34-35, Sullivan 1999.
2    2015, 55.


## Escaping Our Guncrazy Culture

1    Bellesiles 1996, 425; 1999, 17.

# BIBLIOGRAPHY

Abadinsky, Howard. 1997. *Organized Crime*. Chicago, Nelson-Hall.

Ackley, Parker O. 1969. *Home Gun Care and Repair*. Harrisburg, Stackpole Books.

Adams, Alice D. 1973. *The Neglected Period of Anti-Slavery in America (1808-1831)*. Williamstown, MA, Corner House Publishers. Ed. 1, 1908.

Adams, Russell B. et al. 1994.*War for the Plains*. Alexandria, Time-Life Books.

Addington, Larry H. 1994. *The Patterns of War since the Eighteenth Century*. Blooming, Indiana U.P.

Aitkens, Maggi. 1992. *Should We Have Gun Control?* Minneapolis, Lerner Publications.

Alexander, Charles C. 1965. *The Ku Klux Klan in the Southwest*. Lexington, U. of Kentucky P.

Alsop, Fred J., III. 2002. *Birds of North America*. NY, DK Publishing.

Altman, Jack & Marvin Ziporyn. *Born to Raise Hell: The Untold Story of Richard Speck*. NY, Grove P.

Amar, Akhil R. 2000. *The Bill of Rights: Creation and Reconstruction*. New Haven, Yale U.P. 2000.

Amber, John T., ed. 1966. *Gun Digest Treasury: the Best from 20 years of Gun Digest*. Chicago, Gun Digest.

Ambrose, Stephen E. 2000. *Nothing Like It in the World: the Men who Built the Transcontinental Railroad, 1863-1869*. NY, Simon & Schuster.

Ames, Mark. 2005. *Going Postal: Rage, Murder, and Rebellion: from Reagan's Workplaces to Clinton's Columbine and Beyond*. Brooklyn, Soft Skull P.

Ambrose, Jay. 25 June 2017. Gun Control Doesn't Work. *MJS*. Syndicated.

Amory, Cleveland. 1974. *Man Kind? Our Incredible War on Wildlife*. NY, Harper & Row.

Anderson, David L. 1998. *Facing My Lai: Moving beyond the Massacre*. Lawrence, U.P. of Kansas.

Anderson, Fred & Andrew Cayton. 2005. *The Dominion of War: Empire and Liberty in North America, 1500-2000*. NY, Viking.

Anderson, Jack. 1996. *Inside the NRA: Armed and Dangerous—an Exposé*. Beverly Hills, Dove Books.

Aptheker, Herbert. 1943. *American Negro Slave Revolts*. Columbia U.P. 1963. NY, International Publishers.

Armstrong, David A. 1992. *Bullets and Bureaucrats: The Machine Gun and the United States Army, 1861-1916*. Westport CT, Greenwood P.

Aptheker, Herbert. 1943. *American Negro Slave Revolts*. NY, Columbia U.P. 1963.

Asbury, Herbert. 1928. *The Gangs of New York: an Informal History of the Underworld*. NY, Knopf. 2001. NY, Thunder's Mouth P.

— 1936. *French Quarter: an Informal History of the New Orleans Underworld*. Garden City, Garden City Publishing Co.

— 1940. *Gem of the Prairie: an Informal History of the Chicago Underworld*. NY, Knopf.

Associated Press. 30 March 2010. Militia Hoped to Spark Uprising against Government, Officials Say. *MJS*.

Audubon, John J. 1999. *Writings and Drawings*. NY, Library of America.

Bagley, Will. 2002. *Blood of the Prophets: Brigham Young and the Massacre at Mountain Meadows*. Norman, U. of Oklahoma P.

Bain, Donald. 1978. *War in Illinois*. Englewood Cliffs, Prentice-Hall.0

Bakal, Carl. 1968. *No Right to Bear Arms*. Edition 2. NY, Paperback Library. Edition 1, 1966.

Balwin, Leland D. 2003. Whiskey Rebellion (1794). *DAH* **8**, 469-470.

Baldwin, Peter C. 1999. Timothy Daniel Sullivan (1863-1913), politician. *ANB* **21**:126-127.

Banks, Nancy A. 1999. "Lucky" Luciano (1897-1962). Vol. 2, pp. 296-297 in Gottesman 1999.

Barker, Thomas. 2015. *Biker Gangs and Transnational Organized Crime*. NY, Elsevier. Ed. 1, 2007.

Barnes, Gilbert H. 1964. *The Antislavery Impulse: 1830-1844.* NY, Harcourt, Brace & World. Ed. 1, 1933.

Barnet, Richard J. 1990. *The Rockets' Red Glare: When America Goes to War, 200 Years.* NY, Simon & Schuster.

Barger, Ralph with Keith & Kent Zimmerman. 2000. *Hell's Angel: the Life and Times of Sonny Barger and the Hell's Angels Motorcycle Club.* NY, Morrow.

Barnes, Gilbert H. 1964. *The Antislavery Impulse, 1830-1844.* NY, Harcourt & Brothers. Ed. 1, 1933.

Barrow, Thomas C. 1981. The American Revolution as a Colonial War for Independence. Pp.227-236 in Fulton 1981a.

Battison, Edwin A. 1973. A New Look at the Whitney Milling Machine. *Technology & Culture* **14**:592-598.

Beach, Edward L. 1986. *The United States Navy: 200 Years.* NY, Henry Holt.

Bechtel, Stefan. 2012. *Mr. Hornaday's War: How a Peculiar Victorian Zookeeper Waged a Lonely Crusade for Wildlife that Changed the World.* Boston, Beacon P.

Beck, Glenn, Kevin Balfe & Hanna Beck. 2013. *Control: Exposing the Truth about Guns.* NY, Threshold Editions/Mercury Radio Arts.

Bedini, Silvio A. 1990. *Thomas Jefferson: Statesman of Science.* NY, Macmillan.

Behr, Edward. 1996. *Prohibition: Thirteen Years that Changed America.* NY, Arcade.

Berkin, Carol. 2015. *The Bill of Rights: the Fight to Secure America's Liberties.* NY, Simon & Schuster.

Blackmore, Howard L. 1965. *Guns and Rifles of the World.* NY, Viking.

Blee, Kathleen M. 1991. *Women of the Klan: Racism and Gender in the 1920s.* Berkeley, U. of California P.

Bellesiles, Michael A. 1996. The Origins of Gun Culture in the United States, 1760-1865. *J. of American History* **83**:425-455. Reprinted in Dizard et al. 1999:17-46.

—, ed. 1999. *Lethal Imagination: Violence and Brutality in American History.* NY, NY U.P.

— 2003. *Arming America: the Origins of a National Gun Culture.* Ed. 2. Brooklyn, Soft Skull P. Edition 1, 2000. NY, Knopf.

Bellisle, Martha. 14 Jan. 2018. Should Police Sell Guns? Some Chiefs Say No. *JT* A6.

Bennett, David. H. 1988. *The Party of Fear: From Nativist Movements to the New Right in American History*. Chapel Hill, U. North Carolina P. 1990. NY, Vintage Books.

Bergreen, Laurence. 1994. *Capone: the Man and the Era*. NY, Simon & Schuster.

Bigelow, Donald N. 1952. *William Conant Church and the Army and Navy Journal*. NY, Columbia U.P. 1968. NY, AMS P.

Blackmore, Howard L. 1972. *Hunting Weapons*. NY, Walker.

Blackstone, Sarah J. 1986. *Buckskins, Bullets, and Business: A History of Buffalo Bill's Wild West*. Westport CT, Greenwood P.

Block, Alan A. 1999. Organized Crime. Vol. 2, pp. 492-497 in Gottesman 1999.

Bloomgarden, Henry S. 1976. *The Gun: a "Biography" of the Gun That Killed John F. Kennedy*. NY, Bantam Book. Ed. 1, 1975. NY, Viking.

Boatner, Mark M., III. 1959. *The Civil War Dictionary*. NY, David McKay.

—. 1974. *Encyclopedia of the American Revolution*. NY, David McKay.

Bok, Sissela. 1998. *Mayhem: Violence as Public Entertainment*. Reading MA, Addison-Wesley.

Bonanno, Joseph with Sergi Lalli. 1983. *A Man of Honor: the Autobiography of Joseph Bonanno*. NY, Simon & Schuster.

Boorman, Dean K. 2002. *The History of Smith & Wesson Firearms*. Guilford CT, Lyons.

Bordley, James, III. 1976. *Two Centuries of American Medicine*. Philadelphia, W.B. Saunders.

Borneman, Walter R. 2004. *1812: the War that Forged a Nation*. NY, HarperCollins.

— 2006. *The French and Indian War: Deciding the Fate of North America*. NY, HarperCollins.

— 2008. *Polk: the Man Who Transformed the Presidency and America*. NY, Random House.

Bowler, Arthur, ed. 1973. *The War of 1812*. Toronto/Montreal, Holt, Reinhart and Winston of Canada.

Branch, Taylor. 1989. *Parting the Waters: America in the King Years, 1954-63*. NY, Simon & Schuster.

— 1999. *Pillar of Fire: America in the King Years, 1963-65.* NY, Simon & Schuster.

— 2007. *At Cannan's Edge: America in the King Years, 1965-68.* NY, Simon & Schuster.

Brandes, Stuart D. 1997. *Warhogs: a History of War Profits in America.* Lexington, U.P. of Kentucky.

Brands, H.W. 1997. *T.R.: the Last Romantic.* NY, Basic Books.

Brash, Sarah, J. Cave & R. Doyle, eds. 1992. *Mass Murders.* Alexandria, Time-Life Books.

Brashler, William. 1977. *The Don: the Life and Death of Sam Giancana.* NY, Harper & Row.

Breihan, Carl W. 1977. *Great Gunfighters of the West.* Edition 3. NY, New American Library.

Breo, Dennis L. & William J. Martin. *The Crime of the Century: Richard Speck and the Murder of Eight Student Nurses.* NY, Bantam Books.

Briggs, William. 2017. *How America Got Its Guns: A History of the Gun Violence Crisis.* Santa Fe, University of New Mexico P.

Brinkley, Douglas. 2010. *The Last Warrior: Theodore Roosevelt and the Crusade for America.* NY, HarperCollins.

Brooks, Juanita. 1962. *The Mountain Meadows Massacre.* Foreword & Afterword by Jan Shipps. Norman, U. of Oklahoma P. Ed. 1, 1950.

Browder, Laura. *Her Best Shot: Women and Guns in America.* Chapel Hill, U. of North Carolina P.

Brown, Dee. 1962. *Fort Phil Kearny: an American Saga.* NY, Putnam. 1971. Retitled: *The Fetterman Massacre.* Lincoln, University of Nebraska P.

—. 1970. *Bury My Heart at Wounded Knee: an Indian History of the American West.* NY, Holt, Rinehart and Winston.

Brown, M. L. 1980. *Firearms in Colonial America: the Impact on History and Technology, 1492-1792.* Washington, Smithsonian Institution.

Brown, Peter H. & Abel, Daniel G. *Outgunned: Up Against the NRA: the First Complete Insider Account of the Battle Over Gun Control.* NY, Free Press.

Brown, Richard M. 1991. *No Duty to Retreat: Violence and Values in American History and Society.* NY, Oxford U.P.

Browning, Frank & John Gerassi. 1980. *The American Way of Crime.* NY, Putnam's Sons.

Browning, John & Curt Gentry. 1994. *John M. Browning: American Gunmaker*. Ed. 2. Ogden, Browning Arms Co. Ed. 1, 1964.

Bruce, John M. & Clyde Wilcox, editors. 1998. *The Changing Politics of Gun Control*. Lanham, MD, Rowman & Littlefield.

Burbick, Joan. Gun Show Nation: Gun Culture and American Democracy. NY, The New Press.

Bureau of Narcotics, U.S. Treasury Dept. 2009. *Mafia: the Government's Secret File on Organized Crime*. NY, Skyhorse Publishing.

Burke, John. 1973. *Buffalo Bill: the Noblest Whiteskin*. NY, Putnam's Sons.

Burroughs, Raymond D. 1961. *The Natural History of the Lewis and Clark Expedition*. East Lansing, Michigan State U.P.

Bushman, Brad J. & L. R. Huesmann. 2001. Effects of Television Violence on Aggression. Pp. 223-254 in Singer & Singer 2001.

Bushman, Richard L. 1999. Joseph Smith (1805-44), founder of the Church of Jesus Christ of Latter-Day Saints. *ANB* **20**, 230-233.

Caine, Alex. 2009. *Befriend and Betray: Infiltrating the Hells Angels, Bandidos, and Other Criminal Brotherhoods*. NY, Thomas Dunne.

Calhoun, Frederick S. 1989. *The Lawmen: United States Marshals and Their Deputies*. Washington, Smithsonian Institution P.

Calloway, Colin G. 2003. *The Vast Winter Count: the Native American West before Lewis and Clark*. Lincoln, U. Nebraska P.

Caras, Roger A. 1970. *Death as a Way of Life*. Boston, Little, Brown.

Carter, Jimmy. 2005. *Our Endangered Values: America's Moral Crisis*. NY, Simon & Schuster.

Carter, Robert A. 2000. *Buffalo Bill Cody: the Man behind the Legend*. NY, John Wiley & Sons.

Carstensen, Fred. 1999. Philo Remington (1816-89), manufacturer. *ANB* **18**, 334-335.

Cartmill, Matt. 1993. *A View to a Death in the Morning: Hunting and Nature through History*. Cambridge, MA, Harvard U.P.

Catton, Bruce. 1961-65. *The Centennial History of the Civil War*. 3 vols. Garden City, NY, Doubleday.

Cawalti, John G. 1971. *The Six-Gun Mystique*. Bowling Green, OH, Bowling Green U. Popular P.

— 1976. *Adventure, Mystery and Romance: Familiar Stories as Art and Popular Culture*. Chicago, University of Chicago P.

— 1999. *Six-Gun Mystique Sequel.* Bowling Green OH, Bowling Green U. Popular P.

Chadwick, Bruce. 2017. *Law and Disorder: the Chaotic Birth of the NYPD.* NY, Thomas Dunne Books/St. Martin's P.

Chambers, John W., II., ed. 1999. *The Oxford Companion to American Military History.* NY, Oxford U.P.

Chernow, Ron. 2004. *Alexander Hamilton.* NY, Penguin.

Chivers, C.J. 2010. *The Gun.* NY, Simon & Schuster.

Christian, Charles M. with Sari J. Bennett. 1995. *Black Saga: the African American Experience.* Boston, Houghton, Mifflin.

Clark, Ramsay. 1970. *Crime in America: Observations on Its Nature, Causes, Prevention and Control.* NY, Simon & Schuster.

Clepper, Henry. May 1968. The First White House Conference on Natural Resources. *American Forests* 74:28-31, 50-51.

Clifton, Chas S. 1994. The Crime of Piety: Wounded Knee to Waco. Pp. 1-5 in Lewis 1994.

Coates, James. 1985. *Armed and Dangerous: the Rise of the Survivalist Right.* NY, Hill and Wang.

Cohen, Rich. 1998. *Tough Jews.* NY, Simon & Schuster.

Clarke, James W. 1999. Sirhan Sirhan (1944-), vol. 3, pp. 158-159 in Gottesman 1999.

Cole, David. 2016. *Engines of Liberty: the Power of Citizen Activists to Make Constitutional Law.* NY: Basic Books.

Coleman, Loren. 2004. *The Copycat Effect: How the Media and Popular Culture Trigger the Mayhem in Tomorrow's Headlines.* NY, Paraview/ Pocket Books.

Coleman, Ray. 1984. *Lennon: the Definitive Biography.* NY, HarperCollins.

Collier, Peter & David Horwitz. 1984. *The Kennedys: an American Drama.* NY, Summit Books.

Commager, Henry S. & Richard B. Morris, eds., 1967. *The Spirit of 'Seventy-six: the Story of the American Revolution as Told by Participants.* NY, Harper & Row.

Comstock, George & H. Paik. 1991. *Television and the American Child.* San Diego, Academic P.

Cone, James H. 1991. *Martin & Malcolm: a Dream or a Nightmare.* Maryknoll, Orbis Books.

— 1999a. Martin Luther King, Jr. (1929-1968). Vol. 2, pp. 223-226 in Gottesman 1969.

— 1999b. Malcolm X (1925-1965). Vol. 2, pp. 311-313 in Gottesman 1969.

Connell, Evan S. 1984. *Son of the Morning Star*. San Francisco, North Point P.

Cook, Bernie. 1999. Television: Violent Genres. Vol. 3, pp. 275-278 in Gottesman 1999.

Cook, Fred J. 1972. *The Purge of the Greasers*. Pp. 86-113 in Gage 1972. Edition 1, 1966.

Cook, Sherburne F. 1943. The American Invasion, 1848-1870. *Ibero-Americana* **23**:1-115. Reprinted in Cook, *The Conflict between the California Indian and White Civilization*. Berkeley, U. of California P. Pp. 255-361.

Cooley, Robert with Hillel Levin. 2004. *When Corruption Was King: How I Helped the Mob Rule Chicago, then Brought the Outfit Down*. NY, Carroll & Graf.

Cooper, Carolyn & Merrill Lindsay. 1980. *Eli Whitney and the Whitney Amory*. Whitneyville, Eli Whitney Museum.

Cooper, Cynthia A. 1999. Television: Historical Overview. Vol. 3, pp. 258-266.

Cooper, Jerry. 1997. *The Rise of the National Guard: the Evolution of the American Militia, 1865-1920*. Lincoln, U. of Nebraska P.

Corcoran, James. 1990. *Bitter Harvest: Gordon Kahl and the Posse Comitatus: Murder in the Heartland*. NY, Viking.

Cornell, Saul, ed. 2000. *Whose Right to Bear Arms Did the Second Amendment Protect*. NY, Bedford/St. Martin's P.

— 2006. *A Well-regulated Militia: the Founding Fathers and the Origins of Gun Control in America*. NY, Oxford U.P.

— 2013. *The Second Amendment on Trial: Critical Essays on District of Columbia v. Heller*. Amherst, U. of Massachusetts P.

Covey, Herbert C., Scott Menard & Robert J. Franzese. 1992. *Juvenile Gangs*. Springfield, IL, Charles C. Thomas.

Coyle, Marcia. 2013. *The Roberts Court: the Struggle for the Constitution*. NY, Simon & Schuster.

Cramer, Clayton E. 2006. *Armed America: the Story of How and Why Guns Became as American as Apple Pie*. Nashville, Nelson Current.

Cressey, Donald. 1972. The Power Structure. Pp. 191-210 in Gage 1972. Editon 1, 1969.

Crews, Gordon A. & M.R. Counts. 1997. *The Evolution of School Disturbance in America.* Westport CT, Praeger.

Cullen, Dave. 2009. *Columbine.* NY, Twelve/Hachette Book Group.

Curry, G. David & Scott H. Decker. 1998. *Confronting Gangs: Crime and Community.* Los Angles, Roxbury. Cited from Decker & Curry 1999, 13.

Curry, Richard O., ed. 1965. *The Abolitionists: Reformers or Fanatics?* NY, Holt, Rinehart & Winston.

Cutright, Paul R. 1956. *Theodore Roosevelt: the Naturalist.* NY, Harper & Row.

— 1969. *Lewis and Clark: Pioneering Naturalists.* Urbana, U. of Illinois P.

Czitron, Daniel. 1991. Underworlds and Underdogs: Big Tim Sullivan and Metropolitan Politics in New York, 1889-1913. *J.Amer.Hist.* 78:536-558.

Dash, Mike. 2009. *The First Family: Terror, Extortion, Revenge, Murder, and the Birth of the American Mafia.* NY, Random House.

Daumas, Maurice, ed. 1979. *A History of Technology and Invention.* Vol. 3. *The Expansion of Mechanization.* Eileen B. Hennessy, transl. NY, Crown.

Davidson, Osha G. 1993. *Under Fire: the NRA and the Battle for Gun Control.* NY, Henry Holt.

Davis, Burke. 1969. *Yorktown: the Winning of American Independence.* NY, Harper & Row.

Davis, John H. 1993. *Mafia Dynasty: The Rise and Fall of the Gambino Crime Family.* NY, HarperCollins.

Davis, W.W.H. 1899. *The Fries Rebellion, 1798-99: an Armed Resistance to the House Tax Law.* Doyleston, PA, Doyleston Publishing Co. 1969. NY, Arno P.

Davis, William C. 1998. *Three Roads to the Alamo: the Lives and Fortunes of David Crockett, James Bowie, and William Barret Travis.* NY, HarperCollins.

DeArment, Robert K. 1999a. James Butler "Wild Bill" Hickok (1837-1876). Vol. 2, pp. 112-113 in Gottesman 1999.

— 1999b. John Henry "Doc" Holliday (1851-1887). Vol. 2, pp. 123-124 in Gottesman 1999.

DeBrabander, Firmin. 2015. *Do Guns Make Us Free? Democracy and the Armed Society*. New Haven, Yale U.P.

De Bruhl, Marshall. 1933. *Sword of San Jacinto: a Life of Sam Houston*. NY, Random House.

Decker, Scott H. & G. David Curry. 1999. *Gangs*. Vol. 2, pp. 6-13 in Gottesman 1999.

Decker, Scott H. & Barrik Van Winkle. 1996. *Life in the Gang: Family, Friends, and Violence*. NY, Cambridge U.P.

De Conde, Alexander. 2001. *Gun Violence in America The Struggle for Control*. Boston, Northeastern U. P.

Denmark, Florence L., H.H. Kreuss, R.W. Wesner, E. Midlarsky & U.P.Gielen, eds. 2005. *Violence in Schools: Cross-National and Cross-Cultural Perspectives*. NY, Springer.

Denning, Michael. 1987. *Mechanic Accents: Dime Novels and Working-class Culture in America*. London, Verso.

Denton, Sally. 2003. American massacre: the tragedy at Mountain Meadows, September 1857. NY, Knopf.

Derber, Charles & Yale R. Magrass. 2016. *Bully Nation: How the American Establishment Creates Bullying*. Lawrence, U. P. of Kansas.

Derfener, Jeremy. 2003. Shay's Rebellion. *DAH* 7: 338.

De Venanzi, Augusto. 2012. School Shootings in the USA: Popular Culture as Risk, Teen Marginality, and Violence against Peers. *Crime Media Culture* **8,** 261-278.

Devine, John. 1999. Schools: Overview. Vol. 3, pp. 98-112 in Gottesman 1999.

Diaz, Tom. 1999. *Making a Killing: the Business of Guns in America*. NY, New P.

—. 2009. *No Boundaries: Transnational Latino Gangs and American Law Enforcement*. Ann Arbor, U. of Michigan P.

—. 2013. *The Last Gun: How Changes in the Gun Industry Are Killing Americans and What It Will Take to Stop It*. NY, Free P.

Diapoulos, Peter & Steven Linakis. 1976. *The Sixth Family*. NY, Dutton.

Dickinson, Tim. 1 Dec. 2016. All-American Killer. *Rolling Stone*, 50-57.

Diedrich, John & John Fauber. 13 Nov. 2006. Some Wounds Never Heal. *MJS.*

— & —.14 Nov. 06. Gunshot Costs Echo through Economy. *MJS.*

— & —. 15 Nov. 06. Police Confront Rise in Shootings. *MJS.*

Dizard, Jan E. 1999. *Going Wild: Hunting, Animal Rights, and the Contested Meaning of Nature.* Amherst, U. of Massachusetts P.

— 2003. *Mortal Stakes: Hunters and Hunting in Contemporary America.* Amherst: U. of Massachusetts P.

—, Robert M. Muth & Stephen P. Andrews, Jr., eds. 1999. *Guns in America: A Reader.* NY, New York U.P.

Dobyns, Jay & Nils Johnson-Shelton. 2009. *No Angel: My Harrowing Undercover Journey to the Inner Circle of the Hells Angels.* NY, Crown.

Domanick, Joe. 1994. *To Protect and to Serve: the LAPD's Century of War in the City of Dreams.* NY, Pocket Books.

Donald, David H. 1995. *Lincoln.* NY, Simon and Schuster.

Doughty, Robert A. and 7 others. 1996. *American Military History and the Evolution of Warfare in the Western World.* Lexington, MA, D.C. Heath.

Doughty, Robin W. 1975. *Feather Fashions and Bird Preservation: a Study in Nature Protection.* Berkeley, U. of California P.

Downey, Fairfax. 1961. *Texas and the War with Mexico.* NY, American Heritage.

Drago, Harry S. 1973. *Road Agents and Train Robbers: Half a Century of Western Banditry.* NY, Dodd, Mead.

Drain, James A. 11 May 1911. *Arms and the Man* p. 129.

Dreyfuss, Robert. Fall 1995. Political Snipers: How the NRA Exploited Loopholes and Waged a Stealth Campaign Against the Democrats. *American Prospect* 1999 reprint. 233-244 in Dizard et al. 1999.

Droban, Kerrie. 2007. *Running with the Devil: the True Story of the ATF's Infiltration of the Hells Angels.* Guilford, Lyons P.

Dunlap, Thomas R. 1988. *Saving America's Wildlife.* Princeton, Princeton U.P.

Denning, Michael. 1987. *Mechanic Accents: Dime Novels and Working Class Culture in America.* London, Verso.

Dunham, Roger G. & Geoffrey P. Alpert, eds. 1997. *Critical Issues in Policing: Contemporary Readings.* Ed. 3. Prospect Heights, IL, Waveland P.

Dupuy, R. Ernest & Trevor N. Dupuy. 1963. *The Compact History of the Revolutionary War*. NY, Hawthorn Books.

Dyer, Joel. 1997. *Harvest of Rage: Why Oklahoma City Is only the Beginning*. Boulder, Westview Press.

Eccles, W. J. 1972. *France in America*. NY, Harper & Row. Edition 2, 1990.

— 1983. *The Canadian Frontier, 1534-1760*. Albuquerque, U. New Mexico P.

Editorial. 4-11 July 16. *The Nation* **303**, no. 1-2, 3-4.

Editors, Time-Life Books. 1992. *Mass Murderers*. Alexandria VA, Time-Life Books.

— 1994. *Assassination*. Alexandria VA, Time-Life Books.

Egerton, Frank N. 1973. Changing Concepts of the Balance of Nature. *Quart. Rev. Biol.* **48**, 322-360.

— 2007. Understanding Food Chains and Food Webs, 1700-1970. *Bulletin of the Ecological Society of America* **88,** 50-69. at esajournals.org

Eggington, Joyce. 1991. *Day of Fury: The Story of the Tragic Shootings that Forever Changed the Village of Winnetka*. NY, William Morrow.

Elliott, Phililp, Haley S. Edwards & Charlotte Alter. 16 Oct. 2017. After the Massacre. *Time* **190**, no. 15:22-31.

Elman, Robert. 1968. *Fired in Anger: the Personal Handguns of American Heroes and Villains*. Garden City, Doubleday.

Emerson, Everett. 1999. Thomas Morton (*c.* 1580-1647), colonist and writer. *ANB* **15**:963-964.

Emery, Michael C. & Edwin Emery. 1988. *The Press and America: an Interpretive History of the Mass Media*. Ed. 6. Englewood Cliffs, NJ, Prentice-Hall.

Erlebacher, Albert. 1999. Anton Joseph Cermak (1873-1933). *ANB* **4**:607-608.

Eron, Leonard D. 1963. Relationship of TV Viewing Habits and Aggressive Behavior of Children. *Journal of Abnormal and Social Psychology.* **67**:193-196.

— 1992. Impact of Television Violence. *Congressional Record* **88**:S8539.

— & Gunther. 1994. ch.6, n.64

— & L. R. Huesmann. 1984. Television Violence and Aggressive Behavior. *Advances in Clinical Child Psychology* **7**:35-55.

— & —. 1999. Television Programming and Violence, U.S. Vol. 3, pp. 477-486 in Kurtz 1999.

Etcheson, Nicole. 2004. *Bleeding Kansas: Contested Liberty in the Civil War Era*. Lawrence, U.P. of Kansas.

Everitt, David. 1999. Howard Unruh (1920-). Vol. 3, pp. 352-354 in Gottesman 1999.

Evans, Howard E. 1997. *The Natural History of the Long Expedition to the Rocky Mountains, 1819-1820*. NY, Oxford U.P.

Fabianic, David. 1999. J. Edgar Hoover (1895-1972). Vol. 2, pp. 138-140 in Gottesman 1999.

Faragher, John M., M.J. Buhle, D. Czitron & S.H. Armitage. 2000. *Out of Many: a History of the American People*. Ed. 3. Upper Saddle River NJ, Prentice Hall.

Fauber, John & John Diedrich. 12 Nov. 2006. City's Gun Violence Goes beyond Murder. *MJS*.

Fellman, Michael. 1999. Jesse James (1847-1882). Vol. 2, pp. 188-189 in Gottesman 1999.

Filler, Louis. 1960. *The Crusade against Slavery, 1830-1860*. NY, Harper & Brothers.

Finkelman, Paul, ed. 1995. *His Soul Goes Marching On: Responses to John Brown and the Harper's Ferry Raid*. Charlottesville, U.P. of Virginia.

Fischer, David H. 2008. *Champlain's Dream*. NY, Simon & Schuster.

Fitzgerald, Frances. 1972. *Fire in the Lake: the Vietnamese and the Americans in Vietnam*. Boston, Atlantic Monthly Press/Little Brown.

Flaherty, Thomas H., ed. 1992. *Mass Murderers*. Alexandria VA, Time-Life Books.

Flannery, Tim. 2001. *The Eternal Frontier: An Ecological History of North America and Its Peoples*. NY, Atlantic Monthly P.

Fleming, Thomas. 1997. *Liberty! The American Revolution*. NY, Viking.

— 1999. *Duel: Alexander Hamilton, Aaron Burr and the Future of America*. NY, Basic Books.

Fogel, Robert W. & Stanley L. Engerman. 1974. *Time on the Cross: the Economics of American Negro Slavery*. Boston, Little, Brown.

Foote, Shelby. 1958-74. *The Civil War: a Narrative*. 3 vols. NY, Random House.

Fowler, Katherine A. & L.L. Dahlbert, T. Haileyesus & J.L. Annest. 2015. Firearm Injuries in the United States. *Preventive Medicine* **79**:1-27.

Fox, Cybelle, W.D. Roth & K. Newman. 2003. A Deadly Partnership: Lethal Violence in an Arkansas Middle School. Pp.101-131 in Moore et al. 2003.

Fox, James A. and Jack Levin. 2014. *Extreme Killing: Understanding Serial and Mass Murder.* Thousand Oaks, CA, Sage.

— & Jenna Savage. 2009. Mass Murder Goes to College: an Examination of Changes on College Campuses Following Virginia Tech. *American Behavioral Scientist* **52**: 1465-85.

Fox, Stephen. 1989. *Blood and Power: Organized Crime in Twentieth-Century America.* NY, William Morrow.

Frank, Andrew K. 1999. South. Vol. 3, pp. 183-189 in Gottesman 1999.

Frank, Gerold. 1972. *An American Death: the True Story of the Assassination of Dr. Martin Luther King, Jr. and the Greatest Manhunt of Our Times.* Garden City NY, Doubleday.

Franklin, John H. & Alfred A. Moss, Jr. 1994. *From Slavery to Freedom: A History of African Americans.* Edition 7. NY, McGraw-Hill.

— & Isadore Starr, compilers.1967. *The Negro in Twentieth Century America: a Reader on the Struggle for Civil Rights.* NY, Random House.

Frasca, Dom. 1959. *King of Crime.* NY, Crown.

Frazier, Thomas R., ed. 1970. *Afro-American History: Primary Sources.* NY, Harcourt, Brace & World.

Frederickson, George M., ed. *William Lloyd Garrison.* Englewood Cliffs, NJ, Prentice-Hall.

Friedman, Robert I. 2000. *Red Mafiya: How the Russian Mob Has Invaded America.* Boston, Little, Brown.

Fulton, Richard M., ed. 1981a. *The Revolution that Wasn't: a Contemporary Assessment of 1776.* Port Washington NY, Kennikat P.

Furniss, Norman F. 1960. *The Mormon Conflict.* New Haven, Yale U.P.

Gage, Nicholas, editor. *Mafia, U.S.A.* Chicago, Playboy P.

Gallagher, Eugene V. 1999. David Koresh (1959-1993). Vol. 2, pp. 230-231 in Gottesman 1999.

Gallo, Gina. 2001. *Armed and Dangerous: Memoirs of a Chicago Policewoman.* NY, Tom Doherty Associates.

Gambino, Richard. 1977. *Vendetta: a True Story of the Largest Lynching in U.S. History, the Mass Murder of Italian-Americans in New Orleans.* NY, Doubleday.

Gani, Faiz, J.V. Sakrau & J.K. Canner. 2017. Emergency Department Visits for Firearm-related Injuries in the United States, 2006-14. *Health Affairs* **36**:1729-38.

Garraty, John A. & Mark C. Carnes, eds. 1999. *American National Biography*. 24 vols. NY, Oxford U.P.

Garrow, David J. 1986. *Bearing the Cross: Martin Luther King, Jr., and the Southern Christian Leadership Conference*. NY, Random House.

Gates, Daryl, F., with Diane K. Shah. 1992. *Chief: My Life in the LAPD*. NY, Bantam Books.

Gellman, Barton. 11 Oct. 2010. Locked and Loaded: the Secret World of Extreme Militias. *Time* **176, no. 15**, 24-33.

Gentry, Curt. 1991. *J. Edgar Hoover: the Man and the Secrets*. NY, Norton.

George, John & Laird Wilcox. 1992. *Nazis, Communists, Klansmen, and Others: Political Extremism in America*. Buffalo, Prometheus Books.

Giancana, Sam & Chuck Giancana. 1992. *Double Cross: the Explosive Inside Story of the Mobster Who Controlled America*. NY, Warner Books.

Gibson, Arrell Morgan. 1980. *The American Indian: Prehistory to the Present*. Lexington, MA: D.C. Heath.

Gibson, James William. 1994. *Warrior Dreams: Paramilitary Culture in Post-Vietnam America*. NY, Hill & Wang/Farrar, Straus & Giroux.

Giffords, Gabrielle, Mark Kelly, with Harry Jaffe. 2014. *Enough: Our Fight to Keep America Safe from Gun Violence*. NY, Scribner.

Gilmore, Russell S. 1974. *Crackshots and Patriots: The National Rifle Association and America's Military-Sporting Tradition*. Ph.D. dissertation, U. of Wisconsin, Madison.

— 1992. "Another Branch of Manly Sport': American Rifle Games, 1840-1890. Pp.93-111 in *Hard at Play: Leisure in America, 1840-1940*. Kathryn Grover, ed. Amherst, U. of Massachusetts P. Reprinted in Dizard, Muth & Andrews 1999, 105-121.

Goodrich, Thomas. 2005. *The Darkest Dawn: Lincoln, Booth, and the Great American Tragedy*. Bloomington, Indiana University Press.

Gordon, Robert B. 1999. Samuel Colt (1814-62), inventor and industrialist. *ANB* 5:270-271.

Gosch, Martin A. & Richard Hammer. 1975. *The Last Testament of Lucky Luciano*. Boston, Little, Brown.

Gottlieb, Alan. 1986. *The Gun Grabbers*. Bellview, Merril Press.

Gottesman, Ronald, ed. 1999. *Violence in America: an Encyclopedia*. 3 vols. NY, Charles Scribner's Sons.

Gottfried, Alex. 1962. *Boss Cermak of Chicago: a Study of Political Leadership.* Seattle, U. of Washington P.

Gottfried, Ted. 1993. *Gun Control: Public Safety and the Right to Bear Arms.* Brookfield, CT, Millbrook P.

Gottlieb, Alan. 1994. *The Gun Grabbers.* Belleview, WA, Merril P.

Graham, Frank, Jr. 1971. *Man's Dominion: The Story of Conservation in America.* NY, M. Evans.

— & Carl W. Buchheister. 1990. *The Audubon Ark: A History of the National Audubon Society.* NY, Knopf.

Grant, Ellsworth S. 1999. Eli Whitney (1765-1825), inventor and gun manufacturer. *ANB* **23**:298-300.

Gray, Steven. 12 April 2010. Spotlight: the Hutarre Militia. *Time* p.18.

Green, Constance M. 1956. *Eli Whitney and the Birth of American Technology.* Boston, Little, Brown.

Gurr, Ted R., ed. 1989. *Violence in America:* vol. 1: *The History of Crime;* vol. 2: *Protest, Rebellion, Reform.* Newbury Park, CA, Sage.

Haag, Pamela. 2016. *The Gunning of America: Business and the Making of American Gun Culture.* NY, Basic Books.

Haerens, Margaret, ed.2006. *Gun Violence: Oooooopposing Viewpoints.* Farmington, MI, Greenhaven P.

Hagan, John, P. Hirschfield & C. Shedd. 2003. Shooting at Tilden High: Causes and Consequences. Pp.163-197 in Moore et al. 2003.

Haines, Francis. 1970. *The Buffalo.* NY, Thomas Y. Crowell.

Hallahan, William H. 1994. *Misfire: the History of How America's Small Arms Have Failed Our Military.* NY, Charles Scribner's Sons.

Haller, Mark H. 1989. Bootlegging: the Business and Politics of Violence. Vol. 1, pp. 146-162 in Gurr 1989.

Hamilton, James T. 1998. *Channeling Violence: The Economic Market for Violent Television Programming.* Princeton, Princeton U.P.

Hamilton, Nigel. 1992. *J.F.K.: Reckless Youth.* NY, Random House.

Hamm, Mark S. 1999a. Timothy McVeigh. Vol. 2, pp. 307-309 in Gottesman 1999.

— 1999b. Prohibition and Temperance. Vol. 2, pp. 619-622 in Gottesman 1999.

— 1999c. Ruby Ridge. Vol. 3, pp. 69-70 in Gottesman 1999.

— 1999d. Waco. Vol. 3, pp. 389-391 in Gottesman 1999.

Hammer, Richard, ed. 1975. *Playboy's Illustrated History of Organized Crime*. Chicago, Playboy Press.

Hansom, Paul. 1999. My Lai Massacre. Vol. 2, pp. 430-431 in Gottesman 1999.

Harding, David, J. Mehta & K. Newman. 2003. No Exit: Mental Illness, Marginality, and School Violence in West Paducah, Kentucky. Pp.132-162 in Moore et al. 2003.

Harris, Edward. 1951. *Up the Missouri with Audubon*. John F. McDermott, ed. Norman, U. Oklahoma P.

Harris, Robert L., Jr. 1999. African Americans. Vol.1, pp. 38-46 in Gottesman 1999.

Havinghurst, Walter. 1954. *Annie Oakley of the Wild West*. NY, Scribner. 2003. Edison, NJ, Castle Books.

Hawkins, Darnell F. 1999. Race and Ethnicity. Vol. 3, pp. 1-6 in Gottesman 1999.

Hayden, Thomas E. 2004. *Street Wars: Gangs and the Future of Violence*. NY, The New P.

Headley, Joel T. 1873. *The Great Riots of New York, 1712-1873*. NY, E.B. Treat. 2004. NY, Thunder's Mouth P.

Healy, Melissa. 11 March 2018. Fewer Gun Laws, More Gun-related Deaths. Tribune News Service. *JT*.

Heidler, David S. & Joanne T. Heidler. 1996. *Old Hickory's War: Andrew Jackson and the Quest for Empire*. Mechanicsburg, Stackpole Books.

—, — & David J. Coles. 2000. *Encyclopedia of the American Civil War: a Political, Social, and Military History*. Santa Barbara, ABC-CLIO, NY, Norton.

Helmer, William J. 1969. *The Gun that Made the Twenties Roar*. London, Collier-Macmillan.

— & Rich Mattix. 1998. *Public Enemies: America's Criminal Past, 1919-1940*. NY, Checkmark Books/Facts on File.

Henigan, Dennis A. 2009. *Lethal Logic: Exploding the Myths that Paralyze American Gun Policy*. Washington, Potomac Books.

Herman, Daniel J. 2001. *Hunting and the American Imagination*. Washington, Smithsonian Institution P.

Herzog, Todd. 1999. Copycat Violence. Vol. 1, pp. 305-306 in Gottesman 1999.

Hickey, Donald R. 2001. The War of 1812: Still a Forgotten Conflict? *Journal of Military History* **65**, 741-769.

— 2013. *The War of 1812: Writings from America's Second War of Independence.* NY, Library of America.

Hinckley, Jack & Jo Ann Hinckley, with Elizabeth Sherrill. 1985. *Breaking Points.* Carmel, NY, Guideposts.

Hofstadter, Richard. 1965. *The Paranoid Style in American Politics and Other Essays.* NY, Knopf.

— & M. Wallace, eds. 1970. *American Violence: a Documentary History.* NY, Knopf.

Hogeland, William. 2006. *The Whiskey Rebellion: George Washington, Alexander Hamilton, and the Frontier Rebels Who Challenged America's Newfound Sovereignty.* NY, Charles Scribner's Sons.

Horan, James D. 1962. *Desperate Men: Revelations from the Sealed Pinkerton Files.* Edition 2. Garden City, Doubleday. 1997. Lincoln, U. of Nebraska P.

Hosenball, Mark & Michael Isikoff. 12 April 2010. Militias: Extremists Reaction. *Newsweek* p. 14.

Hosley, William N. 1996. *Colt: The Making of an American Legend.* Amherst, U. of Massachusetts P.

Hounshell, David A. 1984. *From the American System to Mass Production, 1800-1932: the Development of Manufacturing Technology in the United States.* Baltimore, Johns Hopkins U.P.

Housenholder, Mike & Corey Williams. 31 March 2010. U.S. Attorney Says Militia Needed to be Taken Down. *MJS.*

Howard, Warren S. 1963. *American Slavers and the Federal Law, 1837-1862.* Berkeley, U. California P.

Huff, C. Ronald, ed. 2002. *Gangs in America.* Thousand Oaks, CA, Sage Publications.

Hummel, Richard L. 1994. *Hunting and Fishing for Sport: Commerce, Controversy, Popular Culture.* Bowling Green OH, Bowling Green State U. Popular P.

— 1999. Hunting. Vol. 2, pp. 151-154 in Gottesman 1999.

Hunnicut, Susan, ed. 2006. *School Shootings.* Detroit, Thomson Gale.

Hunt, Alfred. 1999. Slave Rebellions. Vol. 3, pp. 162-165 in Gottesman 1999.

Isenberg, Andrew C. 2000. *The Destruction of the Bison: An Environmental History, 1750-1920*. NY, Cambridge U.P.

Jacobs, James B. 2002. *Can Gun Control Work?* NY, Oxford U.P.

Jahoda, Gloria. 1975. *Trail of Tears: the Story of the American Indian Removal, 1813-1855*. NY: Henry Holt. 1995. NY: Wing Books.

James, Bill. 2011. *Popular Crime: Reflections on the Celebration of Violence*. NY, Scribners.

Jarrett, William, ed. 1997. *Shooters Bible*. no.88. Wayne NJ, Stoeger Publishing Co.

Jensen, Merrill. 1950. *The New Nation: a History; of the United States during the Confederation, 1781-1789*. NY, Knopf.

Jinks, Roy. 1977. *History of Smith & Wesson: No Thing of Importance Will Come without Effort*. North Hollywood, CA, Beinfield Publishing.

Joerg, W.L.G., ed. 1928. *Problems of Polar Research: a Series of Papers by Thirty-one Authors*. NY, American Geographical Society.

Johnson, Marilynn S. 2003. *Street Justice: a History of Police Violence in New York City*. Boston, Beacon P.

Johnson, Robert U. 1923. *Remembered Yesterdays*. Boston, Little, Brown.

Jones, Stephen, with Peter Israel. 2001. *Others Unknown: Timothy McVeigh and the Oklahoma City Bombing Conspiracy*. Edition 2. NY, Public Affairs. Edition 1, 1998.

Jurgensmeyer, Mark. 10 May 2010. Christian Terrorism Is on the Rebound. *Oklahoma Observer* p. 16.

Kates, Don B., Jr., ed. 1979. *Restricting Handguns: the Liberal Skeptics Speak Out*. Croton-on-Hudson, North River P.

Kauffman, Michael W. 2004. American Brutus: John Wilkes Booth and the Lincoln conspiracies. NY, Random House.

Keenan, Jerry. 1997. *Encyclopedia of American Indian Wars, 1492-1890*. NY, Norton.

Keith, Lee Anna. 2008. *The Colfax Massacre: the Untold Story of Black Power, White Terror, and the Death of Reconstruction*. NY, Oxford U.P.

Kelleher, Michael D. 1997. *Flash Point: the American Mass Murderer*. Westport, CT: Praeger.

Keller, Betty. 1985. *Black Wolf: The Life of Ernest Thompson Seton*. Vancouver, Douglas & McIntyre.

Keller, Julia. 2008. *Mr. Gatling's Terrible Marvel: the Gun that Changed Everything and the Misunderstood Genius Who Invented It*. NY, Penguin Books.

Kelly, Jack. 2004. *Gunpowder: a History of the Explosive that Changed the World*. London, Atlantic.

Kempton, Murray. 5 Nov. 1970. Cops. *New York Review of Books*, 3-7. (Reviews 4 books.)

Kennett, Lee & James L. Anderson. 1975. *The Gun in America: the Origins of a National Dilemma*. Westport CT: Greenwood P.

Kessler, Ronald. 2002. *The Bureau: the Secret History of the F.B.I.* NY, St. Martin's P.

Kheel, Marti. 1995. License to Kill: An Ecofeminist Critique of Hunters' Discourse. Pp.85-125 in *Animals and Women*. C. J. Adams and J. Donovan, eds. Durham, Duke U.P.

Kirkham, James F., Sheldon G. Levy, and William J. Crotty. 1969. *Assassination and Political Violence*. Washington, U.S. Government Printing Office.

Kirkland, K.D. 2007. *America's Premier Gunmakers: Colt*. East Bridgewater MA: World Publications/JG Press.

— 2012. *America's Premier Gunmakers: Remington*. East Bridgewater MA: World Publications/JG Press.

— 2014. *America's Premier Gunmakers: Winchester*. East Bridgewater MA: World Publications/JG Pres.

Kleck, Gary & Don B. Kates. 2001. *Armed: New Perspectives on Gun Control*. Amherst, NY, Prometheus Books.

Klein, Edward. 2003. *The Kennedy Curse: Why Tragedy Has Haunted America's First Family for 150 Years*. NY, St. Martin's Griffin.

Klein, Katherine S. 2012. *The Bully Society: School Shootings and the Crisis of Bullying in American Schools*. NY, New York U. P.

Klein, Malcolm W. 1971. *Street Gangs and Street Workers*. Englewood Cliffs, NJ, Prentice-Hall. Cited from Decker & Curry 1999, 13.

Kleinkecht, William. 1996. *The New Ethnic Mobs: the Changing Face of Organized Crime in America*. NY, Free P.

Knox, Sara L. 1999. Literature: Popular Fiction. Vol. pp. 266-270 in Gottesman 1999.

Kobler, John, ed. 1973. *Ardent Spirits: the Rise and Fall of Prohibition.* NY, Putnam's Sons.

Kohn, Abigail A. 2004. *Shooters: Myths and Realities of America's Gun Culture.* NY, Oxford U.P.

Kohn, Richard H. 1976. The Murder of the Militia System in the Aftermath of the American Revolution. Pp. 110-126 in *The Military History of the Revolution: Proceedings of the Sixth Military History Symposium, USAF Academy.* Washington, Government Printing Office. Reprinted in Skaggs & Browning 1991, 69-81.

Koller, Larry. 1959. *The Fireside Book of Guns.* NY, Ridge P./Simon & Schuster.

— 1974. *The Golden Guide to Guns.* NY, Golden P. Ed. 1, 1961.

Kontos, Louis & David C. Brotherton. 2008. *Encyclopedia of Gangs.* Westport: Greenwood P.

Kranzberg, Milton & Carroll W. Pursell, Jr., eds. *Technology in Western Civilization.* 2 vols. NY, Oxford U.P.

Krech, Shepard III. 1999. *The Ecological Indian: Myth and History.* NY, Norton.

Kurtz, Lester, ed. 1999. *Encyclopedia of Violence, Peace and Conflict.* 3 vols. San Diego, Academic P.

Kutler, Stanley I., ed. 2003. *Dictionary of American History.* Ed. 3., 10 vols. NY, Charles Scribner's Sons.

Lamar, Howard R., ed. 1998. *The New Encyclopedia of the American West.* New Haven, Yale U.P.

LaMay, Craig L. 1999. Children's Television. Vol. 3, pp. 270-275 in Gottesman 1999.

Landau, Elaine. 1991. *Armed America: the Status of Gun Control.* Englewood Cliffs, NJ, Messner.

Lane, Charles. 2009. *The Day Freedom Died: the Colfax Massacre, the Supreme Court, and the Betrayal of Reconstruction.* NY, Henry Holt.

Langman, Peter. 2009. *Why Kids Kill: Inside the Minds of School Shooters.* NY, St. Martin's Griffin.

LaPierre, Wayne. 1994. *Guns, Crime, and Freedom.* Washington: Regnery. 1955. NY: Harper Perennial.

LaPierre, Wayne. Nov. 2000. Standing Guard. *American Rifleman*

LaPierre, Wayne. 2002. *Shooting Straight: Telling the Truth about Guns in America*. Washington: Regnery.

Lardner, James. 1996. *Crusader: the Hell-Raising Police Career of Detective David Durk*. NY, Random House.

Larson, Erik. 1994. *Lethal Passage: How the Travels of a Single Handgun Expose the Roots of America's Gun Crisis*. NY, Crown.

Lavergne, Gary M. 1997. *A Sniper in the Tower: The Charles Whitman Murders*. Denton, U. of Northern Texas P.

Lavigne, Yves. 1987. *Hell's Angels: "Three Can Keep a Secret if Two Are Dead."* NY, Carol Publishing Group.

Lacey, Robert. 1991. *Little Man: Meyer Lansky and the Gangster Life*. Boston, Little Brown.

Leamer, Laurence. 2016. *The Lynching: the Epic Courtroom Battle that Brought Down the Klan*. NY, William Morrow/HarperCollins.

Leckie, Robert. 1981. *The Wars of America*. Ed. 2. NY, Harper & Row.

Leddy, Edward. 1987. *Magnum Force Lobby: the National Rifle Association Fights Gun Control*. Lanham, MD: U.P. of America.

Lefave, Donald G. 1970. *The Will to Arm: the National Rifle Association in American Society, 1871-1970*. Ph.D dissertation. Boulder, U. of Colorado.

Leopold, Aldo. 1933. *Game Management*. NY, Charles Scribner's Sons.

— 1949. *A Sand County Almanac*. NY, Oxford U.P.

Lepore, Jill. 1998. *The Name of War: King Philip's War and the Origins of American Identity*. NY, Knopf.

Levin, Jack & James Alan Fox. 1991. *America's Growing Menace: Mass Murder*. Ed. 2. NY, Berkley Books. Ed. 1., NY, Plenum.

Levine, Madeline. 1996. *Viewing Violence: How Media Violence Affects Your Child and Adolescent's Development*. NY, Doubleday.

Lewis, David L. 1978. *King: a Biography*. Ed. 2. Urbana, U. of Illinois P.

Lewis, James R., ed. 1994. *From the Ashes: Making Sense of Waco*. Landham, MD, Rowman & Littlefield.

Lewis, Stephanie. 1994. *War for the Plains*. Stephen G. Hyslop, ed. Alexandria, VA, Time-Life Books.

Line, Les, ed. 1999. *The National Audubon Society: A Century of Conservation*. Southport, CT, Hugh Lanter Levin Associates.

Livingstone, Harrison E. 1993. *Killing the Truth: Deceit and Deception in the JFK Case*. NY, Caroll & Graf.

— 1995. *Killing Kennedy and the Hoax of the Century*. NY, Caroll & Graf.

Lindop, Edmund. 1992. *Assassinations that Shook America*. NY, Franklin Watts.

Longstreet, Stephen. 1970. *War Cries on Horseback: the Story of the Indian Wars on the Great Plains*. Garden City, Doubleday.

Lott, Dale F. 2002. *American Bison: A Natural History*. Berkeley, U. of California P.

Lott, John R., Jr. 1999. *More Guns, Less Crime: Understanding Crime and Gun Control Laws*. Chicago, U. Chicago P. Edition 2, 2000. Edition 3, 2010.

— 2016. *The War on Guns: Arming Yourself Against Gun Control Lies*. Washington, Regnery.

Lunde, Paul. 2004. *Organized Crime: an Insider Guide to the World's Most Successful Industry*. NY, DK. 2007. NY, Barnes & Noble.

Lutts, Ralph H. 1990. *The Nature Fakers: Wildlife, Science, and Sentiment*. Denver, Fulcrum.

Lynch, Joseph M. 1999. *Negotiating the Constitution: the Earliest Debates over Original Intent*. Ithaca, Cornell U.P.

Maas, Peter. 1968. *The Valachi Papers*. NY, Putnam.

MacDonald, J. Fred. 1987. *Who Shot the Sheriff? The Rise and Fall of the Television Western*. NY, Praeger.

Mackey, Robert R. 1999. Mormons. Vol. 2, pp. 408-410 in Gottesman 1999.

MacLean, Nancy. 1994. *Behind the Mask of Chivalry: the Making of the Second Ku Klux Klan*. NY, Oxford U.P.

McCullough, David. 1981. Mornings on Horseback. NY, Simon & Schuster.

Madley, Benjamin. 2017. *An American Genocide: the United States and the California Indian Catastrophe*. New Haven, Yale U.P.

Malcolm X, with Alex Haley. 1965. *The Autobiography of Malcolm X*. NY, Grove Press. 1999. NY, Ballantine Books.

Mannion, James. 2003. *The Everything Mafia Book: True-Life Accounts of Legendary Figures, Infamous Crime Families, and Chilling Events*. Avon, Adams Media.

Marshall, Bob. Jan. 2009. Why Johnny Won't Hunt. *Field & Stream* 116-119.

Marshall, Slam L.A. 1972. *Crimsoned Prairie: the Wars between the United States and the Plains Indians during the Winning of the West.* NY, Charles Scribner's Sons.

Martinelli, Patricia. A. 2010. *Rain of Bullets: The True Story of Ernest Ingenito's Bloody Family Massacre.* Mechanicsburg PA, Stackpole Books.

Mathiessen, Peter. *Wildlife in America.* NY, Viking P.

Matthews, Chris. 2017. *Bobby Kennedy: a Raging Spirit.* NY, Simon & Schuster.

Mayer, Henry. 1998. *All on Fire: William Lloyd Garrison and the Abolition of Slavery.* NY, St. Martin's Griffin.

McCabe, Kimberly A. & Gregory M. Martin. 2005. *School Violence, the Media, and Criminal Justice Responses.* NY, Peter Lang.

McCullough, David. 1981. *Mornings on Horseback.* NY, Simon & Schuster.

McDowell, Bart. 1967. *The Revolutionary War: America's Fight for Freedom.* Washington, National Geographic Society.

McGrath, Roger D. 1989. Violence and Lawlessness on the Western Frontier. Vol. 1, pp. 122-145 in Gurr 1989.

McIver, Stuart B. 2003. *Death in the Everglades: The Murder of Guy Bradley, America's First Martyr to Environmentalism.* Gainesville, U.P. of Florida.

McMurtry, Larry. 2005. *Oh What a Slaughter: Massacres in the American West, 1846-1980.* NY, Simon & Schuster.

McNab, Chris. 2009. *Deadly Force: Firearms and American Law Enforcement, from the Wild West to the Streets of Today.* NY, Osprey Publishing.

McPhaul, Jack J. *Johnny Torrio: First of the Gang Lords.* New Rochelle, Arlington House.

McPherson, James M. 1988. *Battle Cry of Freedom: the Civil War Era.* NY, Oxford U.P.

McShane, Larry. 1999. *Cops under Fire: the Reign of Terror against Hero Cops.* Washington, D.C., Regnery Publishing.

Mech, L. David. 2002. *Aldo Leopold and the Ecological Conscience.* Richard L. Knight & Suzanne Riedel, eds. NY, Oxford U.P.

Meier, August & Elliott Rudwick. 1970. *From Plantation to Ghetto.* Edition 2. NY, Hill & Wang.

Meine, Curt. 1988. *Aldo Leopold: His Life and Work*. Madison, U. of Wisconsin P.

Melanson, Philip H., with Peter F. Stevens. 2002. *The Secret Service: the Hidden History of an Enigmatic Agency*. NY, Carrol & Graf.

Messick, Hank & Burt Goldblatt. 1972. *The Mobs and the Mafia: the Illustrated History of Organized Crime*. NY, Galahad Books.

Michel, Lou and Dan Herbeck. 2001. *American Terrorist: Timothy McVeigh and the Oklahoma City Bombing*. NY, Regan Books.

Michener, James A. 1990. *The Eagle and the Raven*. Austin, State House P.

Middlekauff, Robert. 2005. *The Glorious Cause: the American Revolution, 1763-1789*. Ed. 2. NY, Oxford U.P.

Midlarsky, Elizabeth & Helen M. Klain. A History of Violence in the Schools. Pp.37-57 in Denmark et al. 2005.

Milan, Michael [pseudonym]. 1989. *The Squad: the U.S. Government's Secret Alliance with Organized Crime*. NY, Shapolsky Publishers.

Miller, Lee. 2000. *Roanoke: Solving the Mystery of the Lost Colony*, NY, Arcade Publishing.

Miller, Walter. 1977. *Violence by Youth Gangs as a Crime Problem in Major American Cities*. Washington, U.S. Government Printing Office. Cited from Decker & Curry 1999, 13.

Milton, Giles. 2000. *Big Chief Elizabeth: the Adventures and Fate of the First English Colonies in America*. NY, Farrar, Straus & Giroux.

Mitchell, John G. 1980. *The Hunt*. NY, Knopf.

Moldea, Dan E. 1995. *The Killing of Robert F. Kennedy: an Investigation of Motive, Means, and Opportunity*. NY, Norton.

Monkkonen, Eric H. 1981. *Police in Urban America, 1860-1920*. NY, Cambridge U.P.

Moore, Leonard J. 1999. Ku Klux Klan. Vol. 2, pp. 231-235 in Gottesman 1999.

Moore, Mark H., C.V. Petrie, A.A. Braga & B.L. McLaughlin, eds. 2003. *Deadly Lessons: Understanding Lethal School Violence*. Washington, National Academies P.

Morgan, Edmund S. &. H.M. Morgan. 1962. *The Stamp Act Crisis: Prologue to Revolution*. Ed. 2. NY, Collier Books.

Morris, Edmund. 1979. *The Rise of Theodore Roosevelt*. 2002. Theodore Rex. 2011. Colonel Roosevelt. NY, Coward, McCann, and Geoghegan.

Morris, Richard B. and Jeffrey B. Morris, eds. 1976. *Encyclopedia of American History*. NY, Harper & Row.

Morrow, Robert D. 1992. *First Hand Knowledge: How I Participated in the CIA-Mafia Murder of President Kennedy*. NY, S.P.I./Shapolsky.

Morton, Thomas. 1637. *New English Canaan*. Amsterdam, Frederick Stam. 1972. NY, Arno P.

Murphy, Edith. 2004. Thomas Morton (1580x95-1646/7), colonist in America. *ODNB* **39**, online.

Myers, A. R. W. & M. B. Pritchard, eds. 1998. *Empire's Nature: Mark Catesby's New World Vision*. Chapel Hill, U. of North Carolina P.

Miller, C. A. 1988. *Jefferson and Nature: An Interpretation*. Baltimore, Johns Hopkins U.P.

Mitchell, John G. Feb. 1978. God, Guns, and Guts Made America Free: The National Rifle Association and the Right to Bear Arms. *American Heritage* **29**:4-17.

— 1980. *The Hunt*. NY, Knopf.

Moore, James. 2001. *Very Special Agents: the Inside Story of America's Most Controversial Law Enforcement Agency—the Bureau of Alcohol, Tobacco, and Firearms*. Ed. 2. Urbana, U. of Illinois P. 1997. NY, Pocket Books.

Mummold, Jonathan. 22 Jan. 2007. Videogames: Defending 'Columbine.' *Newsweek* **149**:10.

Myatt, Frederick. 1981. *An Illustrated Guide to Rifles and Automatic Weapons*. NY, Arco.

Nash, Jay Robert. 1973. *Bloodletters and Badmen: a Narrative Encyclopedia of American Criminals from the Pilgrims to the Present*. NY, M. Evans.

Nash, Roderick F. 1989. *The Rights of Nature: A History of Environmental Ethics*. Madison, U. of Wisconsin P.

*National Television Violence Study*. 1997. Thousand Oaks, Sage Publications.

Navasky, Victor. 1995. Anatomy of a Hoax. *The Nation* **260**:815-817.

Nene, Laurel A. 2009. *Animal Investigators; How the World's First Wildlife Forensics Lab Is Solving Crimes and Saving Endangered Species*. NY, Scribner.

Neiwert, David. 2018. *Alt-America: the Rise of the Radical Right in the Age of Trump*. NY, Verso.

Nelson, Jill, ed. 2000. *Police Brutality: an Anthology*. NY, Norton.

Nelson, Zed. 2000. *Gun Nation*. London, Westzone Publishing.

Nevins, Allan. 1947-71. *Ordeal of the Union*. 8 vols. NY, Charles Scribners Sons.

Newman, Katherine S., C. Fox, D.J. Harding, J. Mehta & W. Roth, eds. 2004. *Rampage: The Social Roots of School Shootings*. NY, Basic Books.

Newman, Paul D. 1999. John Fries (1750-1818), leader of Fries Rebellion of 1799. *ANB* **8**, 490-491.

Newton, Michael. 1999. Mass Murder: Individual Perpetrators. Vol. 2, pp. 329-334 in Gottesman 1999.

Nonte, George C., Jr. 1973. *Firearms Encyclopedia*. NY, Harper & Row.

Norris, James D. 1999. Oliver Fisher Winchester (1810-80), small-arms manufacturer. *ANB* **23**:626-627.

Oates, Stephen B. 1982. *Let the Trumpet Sound: the Life of Martin Luther King, Jr.* NY, Harper & Row.

O'Brien, Joseph F. & Andris Kurins. 1991. *Boss of Bosses: the Fall of the Godfather: the FBI and Paul Castellano*. NY, Simon & Schuster.

Okrent, Daniel. 2010. *Last Call: the Rise and Fall of Prohibition*. NY, Scribner.

Olsen, Jack. 1971. *Slaughter the Animals, Poison the Earth*. NY, Simon & Schuster.

— 1985. *Give a Boy a Gun: A True Story of Law and Disorder in the American West*. NY, Delacorte P.

Onuf, Peter S. 1999. Daniel Shays (1747?-1825), revolutionary officer. *ANB* **19**, 760-761.

O'Toole, Patricia. Nov. 2012. Assassination foiled. Smithsonian pp. 64-65.

Paik, Haejung & G. Comstock. 1994. The Effect of Television Violence on Antisocial Behavior. *Communication Research* **21**, 516-546.

Pan, J.C. March 2018. Alternative History: the Tradition of Conspiracy Theories and Hate Groups behind the Alt-Right. *The New Republic* 60-63.

Parker, Gregory L. 1999. Richard Jordan Gatling (1818-1903). Vol. 2, pp. 15-16 in Gottesman 1999.

Parkman, Francis. 1991. *The Oregon Trail. The Conspiracy of Pontiac*. NY, Library of America.

Paschel, Jarrett. 1999. George "Machine Gun" Kelly (1895-1954). Vol. 2, pp. 209-210 in Gottesman 1999.

Pasco, Craig S. 1999. The Monroe Rifle Club: Finding Justice in an "Ungodly and Social Jungle Called Dixie." Pp. 392-423 in Bellesiles 1999.

Payne, Darwin. 1985. *Owen Wister: Chronicler of the West, Gentleman of the East*. Dallas, Southern Methodist U.P. 2011. Lincoln, U. of Nebraska P.

Pease, William H. & Jane H. Pease, eds. 1965. *The Antislavery Argument*. Indianapolis, IN, Bobbs-Merrill.

Peattie, Donald C. 1942. The Nature of Things. *Audubon Magazine* **44**:266-271.

Perret, Geoffrey. 1989. *A Country Made by War: from the Revolution to Vietnam—The Story of America's Rise to Power*. NY, Random House.

Perry, Douglas. 2014. *Eliot Ness: the Rise and Fall of an American Hero*. NY, Viking.

Peters, Tracy W. 1999a. Butch Cassidy (1886-c. 1909) and Sundance Kid (1870-c. 1909). Vol. 1, pp. 208-210 in Gottesman 1999.

— 1999b. George "Baby Face" Nelson (1908-1934). Vol. 2, pp. 449-450 in Gotttesman 1999.

Petersen, David, compiler. 1996. *A Hunter's Heart: Honest Essays on Blood Sport*. NY, Henry Holt.

Petersen, James R. 2007. Biker Wars. Pp. 276-294 in Playboy Editors. *The Playboy Book of True Crime*. Hanover, NH. Playboy P. Edition 1, 2000.

Peterson, Virgil W. 1983. *The Mob: 200 Years of Organized Crime in New York*. Ottawa, IL, Green Hill.

Petrusich, Amanda. 1 Jan. 2018. Mock Epic: "American Vandal" Captures the True Crime Craze. *New Yorker* 74-75.

Pietrusza, David. 2003. *Rothstein: the Life, Times, and Murder of the Criminal Genius Who Fixed the 1919 World Series*. NY, Carroll & Graf.

Pitch, Anthony S. 2016. *The Last Lynching: How a Gruesome Mass Murder Rocked a Small Georgia Town*. NY, Skyhorse Publishing.

Playboy Editors. 2007. *The Playboy Book of True Crime*. Hanover NH, Playboy Press.

Poe, Richard. 2001. *The Seven Myths of Gun Control: Reclaiming the Truth about Guns, Crime, and the Second Amendment*. NY, Three Rivers P.

Posenwitz, Jim. 1999. *Inherit the Hunt: A Journey into the Heart of American Hunting*. Helena, Falcon P.

Posner, Gerald. 1993. *Case Closed: Lee Harvey Oswald and the Assassination of JFK*. NY, Random House.

— 1998. *Killing the Dream: James Earl Ray and the Assassination of Martin Luther King, Jr.* NY, Random House.

Poten, Constance J. Sept. 1991. A Shameful Harvest: America's Illegal Wildlife Trade. *National Geographic* **180**:106-132.

Potter, W. James. 1999. *On Media Violence.* Thousand Oaks, Sage Publications.

Powell, Jim. 2006. *Bully Boy: the Truth about Theodore Roosevelt's Legacy.* NY, Crown Forum.

Powell, Lawrence N. 1999. Huey Long (1893-1935). Vol. 2, pp. 286-288 in Gottesman 1999.

Powers, Richard G. 1987. *Secrecy and Power: the Life of J. Edgar Hoover.* NY, Free P.

Prall, Stuart E. 1972. *The Bloodless Revolution: England 1688.* Garden City: Anchor Books/Doubleday.

Pratt, Fletcher. 1955. *Civil War in Pictures.* Garden City, Garden City Books.

Prial, Frank J. 1972. Vito Genovese—Power to Spare. Pp. 163-171 in Gage 1972.

Prince, Stephen, ed. 2000. *Screening Violence.* New Brunswick, Rutgers U.P.

Proctor, Nicolas W. 2002. *Bathed in Blood: Hunting and Mastery in the Old South.* Charlottesville, U.P. of Virginia.

Prucha, Paul. 1990. *Atlas of American Indian Affairs.* Lincoln, U. of Nebraska P.

Purcell, L. Edward & S.J. Purcell. 2000. *Encyclopedia of Battles in North America, 1517 to 1916.* NY, Checkmark Books/Facts on File.

Rable, George C. 1999. Ambrose Burnside (1824-1881). P. 97 in Chambers 1999.

Radelet, Louis A. & David L. Carter. 1994. *The Police and the Community.* Ed. 5. NY, Macmillan College Publishing Co.

Rafter, Nicole H. 2000. *Shots in the Mirror: Crime Films and Society.* NY, Oxford U.P.

Rand, Kristen. 1996. *Gun Shows in America: Tupperware Parties for Criminals.* Washington, Violence Policy Center.

Raymond, Emilie. 2006. *From My Cold Dead Hands: Charlton Heston and American Politics.* Lexington, U.P. of Kentucky.

Reagan, Ronald. 1990. *An American Life.* NY, Simon & Schuster.

Reed, John S. 1999. Gun Control. Vol. 2, pp. 66-71 in Gottesman 1999.

Reeves, Richard. 1993. *President Kennedy: Profile of Power.* NY, Simon & Schuster.

Regenstein, Lewis. 1975. *The Politics of Extinction: The Shocking Story of the World's Endangered Wildlife.* NY, Macmillan.

Reiger, John F. 2001. *American Sportsmen and the Origins of Conservation.* Ed.3. Corvallis, Oregon State U.P.

Reisner, Marc. 1991. *Gun Wars: The Undercover Pursuit of Wildlife Poachers.* London, Secker & Warburg.

Remini, Robert V. 1977. *Andrew Jackson and the Course of American Empire, 1767-1821.* NY, Harper & Row.

— 2001. *Andrew Jackson and His Indian Wars.* NY, Viking.

Reppetto, Thomas. 2004. *American Mafia: a History of Its Rise to Power.* NY, Henry Holt.

— 2006. *Bringing Down the Mob: the War Against the American Mafia.* NY, Henry Holt.

Reusswig, William. 1967. *A Picture Report of the Custer Fight.* NY, Hastings House.

Reynolds, David. 2005. *John Brown, Abolitionist: the Man who Killed Slavery, Sparked the Civil War, and Seeded Civil Rights.* NY, Knopf.

Reynolds, Mike. 1999a. Lee Harvey Oswald (1939-1963). Vol. 2, pp. 497-498 in Gottesman 1999.

— 1999b Jack Ruby (1911-1967). Vol. 3, pp. 68-69 in Gottesman 1999.

Richardson, James F. 1974. *Urban Police in the United States.* Port Washington, NY: Kennikat P.

Ridgeway, James. 1990. *Blood in the Face: the Ku Klux Klan, Aryan Nations, Nazi Skinheads, and the Rise of a New White Culture.* NY, Thunder's Mouth Press.

Riley, Carroll L. 1995. *Rio del Norte: People of the Upper Rio Grande from Earliest Times to the Pueblo Revolt.* Salt Lake City, U. Utah P.

Riley, Glenda. 1994. *The Life and Legacy of Annie Oakley.* Norman, U. of Oklahoma P.

Ro, Ronin. 1998. *Have Gun Will Travel: The Spectacular Rise and Violent Fall of Death Row Records.* NY, Broadway Books.

Roberts, David. 2004. *The Pueblo Revolt: The Secret Rebellion that Drove the Spaniards Out of the Southwest.* NY, Simon & Schuster.

Roberts, Gary L. 1999a. Billy the Kid (1859-1881). Vol. 1, pp. 146-147.

— 1999b. Gunfighters and Outlaws, Western. Vol. 2, pp. 71-74 in Gottesman 1999.

— 1999c. William "Bat" Masterton (1853-1921). Vol. 2, pp. 334-335 in Gottesman 1999.

— 1999d. O.K. Coral Gunfight. Vol. 2, pp. 489-490 in Gottesman 1999.

— 1999e. Sand Creek Massacre. Vol.3, pp. 86-87 in Gottesman 1999.

Rodengen, Jeffrey L. 2002. *NRA: An American Legend*. Fort Lauderdale, Write Stuff Enterprises.

Roleff, Tamara L., ed. 2000. *Guns and Crime*. San Diego, Ca., Greenhaven P.

Rolt, L. T. C. 1965. *A Short History of Machine Tools*. Cambridge, MIT P.

Romell, Rick. 15 Sept. 06. Civic Leaders Rebuke Sensenbrenner. *MJS* pp. 1, 15.

Roosevelt, Theodore. 1882. *The Naval War of 1812: or the History of the United States Navy during the Last War with Great Britain, to which Is Appended an Account of the Battle of New Orleans*. NY, Putnam. 1999. NY, Da Capo.

— 1889-96. *The Winning of the West*. 4 vols. NY, Review of Reviews.

— 1924. *Outdoor Pastimes of an American Hunter*. NY, Charles Scribner's Sons. Ed.1, 1905.

Rosa, Joseph G. 1985. *Guns of the American West*. NY, Crown.

Ross, Ron. 2003. *Bummy Davis vs. Murder, Inc.: the Rise and Fall of the Jewish Mafia and an Ill-Fated Prizefighter*. NY, St. Martin's Press.

Rothman, Hal. 1999. West. Vol. 3, pp. 434-441 in Gottesman 1999.

Roy, Lucinda. 2009. *No Right to Remain Silent: the Tragedy at Virginia Tech*. NY, Harmony Books.

Russell, Don. 1960. *The Lives and Legends of Buffalo Bill*. Norman, U. of Oklahoma P.

Russo, Gus. 1998. *Live by the Sword: the Secret War Against Castro and the Death of JFK*. Baltimore, Bancroft P.

Ryan, Patrick J. 1999. Eliot Ness (1903-1957). Vol. 2, pp. 452-453 in Gottesman 1999.

Sabbag, Robert. 1992. *Too Tough to Die: Down and Dangerous with the U.S. Marshals*. NY, Simon & Schuster.

Salerno, Ralph & John Tompkins. 1972a. After Luciano. Pp. 114-146 in Gage 1972. Edition 1, 1969.

Sauer, Carl O. 1980. *Seventeenth Century North America*. Berkeley, Turtle Island.

Scharf, Peter & Arnold Binder. 1983. *The Badge and the Bullet*. NY, Praeger.

Scheim, David E. 1988. *Contract on America: the Mafia Murder of President John F. Kennedy*. NY, Shapolsky.

Schildkraut, Jaclyn & H. Jaymi Elsass. 2016. *Mass Shootings: Media, Myths, and Realities*. Santa Barbara, Praeger/ABC-Clio.

Schlessinger, Arthur M., Jr. 1957. *The Age of Roosevelt*. vol. 1: *The Crisis of the Old Order*. Boston, Houghton Mifflin.

Schoenberg, Robert J. 1992. *Mr. Capone*. NY, William Morrow.

Schoenebaum, Eleanora W., ed. 1979. *Profiles of an Era: the Nixon/Ford Years*. NY, Harcourt Brace Jovanovich.

Schorger, A. W. 1955. *The Passenger Pigeon*. Madison, U. of Wisconsin P.

Schott, Joseph L. 1975. *No Left Turns*. NY, Praeger.

Scott, Anne F. & Andrew W. Scott. 1982. *One Half the People: the Fight for Woman Suffrage*. Chicago, U. of Chicago P.

Schultz, Deanne. 1990. *Month of the Freezing Moon: the Sand Creek Massacre, November 1864*. NY, St. Martin's P.

Schultz, Eric B. & M.J. Tongias. 1999. *King Philip's War: the History and Legacy of America's Forgotten Conflict*. Woodstock, VT, Countryman P.

Scully, Matthew. 2002. *Dominion: The Power of Man, the Suffering of Animals, and the Call to Mercy*. NY, St. Martin's P.

Sedgwick, John. 2015. *War of Two: Alexander Hamilton, Aaron Burr, and the Duel that Stunned the Nation*. NY, New American Library.

Shadoian, Jack. 2003. *Dreams and Dead Ends: The American Gangster Film*. Ed. 2. NY, Oxford U.P.

Shaylor, Andrew. 2004. *Hells Angels Motorcycle Club*. London, Merrell.

Sherrill, Robert. 1973. *The Saturday Night Special and Other Guns with which Americans Won the West, Protected Bootleg Franchises, Slew Wildlife, Robbed Countless Banks, Shot Husbands Purposely and by Mistake, and Killed Presidents—Together with the Debate Over Continuing Same*. NY, Charterhouse.

Shields, Pete. 1981. *Guns Don't Die—People Do*. NY, Arbor House.

Shogan, Robert. 2004. *The Battlle of Blair Mountain: the Story of America's Largest Labor Uprising*. Boulder, CO, Westview P.

Shucard, Alan. 1999. George "Bugs" Moran (1892-1957). Vol. 2, pp. 407-408 in Gottesman 1999.

Shulman, Robert. 1999. Literature: Fiction. Vol. 2, pp. 262-266 in Gottesman 1999.

Sifakis, Carl. 1982. *The Encyclopedia of American Crime*. NY, Facts on File. 1992. NY, Smithmark.

Simon, Ron. 1999. Television: Censorship. Vol. 3, pp. 261-270 in Gottesman 1999.

Singer, Dorothy G. & J. L. Singer, eds. 2001. *Handbook of Children and the Media*. Thousand Oaks, Sage Publications.

Singletary, Otis A. 1960. *The Mexican War*. Chicago, U. of Chicago P.

Skaggs, David C. and Robert S. Browning III, eds. 1991. *In Defense of the Republic: Readings in American Military History*. Belmont, CA, Wadsworth Publishing Co.

Sloan, Irving J. 1970. *Our Violent Past: an American Chronicle*. NY, Random House.

Slotkin, Richard. 1973. *Regeneration through Violence: the Mythology of the American Frontier, 1600-1860*. Middleton CT, Wesleyan U.P.

— 1985. *The Fatal Environment: the Myth of the Frontier in the Age of Industrialization, 1800-1890*. NY, Athenaeum.

— 1992. *Gunfighter Nation: the Myth of the Frontier in Twentieth-Century America*. NY, Harper Collins.

— & J.K. Folsom, eds. 1978. *So Dreadful a Judgment: Puritan Response to King Philip's War, 1675-1677*. Middleton, Wesleyan U.P.

Smith, Anthony. 2002. *Machine Gun: the Story of the Men and the Weapon that Changed the Face of War*. NY, St. Martin's P.

Smith, Brent. 1994. *Terrorism in America: Pipe Bombs and Pipe Dreams*. Albany: State U. of New York P.

Smith, James B. 1980. Simeon North—Patriarch of U.S. Pistol Makers. Pp.69-76 in Cooper & Lindsay 1980.

Smith, Jo Darden. 2003. *A Complete History of the Mafia*. NY, Metrobooks.

Smith, Merritt R. 1977. *Harper's Ferry Armory and the New Technology: the Challenge of Change*. Ithaca, Cornell U.P.

—, ed. 1985a. *Military Enterprise and Technological Change: Perspectives on the American Enterprise*. Cambridge, MA, MIT P.

—, 1985b. Army Ordnance and the "American System" of Manufacturing, 1815-1861. Pp. 39-86 in Smith 1985a.

Smith, Page. 1976. A New Age Now Begins. 2 vols. NY, McGraw-Hill.

— 1980. *The Shaping of America: a People's History of the Young Republic*. NY, McGraw-Hill.

—.1981. *The Nation Comes of Age: a People's History of the Ante-Bellum Years*. NY, McGraw-Hill.

—. 1982. *Trial by Fire: a People's History of the Civil War and Reconstruction*. NY, McGraw-Hill.

Smith, W. H. B. 1968. *Book of Pistols and Revolvers*. Updated by Joseph E. Smith. Harrisburg, Stackpole Books. Ed. 1, 1946.

Snow, Robert L. 1999. *The Militia Threat: Terrorists Among Us*. NY, Plenum Trade.

Sondern, Frederic, Jr. 1972. How the Mafia Came to America. Pp. 78-85 in Gage 1972. Edition 1, 1959.

Sorensen, Theodore C. 1965. *Kennedy*. NY, Harper & Row.

Souter, Gerry. 2012. *American Shooter: a Personal History of Gun Culture in the United States*. Washington, Potomac Books.

Southern Poverty Law Center. *Oklahoma Observer* **41, no. 16**.

Spies, Mike. 5 March 2018. The Arms Dealer: How an N.R.A. Lobbyist Made Florida the Testing Ground for Pro-gun Policies. New Yorker 24-31.

Spitzer, Robert J. 2015. *Guns Across America: Reconciling Gun Rules and Rights*. NY, Oxford U.P.

Stanford, Gregory. 1 Oct. 2006. Gun Lobby Calls the Shots with Sensenbrenner. *MJS* commentary.

Stannard, David E. 1999. American Indian Holocaust. Vol. 1, pp. 76080 in Gottesman 1999.

Starkey, Armstrong. 1998. *European and Native American Warfare, 1675-1815*. Norman, U. of Oklahoma P.

Staub, Ervin. 1999. Mass Murder: Collective Murder. Vol. 2, pp. 320-329 in Gottesman 1999.

Stebbins, Henry M. 1958. *Rifles: A Modern Encyclopedia*. Harrisburg, Stackpole P.

Stein, Barbara R. 2001. *On Her Terms: Annie Montague Alexander and the Rise of Science in the American West*. Berkeley, U. of California P.

Steele, Ian K. 1994. *Warpaths: Invasions of North America*. NY, Oxford U.P.

Stegner, Wallace. 1964. *The Gathering of Zion: the Story of the Mormon Trail*. NY, McGraw-Hill.

Sterling, Keir B. 1977. *Last of the Naturalists: the Career of C. Hart Merriam*. Ed. 2. NY, Arno P.

— 1999. Richard Jordan Gatling (1818-1903), inventor and manufacturer. *ANB* **8**, 792-794.

Stern, Kenneth S. 1996. *A Force upon the Plain: the America Militia Movement and the Politics of Hate*. NY, Simon & Schuster.

— 1999. Militias, Unauthorized. Vol. 2, pp. 400-403 in Gottesman 1999.

Stevens, John Paul. 2014. *Six Amendments: How and Why We Should Change the Constitution*. NY, Little Brown.

Stickney, Brandon M. 1996. *"All-American Monster:" the Unauthorized Biography of Timothy McVeigh*. Amherst NY, Prometheus Books.

Stiles, T. J. 2002. *Jessie James: Last Rebel of the Civil War*. NY, Knopf.

Stock, C. 1999. Agrarian Violence. Vol. 1, pp. 56-58 in Gottesman 1999.

Stockley, Grif, Jr. 2001. Blood in Their Eyes: the Elaine Race Massacres of 1919. Fayettsville, U. of Arkansas P.

Strickland, Rennard. 1999. Trail of Tears. Vol.3, pp. 344-345 in Gottesman 1999.

Subrahmanyam, Koveri, R. Kraut, P. Greenfield & E. Gross. 2001. New Forms of Electronic Media. Pp.73-99 in Singer & Singer 2001.

Sugarmann, Josh. 1992. *National Rifle Association: Money, Firepower & Fear*. Washington, National Press Books.

— 2001. *Every Handgun Is Aimed at You: the Case for Banning Handguns*. NY, New P.

Sullivan, Robert, ed. 2007. *The Most Notorious Crimes in American History*. NY, Life Books.

Sullivan, Robert B. 1999. Benjamin Rush (1746-1813), physician, professor of chemistry and of medicine. *ANB* **19**, 72-75.

Summers, Anthony. 1993. *Official and Confidential: the Secret Life of J. Edgar Hoover*. NY, Putnam's Sons.

Swan, James A. 1995. *In Defense of Hunting*. San Francisco, HarperSanFrancisco.

Swift, Philip J. 2012. *Gangs, Outlaw Bikers, Organized Crime and Extremists: Who They Are, How They Work and the Threat They Pose.* Flushing, NY, Looseleaf Law Publications.

Tabor, James D. 1994. The Waco Tragedy: an Autobiographical Account of One Attempt to Avert Disaster. Pp. 13-21 in Lewis 1994.

— & Eugene V. Gallagher. 1995. *Why Waco: Cults and the Battle for Religious Freedom in America.* Berkeley, U. of California P.

Tartaro, Joseph. 1981. *Revolt at Cincinnati.* Buffalo, Hawkeye Publishing Co.

Taylor, Alan. 2001. *American Colonies.* NY, Penguin Books.

— 2010. *The Civil War of 1812: American Citizens, British Subjects, Irish Rebels, and Indian Allies.* NY, Knopf.

Tebbel, John & Keith Jennison. 1960. *The American Indian Wars.* NY, Harper & Row.

Thomas, Evan & Eve Conant. 19 April 2010. Hate: Antigovernment Extremists Are on the Rise—and on the March. *Newsweek* 44-47.

Thrasher, Frederic M. 1927. *The Gang: a Study of 1,313 Gangs in Chicago.* Chicago, U. Chicago P. Cited from Decker & Curry 1999, 13.

Tobias, Michael. 1998. *Nature's Keepers: the Front Lines of the Fight to Save Wildlife in America.* NY, John Wiley and Sons.

Tolnay, Stweart E. & E.M. Beck. 1995. *A Festival of Violence: an Analysis of Southern Lynchings, 1882-1930.* Urbana, U. of Illinois P.

Tosches, Nick. 2005. *King of the Jews: the Arnold Rothstein Story.* NY, HarperCollins.

Toy, Eckard V., Jr. 1989. Right-Wing Extremism from the Ku Klux Klan to the Order, 1915 to 1988. Vol. 2, pp. 131-152 in Gurr 1989.

Trachtman, Paul. 1977. *The Gun Fighters.* NY, Time-Life Books. Ed. 1, 1974.

Trefethen, James B., compiler. 1967. *Americans and Their Guns: the National Rifle Association Story through nearly a Century of Service to the Nation.* Harrisburg, Stackpole Books.

— 1975. *An American Crusade for Wildlife.* NY, Winchester P.

Treuer, Anton. 2013. *Atlas of Indian Nations.* Washington, National Geographic.

Tucker, Eric & Sadie Gurman (Assoc. P.). 1 Feb. 2018. FBI under heavy Republican Fire. *JT.*

Tucker, Kenneth. 2011. *Eliot Ness and the Untouchables: the Historical Reality and the Film and Television Depictions.* Ed. 2. Jefferson, NC, McFarland.

Turner, William W. 1970. *Hoover's FBI: the Men and the Myth.* Los Angeles, Sherbouorne P.

Tuska, Jon. 1983. *Billy the Kid: a Bio-Bibliography.* Westport CT: Greenwood Press.

Tuttle, Steve. 4 Dec. 2006. The Elusive Hunter. *Newsweek* **148**:50-53. 4 responding letters are in Dec. 18 issue.

Twitchell, James B. 1989. *Preposterous Violence: Fables of Aggression in Modern Culture.* NY, Oxford U.P.

Tyler, Gus, ed. 1962. *Organized Crime in America: a Book of Readings.* Ann Arbor, U. of Michigan P.

Uchida, Craig D. 1997. The Development of the American Police: an Historical Overview. Pages 18-35 in Dunham & Alpert 1997.

Ulanoff, Stanley M., ed. 1984. *American Wars and Heroes: Revolutionary War through Vietnam.* Glen Cove, NY, Baldpate P.

Utley, Lynn Z. Bloom & Arthur F. Kinney, eds. 1964. Ed. 2, 1971. *Bear, Man and God: Eight Approaches to William Faulkner's The Bear.* NY, Random House.

Utley, Robert M. 1973. *Frontier Regulars: the United States Army and the Indian, 1866-1891.* NY, Macmillan. 1984. Lincoln, U. of Nebraska P.

Utley, Robert M. & Wilcomb E. Washburn. 1985. *Indian Wars.* NY, American Heritage.

Uviller, H. Richard and William R. Merkel. 2002. *Militia and the Right to Arms: or, How the Second Amendment Fell Silent.* Durham, NC, Duke U.P.

Van Alstyne, Richard W. 1974. *The Rising American Empire.* NY, Norton.

Van Doren, Carl. 1948. *The Great Rehearsal: the Story of the Making and Ratifying of the Constitution of the United States.* NY, Viking P.

Van Gelder, Arthur P. & Hugo Schlatter. 1927. *History of the Explosive Industry in America.* NY, Columbia U.P. 1972. NY, Arno P.

Vinzant, Carol X. 2005. *Lawyers, Guns, and Money: One Man's Battle with the Gun Industry.* NY, Palgrave Macmillan.

Virgines, George E. 1969. *Saga of the Colt Six-shooter and the Famous Men Who Used It.* NY, Frederick Fell.

Vizzard, William J. 1997. *In the Crossfire: a Political History of the Bureau of Alcohol, Tobacco, and Firearms*. Boulder, CO, Lynne Rienner.

— 2000. *Shots in the Dark: the Policy, Politics, and Symbolism of Gun Control*. Lanham, MD, Rowman & Littlefield.

Vorphal, Ben M., ed. 1972. *My Dear Wister: the Frederic Remington-Owen Wister Letters*. Palo Alto, American West Publishing Co.

Wadman, Robert C. & William T. Allison. 2004. *To Protect and to Serve: a History of Police in America*. Upper Saddle River, NJ, Pearson Prentice Hall.

Wahl, Paul & Don Toppel. 1965. *The Gatling Gun*. NY, Arco Publishing Co.

Wala, Michael. 2003. War of 1812. *DAH* **8**:381-385.

Waldman, Carl. 1985. *Atlas of the North American Indian*. NY, Facts on File. Ed. 2, 2009.

Waldman, Michael. 2014. *The Second Amendment: a Biography*. New York, Simon & Schuster.

Waldrep, Christopher & M. Bellesiles, eds. 2006. *Documenting American Violence: a Sourcebook*. NY, Oxford U.P.

Waldron, Lamar & Thom Hartmann. 2008. *Legacy of Secrecy: the Long Shadow of the JFK Assassination*. Berkeley, Counterpoint.

Waldschmidt-Nelson, Britta. 2012. *Dreams and Nightmares: Martin Luther King, Jr. and Malcolm X, and the Struggle for Black Equality*. Gainesville, U. P. of Florida.

Walker, Ronald W., Richard E. Turley, Jr. & Glen M. Leonard. 2008. *Massacre at Mountain Meadows: an American Tragedy*. NY, Oxford U.P.

Wallace, Anthony. 1993. *The Long Bitter Trail: Andrew Jackson and the Indians*. NY: Hill and Wang.

Walter, Dave. Jan.-Feb. 1985. Swan Valley Shootout, 1908: A Tragic White-Indian Clash Long After the Wars Were Over. *Montana Magazine* **69**:23-31.

Ward, John W. 1962. *Andrew Jackson: Symbol for an Age*. NY, Oxford U.P.

Ware, Eugene F. 1960. *The Indian War of 1864* NY, St. Martin's P. Edition 1, 1911. Topeka KS, Crane.

Warikoo, Nira J. 31 March 2010. Experts: Christian Militia Part of Growing Trend. *JT* p. 4.

Warren, Louis S. 1997. *The Hunters Game: Poachers and Conservationists in Twentieth-Century America*. New Haven, Yale U.P.

— 2005. *Buffalo Bill's America: William Cody and the Wild West Show*. NY, Knopf

Waugh, Daniel. 2007. *Egan's Rats: the Untold Story of the Prohibition Era Gang that Ruled St. Louis*. Nashville, Cumberland House.

Webb, Stephen S. 1984. *1676, the End of American Independence*, NY, Knopf.

Weber, David J. 1992. *The Spanish Frontier in North America*. New Haven, Yale U.P.

Welch, James & Paul Stekler. 1994. *Killing Custer: the Battle of the Little Bighorn and the Fate of the Plains Indians*. NY, Norton.

Welker, Robert H. 1955. *Birds and Men: American Birds in Science, Art, Literature, and Conservation, 1800-1900*. Cambridge, Harvard U.P.

Wellman, Paul I. 1961. *A Dynasty of Western Outlaws*. Garden City, Doubleday.

Werstein, Irving. 1965. *The War with Mexico*. NY, Norton.

White, Richard. 1991. *"It's Your Misfortune and None of My Own:" a New History of the American West*. Norman, U. of Oklahoma P.

— 1991. *The Middle Ground: Indians, Empires, and Republics in the Great Lakes Region, 1650-1815*. NY, Cambridge U.P.

Whitehead, Don. 1956. *The FBI Story: a Report to the People*. NY, Random House.

Whitridge, Arnold. 1965. *Rochambeau*, NY, Collier Books.

Wickwire, Franklin & M. Wickwire. 1971. *Cornwallis and the War of Independence*. London, Faber & Faber.

Williams, Kenneth H. 1999. Eleuthère Irénée Du Pont (1771-1834). *ANB* 7:115-117.

Wiley, Farida A., ed. 1955. *Theodore Roosevelt's America: Selections from the Writings of the Oyster Bay Naturalist*. NY, Devin-Adair.

Williams, Corey & Devlin Barrett. 30 March 2010. Christian Militia Accused of Plotting to Kill Police Officer, then Bomb Funeral. *JT*.

Wills, Gary. 1987. *Reagan's America: Innocents at Home*. Garden City, Doubleday.

Wilson, Alexander & Charles L. Bonaparte. 1832. *American Ornithology; or, the Natural History of the Birds of the United States*. W. Jardine, ed. 3 vols. London, Whitaker, Treacher, & Arnot.

Wilson, R. L. 1991. *Winchester: an American Legend*. NY, Random House. 2004. Edison NJ, Chartwell Books.

Winkler, Adam. 2011. *Gunfight: the Battle over the Right to Bear Arms in America*. NY, Norton.

Wise, William. 1975. *Massacre at Mountain Meadows: an American Legend and a Monumental Crime*. NY, Thomas Y. Crowell.

Wister, Owen. 1902. *The Virginian: a Horseman of the Plains*. Drawings by Charles M. Russell, paintings by Frederic Remington. NY, Macmillan.

Wood, Gordon S. 1969. *The Creation of the American Republic, 1776-1787*. Chapel Hill, U. of North Carolina P.

— 2009. *Empire of Liberty: a History of the Early Republic, 1789-1815*. NY, Oxford U.P.

Woodbury, Robert S. 1960. The Legend of Eli Whitney and Interchangeable Parts. *Technology & Culture* **1**:235-253.

Woods, Elliott. May 2018. How the NRA Sells Guns in America Today. *New Republic*, 16-27 + cover.

Wright, Stuart A., editor. 1995. *Armageddon in Waco: Critical Perspectives on the Branch Davidian Conflict*. Chicago, U. of Chicago P.

— 2007. *Patriots, Politics, and the Oklahoma Bombing*. NY, Cambridge U.P.

Wyatt-Brown, Bertram. 1999. Dueling. Vol. 1, pp. 445-447 in Gottesman 1999.

Yost, Nellie S. 1979. *Buffalo Bill: His Family, Friends, Fame, Failures, and Fortunes*. Chicago, Swallow P.

Zilig, Gerard C. 1974. *Du Pont: Behind the Nylon Curtain*. Englewood Cliffs NJ, Prentice-Hall.

Zimmerman, Brian. 1999. Video Games. Vol. **3**, pp. 374-376 in Gottesman 1999.

Zornick, George. July 2017. Trump and the NRA. *The Nation* **305**, no.2: 12-16, 22.

— 30 April 2018. The Disrupters: How the Youth Activists of #Never Again Are Upending Gun Politics. *The Nation* **306**, no. 13:12-15 + cover.

Printed in the United States
By Bookmasters